Ethical Standards When Conducting Scientific Research

RESEARCH DESIGN

- Design the research study using ethical standards.

- Do not skew the design or slant the questions to elicit a certain response.

TREATMENT OF RESEARCH PARTICIPANTS

- Do not coerce participation in the research study.

- Promise and honor confidentiality to research participants.

- Treat participants with dignity and respect.

- Secure written permission from experimental subjects and debrief them at the conclusion of the experiment.

- Do not misuse research techniques to influence respondents.

- Push polling is unethical and should not be done.

DATA COLLECTION, PROCESSING, AND ANALYSIS

- Disclose when focus group participants are being taped or observed in any way during the discussion.

- Do not falsify or misrepresent data in collection, processing, or analysis.

REPORTING

- Do not represent phone-in, write-in, fax-in, or e-mail-in research results as if they were produced by valid, scientific survey methods and represented the population.

- Disclose question wording, including any filter questions that may have influenced responses, sampling method, sample size and sampling error, response rate, weighting, or any recoding of data when releasing them.

- Disclose the sponsorship of research results when releasing them.

- Do not let others influence you to misuse research methods and analytical techniques, or misrepresent research results.

- Report the results of research accurately and fairly.

Research in

Mass

Communication

A Practical Guide

Research in Mass Communication

A PRACTICAL GUIDE

Paula M. Poindexter

University of Texas at Austin

Maxwell E. McCombs

University of Texas at Austin

Bedford / St. Martin's

Boston ◆ *New York*

For Bedford/St. Martin's

Executive Editor: Patricia Rossi
Developmental Editor: Mark Paluch
Senior Editor, Publishing Services: Douglas Bell
Production Supervisor: Joe Ford
Project Management: Books By Design, Inc.
Marketing Manager: Charles Cavaliere
Text Design: Books By Design, Inc.
Cover Design: Lucy Krikorian
Composition: Thompson Type
Printing and Binding: Haddon Craftsman, an R. R. Donnelley & Sons Company

President: Charles H. Christensen
Editorial Director: Joan E. Feinberg
Editor in Chief: Nancy Perry
Director of Editing, Design, and Production: Marcia Cohen
Manager, Publishing Services: Emily Berleth

Library of Congress Catalog Card Number: 99-62324

Manufactured in the United States of America.

5 4 3
f e d c

For information, write: Bedford/St. Martin's, 75 Arlington Street, Boston, MA 02116   (617–399–4000)

ISBN: 0–312–19162–6

To our students, who learned the relevance of research

To the Instructor

A question that today's communication student often asks is: "What does research have to do with my career goals and the real world?" We feel that our approach to *Research in Mass Communication* will help answer that question.

We have written this book to show your students that research is, indeed, relevant to their major, connected to the real world, and tied to their future career success. In addition to making your students knowledgeable about the research process and competent in conducting and analyzing research, we show your students that research is an integral part of decision making in journalism, advertising, broadcasting, public relations, cable, online information, business, politics, and government. Regardless of your students' majors, this text will help them become accomplished researchers and astute consumers of research who can easily differentiate good research from bad.

This text has been written to make research relevant in several ways. First, a *decision maker/research expert model* has been used to demonstrate that often the person who identifies a need for research and actually uses the results when making decisions is different from the person who has the expertise to conduct the research. The decision maker and research expert are both important in the research process, but they serve different functions. Most of your students will become decision makers, identifying a research need, commissioning the research from a research expert, and making and implementing decisions based on the results of the research. Some of your students will become experts in collecting, analyzing, and reporting scientifically based research data. And a few of your students may even pursue academic careers in which they will function as both the decision maker and research expert in their own program of research.

Even though the decision maker in the communication industry usually does not have the expertise of the research expert, students will learn that effective decision makers must be able to distinguish good research from bad. And as your students learn about the responsibilities of the research expert, they will learn that research is a creative, intellectual, and business-oriented enterprise.

To help illustrate how research is conducted, *Research in Mass Communication* uses a *three-phase research process model* consisting of: (1) a pre-research phase, (2) a research phase, and (3) a post-research phase.

During the pre-research phase, the decision maker, who can be an executive, manager, creative director, editor, producer, practitioner, or university professor, identifies a problem, issue, opportunity, theory, or some research need and the appropriate research method for gathering information to understand the problem.

The research expert actually conducts the research during the research phase, using scientifically based research methods. Finally, during the post-research phase, the decision maker evaluates the research results and decides which results, if any, to use in decisions. Once decisions are implemented, the decision maker carefully monitors the impact of those decisions, paying close attention to the role that research played in understanding an issue, solving a problem, launching a new program, creating a campaign, or developing a new strategy.

By using this three-phase research process, your students will see how research, regardless of the method used, is similar during the pre-research and post-research phases but varies during the research phase. During the research phase, the unique, sequential steps of each research method are treated clearly and comprehensively to make your students comfortable with conducting, analyzing, and evaluating research results and methods.

Another way we have connected research to the real world is by providing interesting, *relevant examples* from the different specialties in the field of communication as well as from familiar sources — the daily newspaper, consumer and trade magazines, television, and the Internet. In addition, we have included research examples from decision makers who have commissioned research and implemented the results, as well as examples from research studies that we have conducted personally. To illustrate the similarities between the academic and industry research process, we have provided examples from scholarly journals.

One important feature of this text is its emphasis on *communicating research results*. As your students will discover, it is not enough to know how to conduct research, they must also be able to communicate the results in written and oral reports. Your students learn that the research method dictates how the research report should be written. For example, as they learn the process for conducting surveys, they learn how survey research reports should be written. And when focus groups are discussed, your students learn how to write a focus group report and how that differs from written survey research reports. They also learn how to write an executive summary, a key component of written research reports in industry.

Another important feature of *Research in Mass Communication* is the integration of ethics throughout the text and the discussions of the various research methods. The emphasis on ethics makes it clear to students that professional standards are an essential ingredient in the research process.

An examination of the table of contents shows that this book has been divided into four parts. Part I introduces the research process. Some questions that will be answered in this section include: Who conducts research and why is it conducted? What is research and what are its roots?

Part II is a comprehensive examination of survey research during the pre-research, research, and post-research phases. By providing such an in-depth examination of survey research from beginning to end, your students will have a solid research foundation for conducting and analyzing surveys as well as other methods of research. In this section, students learn about research concepts and measurement and how to write valid survey questions. They also learn about survey sampling and collecting reliable data.

Part II also introduces data processing, analysis, and statistics. Your students learn how to read computer printouts such as frequencies and cross-tabulations, and they become acquainted with different types of statistics. Your students also learn how to select the right statistic for the type of data that has been collected and how to use statistics as a tool for interpreting the significance of research results. When the post-research phase is examined at the conclusion of Part II, your students learn how decision makers use research results when they make important decisions.

Part III uses the three-phase research process model to examine content analysis, experiments, focus groups, and a multitude of other research methods. Your students learn that concepts such as sampling, measurement, validity, reliability, data processing, statistical analysis, and writing research reports that were discussed as we examined surveys also apply to content analysis, experiments, and other research methods.

Recognizing that valid research should produce a valid representation of a diverse population, Part IV includes a chapter on researching racial and ethnic minorities. Because unique issues must be addressed in drawing a scientific sample, writing an unbiased questionnaire or conducting a professional interview, this chapter focuses on overcoming potential barriers to representing racial and ethnic minorities in research designs. Chapter 16 examines how research is conducted in an academic environment. Chapter 17 includes many examples of how research results have been applied in industry, summarizes the many ethical issues that have been discussed throughout the book, and addresses the future of research in the communication field.

At the end of each chapter, we've suggested activities that will help your students practice what they've learned in the text. Many of these activities are identical to the kinds of research activities that they might encounter once they begin their careers in communication. We have also included recommended readings at the end of most chapters. These readings, which have been carefully selected from books, academic and trade journals, and newspapers and magazines, serve three main purposes. First, we think many should be included in a personal research library. Second, these readings are excellent sources for your students to expand their knowledge of research, its roots, and contemporary practice. Third, for those areas of research that you may want to have a more in-depth treatment, you can assign some of the recommended readings for papers or class discussions.

For your students to benefit fully from the text and suggested activities, we recommend a basic statistics book, the most current version of a computer program that specializes in analyzing research data, and its accompanying manual. To enhance your students' research learning experience, we also recommend that they read newspapers, magazines, and trade publications for their communication specialty, watch and listen to broadcast and cable news and public affairs programs, and search the Internet and online information services, where they will encounter many examples of research as it is used in the real world. Reading the academic communication journals will also provide your students with knowledge about the diverse research and analytical tools that are discussed in the book.

The appendixes, glossary, references, and index that are included in the last part of this book should make the text easier for your students to use. The appendix should be helpful because it provides examples of items that are discussed in the text such as a complete survey questionnaire, survey codebook, research budgets, and frequency and cross-tabulation tables.

Thank you for selecting *Research in Mass Communication* as your research text. We feel that it will enhance your students' research learning experience in many ways. In addition to learning how to conduct and use research, your students will learn that research is an integral part of sound business practices, a necessary part of astute planning, and a prerequisite to effective decision making. Through this text, your students will learn that research is the underpinning of skillful reporting, the backbone of business, marketing, and journalistic success, and the inspiration for creative enterprise. They will also learn that research is the foundation for the scholarly activity that takes place in the classroom and throughout the academic world. Finally, *Research in Mass Communication* will help show your students that research is intellectually stimulating, important to their career aspirations, and — surprisingly — even fun.

To the Student

Research in Mass Communication has been written to take the mystery out of research while making it relevant to you and your career goals in the field of communication. This text has been written to make you knowledgeable about the research process and competent in conducting and analyzing research. It has been written to show you how research is an integral part of good decision making in the business, creative, and journalistic worlds.

Whether you are a journalism, public relations, advertising, broadcast, or integrated communications major, this text can help you become an astute consumer of research who is easily able to differentiate good research from bad. Good research produces quality information that media and public relations decision makers can use to make better decisions, journalists can use to report and write better stories, and advertising professionals can use to write better copy and create more effective campaigns.

Research in Mass Communication has been organized to connect research with the real world in several ways. First, a *decision maker/ research expert model* has been used to demonstrate that often the person who identifies a need for research and actually uses the results when making decisions is different from the person who has the expertise to conduct the research. The decision maker and research expert are both important in the research process, but they serve different functions. Most of you will become decision makers, identifying a research need, commissioning the research from a research expert, and making and implementing decisions based on the results of the research. The research expert may be a vice president of research within your company, the head of an outside research company, or a university professor. Some of you will actually become experts in collecting, analyzing, and reporting scientifically based research data. And a few of you may even pursue academic careers in which you will function as both the decision maker and research expert in your own program of research.

Even though the decision maker in the communication industry usually does not have the expertise of the research expert, the decision maker must be able to distinguish good research from bad. To make effective decisions, the decision maker requires valid information. Knowledge about the research process helps the decision maker evaluate the information produced by the process before deciding to use it. The decision maker may use the results for planning, developing appropriate public relations, advertising, or political campaigns, writing or broadcasting news stories, or evaluating the effectiveness of a campaign.

For the research expert, designing and conducting research is a creative, intellectual, and business-oriented enterprise that is professionally rewarding. The opportunities for the research expert to use his or her creativity are unlimited. Research is built on scientific principles, but *how* the study is designed, the data are analyzed, and the results are reported can really make the creative juices flow.

The intellectual side of research is awesome. From reading and analyzing the latest relevant literature to exploring new communication terrains to analyzing and synthesizing data to communicating significant research results and discussing and debating their implications, the research expert is always stimulated intellectually.

Conducting a research study requires the research expert to employ many of the management skills that are used in the business world. Whether in industry or an academic environment, the research expert must be organized; meet deadlines; stay within a budget; hire, supervise, and motivate staff; delegate responsibilities to assistants; and work with and communicate effectively with other executives. And, like business executives who are involved in launching new products, campaigns, and businesses, the research expert must also be able to translate an idea into reality. The research expert starts with a research idea, but the end product must be a concrete reality with real data from real people with real meaning.

Perhaps, one of the most rewarding aspects of being a research expert is the opportunity to become a feedback channel so that the diverse voices of newspaper and magazine readers, TV and cable viewers, radio listeners and Internet surfers, movie-goers and video renters, consumers and voters, citizens and various other publics can talk back to decision makers. Without that feedback channel that is made possible through research, media moguls and executives, opinion and community leaders, elected and appointed officials, advertisers and computer company chairs, non-profit heads and academic leaders would be uninformed about the opinions, attitudes, aspirations, and activities of their target markets and constituencies.

To help illustrate how research is actually conducted, this text uses a *three-phase research process model* consisting of: (1) a pre-research phase, (2) a research phase, and (3) a post-research phase. During the pre-research phase, the decision maker, who can be an executive, manager, creative director, editor, producer, practitioner, or university professor, identifies a problem, issue, opportunity, theory, or some research need and the appropriate research method for gathering information to understand the problem.

The research expert actually conducts the research during the research phase, using scientifically based research methods. Finally, during the post-research phase, the decision maker evaluates the research results and decides which results, if any, to use in decisions. Once decisions are implemented, the decision maker carefully monitors the impact of those decisions, paying close attention to the role that research played in understanding an issue, solving a problem, launching a new program, creating a campaign, or developing a new strategy.

By using this three-phase research process, you will see how research, regardless of the method used, is similar during the pre-research and post-research phases but varies during the research phase. During the research phase, the unique, sequential steps of each research method are treated clearly and comprehensively to make you comfortable with conducting, analyzing, and evaluating research results and methods.

Another way we have tried to enhance the relevance of research is by providing interesting, *relevant examples* from the different specialties in the field of communication and from such familiar sources as the daily newspaper, consumer and trade magazines, television, and the Internet. In addition, we have included research examples from decision makers who have commissioned research and implemented the results, as well as examples from research studies that we have conducted personally. And to illustrate the similarities between the academic and industry research process, we have provided examples from scholarly journals.

One important feature of this text is its emphasis on *communicating research results*. As you'll discover in this text, it is not enough to know how to conduct research, you must also be able to communicate the results in written and oral reports. In addition, you'll learn that the research method dictates how the research report should be written. For example, as you learn the process for conducting surveys, you'll learn how survey research reports should be written. And when you move to the focus group research method, you'll learn how to write a focus group report and how that differs from written survey research reports. You will also learn how to write an executive summary, a key component of written research reports in industry.

An examination of the table of contents shows that this book has been divided into four parts. Part I introduces you to the research process. Some questions that will be answered in this section include: Who conducts research and why is it conducted? What is research and what are its roots?

Part II is a comprehensive examination of survey research. This section examines survey research during the pre-research, research, and post-research phases. By providing such an in-depth examination of survey research from beginning to end, you will have a foundation for conducting and evaluating a popular and powerful research method. Surveys are popular because they are the only method that can produce data that can represent the total population of newspaper and magazine readers, TV and cable viewers, computer users and Internet surfers, moviegoers and movie renters, consumers, voters, and other publics.

Surveys are powerful because they can predict the outcome of a presidential election, determine the fate of a favorite TV program, set the advertising rates for a new TV season, or even set the agenda for the President of the United States and the U.S. Congress. It is not unusual for survey or poll results to be a front page story in the *New York Times*, a lead story on the "NBC Nightly News," or the centerpiece of the network and cable talking-head public affairs programs. Once you have a thorough grasp of scientific surveys, you will be better able to understand the other research methods, including the similarities and differences in the research process, and the contributions and limitations of the results produced.

Part II also introduces you to data analysis and statistics. You will learn how to read computer printouts such as frequencies and cross-tabulations and become acquainted with different types of statistics. You will also learn how to select the right statistic for the type of data that you have collected and how to use statistics as a tool for interpreting the significance of your research results.

Part III uses the three-phase research process model to examine content analysis, experiments, focus groups, and a multitude of other research methods. Recognizing that valid research should produce a valid representation of a diverse population, Part IV includes a chapter on researching racial and ethnic minorities. Because unique issues must be addressed in drawing a scientific sample, writing an unbiased questionnaire or conducting a professional interview, this chapter focuses on overcoming potential barriers to representing racial and ethnic minorities in research designs. Chapter 16 examines how research is conducted in an academic environment. Chapter 17 includes many examples of how research results have been applied in industry, summarizes the many ethical issues that have been discussed throughout the book, and addresses the future of research in the communication field.

At the end of each chapter, you'll find suggested activities that will help you practice what you have learned in the text. Many of these activities are identical to the kinds of research activities that you might encounter once you begin your career in communication. We have also included recommended readings for most chapters. These readings, which have been carefully selected from books, academic and trade journals, and newspapers and magazines, serve two main purposes. First, we think many should be included in a personal research library. Second, these readings are excellent sources to expand your knowledge of research, its roots, and contemporary practice.

To benefit fully from the text and suggested activities, we also recommend a basic statistics book, the most current version of a computer program that specializes in analyzing research data, and its accompanying manual. To enhance your research learning experience, we also recommend that you read newspapers, magazines, and trade publications for your communication specialty, watch and listen to broadcast and cable news and public affairs programs, and search the Internet and online information services, where you will encounter many examples of research as it is used in the real world. Reading the academic communication journals will also provide you with knowledge about the diverse research and analytical tools that are discussed in the book.

The appendixes, glossary, references, and index that are included in the last part of this book should make the text easier to use. The appendixes should be helpful because they provide examples of items that are discussed in the text such as a complete survey questionnaire, survey codebook, research budgets, and frequency and cross-tabulation tables.

Research in Mass Communication enhances the classroom research learning experience. The text illustrates how research is an integral part of sound business practices, a necessary part of astute planning, and a prerequisite to effective decision making. Research is the underpinning of skillful reporting, the backbone of business, marketing, and journalistic success, and the inspiration for creative endeavors. Finally, research is the foundation for the scholarly activity that takes place in the classroom and throughout the academic world. *Research in Mass Communication* will help show you how research is intellectually stimulating, important to your career aspirations, and—surprisingly—even fun.

Acknowledgments

Paula Poindexter would like to acknowledge the many people who have influenced her interest in research as well as her approach to making research relevant for students. First, she would like to thank her coauthor and colleague, Maxwell E. McCombs, who ignited the spark that lit her career-long interest in research while she was a graduate student at Syracuse University. She would also like to thank the media companies and academic institutions where she was able to practice and refine the three-phase research model that is outlined in the book.

A very special acknowledgment is given to the over 1,200 journalism, advertising, and public relations students whom she has taught how to conduct, analyze, and report research. Students from the academic years 1996–97 and 1997–98 are especially acknowledged because they used draft chapters from *Research in Mass Communication* for their primary text. The positive reception to the ideas in the text suggested that research was indeed becoming relevant for them. A heartfelt thank you is given to her colleague Dominic Lasorsa and the many reviewers who gave enthusiastic and insightful comments on the manuscript.

Development editor Mark Paluch and copyeditor Margaret Hill are also acknowledged. Their sharp editing pencils and format suggestions made the writing clearer, cleaner, and more accessible.

Finally, Paula Poindexter acknowledges her husband, Terry A. Wilson, and daughter, Alexandra, for their love, support, and patience during the writing of this book. An extra special thank you is given to her parents, Dr. and Mrs. A. N. Poindexter, who have always expressed love, support, and pride in everything that she has undertaken or accomplished.

Maxwell McCombs expresses thanks to his wife, Betsy, and sons, Max and Sam.

Paula M. Poindexter
Maxwell E. McCombs

Brief Contents

Contents

Checklists, Sample Materials, and Figures

About the Authors

Paula M. Poindexter first became fascinated with research when she was a graduate student at Syracuse University. While searching the literature on newspaper readers for the American Newspaper Publishers Association News Research Center, she discovered the 1964 Westley and Serverin study on non-newspaper readers. Thinking it was unbelievable that people didn't read newspapers, she wanted to learn why. That question was answered in her first published academic journal article, "Daily Newspaper Readers: Why They Don't Read." Since that initial research endeavor, research has been an important part of Poindexter's life, both professionally and personally.

From 1981 to 1983 at the *Los Angeles Times,* Poindexter conducted surveys on newspaper readers and non-readers in Los Angeles and Orange County for senior executives. When she was promoted to head the division of special projects in 1983, Poindexter commissioned surveys and focus groups to help her make decisions about new programs and projects she launched.

Her first projects were involved in the pioneering electronic publishing projects of the *Los Angeles Times* and its parent company, Times Mirror. In 1983 and 1984, Poindexter developed and managed a market test of Audiotex news services, one of the first four 976 telephone information services to be launched in California. In addition to creating a weekly interactive quiz for Times Mirror's videotex venture, Poindexter was the *Los Angeles Times* Affiliate Representative to Videotex America.

In 1985, Poindexter used research results from one-on-one depth interviews and surveys to help her make decisions about a strategy for launching a new program, the *Los Angeles Times in Education.* The positive results of a field experiment on the effects of using the newspaper in the classroom that she designed and conducted became the centerpiece of the marketing strategy of the *Los Angeles Times'* million dollar newspaper-in-education program in Southern California. As a manager and later executive at the *Times,* Poindexter always relied on primary and secondary research to help her make decisions on the programs that she started and headed until she left in 1991.

Now an associate professor of journalism and advertising at the University of Texas at Austin, Poindexter has been teaching research for nine years. She has also taught at the University of Southern California and the University of Georgia and has been a reporter and producer for KPRC-TV, the NBC affiliate TV station in Houston.

Poindexter is book review editor for *Journalism & Mass Communication Quarterly,* and in 1997, she won the Association for Education in Journalism and Mass Communication (AEJMC) Teaching Standards Competition First Place Award. In her winning paper, Poindexter proposed and tested a model for teaching research in journalism, advertising, and public relations classrooms.

Poindexter received a B.S. degree in Radio-TV-Film from the University of Texas at Austin and M.A. and Ph.D. degrees from Syracuse University.

Maxwell E. McCombs was introduced to communication research by "a benevolent conspiracy." When he first appeared at Stanford University as a beginning graduate student in journalism, Professor Chilton Bush steered him into Wilbur Schramm's theory course, Bush's own content analysis seminar, and psychology courses in statistics and learning theory. In short, McCombs began a Ph.D. program in communication research. It was also during that first year of graduate study when he read Walter Lippmann's *Public Opinion,* the book that he always cites as the intellectual father of agenda setting.

At the end of that academic year at Stanford, an M.A. in hand, McCombs returned to New Orleans and worked as a reporter on the *Times-Picayune.* But that year at Stanford had set his agenda and two years later McCombs returned to Stanford to complete his Ph.D. From there he moved to UCLA and then the University of North Carolina, where he met his long-standing friend and colleague, Donald Shaw. During the 1968 presidential campaign they conducted the seminal Chapel Hill study, which has now generated more than 300 studies of agenda setting worldwide.

McCombs currently holds the Jesse H. Jones Centennial Chair in Communication at the University of Texas at Austin. Also president of the World Association for Public Opinion Research and a fellow of the International Communication Association, McCombs recently received the Murray Edelman Award of the American Political Science Association for his continuing work on agenda setting. In 1998, McCombs was awarded the Deutschmann Award for excellence in research by the Association for Education in Journalism and Mass Communication. McCombs is coauthor of *Contemporary Public Opinion* (1991), which has been translated into Japanese, Korean, and Greek, and coeditor of *Communication and Democracy: Exploring the Intellectual Frontiers in Agenda Setting Research* (1997) and *Agenda Setting* (1991). He also is the author of a dozen recent journal articles and book chapters on public opinion and the influence of the news media.

Prior to joining the University of Texas faculty in 1985, McCombs was the John Ben Snow Professor of Research at Syracuse University and also served simultaneously for ten years as director of the News Research Center of the American Newspaper Publishers Association. McCombs has been on the faculties of the University of North Carolina at Chapel Hill and UCLA.

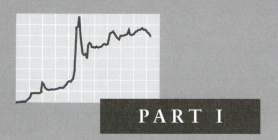

PART I

Introduction

CHAPTER 1

Introduction to Research and the Three-Phase Research Process

- What is research?
- Who conducts research?
- Why is research conducted?
- What are the types of research?
- What is the research process?
- What is the language of research?
- What are the roots of communication research?

Research Is an Essential Tool for Decision Makers

Every executive, manager, creative director, journalist, and practitioner uses research regularly. Some research is informal and unscientific, such as asking a friend's opinion about a new public service campaign to promote recycling. Other research is scientifically structured such as conducting a survey to learn newspaper readers' reactions to a new entertainment section or consumers' responses to a new ad campaign for Grand Cherokee sport utility vehicles. Research helps executives, managers, and practitioners identify and understand consumers' actions and attitudes as well as business opportunities and problems that may be percolating in the communication environment.

Effective managers and professionals in the fields of advertising and marketing, public relations, journalism, broadcasting, film, public opinion, and publishing rely on credible research to enhance their planning, decision making, creative inspiration, and media marketing activities, as well as journalistic and public opinion analysis and reporting. Effective executives, managers, and practitioners also rely on trustworthy research to evaluate the effectiveness of advertising and public relations campaigns, new product launches, and program debuts. Executives and practitioners depend on research to keep them connected to the most powerful constituents on the communication landscape—consumers, readers, viewers, publics, and voters.

What do executives and professionals want to know about consumers, readers, viewers, publics, and voters? Everything. They want to know their levels of awareness and knowledge, attitudes and activities, television viewing, newspaper reading, radio listening, recall of advertised products, shopping patterns, political candidate preferences, turn-ons and turn-offs, hopes and fears, income earned and income potential, educational level, lifestyle, and outlook on future economic prosperity. In sum, executives, managers, and practitioners want to know everything about the hearts and minds and pocketbooks of those who will ultimately determine the success or failure of their communication companies, campaigns, and products.

Rarely do executives, managers, creative directors, and practitioners such as public relations professionals or journalists conduct the research themselves. They usually commission research from a research expert with impressive credentials and years of research experience. In some cases, the research expert is internal, such as the research vice president at a magazine or television network or an account planner or research director at an advertising agency. In other cases, the research expert is an executive of a research company that is in the business of conducting hundreds of research studies a year. In an academic setting, the research expert is a professor who uses various scientific research methods to understand social and human behavior, attitudes, values, and beliefs, as well as media content and its effects on diverse audiences in the communication environment.

Regardless of who has primary responsibility for conducting the research, the decision maker who initiates the research and uses the results must thoroughly understand the research process that ultimately produces credible, reliable data.

Although many of you may not dream of becoming a research director who earns $90,000 or more a year or a university professor who holds an endowed chair, all of you should recognize that your future jobs will require that you rely on research to understand your readers, viewers, consumers, publics, or voters. Understanding the process that produces the data you use for decision making, creative inspiration, reporting, or evaluating the effectiveness of public relations, advertising, and political campaigns may ultimately determine the level of success you achieve in your communication career.

What is research? At the most informal level, research is collecting information. At the most structured level, research is a set of procedures for the systematic and objective observation, collection, processing, analysis, and reporting of information. Research is an approach or technique for identifying relationships, uncovering threats and problems, monitoring programs, evaluating effectiveness, pinpointing opportunities, and describing who is a part of the communication terrain.

Much of the research in the communication industry is directed at solving practical problems or understanding practical issues. Research in communication education is directed toward describing and understanding social and communication issues, behavior, and phenomena through answering research questions, testing hypotheses, or building theories.

Research can be useless or useful. It can be invalid or valid. It can be unrepresentative or representative. It can be the opinion of one or the opinions of many. It can be qualitative and impressionistic or quantitative and grounded in numbers. Overall, the goal of an effective executive, manager, or practitioner is to understand the difference so that he or she can have access to useful, valid, representative research for insight and quality decision making, creative inspiration, and the writing and reporting of unbiased stories about the neighborhood, the country, or the world. Effective managers and professionals rely on research that's found at the far right of the research continuum in Figure 1.1.

FIGURE 1.1   *The Research Continuum*

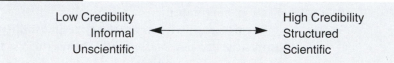

Low Credibility   High Credibility
Informal   Structured
Unscientific   Scientific

The Research Process

The research process can be divided into three distinct but related phases: (1) pre-research, (2) research, (3) post-research. The pre-research phase is initiated by a decision maker who needs relevant and reliable information. The decision maker may be a media manager, a public relations or advertising vice president, a reporter or editor, or a communication professor.

The research phase is handled by the research expert. The research expert has academic training and industry or academic research experience. In industry, the decision maker who initiates the research may hire an outside research expert or supplier or delegate the research task to an internal research expert. In the university, the decision maker and research expert are the same. The professor decides what research will be conducted and then, relying on his or her research expertise, proceeds to carry it out.

The post-research phase returns the responsibility to the decision maker. During this phase, the decision maker receives the research results and analysis from the research expert and decides which, if any, results to use in decisions that have to be made. After implementing the decision, the decision maker evaluates its impact and the role that the research results played. The communication professor's role is slightly different during the post-research phase. The professor evaluates the results from the research phase, then decides how the results should be incorporated into the next stage of his or her program of research. (We'll discuss more about the academic researcher in Chapter 16.)

Figure 1.2 illustrates the three-phase research process. It serves as an outline for our discussion on how the research process works.

FIGURE 1.2   *A Three-Phase Model of the Communication Research Process and the Roles of the Decision Maker and Research Expert*

PRE-RESEARCH PHASE AND THE DECISION MAKER
- Monitor environment and literature.
- Identify problem, trend, opportunity, issue, phenomenon, or theory.
- Specify research topic in research question or hypothesis form.
- Design research study using ethical standards: Specify research method, specify population, and establish budget and timetable.
- Decide who will conduct study.

RESEARCH PHASE AND THE RESEARCH EXPERT
- Consult with decision maker on purpose, background information, research design, measurement instrument, population, sampling, and budget.
- Conduct in-depth literature review.
- Implement research design using ethical standards.
- Draft, pretest, and revise measurement instrument.
- Select participants.
- Secure final approval of measurement instrument from decision maker.
- Train data collectors.
- Collect data.
- Process data.
- Analyze data.
- Write report and prepare oral presentation.
- Share results with decision maker and relevant audiences.

POST-RESEARCH PHASE AND THE DECISION MAKER
- Review and evaluate research results using ethical standards.
- Make decisions based on results and evaluate impact of decisions implemented.
- Decide next step.

Pre-Research Phase

 Identifying a Need for Research

The pre-research phase first requires that the effective decision maker monitor the environment to identify potential problems, opportunities, trends, or issues. Monitoring the environment requires listening attentively, reading widely, and seeing clearly. A tuned-in newspaper executive, public relations professional, advertising creative director, or local TV news reporter realizes that a problem, opportunity, trend, or issue in the organization or on the communication landscape needs to be examined closely.

Having identified a problem or issue, the executive, manager, creative director, or practitioner becomes familiar with everything that is already known about it. Internal background searches, which may take several forms, are conducted to determine institutional knowledge of the issue. Files of previous internal reports on the topic are reviewed. Internal clip files of articles from newspapers, magazines, and trade journals are examined. Online database and World Wide Web searches for recent articles or studies on the topic are conducted. In addition, internal and external experts who have previously been associated with the topic are consulted.

In the academic arena, the communication, social science, or marketing professor begins his or her search with academic journals. This literature review provides the academic researcher with comprehensive knowledge of what is already known about the topic. Although university professors primarily turn to academic journals, they may also examine the popular and trade press for background information on the topic.

Research Questions Guide the Research

Once available information has been collected and synthesized, the topic is formulated as a research question. Examples of research questions include: What is the attitude of 21- to 34-year-olds toward the label "Generation X"? What is the impact of the Internet on newspaper reading? What do television viewers usually do when commercials come on? What perceptions do African Americans have about local news? How does local TV news cover Latinos? What do children learn from prime-time TV? How has prime-time TV's portrayal of women changed since the 1950s? What is the effect of front page news coverage over time?

Well-crafted research questions help executives, managers, creative directors, and practitioners clarify what information is needed to understand an issue, solve a problem, document a trend, or take advantage of an opportunity. Research questions are necessary to design useful research studies. At the conclusion of the research study, the decision maker should have at least a tentative answer to the research question.

Research Hypotheses

Some university professors who conduct research use research questions to determine the relationship between two or more variables, whereas others prefer to use hypotheses to guide their research. Hypotheses use statements instead of questions. Essentially, the researcher predicts the nature of a relationship between two or more variables under investigation. Examples of hypotheses include: As Internet use *increases,* newspaper reading *decreases.* As violent TV viewing *increases,* viewers' fears of becoming a victim of a crime *increase. Greater* newspaper use in elementary and secondary classrooms leads to *more frequent* newspaper reading among adults. As the use of humor in commercials *increases,* recall of the brand *decreases.*

Both research questions and hypotheses serve as guideposts for the research design. They keep the researcher focused on the overall purpose of the research.

Deciding on the Appropriate Research Method

The final components of the pre-research phase include decisions on the best method and population to answer the research question as well as the appropriate research expert to conduct the study. The budget and timetable, which also have to be specified, will influence the complexity of the research design and the number of participants selected from the population. All of the design issues must be planned using ethical standards.

Figure 1.3 (p. 10) lists the various research methods we consider in this book, including surveys, content analysis studies, experiments, focus groups, observation, copy testing, and secondary data analyses. The executive, manager, creative director, or practitioner usually commissions the actual fieldwork from a research expert who may be an internal research vice president or an external research supplier or consultant. In an advertising or public relations agency, the account executive helps facilitate the process of getting the appropriate research, and the research manager or account planner conducts the research to meet the needs of the creative director. In a university, the communication professor may enlist students to serve as interviewers for surveys or subjects in experiments.

FIGURE 1.3   *Some Research Methods Used in
the Communication Field*

- **Survey**
  Telephone survey or poll
  Mail survey
  Face-to-face or in-person survey
  Intercept survey
  E-mail, fax, online, Internet, World Wide Web survey or poll
  Tracking poll or panel survey
  Exit poll
- **Content Analysis**
- **Experiment**
- **Focus Group**
- **One-on-One Depth Interview**
- **Observation**
- **Case Study**
- **Testing**
  Copy testing
  Concept testing
  Trial research
  Market testing
- **Evaluation Research**
- **Syndicated Research**
- **Secondary Analysis**
- **Academic Qualitative Methods**
  Ethnography
  Reception studies
  Cultural studies
  Textual studies
- **Multiple Research Methods**

Research Phase

The research phase is usually handled by the research expert. The research expert may be an internal or external research director, a consultant, or a professor. In industry, the research expert meets with the executive, manager, or practitioner to learn the research question, preferred research method, relevant population, timetable, and budget. The research expert conducts a comprehensive literature review, constructs and pretests a measurement instrument such as a questionnaire, and selects participants using the appropriate sampling techniques. The executive, manager, or practitioner approves the final measurement instrument to ensure that it will, in fact, answer the research question. The account executive represents the creative director's needs during this phase.

After appropriate approvals and participant selection, the research expert trains the data collectors; collects, processes, and analyzes the data; and writes up and reports the results to the decision maker who commissioned the research study. The research expert must adhere to ethical standards in carrying out each aspect of the research design.

In an academic environment, the university professor uses his or her research expertise to complete each task during the research phase. The university professor writes the research results for a scholarly conference presentation or academic journal. The professor's peers review the paper to determine its contribution to the field. Papers that pass the rigorous academic criteria are then presented at conferences or published in the academic communication journals.

Post-Research Phase

The effective executive, manager, or practitioner evaluates the research results and decides whether or not to use them in decisions that will be implemented. As the decision maker, the executive, manager, or practitioner ultimately evaluates the impact of the research-based decision on solving the problem, taking advantage of an opportunity, and better understanding what is happening on the communication terrain.

Although the university professor usually does not have an opportunity to implement the decisions that are based on the research results, he or she assesses the results as well as the limitations of the study to refine future studies on the topic.

Research Relies on Scientific Research Methods

Even though each segment of the communication landscape—journalism, advertising, public relations, television, film, publishing, marketing, political communication, and communication education—has unique practical and theoretical research questions to be asked and answered, the basic research process remains the same. Each segment of the communication field relies on scientifically based research procedures to provide objective, reliable data to make effective decisions. These procedures have roots in the Age of Reason, a period during the eighteenth century in which science was separated from religion and scientific conclusions were based on logic, observation, and experiments (Asimov, 1994, p. 201; *Compton's Interactive Encyclopedia*, 1995).

In their book *An Introduction to Logic and Scientific Method*, philosophers Morris Cohen and Ernest Nagel (1934, p. 192) described scientific method as "the way in which we test impressions, opinions, or surmises by examining the best available evidence for and against them." These philosophers said that the scientific method is one of four methods traditionally relied on for forming opinions or explaining things around us. The other three methods are tenacity, authority, and intuition (Cohen & Nagel, 1934, pp. 194–95). The method of tenacity is an example of holding on to a belief because we have always believed it. The method of authority is a result of believing something because a higher source says we must believe it. The higher source may be religion, tradition, or some other authoritative source. The method of intuition suggests that propositions are believed to be true because they're obvious. Also called *a priori,* this method of knowing is based on theory and not experience (Kerlinger, 1973, p. 5).

The scientific method differs from these other methods of knowing because it uses specific procedures, independent of tenacious beliefs, authoritative sources, and intuition, for objectively observing phenomena to discover evidence that supports or refutes propositions about things around us.

Research Uses a Special Language

Most professionals use a special language that is unique to their fields. For example, professionals in law, astronomy, and computer science use terms that can be understood by their colleagues, but may sound like a foreign language to outsiders. Attorneys talk about depositions and discovery, astronomers refer to light-years and black holes, and computer scientists speak about microprocessors and RAM. Even professional athletes use unique terms to communicate the process, status, or outcome of their sport. To understand and appreciate golf, for example, you need to understand eagle, birdie, par, bogey, and double bogey, to name a few of the terms used in scoring golf. Research also has unique terms that must be understood to communicate the process, status, and outcome of a research project. A look through the terms and definitions in the glossary will show you the language of research that you will encounter as you learn about research and how it is conducted and analyzed. Some of the terms apply to scientifically based research in general; others are applicable to specific research methods.

Let's examine a few of the terms now to understand how the language of research is used. We will discuss most of the terms, however, in the context of examining the various research methods. More than likely you have used the term *theory* in everyday conversation. It would not be unusual for you to have a theory about something. Perhaps, you have a theory about how to stop hiccups. You may theorize that if you drink one glass of water, the hiccups will stop. Your friend's theory might be that eating a teaspoon of sugar stops hiccups. Probably most people have heard the theory about holding your breath or sneaking up on someone and scaring them to stop hiccups. These kinds of theories are commonplace, and they simply mean that you have a guess or conjecture about something.

But when the term "theory" is used in scientific research, it has a specific meaning. Noted research and theory scholar Kerlinger said theory is the basic aim of science. In other words, the goal of science is to explain natural phenomena and these explanations are called theory. Kerlinger (1973, p. 5) defines theory as "a set of interrelated concepts, definitions, and propositions that present a systematic view of phenomena by specifying relations among variables, with the purpose of explaining and predicting the phenomena."

Communication scholars Donohew and Palmgreen (1981, p. 29) emphasized the tentative nature of theory. If consistent, reliable testing of the theory shows the theory to be flawed, the theory will be ignored or discarded. Throughout the history of science and discovery, many theories have been proposed and discarded. During the second century, astronomer Ptolemy theorized that the earth was the center of the universe. Before explorers set out to examine the world, the earth was thought to be flat.

The communication field has had theories proposed and later discarded when research results or logic could not support them. One such theory was the "magic bullet" theory proposed in the aftermath of World War I. Also known as the "hypodermic needle" theory, this theory proposed that the communicator could inject the audience with propaganda and the audience would be persuaded. It wasn't long before this theory was dismissed as naive and simplistic.

Some theories in communication have endured the test of empirical research. In 1922, political columnist and author of *Public Opinion* Walter Lippmann theorized about the agenda-setting effects of the media when he linked the world outside and the pictures in our heads, and fifty years later the theory was empirically tested. Using scientifically based research methods, communication scholars Maxwell McCombs and Donald Shaw found support for the theory that "the pattern of news coverage influences public perception of what are the important issues of the day" (McCombs, 1992, p. 815). Tested over time and under many conditions, this agenda-setting theory of the press endures today.

Another term used in the language of research is *measurement*. In general, when we think of measurement, we think of how many cups of flour are needed for making chocolate chip cookies, how many pounds we want to lose, or how many miles we can drive before running out of gas. Kerlinger (1973, p. 426) borrowed a definition of measurement from mathematics and described it as "the assignment of numerals to objects or events according to rules."

Communication researcher Keith Stamm (1981, p. 90) defined measurement as "a set of rules for assigning numbers to observations." To be even more specific, we'll define measurement as it applies to communication research: measurement is a set of rules for assigning numbers, which represent values of varying degrees of precision, for reported or observed behaviors, attitudes, opinions, and other individual, group, organization, content, or issue characteristics. In communication research, we can measure how much time college students spend on the Internet or reading magazines. We can measure reported attitudes toward the use of humor or emotion in advertising. We can also measure the number of times the term "Generation X" is used in newspapers or what types of violence are showing during prime-time TV. Practically speaking, these measurements are the questions that we ask on questionnaires or rules we use for coding media content or observing media behavior.

In scientifically based research, it is imperative that measurements be valid and reliable representations of the concept being studied. Measurements that lack validity and reliability contain bias and produce error in the measurement of the concept under study. You'll be introduced to these criteria as they relate to measurement when designing a survey in Chapter 3.

Internal validity and *external validity* are terms that are also used in scientifically based research. Internal validity is concerned with whether the measurement is an *accurate* representation of the concept being studied. For example, *access* to the Internet is *not* a valid measurement of *use* of the Internet. Just because an individual has access to the Internet doesn't mean he or she spends time on it. The researcher would need to assess *actual time spent* on the Internet to have a valid measure of Internet use. We'll discuss more about internal validity, concepts, and measurements in Chapter 3.

External validity refers to whether the results of a research study are generalizable to the population of interest. How the participants in a study were selected has a lot to do with how generalizable the results are. But other issues may affect the external validity. For example, can you generalize the results of a study in Austin to the entire nation? Can you generalize the results of a study of college students to baby boomers? Can you generalize the results of a study in which 10 percent of the sample responded to the population as a whole? Can you generalize the results of a study on how people watch TV in a laboratory to how people watch TV at home? The answer to these questions is no.

Results that lack external validity are misleading. We'll address the issues of external validity in more detail as we discuss experiments in Chapter 12. You'll also learn the definitions and accurate use of other terms pertaining to research as we discuss those terms in the context of actually conducting the research.

Communication Research Has a Long and Diverse History

To understand the role, process, institutions, audience, and effects of communication, scientific research methods have been applied across the social and behavioral sciences spectrum. Communication has been scientifically studied in the fields of psychology, social psychology, sociology, political science, anthropology, economics, linguistics, marketing, history, and education as well as the traditional communication disciplines of journalism, advertising, public relations, broadcasting, film, publishing, and speech. Pioneering research in the early twentieth century addressed practical and theoretical issues in the field of communication.

In 1916, the *Literary Digest* magazine used mail surveys to accurately predict who would win the presidential election. The magazine mailed out millions of postcards to names gathered from telephone directories and automobile registration lists, and the returned postcards were used to accurately predict that Woodrow Wilson would become the next President of the United States (Rubenstein, 1995, p. 63). Even though this mail survey method enabled the *Literary Digest* to accurately predict the winner of five presidential elections from 1916 to 1932, their methodology led to their downfall in 1936 when they incorrectly predicted that Republican candidate Alf Landon would beat incumbent president Franklin D. Roosevelt.

In 1922, the *St. Louis Post-Dispatch* hired fifty students to conduct face-to-face surveys with 55,000 St. Louis residents about their newspaper likes and dislikes. One of the students was George H. Gallup (Reeves, 1984). As a result of being involved in this survey of every St. Louis resident, Gallup developed a new research method to measure opinion. Gallup thought it was unnecessary to interview *everyone;* a sample would be sufficient. Gallup tested his sampling theory in his Iowa University Ph.D. dissertation, "A New Technique for Objective Methods for Measuring Reader Interest in Newspapers." Gallup's new research method was published in *Editor & Publisher,* the trade journal of the newspaper industry, on February 8, 1930. By 1932, Young & Rubicam, a new advertising agency, asked Gallup to apply his research procedures to evaluating the effectiveness of advertising.

Psychologist Daniel Starch also applied his research knowledge to practical problems in advertising. He developed a technique for testing readership and recall of advertisements in the early 1920s (Thompson, 1994). Starch also conducted pioneering studies on radio audiences during this period.

Rather than examine practical problems in the communication industry, some early communication researchers focused on more theoretical questions about the media and its effects. A group of social scientists led by Princeton psychologist Dr. Hadley Cantril (1974) conducted one of the first studies on the *effects* of the media. In 1938 on Halloween Eve, Orson Welles broadcast a make-believe invasion from Mars on the radio. After the broadcast, the researchers designed and conducted a study to determine why some radio listeners *believed* the broadcast and became panic-stricken. According to the study, at least six million people heard the radio broadcast and one million of those listeners became frightened that Earth was being invaded by Martians. The researchers did not find one variable that contributed to the radio listeners' panic but a combination of variables, including suggestibility, the lack of critical abilities, and the influence of those around them.

During World War II, psychologists from Yale and Washington Universities conducted field and laboratory experiments for the U.S. Army to determine effective persuasive messages for changing attitudes. For example, Dr. Carl Hovland, chairman of the Yale University Psychology Department, designed an experiment that examined whether one-sided or two-sided arguments were more effective in changing opinions (Hovland et al., 1974).

Content analysis studies were also conducted during World War II. Political scientist Harold Lasswell and Ralph O. Nafziger, professor of journalism at Minnesota, conducted content analysis studies on Allied and Axis news media (Rogers & Chaffee, 1994, p. 26). Lasswell is credited with naming and first systematically using content analysis, a research method we'll talk about in Chapter 11 (Sills, 1996, p. 110).

In 1948, Lasswell (1974, p. 84) synthesized his studies on mass communication and published what has become a classic model of the process of communication:

Who
Says What
In Which Channel
To Whom
With What Effect?

Even though this model has been criticized for the assumed media effects and other models have been proposed to more accurately describe the process of communication, Lasswell's 1948 model still stands as a classic in the field of communication.

Another pioneer in mass communication research was mathematician and psychologist Paul Lazarsfeld, who founded and directed Columbia University's Bureau of Applied Research. In the late 1930s and early 1940s, Lazarsfeld conducted studies on radio audiences, interpersonal influence, and media effects. As a result of presidential election studies conducted during the 1940s, Lazarsfeld put forward a "two-step" flow hypothesis to describe the effects of the media on voting. This hypothesis, which was later discounted by other researchers as too simplistic, proposed that the media's influence flowed from the media to a few opinion leaders to a multitude of followers (Chaffee & Rogers, 1997).

Lazarsfeld also collaborated with Frank Stanton, the director of research at CBS and later president of the network, to study radio listeners during the period in which radio as a communication medium was preeminent. Lazarsfeld and Stanton, who also had a Ph.D. in psychology, developed a machine to simultaneously test the likes and dislikes of radio audiences (Sills, 1996, p. 109).

Many others representing the numerous social and behavioral science fields used scientific research techniques to fertilize the roots of communication study and research. Even though this pioneering research was conducted prior to TV's rise as a mass medium, many of the methods—survey, experiment, content analysis—are still used today. These research methods have also been essential in developing, testing, and refining contemporary communication theories and perspectives such as uses and gratification, agenda setting, cultivation theory, the knowledge gap hypothesis, and the effects of televised violence on children.

Overview of *Research in Mass Communication*

This book will discuss various research methods and teach you how to evaluate research results for their scientific validity. Effective executives, managers, creative directors, and practitioners in the fields of public relations, advertising, journalism, broadcasting, marketing, film, public opinion, and publishing rely on these research techniques to produce credible research to enhance their planning, decision making, creative inspiration, media marketing activities, journalistic reporting, and public opinion analysis. And communication, journalism, advertising, broadcasting, and public relations scholars rely on scientifically based research methods to unearth relationships and build theories to enhance our knowledge about the process, institutions, audience, and effects of communication.

Chapters 2 through 10 of *Research in Mass Communication: A Practical Guide* apply the three-phase research process to survey research. The extensive discussion on the process of conducting surveys will help develop a foundation for understanding all types of research methods. As a result of learning how to apply the three-phase model to conducting surveys, you'll see how all research methods begin with the pre-research phase and end with the post-research phase.

The extensive attention paid to surveys does not mean this type of research is more important than other methods—but it does mean that you should have a thorough grounding in surveys because they are used more than any other research method on the professional and academic sides of communication. Without question, scientifically based surveys are the only method that will allow you to project to the whole population of readers, viewers, consumers, listeners, voters, or relevant publics.

Chapter 11 demonstrates how the three-phase research process can be used with content analysis, a research method for examining media messages such as newspaper editorial or advertising content and TV news, prime-time TV, or commercials. Experiments, you'll discover in Chapter 12, are the only method in which you can sort out causation. In Chapter 13, you'll learn about focus groups, a popular research method in the advertising, newspaper, magazine, and television industries because consumers have an opportunity to give reactions in their own words. One-on-one depth interviews, which rely on individual rather than group interviews, are also discussed in Chapter 13.

Chapter 14 examines an array of other quantitative and qualitative research methods. You'll discover that some of these other methods are variations of surveys, content analysis studies, experiments, and focus groups that you will have already studied.

Chapters 15 through 17 address research issues that affect the process as well as the outcome of research: researching racial and ethnic minorities, research in an academic environment, research applications, ethics, and the future of communication research.

SUGGESTED RESEARCH ACTIVITIES

1. Think about some issues that you have wondered about, read about, or heard about in your area of specialty in the field of communication. Make a list of three to five issues as questions to be answered. For example, often at the end of a commercial, advertisers include their World Wide Web addresses. A question for your list might be: Have consumers noticed these Web addresses and visited the Web sites?

2. After making a list of questions, pick one question on your list. How might you go about answering that question?

3. Spend several days reading newspapers, magazines, and trade journals in your field of specialty, watching TV news, and surfing the Internet looking for examples of research. Describe the examples and sources of research that you found.

4. Examine the list of research methods in Figure 1.3. Which, if any, of these methods are you already familiar with? What was the research study and what was your role in it?

RECOMMENDED READING

For a look at the rich historical background of communication research and pioneering researchers who influenced the field, see:

BRUCE A. AUSTIN, "Audience Research for Motion Pictures: Uncovering the Interests of Moviegoers," in *History of the Mass Media in the United States: An Encyclopedia*, ed. Margaret A. Blanchard, pp. 50–51. Chicago: Fitzroy Dearborn, 1998.

KENNETH R. BLAKE, "Public Opinion Polls: Straw Polls Preceded More Scientific Efforts," in *History of the Mass Media in the United States: An Encyclopedia*, ed. Margaret A. Blanchard, pp. 545–547. Chicago: Fitzroy Dearborn, 1998.

EVERETTE E. DENNIS and ELLEN WARTELLA, Eds., *American Communication Research: The Remembered History*. Mahwah, NJ: Lawrence Erlbaum Associates, 1996.

JOSEPH R. DOMINICK, "Audience Research for Broadcasting: Attempts to Measure Size of Listening Audience," in *History of the Mass Media in the United States: An Encyclopedia*, ed. Margaret A. Blanchard, pp. 49–50. Chicago: Fitzroy Dearborn, 1998.

MICHAEL C. DONATELLO, "Audience Research for Newspapers: Newspapers Seek to Tailor Products to Audiences," in *History of the Mass Media in the United States: An Encyclopedia*, ed. Margaret A. Blanchard, pp. 51–53. Chicago: Fitzroy Dearborn, 1998.

"The Founding Fathers of Advertising Research," *Journal of Advertising Research*, 1977, vol. 17, no. 3, pp. 1–32.

BRADLEY S. GREENBERG and MICHAEL B. SALWEN, "Mass Communication Theory and Research: Concepts and Models," in *An Integrated Approach to Communication Theory and Research*, ed. Michael B. Salwen and Don W. Stacks, pp. 63–78. Mahwah, NJ: Lawrence Erlbaum Associates, 1996.

LYNDA LEE KAID, "Political Communication," in *An Integrated Approach to Communication Theory and Research*, ed. Michael B. Salwen and Don W. Stacks, pp. 443–457. Mahwah, NJ: Lawrence Erlbaum Associates, 1996.

SHEARON LOWERY and MELVIN L. DEFLEUR, *Milestones in Mass Communication Research: Media Effects*, 2nd ed. New York: Longman, 1988.

RICHARD REEVES, "George Gallup's Nation of Numbers," in *Esquire's Fifty Who Made the Difference*, pp. 45–51. New York: Villard Books, 1984.

Everett M. Rogers, *A History of Communication Study: A Biographical Approach.* New York: The Free Press, 1994.

Sondra Miller Rubenstein, "The History of Surveys," in *Surveying Public Opinion,* pp. 49–83. Belmont, CA: Wadsworth Publishing Company, 1995.

Wilbur Schramm, *The Beginnings of Communication Study in America: A Personal Memoir,* ed. Steven H. Chaffee and Everett M. Rogers. Thousand Oaks, CA.: Sage Publications, 1997.

Wilbur Schramm and Donald F. Roberts, *The Process and Effects of Mass Communication,* rev. ed. Urbana: University of Illinois Press, 1971.

Donald L. Thompson, "Daniel Starch," in *The Ad Men and Women: A Biographical Dictionary of Advertising,* ed. Edd Applegate, pp. 313–324. Westport, CT: Greenwood Press, 1994.

Esther Thorson, "Advertising," in *An Integrated Approach to Communication Theory and Research,* ed. Michael B. Salwen and Don W. Stacks, pp. 211–230. Mahwah, NJ: Lawrence Erlbaum Associates, 1996.

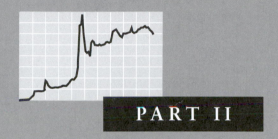

PART II

Applying the

Three-Phase

Research Process to

Survey Research

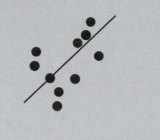

CHAPTER 2

The Pre-Research Phase and the Decision Maker

- When is the most appropriate time to conduct a survey?
- What are the steps in conducting a survey?
- What issues should be considered when deciding whether to conduct a telephone, mail, or face-to-face survey?

Surveys Help Decision Makers Understand Their Market

Imagine that you are attending a national communication convention to assess the future of communication as we know it. The program is filled with prestigious speakers: the Vice President of the United States; Ted Turner, CNN founder and vice chairman of Time Warner; CBS News anchor Dan Rather; Bill Gates, Microsoft founder and chairman; talk-show host and producer Oprah Winfrey; Steven Spielberg, director and co-founder of Dreamworks Studio; the publisher of the *New York Times;* the CEO of Ogilvy & Mather, and many more.

You notice that the press is in attendance in great numbers. The *New York Times,* the *Wall Street Journal,* the *Los Angeles Times, USA Today,* the television networks, *Advertising Age, AdWeek, Editor & Publisher,* National Public Radio, *Dateline,* and CNN are represented.

As you listen to the speakers describe their company's past and predict the future, you are struck by a consistency throughout the speeches. The speakers know their audience inside and out. They may refer to their audience as readers, viewers, listeners, constituents, residents, voters, taxpayers, citizens, or consumers, but they seem to know everything about them—how old they are, how much money they make, their likes and dislikes, their discretionary money and time, their hopes and fears, the number and ages of children who live at home, what cable movie channels they subscribe to, which newspapers they read, what TV programs they like best, whether they own a home computer, their familiarity with the Internet, whether they voted in the last presidential election, whether they voted in the last local election, their racial or ethnic background, their gender, and much, much more.

Clearly, this knowledge has been central to their company's or organization's planning and decisions in the past. And the speakers are using the information to predict the future of their company and the field of communication. How do the speakers know so much about who is reading, watching, listening to, or buying from them, you wonder.

More than likely, as decision makers, the speakers have over the years consulted many surveys, the most popular tool for learning about readers, viewers, listeners, consumers, constituents, or the residents of a city, state, or nation. Specifically a survey is a research technique that uses a standardized questionnaire to collect information about attitudes, opinions, behaviors, and background and lifestyle characteristics from a sample of respondents. The questionnaire can be self-administered or administered by an interviewer.

The Pre-Research Phase Begins with the Decision Maker

The steps involved in conducting a survey fit into the three-phase research process introduced in Chapter 1. According to Figure 2.1, the decision maker has responsibility for the pre-research phase, which involves eight steps.

Decision makers in all industries and academic environments share a common characteristic during the pre-research phase of a survey. All monitor the business, economic, political, and communication environment in which they operate in order to spot new trends and identify problems, issues, opportunities, or theories. Decision makers observe the local, state, national, and international arenas in which they function and keep tabs on their competition to stay ahead.

To monitor the environment, decision makers read widely. They read their local newspapers as well as the *New York Times*, the *Wall Street*

FIGURE 2.1   *Pre-Research Phase of Survey Research and the Decision Maker*

Step 1. Monitor environment and literature.
Step 2. Identify problem, trend, opportunity, issue, phenomenon, or theory.
Step 3. Specify survey topic in research question or hypothesis form.
Step 4. Design study using ethical standards.
Step 5. Specify survey method (telephone, face-to-face, mail) and type (cross-sectional or longitudinal study).
Step 6. Determine population to survey.
Step 7. Establish budget and timetable.
Step 8. Determine who will conduct survey.

Journal and business magazines, the trade press such as *Advertising Age, Editor & Publisher,* and *Presstime.* Decision makers watch the morning and evening news, the Sunday morning news programs, PBS's *Washington Week in Review,* and CNN.

Decision makers also listen to National Public Radio's *All Things Considered* and the local talk radio shows to keep informed of their marketing environment. Decision makers who have targeted specific markets such as people in their twenties or women or African Americans or children must also pay attention to news and information related to these specific markets.

Decision makers attend seminars or conferences to share relevant information with their peers. But, of course, in Step 1 of the pre-research phase, it is not enough to absorb the information. Effective decision makers also analyze and synthesize the information in an objective way. By doing so, decision makers are better able to tackle Step 2 of the pre-research phase in which they identify an issue, trend, opportunity, or problem that needs to be researched.

Let's say that as a result of attending the national communication conference to assess the future of communication, you soaked up the information presented by the numerous speakers. With your new found interest in the subject, you begin to read the trade and business press on the subject. After a reading period, you decide to focus on computers and their impact on traditional media.

You realize fairly quickly that before you can identify any trends, future opportunities, or problems for traditional media and advertising, you need to have a basic understanding of how media consumers are using computers and the various interactive information services that are available through it. You proceed to Step 3, where you formulate a research question.

A good research question attempts to set forth a relationship between two or more variables in question form, for example,

1. Are newspaper readers using interactive computer information services more than non-newspaper readers?
2. Are twenty-somethings using interactive computer information services more than baby boomers?
3. Which interactive information services are used the most and which services are used the least?
4. What is the impact of using interactive computer information services on "free" traditional media and "pay" traditional media?
5. What is the most effective advertising on interactive computer information services?

Standards and Decisions during the Pre-Research Phase

Ethical Standards in Conducting Surveys

Once the research questions are formulated, the decision maker focuses on Step 4, designing the research study using ethical standards. Regardless of the research method, ethical standards must be used in designing and executing the research study. Ethical standards specify that participation is voluntary and ensure that there will be no harm to the participants of the survey or other research study. In addition, participants are promised that the information they provide in the survey will be confidential and not associated with them individually but reported as a part of the complete survey results.

Suppose survey respondent Alvin Jones tells the interviewer that he has a household income of $80,000. If anyone associated with conducting the survey tells a friend, acquaintance, or telemarketing firm that respondent Alvin Jones has a household income of $80,000, the survey researchers have violated the ethical requirement of maintaining the respondent's confidentiality. This breach harms the respondent because confidential financial information will have been disclosed without the respondent's permission. This disclosure may cause the respondent to become a target of unwanted telemarketers or other types of intruders. In addition, if the respondent learns that personal information has been disclosed, he or she will likely decline to participate in future surveys.

Ethical issues and standards such as these are discussed throughout the book in the context of conducting the various research studies. Because of the importance of designing a survey and all research studies using ethical standards, Chapter 17 summarizes all ethical issues into one coherent section.

Deciding Whether to Conduct a Telephone, Mail, or Face-to-Face Survey

Step 5 addresses which type of survey should be conducted—telephone, mail, or face-to-face. (Today surveys are also being conducted by fax, e-mail, and the Internet, which we discuss in Chapter 14.) Although the decision maker may want to consult with the research expert before making a final decision about the best survey method, some issues can be addressed before the research expert is consulted. Figure 2.2 (p. 28) shows that the availability of a comprehensive and current list of prospective survey respondents, amount of time, budget and staff, desired response rate, and security are factored into the decision on which survey method to use.

FIGURE 2.2 *Issues to Consider When Selecting a Survey Method*

Issue	Telephone	Mail	Face-to-Face
1. Comprehensive and current list of people to interview	Yes	Yes	Yes
a. Names required	No	Yes	No
b. Phone numbers required	Yes	No	No
c. Addresses required	No	Yes	Yes
2. Time	Short	Long	Long
3. Budget/staff	Large	Small	Large
4. Response rate	Medium	Low	Medium
5. Security concern	Low	Low	High

All three survey methods require a comprehensive and current list of prospective respondents to produce valid data. A ten-year-old list to select names for a mail survey will not produce valid results. It would be better to use a more current list of phone numbers and conduct a telephone survey instead.

Even so, a telephone survey only requires a valid telephone number, whereas both mail surveys and face-to-face surveys require an address for the respondent to be interviewed. Although it is customary not to use a name for telephone and face-to-face surveys, the failure to use a name for a mail survey may cause the prospective respondent to toss the questionnaire in the trash. So one issue that must be addressed for all types of surveys is: How good is the list of prospective respondents?

Time and budget are also important issues when deciding which survey method to use. If your time is limited, a telephone survey is best. Politicians engaged in a campaign and news organizations on a deadline to publish a poll can conduct and complete a survey or poll in as little as twenty-four hours. More realistically, however, a telephone survey may take three to ten days from formulation of research questions to results. Mail and face-to-face surveys are much more time consuming than telephone surveys. Depending on the size of the survey, both may take several weeks to several months.

A mail survey requires time to mail out a questionnaire, wait for a response, send a reminder, then wait for a completed questionnaire to be returned. For face-to-face surveys in large metropolitan areas, it also takes times to travel to a respondent's home to conduct an interview. If the designated respondent is not home when the interviewer arrives, the interviewer will have to return on another day.

The budget, of course, also affects which survey method is selected. Telephone and face-to-face surveys generally use dozens of interviewers to conduct surveys. This adds to the personnel costs of a budget. A mail survey does not require dozens of interviewers. In fact, a single person can conduct a mail survey with hundreds of respondents. For the same size survey, face-to-face surveys are more expensive than telephone surveys because they require interviewers to travel to the respondents' homes at least once.

Telephone surveys still require interviewers to conduct the survey, but the interviewers are generally calling from a central facility and no gas and mileage costs are involved. For national and international surveys, long-distance telephone calls add to the cost of the survey. (Professional surveying firms, however, have contracts for discounted volume calling.)

As a rule of thumb, twenty-seven dollars per completed interview is used to estimate the cost of a telephone survey (Inchauste, 1999). This figure includes long-distance phone calls, interviewers, data analysis, and the overhead expenses of computer equipment, software, programming, administration, and rent. A telephone survey of 1,000 respondents would therefore cost approximately $27,000. Written and oral reports with analysis and recommendations could increase the cost of the survey by $5,000 or more. (An itemized telephone survey budget can be found in Appendix D.1.)

The costs for conducting a mail survey include printing the questionnaire and first-class postage for sending and returning it. In addition, reminders with additional questionnaires also require first-class postage. And many researchers who conduct mail surveys use advance letters to notify respondents of the forthcoming questionnaire as well as monetary incentives to encourage a response. These efforts to increase the response rate also add to the cost of conducting a mail survey. (An itemized budget for a mail survey can be found in Appendix D2.)

One of the factors involved in assessing the quality of a survey is what percentage of the prospective respondents completed the survey questionnaire. Generally, the higher the response, the more confidence that you can have in the results. Response rate is discussed in detail in Chapter 8, but it is important to mention that in assessing whether to conduct a telephone, mail, or face-to-face survey, the decision maker has to consider that unless they include a major incentive, mail surveys have by far the lowest response rates.

Face-to-face surveys now suffer from lower response rates because of security concerns among residents of large and small cities. Prospective respondents are less willing to let a stranger into their home to interview them for a survey.

In summary, this examination of the different survey methods reveals that the telephone survey, even though it requires a large budget and staff, is the best method for producing valid results during the shortest period of time. Although a mail survey is inexpensive and can be conducted by one person, its small budget and staff cannot make up for a below average response rate, which can reduce the validity of the results. Finally, the high cost of conducting a face-to-face survey and the reluctance of prospective respondents to invite strangers into their homes to conduct an interview have made this type of survey virtually obsolete in today's world.

Deciding Whether to Conduct a Cross-Sectional or Longitudinal Study

Whether or not the telephone, mail, or face-to-face survey will be conducted at one point or several points in time is also decided in Step 5. Are you only interested in consumer, reader, or viewer behavior and attitudes during one period of time or would you like to observe any changes in behavior or attitude over time? These issues dictate whether the survey will be cross-sectional or longitudinal. Figure 2.3 shows that although there is only one type of cross-sectional study, there are three types of longitudinal studies.

As the label suggests, a cross-sectional survey takes the pulse of a cross-section of the population at a specified period of time to gather information about a variety of characteristics. A cross-sectional survey conducted in 1999 is a valid representation of that period only. A longitudinal study might conduct a survey in 1993, 1995, 1997, and 1999 to detect any changes in the population's attitudes, behaviors, lifestyles, life stages, and background characteristics over several distinct periods in time. The most well-known longitudinal study is the U.S. Census, which takes the pulse of the U.S. population every ten years. Census data make it possible to examine changes in the U.S. population on hundreds of variables over time.

To make accurate comparisons in longitudinal studies, the phrasing of the questions asked during each study must match exactly. The differences are in who is asked the questions. When different people are asked questions during each survey, the study is called a trend study. When the

FIGURE 2.3   *Cross-Sectional and Longitudinal Research Studies*

1. Cross-Sectional
2. Longitudinal
   a. Trend
   b. Panel
   c. Cohort

same people are asked the questions, the survey is called a panel study. Sometimes who is asked the questions is determined by a common characteristic such as when the respondents were born or when they graduated from college. This type of survey is called a cohort study. The most well-known cohort today is the baby boom generation, which was born between 1946 and 1964. The post-baby boom cohort has been called twenty-somethings, the MTV Generation, and Generation X. Young adults born between 1965 and 1978 are in this cohort.

The Last Three Steps of the Pre-Research Phase

Who will be surveyed is specified in Step 6 of the pre-research phase. In large part, the research question dictates the population that will be surveyed. A survey that's designed to answer questions about voter attitudes should survey voters and *not* non-voters. A survey to determine the most effective way to advertise soda to eighteen to twenty-nine year olds should study that population group and not baby boomers. A survey to determine attitudes toward and use of TV ratings for monitoring what young children are exposed to on TV should talk to parents of young children and not parents of teens.

Step 7 of the pre-research phase concerns the budget and timetable for the survey. Even though we have already addressed the various issues relevant to selecting among telephone, mail, and face-to-face surveys during this step, the most important question is: Do you have $2,500 or $25,000 to conduct a survey?

If your budget is limited to $2,500, you will only be able to conduct a mail survey. The postage for sending and returning the questionnaire will use much of that budget, but at least you don't have to hire interviewers. A budget of $25,000 would allow you to hire a substantial number of interviewers and conduct a large telephone survey. A longitudinal study will increase the cost of the research study significantly. Conducting the survey during at least two points in time could double the budget.

The timetable varies from survey to survey depending on how soon the information is needed. Political polls can be conducted in as little as twenty-four hours. During a big breaking news story, the news media can even conduct a poll within an hour or two to capture immediate public reaction and report the results on the air during a special edition of a newscast or in the next day's newspaper. Surveys conducted by mail might take four to six weeks or longer.

The final step of the pre-research phase addresses the issue of selecting a research expert to actually conduct a survey. In Chapter 3, you'll learn some of the characteristics of a survey research expert that are important in conducting a valid scientifically based survey. But at this stage, what is important is selecting a survey research expert who is experienced in the type of survey that you want to conduct. Has the survey researcher conducted telephone surveys before? Is the person experienced in mail surveys? Experience that is directly related to the type of survey should be a very important factor in this decision in the pre-research phase.

SUGGESTED RESEARCH ACTIVITIES

1. Read your local newspaper, the *New York Times,* the *Wall Street Journal,* and the trade journals in your field of specialty. Identify a problem, trend, opportunity, issue, phenomenon, or theory in journalism, advertising, public relations, broadcasting, or communication in general. Apply the steps of the pre-research phase to the issue you have identified.

2. Discuss the decisions you made in applying the pre-research phase and the reasons for these decisions. If you need more information in some areas, what are they?

3. Review the research question that you drafted during the pre-research phase. How else might you phrase it? What other relevant research questions might you specify?

4. Examine several surveys that you've found reported in a newspaper or magazine. The article or sidebar should report when the interviews were conducted. What period of time did it take to conduct the interviews for the survey and when were the results reported? What do you think are the reasons, if any, for the differences in the length of time in conducting the surveys?

5. Find a longitudinal survey. What type of longitudinal study did you find? What were the benefits of conducting that kind of survey? What are the major findings?

RECOMMENDED READING

For additional perspectives on surveys, see:

DON A. DILLMAN, *Mail and Telephone Surveys: The Total Design Methods.* New York: Wiley, 1978.

JAMES H. FREY, *Survey Research by Telephone,* 2nd ed. Newbury Park, CA: Sage, 1989.

J. H. WATT and S. A. VAN DEN BERG, *Research Methods for Communication Science.* Boston: Allyn and Bacon, 1995.

For examples of studies using surveys, see:

Recent issues of *Public Opinion Quarterly,* a major research journal published by the American Association for Public Opinion Research, and *International Journal of Public Opinion Research,* the research journal of the World Association for Public Opinion Research. Also see recent annual volumes of the Gallup Poll.

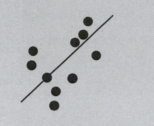

CHAPTER 3

The Research Phase and the Research Expert

- What are the characteristics of a survey researcher?
- What are the steps in the research phase of a survey?
- How is a literature review conducted?
- What are the requirements for valid survey questions?
- What ethical standards are used when writing questions?

Research Know-How and Communication Skills Are Required during the Research Phase

The research phase of a survey is handled by the research expert, who is often commissioned by the decision maker. The research expert may be a vice president or director of a research department within the same company or the president of an outside research firm. In the case of academic communication research, the research expert and the decision maker are the same. The communication scholar decides what survey to conduct and then proceeds to execute it.

The research expert has academic credentials and experience in conducting scientifically valid surveys. Some of the more important attributes of a survey researcher are listed in Figure 3.1. In addition to having a curious and open mind, the researcher is well read and informed about a variety of areas and issues. As an analytical thinker, the research expert is able to sift through large amounts of data to identify relationships and significant variables.

Effective research experts are flexible and organized planners who are capable of conducting valid research studies quickly. Patience, persistence, a sense of humor, and an ability to handle stress are important attributes because some factors are beyond the researcher's control. For example, the research expert can't make people participate in a survey nor even make the decision maker use the results of the study in a certain way.

Research is a people-oriented profession, and the research expert must have people skills. The research expert must be able to manage people on his or her staff as well as work effectively with executives, managers, and creative directors. Understanding and practicing professional and

FIGURE 3.1   *Some Characteristics of a Survey Research Expert*

1. Has academic credentials such as a Ph.D. or other significant graduate education that emphasizes quantitative research and analysis.
2. Is experienced in conducting surveys and analyzing their results.
3. Has a curious and open mind.
4. Is informed about the latest issues in the field as well as the issues of the day. A good researcher pays attention to news and information in newspapers and news magazines, trade journals, network, cable, and radio news.
5. Is an analytical thinker who is able to synthesize diverse and large amounts of data to identify the common threads.
6. Is flexible, organized, able to plan, prioritize, and manage time and projects. An effective research expert is patient, persistent, endowed with a sense of humor, and able to handle stress.
7. Is an excellent manager of people and able to work effectively with people at every level within and outside of the organization.
8. Is professional and ethical.
9. Is able to write and edit clearly.
10. Is able to present research professionally and effectively.

ethical research are also essential attributes of a research expert. Finally, excellent writing and presentation skills are also necessary. It is not enough to be able to conduct research, the research expert must be able to communicate the results and their meaning clearly in both written and oral formats.

Initial Steps of the Research Phase

The research expert uses scientifically based survey research procedures to conduct a survey that produces valid results. Even though the researcher is in charge of this phase of the research study, regular communication with the decision maker is important during Steps 1, 4, and 6 of the research phase, as listed in Figure 3.2 (p. 36). We'll first discuss the research phase as it applies to conducting a telephone survey, and at the end of the chapter, we'll examine how mail surveys differ from telephone surveys during the research phase.

FIGURE 3.2 *Research Phase of Conducting a Telephone Survey and the Research Expert*

Step 1. Consult with decision maker on survey purpose and research question, background on the survey topic, ethical guidelines and design issues, questionnaire, sample size, sampling method, timetable, and budget.

Step 2. Conduct in-depth literature review and background search.

Step 3. Focus on questionnaire, sample, and interviewers.
A. Draft questionnaire using ethical standards.
B. Identify most current and comprehensive source for sampling, then randomly select respondents to be interviewed.
C. Recruit and hire interviewers.

Step 4. Consult with decision maker on questionnaire to be pretested.

Step 5. Pretest questionnaire and revise as needed.

Step 6. Secure final approval of questionnaire from decision maker.

Step 7. Duplicate questionnaires, interviewer instructions, and record-keeping materials for training session and fieldwork. If using a computer-assisted telephone interview system, program the computer with the questionnaire.

Step 8. Train interviewers using ethical standards.

Step 9. Supervise fieldwork in which interviewers conduct interviews.

Step 10. Code and process data using ethical standards.

Step 11. Analyze data using appropriate statistics and possible weighting. Validate sample and evaluate response rate.

Step 12. Write report and prepare oral presentation using ethical standards.

Step 13. Share results with decision maker.

 ## The First Consultation with the Decision Maker

The consultation with the decision maker in Step 1 provides the research expert with an opportunity to gain a clear understanding of the decision maker's goals, expectations, planned use for the survey results, budget, and timetable. During this consultation, the questionnaire, sample size, and sampling method are also discussed. Implicit in this discussion is that the survey will be conducted using ethical standards. Clarifying these issues at the beginning of the survey eliminates potential problems at the conclusion.

During this consultation, the research expert can find out about any research data or other background information that already exists internally. In addition, the research expert will want to see previous reports,

questionnaires, and sampling procedures for similar studies that the decision maker has commissioned. This information may be useful for the next steps of the survey research process.

The Literature Review and Background Search

In reality, Step 2 is used more by the research expert who is conducting academic research to answer a research question, test a hypothesis, or build a theory than by the researcher who is conducting research to solve a practical communication problem in industry. Even so, this step should not be skipped, because it does provide context and guidance for any research study.

During the literature review, or "lit review," the research expert identifies, reviews, and critically analyzes relevant articles in periodicals, academic journals, books, and unpublished reports that contain primary or original research. The research expert attempts to learn what is already known about the research topic and how it was learned. Was a survey or experiment conducted? Who was interviewed and how were they selected? Were the results from a survey at a single point in time or were the results from a minimum of two points in time? Were the results from a panel in which the same people were interviewed during both points in time or were the results from a trend study in which different respondents were surveyed?

While reviewing the literature, the researcher separates research results from opinions and makes notes of consistencies and inconsistencies, especially consistent and different results over time and across different methods of research and samples. The research expert also makes special note of the way questions were phrased in various studies. If the researcher can identify relevant questions in the literature that can be reused in the survey questionnaire being developed, he or she can compare findings from the current survey with previous research results.

Concepts, Variables, and Operational Definitions

As the research expert identifies the relevant questions, he or she also evaluates each question for its ability to represent or measure the concept that is being studied. Often several questions or more are used to represent a single concept.

Behavioral research scholar Fred Kerlinger (1986, p. 26) defined a concept as an expression of an abstraction that is formed by generalization from particulars. Author of *The Elements of Social Scientific Thinking* Kenneth Hoover (1988, p. 18) expanded the definition by adding that concepts are "(1) tentative, (2) based on agreement, and (3) useful only to the degree that they capture or isolate some significant and definable item in reality." Examples of concepts might be achievement, intelligence, aggressiveness, media literate, or status.

Although many people have a mental image of a specific concept such as "status," you can't conduct research on the concept to understand it until you specify variables and operational definitions. Variables have been defined as symbols of the concept that are assigned numerals or values (Kerlinger, 1986, p. 27). Communication scholar Frederick Williams (1992, p. 11) said that a variable is an "observable characteristic of an object or event that can be described according to some well-defined classification or measurement scheme." Whether defined as a symbol or observable characteristic, a review of the literature reveals that different studies may use different variables to represent the same concept.

During the process of examining the research literature, it is also important to keep in mind the distinction between independent and dependent variables. It has been said that the independent and dependent variable categorization is "highly useful because of its general applicability, simplicity, and special importance in conceptualizing and designing research and in communicating the results of research" (Kerlinger, 1986, p. 32). The distinction between the two variables is that the independent variable *influences* and the dependent variable is the one that has been influenced. The variable age, for example, is said to influence the variable newspaper reading because young adults read newspapers less often than older adults. In that example, age is considered the independent variable and newspaper reading is the dependent variable.

Human characteristics such as age, race, or ethnic group are usually considered to be independent variables. Background characteristics such as level of education, income, and marital status are also treated as independent variables. Only in controlled laboratory experiments, which are discussed in Chapter 12, is the independent variable said to cause the dependent variable.

Some concepts can be represented sufficiently by one variable, but other concepts may require multiple variables. For example, the concept "newspaper reader" could be represented by one variable, newspaper reading frequency, which would enable the researcher to classify people according to whether or not they are regular readers, occasional readers, or non-readers.

To represent the concept "media literate" would require multiple variables. The researcher might identify variables that could be used to classify a list of media behaviors such as newspaper reading, magazine reading, television viewing, watching cable programs, paying attention to TV commercials, radio listening, looking at magazine ads, going to the movies, and using the Internet and online information services. To further represent the "media literate" concept, the researcher might add knowledge-based and attitude-based variables that would group people according to their knowledge of and attitudes toward the impact of television, newspapers, magazines, *USA Today,* C-SPAN, CNN, talk radio, and the World Wide Web in society. Ultimately these variables would have to be sorted and combined to symbolize the concept "media literate." When we discuss analyzing data in Chapter 8, you'll learn some techniques for sorting and combining data.

It is important to examine the operational definition of variables during the literature review. An operational definition is used to assign meaning to the variable by specifying the operations or activities required to measure it. While reviewing the literature, you should examine the questions to see how the variables have been specified to represent the characteristics of a concept. For example, you could determine how the concept "media literate" was defined or measured by examining the questions and analytical procedures that were used to sort and combine the variables. You could also determine what media behaviors, media knowledge, and attitudes were used to describe different types of media literates.

A review of the literature will also show that even when variables are the same, researchers may use different operational definitions. When variables and operational definitions vary from study to study, caution must be used when comparing results. Differences that are detected during the literature search may be insignificant if they are due to the use of *different* variables and operational definitions to represent and measure the concept under study.

A Literature Search Example

To better understand the literature review and background search process, let's use a hypothetical example in which the research expert is conducting research on a topic that he or she has not explored before. When the researcher is tackling a topic for the first time, the initial literature search will be very thorough. If the researcher is conducting a study on a topic that he or she has previously researched, the literature search simply focuses on any new studies that may have been published since the last study was conducted.

Suppose in our example that the researcher is conducting a study for the newspaper industry to profile and track the media habits and attitudes of the cohort born between 1965 and 1978—the twenty-somethings, the MTV generation, or Generation X. Although the newspaper industry is aware that newspaper reading among young adults has lagged significantly behind older adults for over two decades, there is hope that the new cohort of young adults can be attracted to the newspaper with special entertainment and technology sections and features that emphasize movies, videos, computers, online services, and the Internet. If this type of editorial content can bring young adults back into the news pages, perhaps advertisers and agencies will stop ignoring newspapers as an effective medium for reaching young adults.

The newspaper industry recognizes, though, that it will not be enough to offer features on movies, technology, and computers. The industry must also develop a campaign to make young adults aware of any new features. Although many angles ultimately need to be addressed in this study on young adults, for now the researcher must collect and analyze data that are a valid representation of the media habits and attitudes of this cohort. So, in this hypothetical case, the research expert will use the steps listed in Figure 3.3 to conduct the literature review.

In Step 1 of the literature search, familiarize yourself with your library's reference resources and tools for retrieving information. If you're unfamiliar with the library, attend an orientation, read printed guides to using the library, or visit with the reference librarian.

Step 2 involves identifying relevant resources, including books, aca-

FIGURE 3.3   *An Example of Conducting a Literature Search and Review*

Step 1. Become familiar with the library and its reference resources and tools for retrieving information.

Step 2. Identify relevant publications, databases, unpublished reports, and Web sites.

Step 3. Find and skim articles to identify those that are relevant. Review the list of references and footnotes to identify additional sources that can be searched.

Step 4. Read relevant articles carefully and summarize.

Step 5. Organize the major findings of articles.

Step 6. Sort results according to consistent and discrepant findings.

Step 7. Identify areas that lack any research.

Step 8. Draft a synthesis of the overall research findings on the topic as well as the areas that have yet to be researched.

demic and professional research journals, newspapers, magazines, trade journals, polling data, and indexes to abstracts, dissertations, and theses. *Communication Abstracts,* which summarizes communication articles in the academic communication, social, and behavior science journals, is very useful at this early stage of the literature review.

To use our example in this second step of the literature search, begin with the most recent issue of *Communication Abstracts* and, working backwards, identify published articles on young adults and their media habits and attitudes in the index. To find articles on young adults, search the following subjects in the index: twenty-somethings, Generation X, the MTV generation, adults in their twenties and early thirties. Once you find the appropriate age group, write down complete citations (author, title, journal, volume, date, and page numbers) for *any* articles that focus on *any* aspect of media habits and attitudes of this age cohort. Major academic journals cited in *Communication Abstracts* include *Journalism & Mass Communication Quarterly, Public Opinion Quarterly, Journal of Advertising Research, Journal of Communication, Journal of Public Relations Research* as well as many others.

Using *Abstracts to Dissertations and Theses,* find relevant studies. Search subjects using the card catalogue to identify relevant books. Libraries with computerized card catalogues make this process easy and fast. Academic journals may also have book review sections that could be a source for relevant books.

During this step of the literature search, you can also use a commercial full-text database such as LEXIS-NEXIS to search for the complete text of previously published articles from newspapers, magazines, and business and trade periodicals. These articles provide background information, context, and up-to-date statistics on the topic. Commercial database services such as LEXIS-NEXIS can be found in the library or accessed for a fee.

Relevant polling data can be found by searching Gallup Poll: Public Opinion Annual Series; Findex: The Directory of Market Research Reports, Studies, and Surveys; and the Public Opinion Online (POLL) database, produced by the Roper Center. Although internal industry studies are often proprietary and unavailable to the public, major communication organizations often publish internal research studies as a service to their advertisers. You can request these studies from a company's marketing department. The *Wall Street Journal,* for example, has published studies on opinion leaders, computer professionals, and the readership of its advertising.

The Internet can also be searched to find a variety of up-to-date statistical information. Narrowly focused key words are helpful in searching this vast array of information. Also, visits to the Web sites of the U.S. Census Bureau, media organizations, advertisers, and national and international polling organizations may provide the most current statistics on the topic of interest. In searching the Internet, you should evaluate Web sites to ensure that they are sources of legitimate information.

Now that you have identified relevant articles, you are ready for Step 3 in Figure 3.3. Find and skim the articles you have identified. Check the bibliography and notes for additional citations of relevant articles. Add these articles to your list of those to find. Make copies of relevant articles for later thorough reading and note-taking.

In Step 4 of the literature review, thoroughly read and summarize relevant articles in a loose-leaf notebook, spiral notebook, or on index cards, depending on your preference. Sorting and organizing relevant material are easier with loose-leaf notebooks and index cards. In the summary, you should include complete citation, purpose of study, how study was conducted (including number and selection of participants), variables (including operational definitions and exact wording of relevant questions), major findings, and any appropriate recommendations.

Because the focus of this literature review example is newspapers and young adults, you need to pay close attention to the variable newspaper reading and the operational definitions that were used to measure it. In other words, what questions did the researchers use to measure Generation X's newspaper reading? Some questions that might be found in the literature are:

1. Do you read newspapers?
2. How often do you read newspapers?
3. Did you read a newspaper yesterday?
4. What part of the newspaper do you read first?

Other variables that might be found in the literature search on this topic may be attitudes about newspapers, reasons for reading newspapers, or reasons for not reading them.

According to Step 5, once all relevant articles have been reviewed and summarized, you should organize the results by placing similar results from different studies together. If three studies have examined this age group and their newspaper reading, then put those together. If five studies have looked at this age group's use of the Internet, put those findings together. If only one study has examined radio listening, make a separate category for that topic.

In Step 6, reexamine the studies on similar topics to see if the findings are the same or if there are contradictions. Flag any relevant contradictions for examination in your current study. The gaps in the literature should be identified in Step 7. Ask yourself: What is unknown about this topic? If there are gaps in the literature, you should determine if that missing data is relevant to your current study. If so, you can use your current study to fill in these gaps. During the final step of the literature search, draft a synthesis of the relevant information that is known on the topic.

Once the literature review has been completed, the three sections of Step 3 of the research phase in Figure 3.2 should begin almost simultaneously. During this step, the questionnaire is being drafted, plans are being made for selecting a sample, and interviewers are being recruited and hired. These steps take place almost simultaneously in order to facilitate collecting the data once the questionnaire has been drafted, pretested, and approved. The literature search will have been helpful in drafting the questionnaire and drawing the sample. Remember, the wording of relevant questions in previous survey studies can be duplicated in this survey questionnaire in order to be able to compare results. Approaches to drawing the sample in previous studies can also be used in this study, which will give more validity to comparisons of different studies.

The Survey Questionnaire

A survey questionnaire is a collection of questions designed to elicit valid information from respondents about the research topic. A questionnaire usually includes questions on attitudes, beliefs, opinions, behaviors, demographics, life cycles, psychographics, and social groups.

With the goals of the decision maker in mind and in-depth knowledge of previous research and background, the research expert is ready to draft a questionnaire to be pretested on respondents who match the respondents who qualify for the study. According to Figure 3.4 (p. 44), a survey questionnaire can be divided into four main sections: record-keeping information, an introduction to the survey, questions, and a closing.

The record-keeping section of the questionnaire is necessary to record information about the respondent, the interviewer, and the survey. The respondent's telephone number, the interviewer's identification number, and the length of time necessary to complete each questionnaire are recorded in this section. The introduction of the questionnaire introduces the interviewer and the survey to the respondent, and the closing thanks

FIGURE 3.4 *Sections of a Survey Questionnaire*

I. Record-Keeping Information
   A. Respondent Information
   B. Interviewer Information
   C. Survey Information
II. Introduction
III. Questions
IV. Closing

the respondent for participating. The questions, which represent the essence of the survey, must conform to scientific principles.

Question Types and Issues

 ### Principles of Valid Survey Questions

Even though the information required for keeping records on the respondent and the interview precedes the questions in the questionnaire, you should begin by drafting your questions first and adding the other sections of the questionnaire later. Before you begin writing your questions, however, you must consider some principles of scientifically based survey questions. These principles, which include ethical standards, types of questions, and measurement issues, apply to all types of scientifically valid surveys, whether telephone, mail, or face-to-face.

 ### Ethical Standards

Ethical standards must be used when writing survey questions. It is unethical to write questions that *intentionally* mislead survey participants or attempt to bias their answers to fit a desired goal. It is also unethical to deliberately write questions that have false information about an individual, organization, or issue in order to influence the opinions or votes of survey participants. An example of a biased question that also contains false information is: *Don't you think the American people should get a tax cut **before** Social Security is fixed since Social Security only benefits the elderly while a tax cut benefits everyone?*

 ### Open-Ended and Closed-Ended Questions

Even though most of a questionnaire's measures are in question form, some of the questions are actually statements. Also, some of the questions are open-ended in which the respondent can supply an answer of his or her choosing and some are closed-ended, in which the research expert supplies responses from which the respondent selects.

Open-ended questions are often used when exploring new territory. An example might be: "What do you like least about the computer as a communication medium?" Because you may not know the possible responses in advance, it would be more useful to let the respondent answer the question in his or her own words. Research experts prefer closed-ended questions, however, because they can be precoded on the questionnaire and are less time consuming during the interview, data processing, and analysis phases of the study.

Mutually Exclusive and Exhaustive Response Choices

Another important principle that governs the writing of survey questions is that response choices for closed-ended survey questions must be mutually exclusive and exhaustive. The respondent should be able to pick only one of the possible choices provided in closed-ended questions. In addition, the respondent should be given an exhaustive or comprehensive list of possible response choices from which to choose. Exhaustive response choices are often accomplished by listing "other" as a possible choice.

Let's now look at a closed-ended question that fails the mutually exclusive and exhaustive requirements of valid questions. Suppose that you draft the following question for your questionnaire:

Which generation are you a member of?
   1. Twenty-Somethings
   2. Generation X
   3. Baby Boomers
   4. World War II

This question is not mutually exclusive because respondents who are in their twenties could fit into both the twenty-somethings and Generation X categories. You would need to eliminate one of the response choices to avoid the overlap. The other problem with the question is that it is not exhaustive. What response would someone in the World War I generation choose? And what about the young adults born after Generation X? They're being called Generation Y or the Millennium Generation (Neuborne & Kerwin, 1999, pp. 80–88). By adding a response choice of "other," you would provide an option for every possible generation over eighteen years of age.

Validity and Reliability

As you draft your questions, you must also consider the validity and reliability of the questions. Validity addresses whether or not you have asked the right question to get the answer that represents the phenomenon you are researching. Suppose you want to determine what percentage of your market or community uses the Internet and then you draft a question that asks: "Do you use a computer at least once a week?" Although respondents who use a computer regularly may use the Internet, the question is not a valid representation of Internet use. A valid question might be: "Do you use the Internet at least once a week?"

The response choices are also related to the validity of the question. For a question to be valid, its response choices must be mutually exclusive and exhaustive.

The reliability of the question is also important for conducting scientifically valid research. Reliability addresses the issue of the consistency of the question that measures the concept being studied. If you use the same question that is an accurate measure of the concept studied in different surveys at different points in time, you should have consistency in responses because the respondents are answering the same question.

What question would you ask to obtain a reliable measure of Internet use? What if this month, you ask: "Do you use the Internet at least once a week?" and six months later, you ask: "Do you use the World Wide Web at least once a week?" Because you replaced the term "Internet" with "World Wide Web," you should *not* expect consistency in the responses. More important, you will not be able to compare the responses because you have used different wording. In other words, the measurement instrument lacks reliability or consistency, which violates one of the principles of writing scientifically valid questions.

The reliability of a survey question is critical in studies that are conducted at two or more points in time. As we discussed in Chapter 2, researchers call these longitudinal studies panel, trend, or cohort studies. Unlike cross-sectional studies, which are conducted at one point in time, the results from trend, panel, and cohort studies permit the research expert to analyze change over time, as long as the question has reliability.

Precision

The concept of precision must also be considered when drafting survey questions. Precision refers to how precise you want your responses to be. In scientifically based research, there are four levels of measurement precision in questions: nominal, ordinal, interval, and ratio. Nominal

FIGURE 3.5   *Characteristics of Levels of Measurement Precision Used in Survey Questions*

Characteristic	Level of Measurement Precision			
	Nominal	*Ordinal*	*Interval*	*Ratio*
Sort Attributes into Groups and Assign Labels	Yes	Yes	Yes	Yes
Rank Attributes or Values	No	Yes	Yes	Yes
Equal Distance between Attributes	No	No	Yes	Yes
True Zero	No	No	No	Yes

questions are the least precise and ratio questions are the most precise measurements. Figure 3.5 shows the characteristics that make the different levels of measurement less or more precise.

Let's say that you are concerned about the impact of home computer use on prime-time TV viewing. You will need to ask many questions in a survey to sort out the impact, if any, of home computers on prime-time TV viewing, but let's focus on one to illustrate the four levels of precision.

At the nominal level, you could draft the following closed-ended question: "Do you use a home computer between the hours of 7:00 and 10:00 P.M.?" The response choices would be "yes" or "no." At this low level of precision, you would only learn whether or not respondents were using their home computers during this three-hour block of prime-time TV. This question would not tell you during how much of the three-hour block the respondents are using a computer. At the lowest level of precision, the attributes or values must be mutually exclusive and exhaustive. Examples of other nominal measures are gender, marital status, political party, and college major.

A question at the ordinal level, which allows you to place the attributes in some kind of order, would provide you with more precise data. You might draft the question: "How much are you using a home computer between the hours of 7:00 and 10:00 P.M.?" The mutually exclusive response choices could be "none," "some," and "a lot."

Although this question provides you with enough information to sort the respondents into groups from low to high, you still do not have enough information to determine exactly how much they are using computers during this time period. You also are unable to determine whether the distance between the "none" and "some" group is the same as the distance between the "some" and "a lot" group. In other words, these response choices are limited in their ability to provide precise data on the relationship between the categories.

Interval and ratio questions have the same characteristics as nominal and ordinal questions, plus the distance between the attributes is the same. For example, in both interval and ratio measures with values A, B, C, and D, you can say that the distance between A and B is the same as the distance between C and D. So why are ratio questions more precise than interval questions?

Ratio measures have a true or absolute zero, but interval questions do not. With a true zero, you can add, subtract, multiply, and divide the values on the measurement scale. In addition to saying the distance between A and B is the same as the distance between C and D, you can also say the distance between A and D is twice the distance between A and B. Because the zero in interval scales is arbitrary and not absolute or natural, you cannot multiply and divide. A well-known example of an interval scale in which the zero is arbitrary is a Fahrenheit thermometer scale: 32 degrees is freezing, 212 degrees is boiling, and 96 degrees is extremely hot but not three times as hot as the freezing temperature of 32 degrees.

An example of a ratio-level question for measuring computer use during prime time in which the criteria are met would be: "Approximately how many minutes do you use a home computer between the hours of 7:00 and 10:00 P.M.?" The exhaustive response choices include 0 minutes up to 180 minutes. As a result of using this ratio question, the research expert would be able to determine that the respondent who uses the computer for 60 minutes uses it twice as long as the person who uses it for 30 minutes. Of course, this precision would not be possible with questions using nominal, ordinal, or interval measurement levels.

This ratio question may also be downgraded to an ordinal question. The research expert may not need the level of precision of a ratio question but may need more precision than such response choices as "none," "some," and "a lot" would yield. The research expert may simply group the response choices: "none," "1 to 9 minutes," "10 to 19 minutes," "20 to 29 minutes," and "30 minutes or more." The level of precision that the research expert chooses is based on the purpose of the survey and the type of data analysis that is required to answer the research question.

All scientifically based survey questions have validity, reliability, and some level of precision. An open-ended question's level of precision is determined after the data have been collected and reviewed for coding, which we'll discuss in Chapter 7.

Phrasing Valid Survey Questions

The actual wording of the questions is one of several keys to valid survey results. As we discuss writing survey questions, you'll see that many of the rules are designed to elicit honest and meaningful answers from respondents.

Valid survey questions must use *clear* phrasing. The language should be as plain as the words in the local newspaper so that respondents of any educational level can understand and answer the question.

Questions must also be *unbiased*. The question should be worded objectively so the respondent is not swayed to answer in a certain way. The response choices must also be unbiased to elicit valid responses. As we noted earlier, it is unethical to intentionally write biased questions to influence survey respondents so they will respond in a certain way. Remember that the goal of scientifically based research is to gather accurate data that capture honest opinions. Questions that attempt to influence the answers of respondents produce erroneous information. An example of a biased question would be: "Don't you agree that local TV news covers too much violent crime?"

Questions need to be *specific*. Vague questions produce hazy answers that are unusable in survey results. Avoid vague questions such as: "Do you agree or disagree that shopping on the Internet has the same pitfalls as catalog shopping?" Since the pitfalls have not been specified, it is unclear what problems the respondents are being asked to compare.

Short questions are better in questionnaires because they are easier to understand than long questions. This is especially true in telephone surveys in which respondents are expected to listen, then respond. Long questions can confuse respondents and cause them to ask the interviewer to repeat the question, which can be time consuming. The following question should be shortened: "Do you agree or disagree that the impeachment of President Bill Clinton following the White House sex scandal will affect the importance that voters attach to private behavior in future presidential elections?"

Response choices to closed-ended questions should be *simple* and *uncomplicated*. Again, complicated response choices can confuse respondents and cause them to provide an invalid response or ask the interviewer to repeat the choices.

As we discussed earlier in the chapter, response choices must also be *mutually exclusive*. There should be no overlap in the possible responses that respondents can pick. *Exhaustive* response choices must also be included with closed-ended questions. Non-exhaustive response choices can bias the respondents' answers.

Response choices must also *match* closed-ended questions. It is more appropriate to ask respondents to agree or disagree to survey questions that are written as a statement than those written in a question format. Appropriate response choices for survey questions using a question format might be: "yes" or "no"; "definitely," "probably," "probably not," "definitely not"; and so on.

Some researchers prefer to avoid offering "undecided," "don't know," and "no opinion" as response options in closed-ended questions. Others prefer to include these choices, but you should *use caution when offering them.* The type of question asked should influence your decision about offering such choices. Is the question soliciting information about knowledge, opinions, attitudes, behaviors, behavioral intentions, lifestyles, or the social, economic, physical, and geographic characteristics of the respondents? For example, if you're conducting a poll among voters prior to a presidential election to find out which candidate voters intend to vote for, "undecided" and "don't know" would be legitimate responses to offer. Or, during President Bill Clinton's impeachment trial in the Senate, "don't know" would have been a legitimate response choice to offer respondents who were asked their opinion about whether the President's conduct constituted high crimes and misdemeanors.

But sometimes by offering the response choices of "undecided," "don't know," and "no opinion," you are simply providing easy answers for respondents who haven't thought about the issue before, are not familiar with it, or don't want to tell you their opinion. By including a filter question to determine if respondents are familiar with the topic, you should be able to weed out those who don't have an opinion because they are unfamiliar with the topic from those who are familiar with the issue but haven't formed an opinion or legitimately don't know. A filter question can help to ensure that questions are relevant and that the respondent is qualified to provide a meaningful response. If, for example, you want to find out what consumers like *least* about shopping on the Internet, first ask: "Have you ever shopped on the Internet?" Only respondents who have shopped on the Internet will be asked to express their opinion.

As a rule of thumb, "don't know" is a legitimate response for questions on knowledge, attitudes, opinions, and future behavior. "Don't know" would not be a legitimate response for questions about past behavior, lifestyles, and social, economic, and geographic characteristics. When asking about past behavior, ask respondents to approximate. Do not try to get *exact* behavior. How many people know exactly how many hours of TV they watch per day? It's better to ask: "Approximately, how many hours of TV do you watch a day?" Response choices that include a range rather than an exact number make it easier for respondents to choose a response other than "I don't know."

When asked their household income, a standard question on surveys, a significant percentage of respondents refuse to answer. You certainly do not want to encourage them to refuse to answer. We'll learn in Chapter 4 how to include "refuse" on the questionnaire without giving it as an option.

Avoid using "not" in survey questions to reduce confusion. Because the word "not" turns an affirmative question into a negative one, the respondent may get mixed up in providing a response. Avoid a question like: "Do you not like to surf the Internet?"

Do not ask two or more questions in one. Commonly called double-barreled or even triple-barreled, these questions lack validity because some respondents may answer the first question and others may answer the second. You can tell a double-barreled question because a conjunction such as "and" or "or" combines two sentences. An example of a double-barreled question is: "How much impact do the Internet and cable have on your prime-time TV viewing?" Stick to a *single topic* in each question.

Eliminate emotionally loaded words or phrases when writing survey questions. Respondents may react to these emotionally charged words and not necessarily respond honestly to the question. For some, any question on abortion causes an emotional reaction. Questions that emphasize life will elicit certain reactions, whereas questions that focus on choice will awaken other emotional responses. By asking a *neutral* open-ended question such as "What is your opinion of abortion?" respondents should be able to frame their answers in a way that reflects their honest opinion.

Make sure that when questions are written about new concepts or technical terms that respondents understand the concepts and terms that are being asked about. For example, if you ask the general population about e-mail, e-commerce, surfing the Internet, the World Wide Web, Generation X, or Generation Y, make sure that respondents are *familiar* with the terms before soliciting their opinions about them.

Now that we've reviewed guidelines for writing valid survey questions, let's see why questions in Figure 3.6 (p. 52) rate low on the scientific validity scale.

Question 1 in Figure 3.6 breaks the rule of writing questions in language that is simple and plain enough that respondents of any educational level would be able to understand and respond to the question. The word "culpability" and the term "antisocial behavior" may not be understood by everyone and should therefore be avoided. The response

FIGURE 3.6   *Some Survey Questions That Lack Validity*

1. TV's culpability in causing antisocial behavior among low-income preschool and elementary school children has yet to be proven. Do you?
   1. Agree
   2. Disagree
2. Don't you agree that the press is unfair in reporting the news?
   1. Yes
   2. No
3. Are the announcements at the beginning of programs?
   1. Helpful
   2. Unhelpful
4. Which of the many policies that were announced as part of a settlement with the tobacco companies on cigarette advertising do you think will make a difference in smoking cigarettes?

   _____

5. Do you buy the products of the commercials you like?
   1. When you're in the market for a particular product
   2. When you're not necessarily in the market for a particular product but you still have an open mind to buying a new product
6. How many days a week do you not watch CNN?
   1. 0 days a week
   2. 1 or 2 days a week
   3. 2 or 3 days a week
7. Do you like humor and emotion in commercials?
   1. Agree
   2. Disagree
8. How satisfied are you with shopping on the Internet?
   1. Very satisfied
   2. Satisfied
   3. Somewhat satisfied
9. Are you?
   1. Pro-life
   2. Pro-abortion
10. What movies have you seen that used product placement?

    _____

choices are also a problem. Because the range of responses is limited to "agree" or "disagree," some respondents may not be able to choose. If a respondent somewhat agrees or somewhat disagrees with the statement, those responses are not available.

Question 2 is clearly biased. It is leading the respondent to a certain attitude by suggesting that the press is unfair in reporting the news.

Question 3 is vague. What announcements? What programs? Also, the response choices of "helpful" and "unhelpful" are vague. Helpful in what way? Because the question is vague, each respondent may interpret the question in his or her own way and the research expert will not really know what is being responded to.

The long length of Question 4 in Figure 3.6 is a problem because it will be difficult for some respondents to remember what is being asked. More than likely, the respondents will ask the interviewer to repeat the question several times. Also, the question is vague, which may cause each respondent to interpret it in his or her own way.

The response choices of Question 5 are long and complicated, which can confuse respondents. Again, respondents will likely ask for the response choices to be repeated.

Question 6 has a couple of problems. First, the word "not" can be confusing. The question is asking respondents to indicate the number of days they *don't* watch rather than the number of days they *do* watch. Not only will respondents have to translate the question in their minds, some will not even hear the word "not" when the question is read over the telephone.

Notice in question 6 that the response choices for that question are *not* mutually exclusive. The response choice of "1 or 2 days a week" overlaps with "2 or 3 days a week." Respondents can answer either way, and the research expert will not know how to interpret the results. Another problem is that the response choices in Question 6 are not exhaustive. Where are response choices for four to seven days?

Question 7 in Figure 3.6 is double-barreled. It asks respondents to respond to humor *and* emotion. Some respondents may respond to humor; others may respond to emotion; still others may respond to both. The research expert will not know what respondents are responding to. Also, notice that the response choices do not match the question. Appropriate response choices would be "yes" or "no." It is inappropriate to use "agree" or "disagree," which would be more appropriate response choices for statements.

Question 8 can be a problem because it is not going to be applicable to many people who might be asked the question. One or two filter or qualifying questions should precede Question 8 in order to determine that respondents have access to computers, use the Internet, and actually shop on it. The other problem with Question 8 is that its response choices are not exhaustive. More important, only responses that address different levels of satisfaction are included. Respondents are unable to choose a level of dissatisfaction. By offering only a positive or even a negative side of the scale, you are writing a biased question.

Question 9, because of its use of the emotion-filled term "pro-abortion," is biasing. Some respondents may react to the term without really considering the question. Also, the term "pro-abortion" is not a synonym for pro-choice or a woman's right to choose. The different terms would produce different answers. Similarly, "reverse discrimination" is not a synonym for "affirmative action." The different terms would produce different responses.

Question 10 in Figure 3.6 asks about a term that is known in the movie industry and advertising circles. Although advertising products by placing them in movies is known in the industry, it is not widely known or understood among the general public. By asking the question using the insider term "product placement," you are unlikely to get a meaningful answer from respondents.

All of the survey questions in Figure 3.6 have at least one problem that negatively affects the validity of the question. As we discuss the overall survey questionnaire in Chapter 4, keep in mind that the validity of the questionnaire is determined by the quality of the individual questions that are written to ascertain consumer characteristics, attitudes, and behavior.

SUGGESTED RESEARCH ACTIVITIES

1. Select an issue, problem, opportunity, or theory in journalism, advertising, public relations, radio, TV, film, or other aspect of communication and media about which you need more information. Write a research question that could be used in designing a survey to gain valid information.

2. Using the guidelines for a literature review, conduct a literature search for relevant studies on the topic in academic journals. Find at least three articles, read them, and synthesize the major findings in two or three paragraphs. Include complete citations in your list of sources. Several topics have been listed as idea starters.

A. Press credibility

B. Perceptions of the public when companies or organizations experience a crisis

C. Attitudes of consumers toward advertising

D. Nonreaders of newspapers

E. Media habits of Generation X or Generation Y

F. Attitudes of the press toward spin doctors

G. Attitudes toward and use of television ratings

H. Consumer attention to political advertising

I. Media use and attitudes of African Americans, Latinos, Asian Americans, or Native Americans

3. Revise the questions in Figure 3.6 to make them valid. Explain the reasons behind your revisions.

RECOMMENDED READING

For a more detailed discussion on levels of measurement, see:

FRED N. KERLINGER, *Foundations of Behavioral Research,* 3rd ed., pp. 397–403. New York: Holt, Rinehart and Winston, 1986.

For more perspectives on writing survey questions, see:

PHILIP MEYER, *The New Precision Journalism,* Chapter 5. Bloomington: Indiana University Press, 1991.

STANLEY PAYNE, *The Art of Asking Questions.* Princeton, NJ: Princeton University Press, 1951.

SAM ROBERTS, "Conversations/Burns W. Roper: Private Opinions on Public Opinion: Question Is, What Is the Question?" The *New York Times,* August 21, 1994.

REBECCA RUBIN, PHILIP PALMGREEN, and HOWARD SYPHER, eds. *Communication Research Measures. A Sourcebook.* New York: Guilford, 1994.

HOWARD SCHUMAN and STANLEY PRESSER, *Questions and Answers in Attitude Surveys: Experiments on Question Form, Wording, and Context.* Thousand Oaks, CA: Sage, 1996.

For more information on searching academic, professional, poll, and Internet sources, see:

MARY McGUIRE, LINDA STILLBORNE, MELINDA McADAMS, and LAUREL HYATT, *The Internet Handbook for Writers, Researchers, and Journalists.* New York: Guilford, 1997.

R. B. RUBIN, A. M. RUBIN and L. J. PIELE, *Communication Research: Strategies and Sources,* 3rd ed. Belmont, CA: Wadsworth, 1993. See Chapters 5 and 6 for detailed lists of scholarly communication research journals, professional and trade journals, periodicals, and indexes to abstracts. Chapter 2 has additional suggestions for conducting a literature search.

JEAN WARD and KATHLEEN A. HANSEN, *Search Strategies in Mass Communication,* 3rd ed. New York: Longman, 1997. See Chapter 8 for a detailed list of poll sources.

The Survey Questionnaire

- How is a questionnaire organized?
- What information should be included in the introduction?
- Why is a promise of confidentiality necessary?
- Why is the first question important?
- What are valid response choices for closed-ended questions?
- What is a contingency question?
- What is a matrix question?
- Why are transitions important?
- How do you precode a questionnaire?
- How do you lay out a questionnaire?
- How does the format of a mail questionnaire differ from a telephone survey questionnaire?

Overview of the Questionnaire Format

It is not sufficient to have valid survey questions. A questionnaire must also be organized and formatted in such a way that it can serve as an easy-to-use comprehensive tool for reliable data collection. As outlined in Chapter 3, the questionnaire includes record-keeping information on the cover page, an introduction, precoded questions, and a closing. We'll devote most of this chapter to the format of a telephone questionnaire and we'll conclude by discussing format issues that are unique to mail surveys.

 ### Record-Keeping Information

The first or cover page also serves as a record-keeping form. This section of the telephone questionnaire includes spaces to record a unique identification number for the respondent who was interviewed, the respondent's phone number, the date of the interview, the time the interview began and ended, and comments from the interviewer.

Questionnaire Introduction

The introduction to the survey should be brief, reassuring, and conversational. The introduction should indicate the purpose and sponsor of the survey and explain how the respondent was selected.

Sometimes the person who has been randomly selected to participate in the survey feels that he or she doesn't know enough to participate. Explaining that the respondent's participation is important to the survey's accuracy may increase the likelihood that the respondent will participate.

Promising confidentiality is one of many requirements of ethical research. This promise, which is made in the introduction, must be kept by all those involved in conducting the research. The research expert reports the responses as part of the overall data, but individual responses must never be associated with the individuals who provided the answers. Because some survey questions are personal and others are very sensitive, the promise of confidentiality also helps increase overall participation and honest and accurate responses. Remember that questions on whom the respondent voted for or household income are personal and those responses must be kept confidential.

Finally, the tone of the introduction should be conversational and respectful of the respondent. The conversational and respectful tone also helps increase participation in the survey. Higher response rates produce more valid data, and every aspect of the survey questionnaire can play a role in greater participation.

The following introduction was used in a survey of Austin, Texas, residents:

> Hello, my name is _____ and I'm a University of Texas student. The College of Communication is conducting a public opinion poll of Austin-area residents. We randomly selected your home to ask your opinions about the media and several subjects in the news. Your opinions are important to the accuracy of our survey and we would appreciate your help. Your answers, of course, will be confidential.

In the introduction, you also have to verify that you are interviewing the *correct* person. Since most telephone surveys do not have a name but are seeking to complete an interview with a randomly selected male or female, it is imperative to establish that the right person is being interviewed during the introduction. The following verification was used in the Austin survey:

> My instructions say that at your house, I'm to interview a (SEX) adult head of the house. (If SEX matches person on the phone, say:) Are you that person? (Otherwise, say:) May I speak to that person? (If you are

already speaking to the correct person, ask your first question. If a new person comes to the telephone, repeat your introduction, then begin.)

You'll notice that the introduction of the questionnaire does *not* explicitly ask the respondent for permission to proceed with the interview. It is better to ask the first question after a brief pause at the end of the introduction. If your respondent feels strongly about not participating, he or she will say so at this point. Asking for explicit permission causes many more respondents to decline to be interviewed, and because your goal is to complete the interview, you want to minimize the chances for refusals. In Chapter 6 on training interviewers, you'll learn techniques for decreasing refusals and encouraging voluntary participation in the survey.

Issues That Influence the Questionnaire's Validity and Organization

Following the record-keeping information and introduction, the questionnaire includes questions that measure behavior, attitudes, motivations, avoidances, knowledge, sources relied on, group memberships, psychographics, life cycle data, and demographics. These areas should be organized so that the questionnaire flows logically and earlier questions do not bias responses to later questions. In addition, you should take special care in selecting the very first question to be asked of your respondent.

First Question

The first question in the questionnaire is important because it may make the difference between a completed interview and one that the respondent terminates early. If the respondent is bored or offended by the first question, he or she may hang up the phone. If the question is difficult and your respondent feels stupid or unqualified to answer, he or she may hang up. If the first question is sensitive, embarrassing, or intrusive, your respondent may hang up. It's best to begin with an interesting question that's easy to answer. Make sure your first question does not offend, embarrass, or intrude on the respondent's privacy if you want to keep your respondent on the phone to complete the questionnaire.

This does not mean that you *can't* ask a question that some may perceive as boring or sensitive or a test of knowledge. You simply do not want to ask those types of questions until after you've established some rapport with your respondent. The questions listed in Figure 4.1 (p. 60) are examples of first questions that may cause an otherwise cooperative respondent to terminate the interview.

FIGURE 4.1   *First Questions to Avoid*

1. How much money do you make?
2. Do you have an alarm system on your home?
3. Have you ever driven while intoxicated?
4. Do you use illegal drugs?
5. Have you ever been tested for HIV?
6. Who is the Speaker of the House of Representatives?

A safe first question in a questionnaire on the media might be: "How often do you watch local evening TV news?" Everyone should be able to answer that question. It doesn't test anyone's knowledge or intrude on privacy. This question qualifies as a question about behavior because you've asked a respondent to report his or her actions with local TV news.

Other Questions

Subsequent behavior questions might ask about watching network TV news, reading daily newspapers, paying attention to TV commercials, watching prime-time TV, listening to talk radio, watching cable, buying merchandise promoted on home shopping channels, and interacting with computer-related services. Putting all of the media behavior questions together gives the questionnaire a logical flow.

After the behavior questions, you may ask attitude questions. Attitude questions measure a favorable or unfavorable orientation toward an object, individual, or even behavior. An example of an attitude question might be: "How do you feel about the amount of violence portrayed on television programs today, not including news programs?"

You may also ask questions to determine the motivations for using or avoiding the various media. The question, "What is the main reason that you watch TV commercials?" taps into motivations. You might also ask questions about the sources the respondent relies on for various types of information. An example question is: "What is your primary source of information for learning about computer-related information services?"

Social group membership can influence behaviors, attitudes, and opinions. An example would be: "Do most, some, or none of your friends use the Internet?"

Psychographics go beyond standard demographics. Dozens of questions might be asked to segment consumers into lifestyle groups that represent a composite of a person's "attitudes, beliefs, opinions, hopes, fears, prejudices, needs, desires, and aspirations" (Townsend, 1988, p.60).

A question to determine a respondent's life cycle might be: "How many children, under 18, are there in your home?" Following up with a question to determine the ages of the children under eighteen would help pinpoint where the respondent is in his or her life cycle. By pinpointing the stage in the life cycle, you would be able to predict a variety of attitudes, media behaviors, lifestyle choices, and even purchase behaviors. People with preschool children, for example, generally have different concerns, interests, and media and purchase behaviors than people with children who are grown and independent.

You would conclude your questions with demographics or background questions. Examples are: "How old are you?" What is your race or ethnic group? What is the highest level of education that you've completed?" These questions are another way of categorizing and analyzing your respondents. Demographic questions are very important to your questionnaire because they help you better understand the relationship of background variables such as age, income, or educational level to behaviors or attitudes. Demographic questions are asked at the conclusion of the questionnaire because they are factual and include sensitive questions such as household income and even age.

Socially Desirable Questions

For all questions, whether attitude, behavior, knowledge, psychographics, life cycle, or demographics, you have to be sensitive to questions about areas that are socially desirable or even socially undesirable. Voting, reading a daily newspaper, reading a book, watching the news—these are socially desirable behaviors. Watching TV twenty hours a day is looked down on as "couch potato" behavior.

The research expert must phrase questions about socially desirable and undesirable behavior in a nonjudgmental way so the respondent will answer honestly and not inflate or deflate the amount of participation in the behavior. Often a brief lead-in to the question that indicates it's okay if you do and it's okay if you don't helps with questions about socially desirable and undesirable behavior.

The following is an example of a question about the socially desirable behavior of reading the editorial page:

Some people read the editorial page; others don't. How often do you read the editorial page?

1. Seldom or never
2. One or two days a week
3. Three or four days a week
4. Five or six days a week
5. Every day

Combining "seldom" and "never" into one response choice of "seldom or never" also addressed the issue of socially desirable behavior. For socially desirable behavior, it is a little easier to admit to *seldom* rather than *never* engaging in behavior that society considers desirable. Because "seldom" and "never" are combined into one response category, it will not be possible to separate those who never read the editorial page from those who seldom read it. But the loss of that distinction is minimal compared to what might otherwise be an exaggeration of the number of people who say they read the editorial page regularly.

Issues That Affect Response Choices and Their Validity

All closed-ended questions require response choices that are objective, mutually exclusive, and exhaustive. Response choices can be written as a nominal, ordinal, interval, or ratio scale depending on the precision in response that is needed. Notice in the telephone survey questions listed in Figure 4.2 that the numbers adjacent to the response choices are precodes. Precodes, which are used when computer analyzing survey data, are discussed later in the chapter.

Question 1 in Figure 4.2 measures news discussion behavior and was written as an ordinal level scale. That same question could have been written as a nominal scale: "Do you discuss the news with your friends or family?" with response choices of "yes" or "no." Although it is certainly a valid question at the nominal level, the response choices do not provide much precision.

A ratio scale question provides significantly greater precision. Using the same question but providing the response choices of "0 days, 1 day, 2 days, 3 days, 4 days, 5 days, 6 days, and 7 days, the research expert can learn *exactly* how frequently the news is discussed. Of course, the research expert is relying on the respondent to provide the information, which may be an approximation. Even so, this information would still be more precise than an ordinal measurement.

The amount of response precision that's needed and the type of statistical analysis should determine whether the question is written as a nominal, ordinal, interval, or ratio scale. It is important to remember that if the question is written as a ratio scale, the research expert can always recode the data to the less precise ordinal level. However, once the question has been written as an ordinal scale, the detail is lost and the responses *cannot* be changed to a ratio scale.

Notice in Question 4 in Figure 4.2 that age has been written at the ordinal level of measurement. Without the age groupings, the question

FIGURE 4.2   *Response Choices for a Variety of Survey Questions*

1. How often do you discuss the news with your friends or family?
Would you say:
1. Never or seldom
2. 1 or 2 days a week
3. 3 or 4 days a week
4. Nearly every day
5. Every day

2. Which movies do you restrict?

	Yes	No
A. PG	1	2
B. PG-13	1	2
C. R	1	2
D. NC-17	1	2
E. X	1	2

3. Based on the information you received on the O. J. Simpson trial, what grade, A, B, C, D, F, would you give:

	A	B	C	D	F	(Don't Know)
A. The fairness of Judge Ito's rulings	1	2	3	4	5	6
B. The quality of media coverage	1	2	3	4	5	6

4. How old are you? (If respondent does not volunteer age, read categories.)

01. 18–22	07. 45–49
02. 23–24	08. 50–54
03. 25–29	09. 55–59
04. 30–34	10. 60–64
05. 35–39	11. 65–69
06. 40–44	12. 70 or older
	(13. Refused)

would be at the ratio scale. The age groups have been used to make it easier for respondents who might otherwise refuse to answer the question with their exact age. Also, the specific age categories have been used because the data will be analyzed by comparing younger age groups with older age groups on various questions. The age breakdowns also make it possible to compare the youngest group (18–22) with the older twenty-somethings (25–29). Or the three age groups in the twenties can be combined into one age group, 18–29, then compared with respondents in their thirties.

A different combination of the age groups would even make it possible to compare the survey results with census data. Standard census age categories include 18–24 years, 25–34 years, 35–44 years, 45–64 years, and 65 years and over. These issues are discussed further in Chapter 8 on analyzing data and statistics.

Response Choices for Measuring Behavior

When writing a question to measure behavior, the response choices should be consistent with how people think about the behavior. For example, it is easier for a respondent to answer a question about the number of hours of television watched during the *day* than the number of hours watched during the *week*. It is easier for a respondent to recall the number of *hours* listening to radio than the number of *minutes*. Phrasing that is consistent with how respondents participate in the behavior is more reliable.

In writing a question to measure frequency of behavior, it is more reliable to determine how many *days* the behavior is engaged in than how many *times*. If a respondent is asked how many times he or she exercises, you still do not know if the respondent exercises daily, occasionally, or seldom. Reliable measures are also commonsense measures. Phrase the question in a way that is valid both for the research expert and the respondent who has to answer the question.

Response Choices in Ordinal Scales That Measure Attitudes

The first two questions in Figure 4.2 measure behavior, whereas the third question measures attitude at the ordinal level. The grading scale is a valid measure because most people are familiar with a grading system of A to F, with A meaning "excellent" and F meaning "very poor." Also, the interval between A and B is equal to the interval between C and D. In fact, instead of using grades, the words excellent, very good, average, poor, and very poor could have been used as points on the attitude scale. These words represent degrees of favorability or unfavorability on an attitude scale. When words are used as gradations on an attitude scale, they should be equal intervals apart. Without this equal distance, the response choices would be biased and the question would be invalid.

Compare the two scales in Figure 4.3. Which is biased? Responses for the first scale are biased because the respondent is *not* offered "good" as a response choice. Because "good" is not an option, the respondent is forced to choose "excellent" or a response that represents average or poor. It would be equivalent to your professor saying that in this class you can either make an A or a C or below, which would be unfair.

Sometimes the question is a statement with the points on the scale measuring intensity of agreement or disagreement. When several of these statements are used to measure intensity of agreement or disagreement toward an individual or object, the statements can be analyzed as a Likert-type scale, one of several types of attitude scales (Kerlinger,

FIGURE 4.3   *Biased and Unbiased Points on an Attitude Scale*

A.

1. Excellent   2. Fair   3. Poor   4. Very Poor

B.

1. Excellent   2. Good   3. Fair   4. Poor   5. Very Poor

1986, pp. 453–454). An example of a Likert-type scale is displayed in Figure 4.4. These questions were used in a telephone survey two months after President Clinton was first sworn into office. The responses to the questions would be analyzed in such a way that a composite attitude, reflecting both positive and negative feelings toward President Clinton, would be produced.

Notice in Figure 4.4 that the research expert has provided the respondent with two levels of agreement, strongly and somewhat agree, and two levels of disagreement, strongly and somewhat disagree. The researcher did not provide a neutral point, thereby forcing the respondent to choose a level of agreement or disagreement. The "don't know" response choice is surrounded by parentheses, which means that the interviewer will *not* read the response aloud but will circle it if the respondent volunteers "don't know" as an answer.

To ensure the validity of the measurement, the level of agreement and disagreement must be balanced. Some researchers recommend including a neutral point on the scale. Others recommend having at least seven points on the scale by adding "agree" as an option between "strongly agree" and "somewhat agree" and coding the neutral response. Providing seven levels

FIGURE 4.4   *Agreement and Disagreement Response Choices*

I'm going to read a list of words that have been used to describe President Clinton. Please tell me whether you strongly agree, somewhat agree, somewhat disagree, or strongly disagree with these words.

	Strongly Agree	Somewhat Agree	Somewhat Disagree	Strongly Disagree	(Don't Know)
A. Youthful	1	2	3	4	(5)
B. Incompetent	1	2	3	4	(5)
C. Trustworthy	1	2	3	4	(5)
D. Ineffective	1	2	3	4	(5)
E. Fair	1	2	3	4	(5)
F. Unrealistic	1	2	3	4	(5)

of agreement and disagreement to a list of attitude items can be very tedious over the telephone and in some cases cause some respondents to hang up before completing the interview. The pretest of the questionnaire can provide some guidance as to how many options respondents will tolerate during a telephone survey.

Also notice that the list of attributes in Figure 4.4 alternates positive and negative words. It is important to mix positive and negative attributes so the respondent is forced to think about the choices and react accordingly. Some researchers have worried about response set when respondents give the same answer regardless of the question, but others have argued that this problem may be overrated (Kerlinger, 1986, p. 454).

Some research experts prefer to use number points to measure agreement or approval. In telephone interviews, it is generally easier for respondents to respond to a word that represents a point on a scale rather than a number. This ease increases the reliability of the measure. Most respondents translate "agree somewhat" in a similar manner. But translating "4" on a five-point scale may vary across respondents, which decreases the question's reliability.

The semantic differential has also been used to measure attitudes. But instead of determining whether a respondent is favorable or unfavorable toward an object, concept, individual, or institution, the semantic differential attempts to measure the meaning a respondent assigns to an object, concept, individual, or institution in three dimensions. In addition to measuring a respondent's perception of an object's favorability, the semantic differential also assesses a respondent's perception of an object's potency and activity. For example, the semantic differential could be used to measure favorability, potency, and activity of the Internet, FOX TV network, or the tobacco companies by asking respondents to rate these institutions on seven-point scales that use bipolar or opposite adjectives such as good-bad, weak-strong, and fast-slow (Miller, 1977, pp. 95–96). In other words, a question to measure favorability would ask on a scale of 1 to 7, where "7" equals good and "1" equals bad: "How would you rate the Internet?"

 ## *Don't Know, Undecided, No Opinion, Neutral*

Some research experts include "don't know," "undecided," "no opinion," and "neutral" as response choices for attitude and opinion questions to be read aloud to respondents; other researchers enclose these response options in parentheses so the interviewer will *not* read the option out loud but will be able to indicate it on the questionnaire in case the respondent volunteers the answer.

These response options can be valid choices when asking attitudes, opinions, knowledge, or behavior intentions but not when asking past behavior or background characteristics. There are some subtle differences among the four response choices, and you should carefully consider whether or how the different response options should be used in a telephone survey.

In general, "don't know" means because the respondent is unfamiliar with the topic, he or she doesn't know. "Undecided" generally means the respondent is familiar with the topic but hasn't made a decision yet. A good example is during political campaign seasons, the voter is likely to be familiar with the candidates but has not decided which one to vote for. The response choices of "no opinion" and "neutral" have similar meanings. More than likely the respondent has some familiarity but hasn't formed an opinion. Perhaps, an opinion has not been formed because the respondent doesn't care or hasn't thought about the topic, or because the topic doesn't have any effect on the respondent. The respondent simply lacks an opinion or is neutral about the topic.

Figure 4.5 (p. 68) displays an example of four options for handling "don't know." Similar options could be used for "undecided," "no opinion," or "neutral." In this survey question, respondents are asked their opinion about the effectiveness of the TV ratings at the beginning of programs to provide information about the appropriateness of content for children.

In Option 1, the "don't know" group will likely go into the "not helpful" category or be treated as "no response" because the question lacks a viable option for respondents who are not knowledgeable about the topic. In Option 2, the parentheses indicate that the interviewer will not read the "don't know" response choice aloud. If a "don't know" response is volunteered, it will be coded as such. Option 3 presents "don't know" as a legitimate response choice. Unfortunately some respondents may rush to give "don't know" as a response without taking time to think about the other options. Option 4 provides a filter question to determine if the respondent should be asked the follow-up or contingency question on the helpfulness of the TV ratings. This is the best option because you are asking the follow-up question only of those who have familiarity with the topic.

(Refused)

It is not unusual for respondents to refuse to answer very personal or sensitive questions. In anticipation of this, refused should be enclosed in parentheses and included as an option. By listing "refused" in parentheses, the interviewer will know not to read the question aloud. At the

FIGURE 4.5   *Don't Know Options in Survey Questions*

Option 1. How helpful are the ratings that appear at the beginning of TV programs?
   1. Very helpful
   2. Helpful
   3. Somewhat helpful
   4. Not helpful

Option 2. How helpful are the ratings that appear at the beginning of TV programs?
   1. Very helpful
   2. Helpful
   3. Somewhat helpful
   4. Not helpful
   (5. Don't know)

Option 3. How helpful are the ratings that appear at the beginning of TV programs?
   1. Very helpful
   2. Helpful
   3. Somewhat helpful
   4. Not helpful
   5. You don't know

Option 4. 1. How familiar are you with the ratings that appear at the beginning of TV programs?
      1. Familiar
      2. Somewhat familiar
      3. Not familiar (Skip to Question 3.)
   2. How helpful are the ratings that appear at the beginning of TV programs?
      1. Very helpful
      2. Helpful
      3. Somewhat helpful
      4. Not helpful

same time, the researcher is able to record the number of people who refuse to answer that particular question.

Format Issues

 ### *Qualifying and Contingency Questions*

Option 4 of Figure 4.5 is an example of a qualifying or filter question with a follow-up contingency question. As you write your questions, you want to be sensitive to whether or not the respondent is familiar with the topic or if the question is relevant to the respondent. If the respondent is unfamiliar with the topic, the respondent's answer will be uninformed and lack validity. If the question is not relevant to the respondent, he or she may become annoyed and terminate the interview. Asking a qualifying or filter question is the best way to determine if the respondent is familiar with the topic or if the question is relevant.

If the filter question determines that the respondent is familiar with the topic or the subject is relevant, the follow-up contingency question should be asked. If the filter question determines that the respondent is unfamiliar with the topic or it is not relevant, the contingency question should be skipped. Figure 4.6 displays examples of four different qualifying or filter questions that were asked in a telephone survey.

These qualifying or filter questions in Figure 4.6 were used to determine whether to proceed to the follow-up contingency question in the questionnaire. For example, the follow-up contingency question for question A would require that the respondent have cable. If the respondent does not have cable, it would be inappropriate to ask a question that required cable to answer. By skipping the non-cable subscriber over the cable questions, you can avoid annoying the non-cable respondent

FIGURE 4.6   *Qualifying or Filter Questions*

A. Do you have cable?
   1. Yes
   2. No (Skip to Q12.)
B. How many times have you ordered merchandise from a home shopping channel?
   1. 0 times (Skip to Q12.)
   2. 1 time
   3. 2 to 5 times
   4. 6 to 9 times
   5. 10 times or more
C. How familiar are you with the O.J. Simpson murder case? Would you say:
   1. Very familiar
   2. Familiar
   3. Somewhat familiar
   4. Not familiar at all (Skip to Q54.)
D. How often do you use the Motion Picture Association of America movie ratings, such as G, PG, PG-13, NC-17, R, as guides to help you decide whether to let your child view a movie?
   1. Never (Skip to Q46.)
   2. Rarely
   3. Sometimes
   4. Often

by asking a series of irrelevant questions. In other words, if the filter question shows that the respondent qualifies, ask the follow-up contingency question. If the respondent does not qualify, skip the follow-up contingency question because it would not be relevant.

Notice that each qualifying question has "skip" instructions adjacent to the response choice that indicates that the respondent does not qualify for the follow-up contingency question. These skip instructions are included in parentheses so the interviewer knows not to read the instructions out loud to the respondent. Sometimes arrows and brackets are used to point the interviewer to the contingency question that should be asked next.

Figure 4.7 displays examples of qualifying questions plus the follow-up contingency questions that were used in two surveys. Notice the use of parentheses, arrows, and brackets to guide the interviewer to the follow-up contingency question.

Matrix Format

Once the questions have been drafted and organized from the first question to the demographics, you should examine the questionnaire to see if you can use a matrix format. A matrix, which saves space and time, combines individual questions on a related topic. The response choices must be the same to be appropriate for a matrix format. The matrix format in Figure 4.8 (p. 72) was used in a telephone questionnaire.

You should also examine the questionnaire to determine where transitions should be inserted. Generally a survey questionnaire includes several different topics and a transition statement will smoothly move the respondent from topic to topic. Questionnaires without transitions are abrupt and disjointed and should be avoided.

In the telephone questionnaire, several questions were asked about computers and then followed with a new topic about the most important problem facing people in the United States. By adding the simple transition statement, "Now, I'm going to ask your opinions about some national and local issues," the interview flowed smoothly to a new topic.

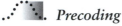 Precoding

Before finalizing the questionnaire for pretesting, you should make sure that all closed-ended questions have been precoded. Precodes are numerical values adjacent to the response choices that speed the processing of the data. For questions with nine or fewer response choices, single-digit numerical values from one to nine are used. Questions with ten to ninety-nine response choices use two-digit numerical precodes. Open-ended questions are coded after questionnaires have been completed. A

FIGURE 4.7   *Qualifying with Follow-Up Contingency Questions Format Issues*

Example A:

15. During the past three months, about how many times have you tried to call in on a "talk radio" show? Would you say:

1. 0 or no times (Skip to Q 18.)
2. 1 time
3. 2 to 5 times
4. 6 to 9 times
5. 10 times or more

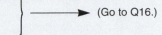 (Go to Q16.)

16. About how many times have you talked on the air?

1. 0 or no times
2. 1 time
3. 2 to 5 times
4. 6 to 9 times
5. 10 times or more

17. People have different reasons for listening to talk radio. In general, what is the main reason that you listen to talk radio?

_____

Example B:

23. How often do you watch network TV evening news? Would you say:

1. Never or seldom
2. 1 or 2 days a week
3. 3 or 4 days a week
4. Nearly every day
5. Every day

→ **23A.** People have many reasons for not watching network TV news. Why do you seldom watch network TV evening news?

_____

_____

_____

24. How often do you watch CNN, the 24–hour cable news channel? Would you say:

1. Never or seldom (Go to Q. 25.)
2. 1 or 2 days a week
3. 3 or 4 days a week
4. Nearly every day
5. Every day

→ **24A.** People have many reasons for watching CNN. Why do you watch CNN?

_____

review of the previously discussed questions in Figures 4.2 through 4.8 shows that all of the closed-ended questions were precoded.

You should also make sure that all necessary instructions for the interviewer have been inserted into the questionnaire. As mentioned earlier, interviewer instructions should be placed inside parentheses so they are not read aloud. Instructions may tell the interviewer to skip a question, define or clarify a phrase, or encourage a probe for an open-ended

FIGURE 4.8   *Matrix Format*

Which of the following computer-related services do you use at least three times a week?	Yes	No
A. Word processing	1	2
B. Electronic mail	1	2
C. The Internet	1	2
D. Computer games	1	2
E. CD-ROM	1	2
F. Online information services such as Prodigy, America Online, or CompuServe	1	2

question. The response choices "don't know," "no opinion," "neutral," and "refused" are best used in parentheses. The interviewer then knows that if these responses are volunteered, he or she has a place to record these answers. Without the parentheses, the interviewer would offer these as possible choices.

Layout and Style

 ### Questionnaire Closing

The questionnaire should end with a brief conclusion, thanking the respondent for his or her participation. The following closing was used in a telephone survey:

> "That's the end of our survey. Thank you very much for participating."

Before finalizing the questionnaire for pretesting, you should verify that everything is in order: cover page with record-keeping information, introduction, questions, and closing. You should also make sure that there is plenty of white space and the interviewer instructions stand out so they will not be skipped. The response choices should be laid out clearly and not squeezed. Check to make sure that the question and the response choices are on the same page and that each page has been numbered.

Grammar and Spelling Check, Tone, and Style

Once the questionnaire is finished, it should be carefully proofed for grammar and spelling. In addition, it should be checked for a conversational style that is objective and respectful in tone. By reading the completed questionnaire out loud, you should be able to identify the questions that lack a conversational style. Often adding a conversational style is as simple as changing some words into contractions. For example, in the introduction, it is more conversational for the interviewer to introduce him or herself using the contraction "I'm" instead of "I am." It is also more conversational to ask how often the respondent *uses* a computer instead of *utilizes*. To achieve a conversational style, questions should be written in the manner in which people talk, but without slang or jargon. In explaining the selection process to the respondent, it's more conversational to say: "You were randomly selected. . . ." If you say: "You were selected by using a systematic random sample with a skip interval of 100 and a random start point of 17," the respondent will likely hang up before you ask your first question.

Pretesting the Questionnaire

Before proceeding with the pretest, the research expert should review the questionnaire with the decision maker for approval. Then copies can be made for a few experienced interviewers to use to conduct the pretest on approximately two dozen respondents who are similar to those who will be used for the actual survey.

The questionnaire should be pretested on male and female adults who vary in age, income, and education. Of course, if the survey is being conducted on college students, it should be pretested on that age group. The pretest is an essential part of the research process that should not be skipped. You want to find and fix any problems with the questionnaire *before* you interview 500 people or more—not after.

During the pretest, you can identify problem words, phrases, and questions. You may even learn that the response choices are neither exhaustive nor mutually exclusive for some questions. Pretesting also helps you find places where you may need to add a qualifying or filter question before a question. Finally, the pretest gives you an opportunity to time the interview.

To obtain accurate information about how well the questionnaire works, the pretest should simulate the real interview situation. After the pretest interview has been conducted, the interviewer should complete a standardized pretest form similar to the one in Figure 4.9 (p. 74). Some researchers may also include a question at the end of the pretest that asks specifically if the pretest respondent had trouble answering any questions.

After the questionnaire has been pretested on approximately twenty-four respondents, the research expert should review the pretest forms looking for consistency in problems. As a rule of thumb, if a question is

FIGURE 4.9   *Pretest Form*

1. Name of interviewer pretesting questionnaire

_____

2. Who was pretested? Male or Female_____

3. Age of person pretested:_____

4. Please check types of problems, if any, that you had during the
pretest:
A. Introduction _____
B. Questions _____
C. Instructions _____
D. Other _____

5. Please list page number and specific problem that you found during
the pretest:
A. Page_____/Problem_____
B. Page_____/Problem_____
C. Page_____/Problem_____
D. Page_____/Problem_____
E. Page_____/Problem_____
F. Page_____/Problem_____
G. Page_____/Problem_____

6. Total interview time:_____

   Please attach this form to front of questionnaire.

posing a problem for at least one-third of those interviewed during the
pretest, the question should be revised for clarity. Sometimes the research
expert decides it's better to simply eliminate the problem question from
the questionnaire.

Sometimes the problem that's discovered in the pretest is that a question should not be asked of everyone. If, for example, the questionnaire
asks about watching *CNN* or *Comedy Central,* you'll quickly discover
during the pretest that some respondents will say they don't watch *CNN*
or *Comedy Central* because they don't have cable. In that case, it is appropriate to insert a qualifying question to determine who subscribes to
cable and who does not. As a result of inserting the qualifying question
with interviewer instructions, non-cable subscribers will be skipped out
of the cable questions.

Other times during the pretest, it is discovered that the qualifying
question has been included, but there are no skip instructions for the interviewer. As a result of the pretest, the interviewer instructions are
added to the questionnaire. Often the pretest reveals a simple problem
such as the one in Figure 4.10. But even simple problems must be corrected to obtain the most valid results.

FIGURE 4.10   *Original and Revised Question after Pretest*

Original:

Which local TV news do you usually watch?

    1. Channel 36, KXAN-TV

    2. Channel 24, KVUE-TV

    3. Channel 7, KTBC-TV*

    4. Channel 42, FOX-TV

    (5. Other_____)

    (6. Don't Know)

Revised after Pretest:

Which local TV news do you usually watch?

    1. Channel 36, KXAN-TV, (Cable 4)

    2. Channel 24, KVUE-TV, (Cable 3)

    3. Channel 7, KTBC-TV, (Cable 2)

    4. Channel 42, FOX-TV, (Cable 5)

    (5. Other_____)

    (6. Don't Know)

*Channels 7 and 42 switched network affiliations after the survey was conducted. Channel 7 is now affilated with Fox and 42, which also changed its call letters, is affiliated with CBS.

In the original question, respondents were asked which local TV news they usually watched and the channel and call letters were provided as response choices. During the pretest, it became clear that many cable subscribers referred to the stations by their cable number and not their TV channel number. After learning this, the cable number with parentheses was added to the response choices. By including the additional information within parentheses, the interviewer would know the appropriate response to circle.

It is not unusual for the pretest questionnaire to run five to ten minutes longer than reasonable for a survey. After timing the pretest, the research expert is in a position to shorten the questionnaire. Without information on the length of the questionnaire, the research expert may have a questionnaire that is too long and consequently annoying to the respondent, which may cause the respondent to terminate the interview before completion. A ten- to fifteen-minute questionnaire is a reasonable amount of time to conduct an interview. Shorter questionnaires are even better.

After deciding which, if any, revisions to make, the research expert makes changes in the final questionnaire, secures final approval from the decision maker, then makes copies of the final questionnaire for the interviewer training session.

If a computer-assisted telephone interviewing (CATI) system is used for the telephone survey, the questionnaire is programmed into a computer system. Even though the questionnaire is displayed on a computer screen, the same organization and layout principles apply. One advantage of having a computer assist with the interviewing is that once responses to qualifying or filter questions are recorded, the computer automatically skips to the correct follow-up contingency question.

Format for a Mail Survey Questionnaire

Many of the issues that we addressed for a telephone survey questionnaire apply when developing a mail survey questionnaire, but there are a few differences. Instead of a questionnaire cover sheet and introduction, the mail questionnaire should have a cover letter giving the purpose and sponsor of the questionnaire, a compelling reason for the respondent to complete the questionnaire and return it, the procedure and deadline for completing and returning the mail questionnaire, and a promise of confidentiality. If an incentive is used to encourage respondents to complete and return the questionnaire, it must also be explained in the cover letter. Incentives such as money or donations to favorite charities have been offered to encourage a higher response rate. Some researchers also send a letter in advance of the questionnaire to notify respondents that they have been selected for the survey and that a questionnaire is forthcoming. This technique also helps increase a mail survey's response rate.

Because a mail survey questionnaire is self-administered and under the complete control of the respondent, the questionnaire must be inviting. What would encourage a respondent to take a look at a mail questionnaire and actually fill it out and return it? In addition to a topic of interest to the respondent and a good reason for completing it, the mail questionnaire must have a professional but non-intimidating look. Even though some of the research on mail surveys shows that the length of a mail questionnaire does not matter (Dillman, 1978, p. 6), we recommend that mail questionnaires be short and easy to complete. In today's busy world, who has time to answer long, complicated questionnaires with lots of open-ended questions? We feel shorter questionnaires with mostly closed-ended questions have a greater chance of being answered and returned.

Mail survey questionnaire instructions should be simple and clear, and filter and follow-up contingency questions must be clearly laid out. Because the self-administered mail questionnaire has no interviewer, interviewer instructions enclosed in parentheses are unnecessary. And, of course, because there is no interviewer to guide the respondent through the questionnaire, it is even more imperative that the questions, instructions, and layout make the questionnaire easy to complete and return.

SUGGESTED RESEARCH ACTIVITIES

1. In Appendix A.1, you'll find a questionnaire titled, "What's Wrong with This Questionnaire." Examine the questionnaire, then list everything you can find wrong with it and the reasons why. How would you correct the things that you found to be wrong?

2. Select an audience, reader or consumer group, or public relations public of interest to you. Using the guidelines for writing valid survey questions and response categories, write a four- to six-page telephone survey questionnaire that would help you understand your selected audience's characteristics, attitudes, media behavior, buying patterns, responses to your message, etc. Your telephone survey questionnaire should include the following items:

A. Introduction

B. At least one contingency question

C. At least one matrix question

D. At least one open-ended question

E. At least one nominal level question

F. At least one ordinal level question

G. Five to seven relevant demographic questions that will help you better understand your consumer market segment

H. Closing for the questionnaire

You may use the telephone survey questionnaire in Appendix A.2 as a guide for a correct questionnaire format. Except for demographic questions, your telephone survey questions must be original. Make sure you have numbered each page and question. Include numeric precodes to response choices for all closed-ended questions .

3. Using the pretest form in Figure 4.9, pretest and time your questionnaire on several test respondents.

4. Revise any problems with the questionnaire to produce a final questionnaire. Explain your revisions.

RECOMMENDED READING

For examples of questionnaires used by journalists as well as other communicators, see:

DONALD L. SHAW, MAXWELL MCCOMBS, and GERRY KEIR, *Advanced Reporting: Discovering Patterns in News Events,* 2nd ed. Prospect Heights, IL: Waveland, 1997. See Chapters 7–9.

For more perspectives on mail surveys, see:

DON A. DILLMAN, *Mail and Telephone Surveys: The Total Design Method.* New York: Wiley, 1978.

PAUL L. ERDOS, *Professional Mail Surveys.* Malabar, FL: Robert E. Kreiger, 1983.

F. YAMMARINO, S. SKINNER, and T. CHILDERS, "Understanding Mail Survey Response Behavior: A Meta-Analysis," *Public Opinion Quarterly,* 1991, vol. 55, pp. 613–639.

For more on different types of attitude scales and how to construct them, see:

DELBERT C. MILLER, *Handbook of Research Design and Social Measurement,* 3rd ed. New York: David McKay, 1977.

CHAPTER 5

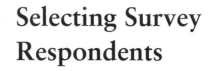

Selecting Survey Respondents

> - How are survey participants selected?
> - Why and how are survey respondents selected randomly?
> - How does a sample for a mail survey differ from a telephone survey sample?

Methods of Selecting Survey Participants

Equally as important as the survey questionnaire is the method of selecting the respondents who will be asked the survey questions. The survey expert can attempt to question *all* of the population (which would be a census) or just a sample of the population. Figure 5.1 describes the three primary methods for selecting respondents to participate in a survey: census, random sample, non-random sample.

 ### Census

Article 1, Section 2, of the U.S. Constitution requires the U.S. government to enumerate the population, to conduct a census of all the states, every ten years. The federal government uses this population enumeration to determine the number of representatives that each state should have in Congress as well as the disbursement of revenues or federal taxes that are collected. The census data also provide a demographic profile of

FIGURE 5.1   *Selection Methods for Survey Participants*

Census	Random or Probability Sample	Non-Random or Non-Probability Sample
Every member of the population is surveyed	Simple random sample	Convenience
	Systematic random sample with random start point	Quota
	Stratified random sample	Voluntary self-selection through call-in or write-in
	Cluster	People on the street
	Plus-one random sample	
	Random digit dialing	

the total U.S. population that is used by government agencies, businesses, advertisers, news organizations, and various other groups.

Civic, educational, business, religious, and political organizations often attempt to conduct a census of their memberships to develop a profile of their constituencies. Asking questions of every member of a small organization is relatively easy, but attempting to contact and complete a questionnaire for several hundred members or more of an organization is often difficult. Imagine what it's like to contact every household in the United States to get an accurate count and profile of the U.S. population. A census can be time consuming and expensive. And when the completion rate of a census is low, the results can be less valid than a study that uses a carefully selected sample of the population.

Random Sample

A random sample, which is also called a probability or scientific sample, uses statistical assumptions to select respondents from the population of interest and the results from the sample are representative of the population within a known amount of error even though every member of the population is not surveyed. The statistical assumption in a simple random sample is that every element of the population has an *equal chance* of being selected for the survey. If this is so, the research expert can be confident that the results represent the whole population within a calculated margin of error.

Having a sample that represents the population of interest is critical if the results of the survey are to be valid. If the results are invalid, important decisions may be made on incorrect information or news stories can be reported using flawed data. Bad data can cause decision makers to make mistakes, companies to lose money, and the press to damage its reputation. To avoid these problems, make sure that the survey is conducted with a random sample that represents the population within a known amount of error.

Figure 5.1 lists several types of random samples, including simple, systematic, stratified, cluster, plus-one, and random digit dialing. Each gets its name from the way survey participants are selected. But before we illustrate the selection process, let's understand the implications of a random sample in terms of the survey results.

Randomly selecting 1,000 adults, for example, to participate in a survey would produce results that are representative of the population within "plus or minus 3.1 percentage points." In other words, if a census were conducted and everyone were interviewed, a statement of sampling error would be unnecessary because an accurate portrait of the population would have been produced. But a random sample of 1,000 adults can only produce a representative picture of the total population within an expected amount of sampling error. (We discuss how sampling error is calculated later in this chapter.)

If 20 percent of a random sample say that they use online computer services at least three times a week, that percentage, because it is representative of the population, could be as large as 23 percent or as little as 17 percent after the sampling error is factored into the results. The research expert knows that a random sample can never produce an *exact* replica of the population under study, but it can certainly yield a valid impression of the population of interest. And it can yield that information at a much lower cost in time and money. The process of picking a random sample is systematic to ensure that the respondents are indeed representative of the population of interest.

 ### Non-Random Sample

A non-random sample, which is also referred to as a non-probability or non-scientific sample, cannot produce a valid impression of the population. Because statistical assumptions are ignored when picking a non-random sample, the resulting sample is usually biased, yielding a distorted picture of the population of interest. In a non-random sample, every individual does not have an *equal* chance of being selected and there may be too many of some individuals and not enough of others. Although it is relatively easy to obtain survey participants through non-random sampling methods, the results are unreliable and should not be used for making decisions.

Non-random samples select participants based on convenience, quotas, or some type of self-selection. Suppose the purpose of the research study is to determine the future career goals of communication students and then the researcher conducts the survey with your class. Your class clearly would have been selected because it was conveniently available to the researcher. The problem with this type of study is that the results would not be representative of the population of *all* communication students.

Another type of non-random sample is a quota. For quota sampling, it is necessary to first know the characteristics of the population that is being sampled. Once you know the characteristics, you need to represent those characteristics in the sample. If, for example, you know that 90 percent of undergraduate communication majors are under twenty-three years of age and 10 percent are twenty-three years of age or older, your quota sample would represent those age proportions.

Voluntary self-selection is another type of non-random sample. Probably most of you have seen a survey questionnaire published in a newspaper or magazine or a telephone number to call and give your opinion on a topic. The participants in these surveys are self-selected and are un-representative of the population as a whole. The opinions of those who saw the questionnaire but didn't even call or send in their opinion as well as those who didn't even see the questionnaire are not represented in the sample.

Sometimes network or local TV will "sample" public opinion by stationing a camera at a mall or bar to find out what the people on the street think about a major issue or event. The results from these non-random "people-on-the-street" surveys are also unrepresentative of the population they claim to describe. Phone-in, and now e-mail-in, polls that television stations love to conduct and then report as viewer opinion are equally unscientific and unrepresentative.

Identifying a List for Drawing a Sample

Available Lists

To survey respondents who represent the population, the survey expert needs a list, which is also called a sampling frame, of all possible members of the population. In surveying the membership of an organization, such as Women in Communication or the Public Relations Society of America, the most up-to-date list of the membership can be used. A voter registration list might be appropriate for a survey of voters. Although a survey of Columbus, Ohio, could use that city's most recent telephone directory as a starting point, finding a comprehensive list to survey residents of, say, the state of California—or the nation—would be difficult if not impossible.

Criteria for Evaluating Lists

In deciding the appropriate list to use for a survey, the research expert has to consider the availability of a comprehensive, up-to-date list or the feasibility of either modifying a list that has some shortcomings or constructing a new, usable list. A useful list should be comprehensive and current as well as provide the necessary information for a survey. For example, a voter registration list without telephone numbers is not a useful list for a telephone survey of registered voters. Likewise, a list without addresses would be useless for a mail survey.

When No List Is Available

The research expert who conducts a statewide or national survey often generates a list of telephone numbers from all available telephone area codes, exchanges, and numbers. He or she may use a random digit dial computer program or buy the numbers from a service that specializes in providing survey sample numbers. Regardless of which list is used, a perfect sampling frame rarely exists. The sampling frame usually has names or numbers that are out of date, or the most recent names, numbers, or addresses have not been added to the list.

If the phone directory is used as the survey sampling frame, it does not include people who asked to be unlisted or people without phones. Even a list generated from a random digit dial program has shortcomings. It includes nonworking numbers as well as numbers for modems and fax machines. The researcher recognizes the potential shortcomings of any list and makes necessary modifications to produce the best, if not perfect, sampling frame to conduct the survey.

Assumptions about Sample Size

Sample Size

The size of a random or probability sample is another important issue that the research expert must address. The sample size should be large enough that the research expert and decision maker will feel confident in the results of the survey, but not so large that money and time will be wasted in an effort to decrease the sampling error by a minuscule amount.

But how do you know how large is large enough? Figure 5.2 (p. 84) lists random sample sizes that range from a small of ten to a large of 50,000 as well as the sampling error or confidence interval for each sample size. Remember that when using a random sample instead of a census in which every member of the population is surveyed, the research expert never knows what the true response of the population would have been if each and every member of the population had been interviewed. But when drawing a random sample to estimate the population statistic, the researcher can feel confident that in ninety-five random samples out of one hundred, the results from the sample would fall within the sampling error or confidence interval.

Assumptions behind the Sample Sizes and Sampling Errors

Those of you who have already taken an introductory statistics course will recall that the sample size, sampling error or confidence interval, and confidence level are based on probability theory and the assumptions of a normal curve. A normal curve is a theoretical representation

FIGURE 5.2 *Sampling Errors for Random Samples of Various Sizes at the 95 Percent Confidence Level*

Sample Size	Sampling Error (Plus or Minus Percentage Points)
10	30.1
25	19.65
50	13.9
100	9.8
150	8.0
200	6.9
250	6.2
300	5.7
350	5.2
400	4.9
450	4.6
500	4.4
550	4.2
600	4.0
650	3.8
700	3.7
750	3.6
800	3.5
850	3.4
900	3.3
950	3.2
1,000	3.1
1,200	2.8
1,500	2.5
2,000	2.2
2,500	2.0
3,000	1.8
5,000	1.4
10,000	1.0
25,000	0.6
50,000	0.4

Adapted from the 1990 handbook for journalists, *Newsroom Guide to Polls & Surveys,* by Indiana University journalism professors G. Cleveland Wilhoit and David H. Weaver. Used with permission. The table assumes simple random sampling and maximum sampling error. According to social science research scholar Earl Babbie (1995), simple and systematic random samples are virtually identical empirically.

of population means and their standard deviations. If you drew 100 random samples, and calculated the means of each sample, the means would be distributed in a known way. Figure 5.3 shows what a normal curve would look like.

Remember that because you are surveying a random sample and not the actual population, you do not know what the actual population mean would be. You use the sample mean to *estimate* the population mean. The mean from your sample may be the actual population mean or it may deviate from the population mean. The best guess you can have is that the sample mean falls within a certain interval. This interval, known as a confidence interval, takes into consideration values above the mean and those below, as in plus or minus. Normal curve theory tells us the likelihood that the actual population mean would fall within the confidence interval. Normal curve theory says that ninety-five times out of one hundred, the sample mean will fall within

FIGURE 5.3 *Normal Curve and Percentage of Cases That Would Fall within 68 Percent and 95 Percent of the Area under the Normal Curve*

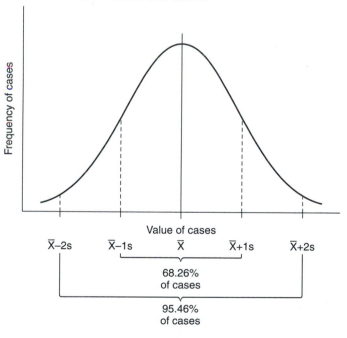

Areas under the normal curve

From: D. H. Weaver (1981). Basic Statistical Tools. In G. H. Stempel, III, & B. H. Westley (Eds.), *Research Methods in Mass Communication* (p. 58). Englewood Cliffs, NJ: Prentice-Hall. Used with permission.

plus or minus two standard deviations of the population mean. This knowledge can be applied to calculating the confidence interval for various sample sizes at the 95 percent confidence level.

To calculate the confidence interval, use the following formula:

$$s = \sqrt{\frac{P \times Q}{n}}$$

where P represents one proportion of the results and Q represents $1- P$, or the remaining proportion of what the results would have been if everyone in the population had been surveyed. But remember that because you don't know the exact population statistic, since you conducted your survey on a random sample, you must insert the sample statistics in the formula. The n in the formula represents the size of your sample. The s represents one standard deviation, also known as standard error for a sampling distribution. To calculate the sample error for two standard deviations, you would need to multiply that number by 2. Remember from Figure 5.3 that 95 percent of the cases fall within plus or minus two standard deviations of the mean.

Doubling the standard deviation is appropriate when the level of measurement is ratio and you can calculate a mean because there is a real zero and the intervals between the values on the measurement are equal. But most of the measurements used in surveys are at the nominal and ordinal levels, which means that one measurement scale is not equivalent to another. To address this limitation, the standard deviation for the theoretical normal curve is converted into a standard score, also called a Z score. When the normal curve is standardized, the mean is always zero and the standard deviation is Z. A Z standard deviation table in a statistics book shows that ninety-five percent of the cases fall within plus or minus 1.96 Z standard deviations of the mean. Remember that, before converting to the standard Z score, 95 percent of the cases fell within plus or minus two standard deviations.

Let's see how this applies to real survey data. Suppose you conducted a survey of a random sample of 454 adults and asked: "Do you have cable?" If 76 percent said yes and 24 percent said no, you could plug these numbers into the formula and have:

$$s = \sqrt{\frac{.76 \times .24}{454}}$$

$$s = .02$$

The number .02 represents only one standard deviation. But remember you are interested in a confidence interval that encompasses 95 percent of the cases and 95 percent of the cases fall within two standard deviations above and below the mean. To have a confidence level of 95 percent, you would need to double the standard error of .02, which would produce a standard error of .04. To represent the interval above and below the unknown population value, the confidence interval would be plus or minus .04. But if you use a Z standard deviation, you would multiply the standard deviation by 1.96 instead of 2. So the formula would be:

$$s = 1.96 \sqrt{\frac{P \times Q}{n}}$$

$$s = .039$$

The correct interpretation of the percentage of the population that has cable would be 76 percent with a margin of error or confidence interval of plus or minus 3.9 percentage points at the 95 percent level of confidence. In other words, by calculating the sampling error or confidence interval, we can determine the interval in which the real population value would fall ninety-five times out of one hundred. Thus as much as 80 percent or as little as 72 percent of the population could have cable.

What does this mean for sub-samples? Is the sampling error calculated on the total sample or the sub-segments? If you find that 60 percent of males and 40 percent of females have cable, how would you treat the sampling error for these sub-segments? According to one method, you would take the sampling error for each group and sum them (Wilhoit & Weaver, 1980). If the difference between males and females (20 percent) exceeds the sampling error for the two sub-samples, you can assume the differences are significant.

If you compare the calculation of the sampling error for the cable example with Figure 5.2, you will notice a slight difference. The calculation was based on plugging in actual percentages from the sample survey. The sample sizes and sampling errors in Figure 5.2 assume that the percentage "yes" and percentage "no" are evenly split at 50 percent and 50 percent, which would make a constant value of .25 in the numerator. (i.e., $P \times Q$ in this case is .50 × .50—which equals .25) By using this constant of .25, you can use Figure 5.2 as a rule of thumb for the maximum amount of sampling error for any given sample size at the 95 percent level of confidence. This rule of thumb will help you estimate an appropriate sample size for your survey needs. And, of course, once the survey has been completed, you can always insert exact numbers from the sample to calculate the sampling error.

Although the research expert determined that a random sample of 452 was sufficient for the study, a look at a larger sample size of 900 shows that the sampling error or confidence interval decreases only plus or minus 1.3 percentage points.

Sometimes, though, reducing the margin of error plus or minus 1.3 percentage points is worth the additional time and expense of drawing and interviewing a larger sample. Certainly, during a presidential election year, the presidential candidates, campaign strategists, and news organizations that poll likely voters want as small a margin of error as possible for predicting the outcome of the election.

This discussion focused on the 95 percent confidence level because it is the standard that is used. The same discussion would hold for a 99 percent confidence level in which you can be 99 percent certain that the population statistic would fall within three standard deviations of the mean. The standardized Z deviation would be 2.58 in the formula, rather than 1.96.

Different Methods for Drawing a Random Sample

Drawing a Simple Random Sample

Once the best sampling list has been identified or constructed and the sample size determined, the research expert is ready to draw the random sample. The research expert will probably select from one of the following random sampling methods: simple random sample, systematic random sample with a random start point, stratified random sample, cluster sample, plus-one random sample, or random digit dialing.

Let's say your research professor wants to determine what aspect of the research class has been useful in subsequent classes, internships, summer jobs, or jobs after graduation. The professor compiles a list or sampling frame of 188 students who have taken the research class over the past three semesters. The professor decides to randomly select forty-seven students to survey. Figure 5.4 shows the first sixteen names of the 188 on the compiled list.

FIGURE 5.4 *The First Sixteen Research Students during Past Three Semesters*

Nissa A.	Ginger C.
Robert A.	Khawh D.
Misty B.	Sarah D.
Cari B.	Robert D.
Sean B.	Melissa D.
Jason B.	Amy E.
Lori B.	Sandi E.
Teri C.	Leigh F.

To draw a simple random sample from the list, the research expert could write each name on a small slip of paper, place the paper in a hat or brown paper bag, shake it, then draw a name. It is not necessary to replace the name as long as the remaining names have the same chance of being selected. According to statistician Hubert Blalock (1972), sampling with replacement is necessary only when the sample exceeds one-fifth of the population. But because survey samples are usually small in relation to the population, this correction is unnecessary.

Even though the process of picking a simple random sample is not the most efficient use of time and resources, those names would constitute a random sample of the complete list of research students. A fair coin could also be tossed to determine which names get picked for the random sample. For example, "heads" could mean the name is added to the random sample and "tails" could mean the name is skipped. Practically speaking, the coin toss may produce more than or fewer than forty-seven names, but it would still be a random sample.

Drawing a Systematic Random Sample with a Random Start Point

A systematic random sample with a random start point is a far more practical way of randomly selecting respondents from a large population. To use this method, the number of elements on the population list or sampling frame must be determined in order to calculate a skip or sampling interval. The skip interval is calculated by dividing the sampling frame total by the desired sample size:

$$\frac{\text{Sampling Frame}}{\text{Sample Size}} = \text{Skip Interval}$$

The research professor's list consisted of 188 students who had taken the research course. The professor wanted a random sample of forty-seven, so the skip interval would be:

$$\frac{188}{47} = 4$$

Thus the research professor would survey every fourth student on the list. But where should the professor start in drawing names? That's where the random start point becomes relevant. The professor should randomly pick the start point to eliminate any bias in picking names. The random start point can be selected from 1 through the number that represents the skip interval. Therefore, the professor's random start point should be a number from 1 through 4.

To randomly select this number, the professor could write the numbers 1, 2, 3, and 4 on a small piece of paper, place all four numbers in a hat, shake them up, then draw a number randomly. Or the research professor could consult a table of random numbers such as the one in Figure 5.5. A table of random numbers contains numbers listed horizontally and vertically without any order or pattern. Because the numbers have been generated randomly, the professor can close his or her eyes and point an index finger on the chart. The first single-digit number between 1 and 4 would be the random start point.

Let's say the professor picks the number 3 as the random start point. The third name on the list is picked first for the sample, followed by the seventh name on the list, then the eleventh name, continuing on through the entire list until forty-seven names have been drawn. So from the random start point, every fourth name is picked for the sample. From Figure 5.4, the following students would be randomly selected: Misty B., Lori B., Sarah D., Sandi E., etc. If the list in Figure 5.4 were numbered, the process of randomly drawing the sample would be much faster.

Although a straight systematic random sample with a random start point would ensure that the sample is representative of all students who have taken the class over the three semesters, the research professor may decide that the results of the survey would be more useful if a stratified random sample were used. This type of sample first sorts the population list by some key characteristic and draws sub-samples that are proportionate to the representation in the overall population.

For example, a survey of newspaper executives may stratify the sample according to large, medium, and small circulation papers. Since there are many more small newspapers than large newspapers, more small newspapers would be represented in the sample than large. Advertisers could be stratified according to their advertising expenditures.

In the case of the research class, the professor decides to stratify the list by grades, A, A−, B+, B, B−, C+, C, C−, Below C−. The professor then reorganizes the list to determine the number of students in each grade category. With twenty-one As over three semesters, the professor uses the same skip interval of four to randomly select five students from the A group.

Cluster sampling, which differs from simple and systematic random sampling, is the successive sampling of clusters and sub-samples of those clusters. For a citywide survey, clusters and sub-samples might include census blocks, street addresses, and household heads. After a list of census blocks is compiled, a random sample of census blocks would be picked. From the random sample of census blocks, a sub-sample of street

FIGURE 5.5   *Table of Random Numbers*

63012	92410	45545	53116	79455	53300	81857	16736	91161
19533	18542	65429	39662	50441	52949	28455	31231	88939
70224	44235	32021	90900	37531	92497	65298	37591	84985
73718	89788	51705	85008	75510	68167	59894	75528	55586
66031	42701	66713	97208	75995	33058	31429	84385	56099
38844	87669	90412	58421	14212	68809	10441	80744	11591
64569	61247	27404	28109	18560	75395	46673	82615	60453
26164	58905	15309	50958	74521	63849	53177	44521	50782
67527	27590	97299	17052	97857	32781	24236	37288	82017
15743	46932	33700	85326	90712	25590	86808	92491	56495
37177	23612	58894	64446	29774	17097	85230	60721	53063
49495	17261	85358	54400	61176	15750	19919	88933	91370
59676	75299	28149	83494	88996	68219	63514	24986	17141
38317	26041	61612	75443	99298	38191	42133	12514	13268
66715	57245	75981	72216	32957	42007	92151	50191	72137
54442	10070	87520	84804	40078	31264	15899	19619	51985
33163	79267	96886	87501	51959	31084	16389	44926	39863
84312	19410	39686	24285	17672	61520	26068	90326	87626
18320	88428	61801	47003	64642	12968	80128	97752	28350
40535	29187	96820	41764	63073	31278	96124	42395	62816
22027	88276	37335	43705	88696	47945	80489	39519	34822
74841	89305	16119	35947	95263	35042	12159	96310	22567
31418	55481	61198	15557	91760	20023	89465	11796	98392
38667	80126	61603	18147	84563	43872	41753	56285	16854
27082	88108	69106	31299	98070	58803	96957	39939	50424
65869	88229	94649	24840	83025	27547	79423	82852	29628
90253	65573	44161	14629	73257	62081	38170	45141	12432
38866	97398	10398	31556	45304	17855	36164	60948	75692
26749	86529	34489	87608	71150	50604	11771	40515	65296
42324	87827	13437	89740	33452	95167	79882	66875	26107
64253	78722	61945	75535	28739	47740	40171	28400	74090
25035	43773	12455	61732	25070	40695	33923	59329	70360
28825	34634	96134	24955	97840	78854	61066	52257	95360
54215	92248	70568	43968	35819	43611	52184	11873	46597
63174	40977	16103	93960	77576	99048	34001	88787	90350
72266	50258	53218	42471	18447	63900	86697	67524	89505
41115	90746	61987	34870	77875	23599	91183	24888	78744

Random numbers generated by the Office of Survey Research, the University of Texas at Austin.

addresses would be randomly selected. And finally from this sub-sample of addresses, a household head would be picked randomly to participate in the survey.

Plus-One Random Sampling

Plus-one random sampling, another random sampling method, is appropriate for surveying a city or metropolitan area in which the best list available is the telephone directory. This method draws a phone number directly from the phone book, then alters the last digit by adding one to it. This alteration makes it possible to correct some of the shortcomings of a telephone directory, but not all of them. Of course, one of the most obvious deficiencies of a telephone directory for a survey is that it does not include households without phones.

Another limitation is that because the phone book is published annually, recent residents to the city are not listed and the people who have moved out of town still are. Finally, the phone book only contains people who prefer to be listed. Unlisted numbers, of course, are not included. The plus-one method can correct the problem of new residents who have just moved into the calling area but have yet to be listed in the published directory as well as make it possible to reach unlisted phone numbers.

Phone directories include names and phone numbers, like the ones in Figure 5.6, but in the case of the plus-one sampling method, names are ignored, and the phone numbers that are listed in the phone book are used as a base for the number that will be called as part of the sample.

When drawing a random sample from the phone book or any other list, it is necessary to over-sample with alternate numbers in case an in-

FIGURE 5.6   *Sample Telephone Numbers*

447-2278	323-6362	331-1420	331-0388
292-1704	255-3834	335-8518	247-3036
794-6369	453-9633	346-9568	467-9579
472-5021	255-0405	442-4243	707-0909
288-8308	331-6290	441-4502	502-9618
467-9041	255-2783	371-1631	990-9579
499-8902	477-1260	376-4904	326-4194
482-8542	708-1422	495-9993	480-0276
499-3212	708-8420	833-6891	892-2918
928-9508	247-3769	380-8954	327-8101

terview cannot be completed with the primary sample number. Some obstacles that hinder completion of the interview with the primary sample number include: the respondent refuses to participate; the respondent is not home after multiple callbacks; the number is disconnected, the number is non-residential or connected to a modem or fax machine; an answering machine always answers the phone even after multiple callbacks; the person does not speak the language that the interview is being conducted in.

The amount of over-sampling varies with the list being used. A membership list or class roster may only need one alternate name for every primary name drawn, whereas the phone directory may need four alternate phone numbers for every primary number drawn. Although over-sampling may take extra time, it is preferred to running out of phone numbers before reaching the desired sample size.

When calculating the skip interval of a systematic random sample with a random start point, the research expert uses the sample size plus the over-sample to draw the desired amount of numbers. When the numbers are drawn, the primary sample number is identified, as are the alternate numbers. If the interview is completed with the primary number, the alternate sample numbers for that specific primary should be discarded.

Let's say that calculations determined that a skip interval of five should be used and the random start point, determined from the table of random numbers, was three. The research expert plans to draw two alternate numbers for every primary number. With this information determined, the research expert proceeds to draw the random sample. The research expert draws the third number on the list, 794-6369, as the primary, the eighth number, 482-8542, as an alternate, and the thirteenth number, 453-9633, as another alternate. The next number to be drawn, 708-1422, is another primary.

Although these numbers have been drawn from the list of phone numbers, they are *never* called for the survey. The research expert adds one to the last digit of each number to produce the number that will actually be called. Figure 5.7 (p. 94) shows how the numbers have been altered with the plus-one method.

Unlike the original number, the new plus-one number does not have a name associated with it. Therefore, the research expert has to develop a plan for randomly selecting the person who should be interviewed at the household. It is not random to have the person who answers the phone complete the survey. One method is to randomly assign male or female household heads to each number before the number is actually dialed.

FIGURE 5.7   *Applying Plus-One to Original Phone Numbers*

Original	Plus-One
794-6369	794-6370
482-8542	482-8543
453-9633	453-9634
708-1422	708-1423

Figure 5.6 makes the process of picking numbers from a telephone book fairly easy. But a look through the phone book for Houston or Los Angeles can be very intimidating. Even Bloomington, Indiana, has lots of numbers per page. The straight skip interval method is not as easy when it is applied to a large phone book. It is far easier to first randomly select the columns on the page of the phone book to be included in the sample, and then use a ruler to measure inches down the column.

Let's apply this to a phone book that has four columns on every page. Suppose you randomly select the second and fourth column of each page for the sample. And you need to draw three numbers from each column. By measuring the columns, you determine that each column is twelve inches long, which means that your skip interval would be four inches. Your random start point would be within the four-inch interval. If there are forty numbers in that four-inch interval, you can pick the random start point using a table of random numbers.

Suppose your random number table indicates that you should start with the seventeenth number. That number becomes your first number in the sample, and each additional number is taken at four-inch intervals. This same process can be used for the second and fourth columns of each page. To facilitate this process, you can make a transparent overlay for each telephone book page, which marks the second and fourth columns, the seventeenth phone number from the top of the page, and the four-inch skip intervals from the random start point.

Phil Meyer, a research expert at the University of North Carolina at Chapel Hill and author of *The New Precision Journalism,* recommended avoiding using the phone book as a base for picking a random sample because of the underrepresentation of high-income areas (Meyer, 1991, pp. 106–107). Even though he acknowledged that by altering the last digit, you can reach high-income unlisted phone numbers, he expressed concern that there will still be underrepresentation of high-income areas because more households in these areas have unlisted numbers. In other words, because the three-digit prefixes are assigned geographically, it is likely that in high-income areas, many numbers will be unlisted, which will significantly decrease the representation of phone numbers from high-income areas.

One alternative to ignoring the plus-one method completely is to conduct the survey and then compare the representation of high-income homes with the most recently available census data. If high-income homes are underrepresented in the survey, the data can be weighted, an issue we will discuss more in Chapter 8.

Random Digit Dialing

Random digit dialing can compensate for many of the shortcomings of a phone book. By using random digit dialing to pick a random sample, you can use a computer program to combine the three-digit telephone exchanges, or prefixes for the calling areas, and the four-digit root number to produce completely random numbers. Of course, you will need to find out from the phone company which and how many three-digit exchanges are in the survey area. The phone numbers in your random sample must be a proportionate representation of the exchanges assigned to the geographic area.

If you are conducting surveys regularly, you may want to invest in developing a procedure for selecting a sample from random digit dialing. Otherwise you can pay a fee to a professional service that specializes in generating random samples through random digit dialing for any geographic region in the country. (These companies can be found in publications such as *Marketing News*.) Because no names are associated with these computer-generated phone numbers, you will still have to develop a plan for determining which person at the household should be interviewed.

In summary, random sampling is the best method for selecting people to interview. You can have a certain level of confidence that the random sample is representative of the population of interest within a known amount of error. In general, researchers use the 95 percent probability level, which is a level of certainty ninety-five times out of one hundred. The key to increasing the validity of the sample is to start with the most accurate sampling frame possible. The plus-one method, which draws a sample from the phone book by using systematic random sampling with a random start point, is one cost effective way of producing a valid sample of respondents to interview. Random digit dialing, which generates a random sample of numbers based on the three-digit exchanges and four-digit root numbers in a geographic area, produces the best sample of phone numbers.

Sample for a Mail Survey

How does a sample for a mail survey differ from a telephone survey sample? One of the major concerns in selecting a sample for a mail survey is the sampling frame or list. It is necessary to have current and complete names, addresses, and zip codes of the population that is being surveyed by mail. Unlike a phone survey in which a male or female adult household can be requested, a mail survey sent to "resident" will most likely be ignored.

Mail surveys that are conducted with specific populations generally yield the best response rates. An up-to-date membership list of professional or nonprofit organizations, the directory of employees for a specific organization, or subscribers to a magazine or newspaper will certainly provide an adequate sampling frame for drawing a random sample. Of course, permission of the organization must be requested and, in some cases, a fee will have to be paid to obtain the list.

The researcher may conduct a census and send questionnaires to all of those on the list or the researcher may use a systematic random sample with a random start point or a stratified random sample, depending on the specifications of the mail survey.

SUGGESTED RESEARCH ACTIVITIES

1. In sixty seconds, write down the names of people you know, including friends, family, classmates, and professors. Draw a simple random sample of five names.

2. Using the same sampling frame, now draw a systematic random sample with a random start point of five names. Which method was faster and why?

3. Using the telephone book from your city as a sampling frame and the plus-one method, describe the procedure you would use to draw a systematic random sample with a random start point of 1,000 primary numbers and three alternates for each primary. Now draw the first ten primary numbers and their alternates.

4. What sampling frame would you use to conduct a mail survey of the following: newspaper publishers, magazine photojournalists, advertising agency creative directors, public relations professionals, and communication professors. Discuss the process you would use to find the appropriate sampling frame.

5. Find one or two random sample surveys or polls that have been published in newspapers or magazines. Read the description of the sample size, sampling error, and confidence level. How does this information compare to Figure 5.2?

RECOMMENDED READING

For more perspectives on different sampling methods, see:

FLOYD FOWLER, *Survey Research Methods,* 2nd ed., Applied Social Research Methods Series, Volume I. Newbury Park, CA: Sage, 1993.

GRAHAM KALTON, *Introduction to Survey Sampling.* Beverly Hills, CA: Sage, 1983.

LESLIE KISH, *Survey Sampling.* New York: Wiley, 1965.

E. LAIRD LANDON JR. and SHARON K. BANKS, "Relative Efficiency and Bias of Plus-One Telephone Sampling," *Journal of Marketing Research,* 1977, vol. 14, pp. 294–299.

RICHARD POTHOFF, "Some Generalizations of the Mitofsky-Waksberg Technique of Random Digit Dialing," *Journal of the American Statistical Association,* 1987, vol. 82, pp. 409–418.

MADHAV N. SEGAL and FIROOZ HEKMAT, "Random Digit Dialing: A Comparison of Methods, *Journal of Advertising,* 1985, vol. 14, no. 4, pp. 36–43.

SEYMOUR SUDMAN, "Applied Sampling," in *Handbook of Survey Research*, ed. Peter H. Rossi, James D. Wright, and Andy B. Anderson, pp. 145–194. New York: Academic Press, 1983.

DENNIS TREWIN and GEOF LEE, "International Comparisons of Telephone Coverage," in *Telephone Survey Methodology,* ed. Robert Groves et al., pp. 9–24. New York: Wiley, 1988.

JOSEPH WAKSBERG, "Sampling Methods for Random Digit Dialing," *Journal of the American Statistical Association,* 1978, vol. 73, pp. 40–46.

For a more detailed discussion of normal curve theory and sampling theory, see:

EARL BABBIE, *The Practice of Social Research,* 7th ed., pp. 195–203. Belmont, CA: Wadsworth, 1995.

HUBERT M. BLALOCK, JR., *Social Statistics.* New York: McGraw-Hill, 1972.

FRED N. KERLINGER, *Foundations of Behavioral Research,* 2nd ed., pp. 191–197. New York: Holt, Rinehart and Winston, 1973.

DAVID H. WEAVER, "Basic Statistical Tools," in *Research Methods in Mass Communication,* ed. Guido H. Stempel, III, and Bruce H. Westley, pp. 55–61. Englewood Cliffs, NJ: Prentice-Hall, 1981.

For poll results and discussions on how well random sampling predicted the outcomes of the 1992 and 1996 presidential elections, see:

MICHAEL R. KAGAY, "Experts See a Need for Refining Election Polls," The *New York Times,* December 15, 1996, National Edition, Sec. A22.

"The Poll Findings Converge," The *New York Times,* National Edition, November 3, 1992, Sec. A9.

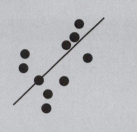

CHAPTER 6

Interviewer Training and Survey Data Collection

- What is the role of interviewers in collecting survey data?

- What are the characteristics of effective interviewers?

- How are interviewers trained?

- What procedures are used for collecting valid survey data?

- What are the rules for good interviewing?

- What are the ethical standards for survey interviewers?

- How is data collection different for mail surveys?

Interviewers Play an Important Role in Surveys

In telephone and face-to-face surveys, interviewers are used to collect the data. Interviewers must be trained to ask survey questions and record responses so that reliable data is collected. Although interviewers are not used in mail surveys, the research expert must follow certain steps to ensure that valid data is collected, which we'll discuss later in this chapter.

 Hiring

Figure 6.1 lists the steps involving training interviewers. Once the research expert has determined that a survey will be conducted, he or she needs to begin the interviewer hiring process. If the research expert has interviewers on staff or intends to subcontract the interviewing to a research supplier, the hiring step can be skipped and the research expert can proceed to prepare for the training session.

If the survey expert has to hire interviewers, he or she can advertise in the local newspaper and post notices at local or nearby colleges. Appli-

FIGURE 6.1   *Steps in the Interviewer Phase of the Survey*

Step 1. Hire qualified interviewers.
Step 2. Organize training session.
Step 3. Conduct training session.
Step 4. Supervise interviewers during fieldwork.

cants who respond to the ad should be interviewed in person and references should be checked.

 ### Characteristics of Effective Interviewers

Survey interviewers are often part-time workers who have a high school degree or some college education and are paid an attractive hourly rate. Effective interviewers are dependable, honest, persistent, and detail oriented. A pleasant, friendly voice is important. The interviewer needs to be able to quickly establish rapport with the respondent and gain his or her confidence.

A good interviewer should be able to work at a fairly fast pace in order to complete as many interviews as possible during the allotted time. Experienced interviewers are ideal, and you may want to pay them more than inexperienced interviewers who have to be trained. Interviewers generally need to have evening and weekend hours available for interviewing because those times are best for reaching respondents today.

The survey expert may hire twenty to eighty interviewers, depending on the number of people to be interviewed, the budget, and amount of time to complete the interviews. The interviewers need to attend a mandatory two- to four-hour training session, which is an essential step in ensuring that reliable data are collected.

The Training Session

Organizing a Training Session

Interviewers should be notified of the required training session when they are interviewed for the job. The date, time, and location of the session should be communicated when the interviewers are hired. A classroom style training facility is ideal for discussing the purpose of the study, the questionnaire, interviewer instructions, record-keeping, and the demonstration and role-playing of an interview. All written materials must be prepared in advance for distribution at the beginning of the training session. The written materials and supplies required for the session can be found in Figure 6.2.

If computer-assisted telephone interviewing (CATI) equipment is being used for the survey, it should be programmed with the questionnaire prior to the training session so that interviewers can be trained to use the equipment during the session.

FIGURE 6.2   *Materials for a Training Session*

☐ Name tags
☐ Agenda
☐ Practice questionnaire
☐ Written instructions and timetable
☐ List of respondents to be called
☐ Record-keeping forms
☐ Pencils
☐ Notepad

 Conducting a Training Session

Five goals of the interviewer training session are to:

1. Acquaint interviewers with the goals and timetable of the study.
2. Familiarize interviewers with the questionnaire and correct procedures for conducting interviews.
3. Make interviewers aware of good interviewing techniques and ethical standards that must be followed.
4. Inform interviewers about the sample of respondents, required call-backs, and record-keeping.
5. Develop proficiency in conducting interviews and using any special equipment.

Figure 6.3 (p. 102) displays a sample agenda that describes a typical interviewer training session. Beginning with the welcome and ending with the closing, interviewers will learn the skills necessary to complete valid interviews.

Rules for Calling the Sample of Respondents

 Who Should Be Called

After discussing the survey's purpose and the materials that will be used to conduct the survey, the researcher reviews the sample of respondents to be called. Remember from Chapter 5 that the sample includes primary and alternate numbers. There may be three or more alternate numbers for each primary number, depending on how much over-sampling was done. The primary number should be called first. Only if the interview

FIGURE 6.3   *Training Session Agenda*

Welcome
Purpose of Survey
Materials

The Sample
Which People to Call and When
Callbacks
Record-Keeping

Interviewer Protocol

The Questionnaire
Interviewer Instructions in the Questionnaire

Professional Interviewing Techniques
Demonstration of an Interview
Interviewing Practice

Training on Special Equipment

Closing

cannot be completed with the primary respondent should the first alternate be called. If an interview cannot be completed with the first alternate, the second alternate should be called. Later in the chapter, we'll discuss keeping records on primary and alternate numbers. In general, the primary and alternate numbers represent one of three categories:

1. Randomly selected person at the residence of a number selected through random digit dialing.
2. Randomly selected person at the home of a "plus-one" phone number.
3. Randomly selected name from a directory, membership list, business, or organization

For phone numbers that have been randomly selected through random digit dialing or the plus-one method, a name is not connected to the phone number. Consequently the interviewer is unable to ask to speak to Mary Smith or John Jones. The interviewer has to ask for a male or female household head. The research expert randomly determines whether to interview a male or a female, and interviewers must *not* deviate from this selection. Randomly designating which person to interview ensures that the sample will indeed be random and not just a sample of respondents who were conveniently available when the interviewer called. Because of time and budget constraints, some research experts allow a substitution of a male for a female or vice versa *only* when the designated sex does not live at the household. Note that some surveys use a designation other than male or female household head. For example, the interviewer may be instructed to ask for the person over eighteen who has the next birthday.

Whatever method the research expert developed for the sample must be communicated to the interviewers during the training session, and interviewers must understand that they are *not* to deviate from the procedures. Any deviation from the established method can reduce the validity of the survey results.

 When Calls Should Be Made

During the training session, interviewers are supplied with sample phone numbers or names that are to be called as well as record-keeping forms for tracking the sample. Tell the interviewers that the best times to call sample respondents are evenings from 5:30 P.M. to 9:00 P.M. and weekends from 11:00 A.M. to 9:00 P.M.

With the majority of adult household heads working, calling during the day is unproductive and calling after 9:00 P.M. can annoy prospective respondents and cause them to refuse participation in the survey. Of course, if the survey is being conducted with people who work in certain businesses or industries, and business phones, not home phones, are used in the sample, calls should be made during business hours.

During the training session, interviewers should be instructed to attempt to conduct the interview *when* contact is made with the respondent. If the respondent insists that he or she is unable to do the interview, the interviewer should try to schedule an alternate time for a callback.

Callbacks

Callbacks are often required to reach the person who has been randomly selected for the sample. If the interviewer is unable to reach the person selected for the sample, the interviewer must call back at a later time or on a different day. If, for example, the original call is made at 6:00 P.M., the interviewer should not call back until at least 8:00 P.M. to allow time for the prospective respondent to arrive home. The research expert designates whether two or three callbacks or more are to be made. Up to a certain point, more callbacks increase the chances of reaching busy people. The number of required callbacks is also determined by time and budget constraints.

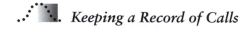 *Keeping a Record of Calls*

Accurate records are required for all primary and alternate phone numbers called. The number must be tracked from its original to final status. Figure 6.4 displays a Call Record Form to record information about sample numbers for a telephone survey that used the plus-one method. A variation of this form can be hard copy or computerized. Although this form is recommended for tracking only the primary and alternate numbers actually called, it can also be used to keep a record of all numbers picked for the random sample.

FIGURE 6.4   *Call Record Form*

A. Original Phone Number: _____

B. Primary or Alternate Sample Number:
   1. Primary
   2. Alternate

C. Location in Phone Book:
   Page _____
   Column _____

D. **Plus-One Number (Add "1" to Original Number):** _____

E. First Call:
   1. Day_____
   2. Time_____

F. First Callback:
   1. Day_____
   2. Time_____

G. Second Callback:
   1. Day_____
   2. Time_____

H. Interview Status:
   1. Completed ————▶ Person Interviewed:
                       1. Male
                       2. Female

   2. Incomplete ————▶ Reason for Incomplete Interview:
                       01. Never home
                       02. Refusal
                       03. Business
                       04. Nonworking number
                       05. Modem
                       06. Fax
                       07. Language barrier
                       08. Designated sex does not live there
                       09. Did not use number
                       10. Other_____

Rules for Interviewing

Prior to demonstrating the correct method of conducting a survey interview, the research expert should review the format of the questionnaire and the interviewer's protocol. By following the rules for interviewing, which are listed in Figure 6.5 (p. 106), the interviewer collects valid data in a professional and ethical manner. The rules for interviewing can be divided into three areas: (1) following directions and recording responses, (2) conducting the interview, and (3) ethical interviewing. By following directions on whom to call and when, as well as accurately recording responses, the interviewer will collect accurate data during the course of the survey. Interviewers will also learn that instructions that are placed in parentheses throughout the questionnaire are for their benefit only. These instructions are *not* to be read aloud.

Discuss Rules for Interviewing during the Demonstration

Be Conversational, Objective, and Accurate

The rules on how to ask the questions can make a significant difference in the respondents' participation in the survey and the quality of the data collected. As the research expert demonstrates how to conduct a valid interview, he or she can discuss the guidelines for asking questions and recording responses. One of the first rules in conducting the interview is to be familiar with the questionnaire. The greater the familiarity, the greater the chance the interviewer can ask questions in a conversational manner and establish a good rapport with the respondent.

Good rapport can facilitate completion of the interview, and an objective manner aids the collection of valid data. For example, during the demonstration, the research expert can show interviewers the difference between asking a question objectively versus asking a question as if the respondent were being investigated for misdeeds or felony crimes. The interviewer is not an investigative reporter cornering a government official or a prosecutor cross-examining a hostile witness in a criminal trial. On the contrary, an objective tone will elicit honest responses, which is the goal of the survey. A combative tone, which can cause the respondent to terminate the interview or produce less than candid responses, should be avoided.

Interviewers must also record respondents' answers accurately. Responses to open-ended questions should be recorded exactly and *not* paraphrased. Paraphrasing could change the meaning of answers, which would have a negative impact on the survey's validity.

FIGURE 6.5 *Interviewer's Protocol*

Following Directions and Recording Responses

1. Follow directions on whom to call and when.
2. Complete required number of callbacks for hard-to-reach respondents.
3. Complete all records on sample numbers and respondents and the individual interview.
4. Read and follow instructions in the parentheses. These instructions are for you and should not be read aloud to the respondent.
5. When using a paper questionnaire, record responses with a pencil.
6. Mark only one response unless instructions indicate otherwise.
7. Record responses accurately and completely. Do not paraphrase responses to open-ended questions.

Conducting the Interview

8. Familiarize yourself with the questionnaire in order to ask questions in a conversational and objective manner.
9. Follow wording of the introduction and questions, and order of questions on questionnaire exactly. Do not deviate from the wording or order of the introduction and questions. Do not paraphrase or explain the meaning of a question.
10. Do not suggest answers to the respondents or give your opinions about the questions.
11. Do not react to respondents' answers. Do not respond with approval, disapproval, or surprise. Act as a neutral recorder.
12. Be respectful of all respondents regardless of age, income, education, race, ethnicity, gender, sexual orientation, or religion.
13. Keep the respondent focused on the interview in order to move the interview along at a reasonable pace.
14. When conducting face-to-face interviews, dress professionally.

Ethical Interviewing

15. Do not reveal the identity or answers of individual respondents. You have promised confidentiality to the respondents and you must *not* violate that trust.
16. Never falsify information on a questionnaire. Always be thorough, honest, and professional in your work as an interviewer.
17. Participation is voluntary. Do not coerce the respondent into participating in the survey.

Follow the Wording and Order of Questions

During the demonstration, the research expert should discuss the importance of following the wording of the introduction and questions as well as the exact order of the questions in the questionnaire. It would be impossible to produce reliable data if each interviewer reworded the questions and changed their order.

Because reliable and valid results are produced through consistency, all interviewers must ask the questions in the same objective manner. Even when respondents do not understand a question, interviewers cannot explain its meaning. If the respondent does not understand a question, the interviewer should ask it again. If, after a second reading, the respondent still does not understand, the interviewer should quickly move on to the next question. Likewise, interviewers must *not* indicate that they approve of or agree with responses they like, and they must not suggest answers. The focus of the survey is the respondent's opinions—not the interviewer's.

Respect Respondents

Interviewers should be reminded that respondents represent a variety of backgrounds. Interviewers must be respectful of all respondents regardless of age, income, education, race, ethnicity, gender, religion, or sexual orientation. Sometimes interviewers have a respondent who has opinions that are offensive. The respondent may be racist, sexist, or anti-Semitic. An interviewer who is pro-choice may learn that the person on the other end of the phone is pro-life or vice versa. It is imperative that interviewers conduct all interviews in an objective manner and never respond with disapproval or disgust.

Follow Ethical Standards

The last section of the Interviewer's Protocol in Figure 6.5 addresses ethical interviewing. It is imperative that interviewers conduct the interviews using ethical standards. The introduction to the questionnaire promises the respondent that his or her answers will be confidential, and the interviewer must keep this promise. Not only would it be wrong and unethical to reveal individual responses to questions on questionnaires, divulging information about individual respondents could have a chilling effect on scientific surveys that ask questions about voting behavior, sexual behavior, drug use, HIV and AIDS infections, a respondent's financial profile, or any other sensitive or private topic.

Finally, never falsify questionnaires or respondents' answers. Remember that participation is voluntary, so do not try to force respondents to answer questions.

Strategies to Encourage Participation

In addition to the rules for collecting reliable survey data, the interviewer may have to rely on a variety of strategies to persuade the respondent to participate in the survey. Even though participation is voluntary, it is important for interviewers to encourage everyone's participation. Strategies are also necessary to encourage respondents to answer every question in a meaningful way as well as complete the interview in reasonable time. The research expert should discuss these strategies, which are listed in Figure 6.6, after demonstrating how the questionnaire should be conducted.

Experience teaches that most of the respondents who are actually reached will complete the questionnaire. A minority of respondents decline to participate. The interviewer's goal should be to persuade all reluctant respondents and refusals to participate in the survey and answer all questions for the accuracy of the survey. By gaining the respondent's confidence, establishing rapport, keeping the respondent focused on the questionnaire, and working as quickly as possible through the questions, the interviewer should succeed in having a high percentage of respondents complete the questionnaire. The higher the response rate, the more valid the survey results.

After completing the demonstration, reviewing the interviewer protocol and strategies, and answering questions, the research expert should pair up the interviewers and have them role-play conducting the questionnaire. Role-playing should be approached as an actual interviewer situation. This process not only prepares interviewers for the real interview, it also helps them identify questions or problems that need to be addressed.

Before starting the actual fieldwork with the real sample, the research expert should have the interviewers practice on a real person who has been selected from a practice sample. After completing a couple of interviews from the practice sample, the interviewers are ready to question the real respondents.

When the Interviewer Is Assisted by Computer

Some telephone surveys are conducted with paper questionnaires and pencils; others are conducted using computer-assisted telephone interviewing equipment known as CATI. When CATI equipment is used, the

FIGURE 6.6   *Interviewer Strategies*

1. If the person who has been randomly selected to be interviewed does not want to be interviewed, say, "Your opinions are very important to the overall accuracy of the survey and we would very much appreciate your taking time to answer the questions." If the respondent says he or she is too busy, suggest alternative times to call back. If the respondent says his or her spouse would be better able to answer the questions, say, "You were selected using scientific procedures and your opinions are the ones that are important." If the respondent outright refuses or rudely hangs up the phone, the interviewer should not take the rejection personally.

2. If the respondent does not want to answer a specific question because it is too personal, tell the respondent that his or her response will be kept confidential and it will only be included as part of the total responses.

3. If respondent continues to refuse to answer a question, explain that the overall survey will produce a more valid profile of everyone's opinions if all questions are answered. If respondent still does not answer, go on to the next question.

4. If respondent tends to ramble or wants to talk about areas that are unrelated to the questionnaire, politely say, "My next question is:" and go to the next question.

5. Do not change an answer after it has been recorded. You should, however, inform the research expert about the change that the respondent wanted to make. The research expert should also be informed about responses that are followed by "but." In both cases, respondents' comments should be recorded in the margin of the questionnaire.

6. Do not record a "don't know" or vague response too quickly. Allowing the respondent a few extra seconds before moving on to the next question may help the respondent offer a meaningful response. When vague responses are offered, the interviewer should politely add, "Can you be a little more specific?"

7. If respondent does not want to pick one of the response choices provided in a closed-ended question, the interviewer should say, "But which of these choices best fits your response to the question?" and read the question again. If the respondent still wants to supply his or her own response choice, the interviewer should not mark one of the given response choices but make a note of the respondent's preferred answer.

8. Ask the questions in the questionnaire at a moderate pace—fast enough to keep the questionnaire moving along so the respondent will not lose interest, but slow enough so the questions can be understood.

interviewer reads the questionnaire from the computer screen and uses a keyboard to input the responses directly into the computer. Interviewers must be thoroughly trained to use this equipment until it becomes second nature so that they can focus on reading the questions and accurately inputting respondents' answers into the computer.

Fieldwork Must Be Monitored to Produce Valid Results

After the training session is over, the fieldwork is ready to begin. The research expert or an assistant supervises the collection of the data during the survey period. It is imperative that the supervisor check over the first completed questionnaires to ensure that they are being filled out correctly. In addition, the supervisor should identify and correct any problems immediately. The supervisor should monitor the interviewers' work to make sure that they are following protocol. Interviewers should also be monitored for problems with refusals. An interviewer who is being turned down a lot is a problem. Further training may be necessary or the interviewer may have to be terminated. Because high refusal rates negatively affect the overall validity of the survey, refusals must be kept to a minimum.

Mail Surveys Have Special Requirements

Even though the research expert does not have to worry about hiring and training interviewers for a mail survey, he or she does have to conduct the mail survey in such a way as to encourage a good response. As mentioned in Chapter 4, when conducting a mail survey, the research expert prepares a cover letter, self-administered questionnaire with an incentive, a stamped, addressed envelope to send the questionnaire, and a stamped, self-addressed envelope for the respondent to return the completed questionnaire. In addition, the research expert must prepare a reminder postcard and replacement questionnaires and cover letters for follow-up mailings to the respondents. If an advance letter announcing the forthcoming questionnaire is used to increase the response rate, it must also be prepared.

It has been suggested that a reminder postcard that also serves as a thank you be sent one week after the initial mailing (Dillman, 1978, p. 183). Three weeks after mailing the original questionnaire, a new cover letter and replacement questionnaire should be sent to those who have yet to reply. A final replacement questionnaire should be sent approximately five weeks after the original mailing to those who have not returned a questionnaire.

The research expert should monitor the questionnaires daily, keeping track of the number of questionnaires returned on each day. The pattern of returns will certainly be helpful in planning future mail surveys. In addition, the research expert must record the identification numbers of the returned questionnaire. Respondents who have not returned a questionnaire will receive a replacement questionnaire and new cover letter within three weeks of the original questionnaire. Even with all of the effort to increase response rates, mail survey response rates are significantly lower than telephone survey response rates. We'll discuss acceptable survey response rates in Chapter 8.

SUGGESTED RESEARCH ACTIVITIES

1. Discuss the similarities and differences between interviewing for a survey versus interviewing for a journalism assignment.
2. Visit a survey research center that uses CATI equipment for conducting telephone surveys. Ask the director of the research center to explain the process of training interviewers for that computer-assisted equipment.
3. Search the academic journals in communication to identify two or three mail surveys. What procedures did those studies use for increasing response rates?
4. Find a partner in your class and role-play the interviewer strategies in Figure 6.6. What did you learn as an interviewer from this role-playing?

RECOMMENDED READING

For more perspectives on telephone, mail, and computer-assisted surveys, see:

CHARLES H. BACKSTROM and GERALD HURSCH-CESAR, *Survey Research,* 2nd ed. New York: Wiley, 1981.

CHARLES F. CANNELL and ROBERT L. KAHN, "Interviewing" in *Handbook of Social Psychology,* Volume II, ed. Gardner Lindzey and Elliot Aronson. Reading, MA: Addison-Wesley, 1968.

DON A. DILLMAN, *Mail and Telephone Surveys: The Total Design Method.* New York: Wiley, 1978.

PAUL L. ERDOS, *Professional Mail Surveys.* Malabar, FL: Robert E. Kreiger, 1983.

ROBERT M. GROVES and N. MATHIOWETZ, "Computer-Assisted Telephone Interviewing. Effects on Interviewers and Respondents," *Public Opinion Quarterly,* 1984, vol. 48, pp. 356–369.

ROBERT M. GROVES and WILLIAM L. NICHOLLS, II, "The Status of Computer-Assisted Telephone Interviewing, Part 2: Data Quality Issues," *Journal of Official Statistics,* 1986, vol. 2, no. 2, pp. 117–134.

WILLIAM L. NICHOLLS, II, and ROBERT M. GROVES, "The Status of Computer-Assisted Telephone Interviewing, Part 1: Introduction and Impact on Cost and Timeliness of Survey Data," *Journal of Official Statistics,* 1986, vol. 2, no. 2, pp. 93–115.

For an example of a mail questionnaire, see:

LYNETTE MARIE CHEWNING, "Technology, Roles and Gender in the Business Communication Environment." Master's thesis, The University of Texas at Austin, 1995.

CHAPTER 7

Coding and Processing Survey Data

- How are data prepared for tabulation and analysis?
- How are data tabulated?
- How are data cleaned?
- What information is included on a frequency printout?

Precoding and Computers Facilitate Tabulating Survey Results

As the questionnaire is being developed, the research expert is anticipating the computer data processing and analysis that will follow the data collection phase. To facilitate data processing and analysis, the researcher precodes the questionnaire by assigning numerical codes to response choices for closed-ended questions. If the research expert is using a computer-assisted telephone interviewing system, the CATI system needs to be programmed with the questionnaire and coding information *before* the survey begins.

Before the development of computers, answers on survey questionnaires were tabulated by hand. Imagine how tedious and time consuming it would be to count the responses for each and every question for a sample of 500 respondents. In addition to being tedious and time consuming, hand tabulation was prone to human error, which could produce unreliable results. With today's computers and software programs designed for tabulating survey data, tabulation of survey data is fast and accurate, that is, once the responses have been coded and entered into the computer program that is being used.

When paper questionnaires are used for telephone, face-to-face, and mail surveys, the research expert develops a master codebook. The codebook is a document that will be used for coding, processing, cleaning, and intepreting the data for the survey. Every survey has its own unique codebook that is based on the questionnaire; it is created for the survey and computer software program that will be used to tabulate the data. The codebook includes unique respondent identification numbers, precodes for response choices for closed-ended questions, and variable, column, and record information. As the questionnaires are completed, the research expert develops codes and descriptions for any open-ended questions. This information is added to the codebook.

Coding Starts with a Master Codebook

Although programming a CATI system is beyond the scope of this text, the logic of coding and processing data from paper questionnaires is certainly beneficial to those who use CATI systems for conducting surveys. Figure 7.1 lists the steps in coding data for computer processing.

 Preparing Data for Coding

To input the questionnaire responses into the computer, the responses for each question must be translated into a numerical code. Each numerical code must have an assigned place in the computer data file. By completing Step 1 in Figure 7.1, converting the questionnaire to a master codebook, the research expert is able to translate each respondent's answers into meaningful numbers that can later be interpreted with a computer program that tabulates and analyzes survey data.

Figure 7.2 shows the first two pages of a questionnaire that has been transformed into a master codebook. (The complete codebook is in Appendix B.) In the left margin, variable numbers have been added, and in the right margin, column numbers have been added. The variable numbers, V1, V2, V3, etc. are arbitrary names that have been assigned to each piece of information that the research expert wants to have tabulated.

FIGURE 7.1   *Steps in Coding Data for Computer Processing*

Step 1. Convert a copy of the final precoded questionnaire into the master codebook by adding variable numbers and column numbers to *each* question.

Step 2. Develop responses and codes for open-ended questions for the master codebook.

Step 3. Write coding instructions that include information on: (1) assigning unique respondent identification numbers; (2) handling nonresponses; (3) coding multiple responses for open-ended questions; (4) editing questionnaires that are inconsistent with the skip patterns.

Step 4. Train at least two coders to code the questionnaires.

Step 5. Code a random sample of at least ten questionnaires, then evaluate the reliability of the coding with special attention given to open-ended questions.

Step 6. Once the inter-coder reliability is acceptable, code all questionnaires onto a separate codesheet or directly into a computer data file.

FIGURE 7.2   *Master Codebook for Media Use Survey*

Variable		Column
V1	Respondent I.D. No.	**(1–3)**
V2	Interviewer I.D. No.	**(4–8)**
V3	Respondent: 1. Primary 2. Alternate	**(9)**

V4   1. How often do you watch local evening TV news?   **(10)**
Would you say:
(Local evening TV news comes on at 6:00 P.M.
and 10:00 P.M.)
1. Never or seldom (Skip to Q4.)
2. 1 or 2 days a week
3. 3 or 4 days a week
4. Nearly every day
5. Every day

V5   2. Which local TV news do you usually watch?   **(11)**
1. Channel 36, KXAN-TV, (Cable 4)
2. Channel 24, KVUE-TV, (Cable 3)
3. Channel 7, KTBC-TV, (Cable 2)
4. Channel 42, FOX-TV, (Cable 5)
(5. Other _____)
(6. Don't know)

V6   3. Why do you usually watch that local TV news?   **(12–13)**
_____

V7   4. How often do you watch network TV evening news?   **(14)**
Would you say:
(Network TV evening news comes on at 5:30 P.M.)
1. Never or seldom
2. 1 or 2 days a week
3. 3 or 4 days a week
4. Nearly every day
5. Every day

V8   5. How often do you read a daily newspaper?   **(15)**
Would you say:
1. Never or seldom
2. 1 or 2 days a week
3. 3 or 4 days a week
4. Nearly every day
5. Every day

V9   6. How often do you discuss the news with your friends or
family?   **(16)**
Would you say:
1. Never or seldom
2. 1 or 2 days a week
3. 3 or 4 days a week
4. Nearly every day
5. Every day

(continued)

FIGURE 7.2   *(continued)*

Variable		Column

V10	7. Do you have cable?
	   1. Yes
	   2. No (Skip to Q12.)
		(17)

V11	8. How often do you watch a home shopping channel on cable?
	   Would you say:
	   1. Never or seldom (Skip to Q12.)
	   2. 1 or 2 days a week
	   3. 3 or 4 days a week
	   4. Nearly every day
	   5. Every day
		(18)

V12	9. How many times have you ordered merchandise from a home shopping channel? Would you say:
	   1. 0 times (Skip to Q12.)
	   2. 1 time
	   3. 2 to 5 times
	   4. 6 to 9 times
	   5. 10 times or more
		(19)

V13	10. What merchandise did you buy? Do not code. Leave Blank.	**(20–21)**

V14	11. How satisfied were you with shopping from a home shopping channel? Would you say:
	   1. Very satisfied
	   2. Satisfied
	   3. Somewhat satisfied
	   4. Not satisfied
		(22)

V15	12. How often do you listen to radio?
	   1. Never or seldom (Skip to Q18.)
	   2. 1 or 2 days a week
	   3. 3 or 4 days a week
	   4. Nearly every day
	   5. Every day
		(23)

The column numbers are place assignments that have been given on the computer record so the variables can be found. V1, which represents the respondent's identification number, is a three-digit number that can be found in columns 1 through 3 on the record. The interviewer identification number is five columns long, from columns 4 through 8.

The first question has been renamed V4 and takes up one column on the computer record. The number of columns is determined by how many values the variable or question will have. In the case of V1, the respondent's ID number, unique numbers can be assigned from 001 to 999. That's fine for a sample of 500, but if the sample contained 1,200 respondents, the research expert would have to assign four columns to handle unique ID numbers from 0001 to 9999.

For open-ended questions such as Question 3, the research expert must develop the codes for that question before finalizing the number of columns to be assigned. For nine or fewer response codes, one column is assigned. For ten to ninety-nine responses, two columns are assigned to the codebook.

Coding Open-Ended Questions

Question 3 is an open-ended question, which means the respondents are able to answer the question in their own words. Although the personalized responses provide insight that closed-ended responses cannot, the research expert needs to convert the open-ended responses to numerical codes that the computer tabulates. This process is similar to one step of the content analysis research method that is discussed in Chapter 11.

To develop codes for open-ended questions, the research expert reviews approximately 100 questionnaires and writes the verbatim responses on a separate sheet of paper. The researcher quickly discovers that the language may vary among respondents, but the intent of many responses is similar. Figure 7.3 lists the various responses for Question 3, "Why do you usually watch that local TV news?"

When ten or more responses have a similar meaning, the research expert assigns a numerical code and a two- to three-word description that encompasses the similar responses. The goal of the researcher is to include a sufficient number of descriptions and codes that the range of responses to the open-ended question will be reflected in the codebook. But there should not be so many descriptions and codes that the data will lose their meaning.

Next to each verbatim response, the research expert should include one or two identifying pieces of information about the respondent such as sex, age, or marital status. This information may prove helpful when the report is written. Reporting the data from open-ended questions will be discussed in Chapter 9 on writing research results.

FIGURE 7.3   *Some Responses to the Open-Ended Question: Why Do You Usually Watch That Local TV News?*

1. "I like the anchor person."
2. "Sports."
3. "News is very good and to the point."
4. "The feature stories."
5. "Like Sally Holiday (the anchor)."
6. "To find out what's happening in the world."
7. "Because my TV is usually on that channel."

FIGURE 7.4   *Coding for an Open-Ended Question*

V6   3. Why do you usually watch that
local TV news?   **(12–13)**
01 News anchors
02 Already tuned to station
03 Coverage of events/quality of coverage
04 Habit
05 Sports
06 Weather
07 No particular reason

97 No response/No opinion
98 Don't know
99 Other

The responses that are developed for the open-ended questions must conform to the same rules as responses or values for closed-ended questions. The responses or values must be mutually exclusive and exhaustive. After checking that the responses do not overlap, the researcher adds an "other" value to make the responses exhaustive. The research expert also adds "no response" and "don't know" for respondents who didn't or couldn't answer the open-ended question. Figure 7.4 shows what the open-ended Question 3 looks like after the codes have been developed for the codebook.

Two-digit columns have been assigned to Question 3 because there are ten possible values. Also, note that the research expert has left space in the codebook to add a few codes if necessary. Remember that the research expert developed the coding for the open-ended questions after reviewing only 100 questionnaires. Although it is unlikely, it is still possible that the researcher will determine during the coding process that another code needs to be added rather than code the response as "other."

The research expert has assigned "no response/no opinion," "don't know," and "other" to 97, 98, and 99, respectively. These number assignments are arbitrary but can facilitate the coding process when it's possible to have a consistent numerical code across all the questions for "no response," "don't know," and "other."

Finally, a lengthy questionnaire may require that the coding stretch over two or more records or rows of data. In that case, the researcher must assign a record number in the codebook. The record number is usually assigned at the end of the record and the following record begins again with the respondent's unique identification number before ending with the record number. These record numbers, which will become important during the computer processing, are discussed in more depth in Chapter 8.

Written Instructions and Coder Training Produce Reliable Coding

Written Instructions

In Step 3 of Figure 7.1, the research expert develops written instructions for the coders. To achieve reliable coding, the researcher needs to ensure that all coders are consistent in their coding. Written rules and coder training contribute to reliable coding. Figure 7.5 displays instructions for coding paper questionnaires.

Coder Training

Just as interviewers are trained to conduct valid survey interviews, coders are trained to complete valid coding. Unlike the training for telephone survey interviewers, the training for coders is informal because it involves only one or two people.

FIGURE 7.5   *Instructions for Coding Paper Questionnaires*

1. Assign a unique respondent identification number to the cover page of every completed questionnaire. These sequential numbers should begin with "001."
2. Check each questionnaire before coding begins to ensure that the questions answered are consistent with the skip patterns. Delete any responses that are inconsistent with skip patterns. Initial and date any changes made to the questionnaire.
3. Rather than leave the coding space blank when there is no answer, you can write in a space holder such as a zero with a slash through it.
4. If a respondent has given more than one answer to an open-ended question, code the first response.
5. Code questionnaires on the coding grid with a pencil. Erase; don't write over changes in coding.
6. If you are unsure how to code a particular response, ask the coding supervisor.
7. If you find notes on the questionnaires that have been written by the interviewers, bring them to the coding supervisor's attention.

The necessary materials for coding—written coding instructions, a copy of the codebook, a copy of a completed questionnaire, a blank coding spreadsheet, and a pencil with an eraser—are distributed. Using the sample completed questionnaire, the research expert demonstrates how the codes for the responses must match the columns on the coding grid and how to code open-ended questions with multiple responses. The coders then code the sample questionnaire.

To evaluate the reliability of the coding, the research expert calculates the level of agreement between coders, also called inter-coder reliability. Because most of the coding is probably on closed-ended questions, a high degree of agreement, of 95 percent or above, is expected. Special attention should be given to the coding of the open-ended questions because the coders' judgment is involved in deciding how to reliably code those responses.

Coding Follows the Training

Once the research expert finds the coding at an acceptable level of agreement, the coders can code all questionnaires onto a separate coding spreadsheet or directly into a computer data file. Figure 7.6 displays four lines of a twenty-four-line coding spreadsheet.

Because of the length of the questionnaire, the codebook was set up so that each respondent would take up two lines or records. The codebook set aside columns 1 through 3 for the respondent's identification number. Notice that the first respondent has an identification number of "031," which is found in the first three columns of the first two records. The next respondent coded has an identification number of "032." Note that there are no blank spaces between records or lines. Although double-spaced lines would be easier to read, the computer would incorrectly "read" blank lines as a record, so single-spaced lines are used.

If a space holder, such as a zero with a slash through it, is used to hold a blank place on the coding spreadsheet, it is not entered into the computer data file. Leaving the space blank or entering a zero indicates no response in the computer data file. Rather than deal with no response during the coding phase, many researchers designate a code such as 9 or 99 on the questionnaire for no response. This code essentially serves as a space holder for no response. Regardless of which method is used to indicate no response, the missing data must be deleted from the tabulation during the computer run in order to accurately report the results of those who responded to the question.

FIGURE 7.6   *A Partial Coding Spreadsheet of the Raw Data*

```
031360012359944511   41432010242122221    2912022039702081
0311311059721311                 22010222299299130474523323212
032360012340213311   121  0212222221    6720621    298971
0321111989722321                 21019924204297220175352354322
```

Computer Processing Data

 ## Special Computer Software Makes Tabulating Fast and Easy

Once all questionnaires have been coded, the researcher is ready to process the data using a computer program specializing in tabulating and analyzing survey data. Several easy-to-use computer software programs have been designed to process and analyze survey data. In addition, these survey data computer programs calculate statistics that can be used to interpret the significance of the survey results. We'll discuss various statistics for analyzing data in Chapter 8. But regardless of which survey data analysis program is used, they will all produce a basic frequency printout, a report on the percentage responding to each response choice of a survey question. Figure 7.7 (p. 122) lists the steps necessary for computer tabulating data for a survey data analysis software program known as Statistical Package for the Social Sciences, or SPSS. Similar steps would be used for other programs specializing in tabulating survey data.

Become Familiar with the Computer Software

According to the first step of Figure 7.7, you should familiarize yourself with the computer software program that you will use to tabulate your data. You can do this by reading the manual, attending a class, or viewing the software program's tutorial. During this step, you "inform" the computer program about your data and the variables and codes from your codebook. In Step 2, you actually enter the data into the computer so that it can be tabulated. As listed in Step 3, you instruct the program to produce a frequency printout, which reports the responses to the survey questions in percentages.

According to the remaining steps of Figure 7.7, the frequency printout should be inspected carefully to make sure that the information is correct. In Step 4, verify that the number of cases being read by the

FIGURE 7.7   *Steps in Tabulating Data with SPSS*

Step 1. If you are unfamiliar with the computer program that you will use to analyze your survey data, review the manual or tutorial or attend a training class. Using your codebook as a guide, you must first "inform" the program about your data, the names that you will use for the variables and the labels that you will use to describe the variables and values. Once you have entered this information into the computer, save the file. Now you're ready to enter your data, the numer-ical codes that represent the responses of each respondent.

Step 2. You can enter your data into the computer program directly or from a text file. Once you have entered the data, you are ready to run the program.

Step 3. Run a frequency printout.

Step 4. Verify that the number of cases is correct.

Step 5. If you entered your data from a text editor, verify that the records have been read in the correct order. If you entered your data directly into SPSS, you will likely skip this step. Because of the unlimited number of columns on each record in SPSS, it's not necessary to input the data from each questionnaire on more than one record.

Step 6. Verify that variables have been read in the columns that you indicated on the codebook.

Step 7. Scan the output to make sure that the tabulations appear logical.

Step 8. Print a hard copy of the frequency output.

computer is correct. If you have more than one record per case, also check that the records are being read in the correct order. Do this by checking that the number of cases in the last variable, V88 for record 2, matches the number of respondents interviewed and coded for the computer tabulation. (This variable, V88, can be found in the complete codebook in Appendix B.)

If there were 500 cases, the printout should show that there are 500 "2's." If the printout indicates that there are, for example, 251 "2's" and 249 "1's," the computer is not reading the records in the correct order. A search through the raw data in the computer should quickly identify the problem that needs to be corrected.

You must also verify that the variables have been read in the correct columns. If you coded V5 in column 11, but the printout shows that V5 is being read in column 13, the data are being read incorrectly. Finally, scan through the printout to make sure that the tabulations appear logical.

Cleaning and Recoding May Be Necessary before Final Computer Runs

Cleaning "Dirty" Data

Once these steps have been completed, you can prepare for the final computer run, which is described in Figure 7.8. Steps 1 and 2 address procedures for handling dirty data. It is not unusual for newly run printouts to contain "dirty" data, that is, numbers that do not match the values listed in the codebook. These dirty data may be a result of either coding or data input errors. Regardless of the source, the research expert needs to identify the location of the dirty data in the raw data file and correct it. A computer or manual search can trace the dirty data back to the unique respondent's identification number, which can then be used to retrieve the original questionnaire for checking. The incorrect code must be corrected in the raw data file, making sure that the correction is made on the right case, record number, and column.

FIGURE 7.8   *Preparations for the Final Computer Runs*

Step 1. Carefully examine each variable in the printout searching for "dirty" data, any values that do not match the codebook.

Step 2. To "clean" the dirty data, return to the original questionnaire to find the correct response that had been given, and then correct the wrong response in the computer data file.

Step 3. Identify any responses that should be combined, then instruct the computer to combine the values into one by using a recode procedure.

Step 4. Run a clean final SPSS frequency printout.

Step 5. Examine the printouts and mark the frequency tables that will be used in the final research report.

Step 6. Plan the cross-tabulations and statistics that need to be run.

Recoding Decisions

Step 3 of Figure 7.8 recommends that the printout be examined for opportunities to recode or combine data. When the questionnaire is written, the research expert includes response choices that sometimes provide more detail than will eventually be reported. For example, variable 79, age, provided thirteen different age categories for the respondent to respond to. But once the frequency printout is examined, the research expert may decide to combine the age groups, 18 to 22 and 23 to 24, into a new age category, 18 to 24. Or perhaps the researcher may decide to have just one age category of 18 to 29.

These recoding decisions are usually made because of the research question or the distribution of the data. If you're interested in how the "under-30" group compares with the "30 and over" age group, it is unnecessary to have three separate age categories under 30 years old. Or if 11 percent of the respondents are in the 18–22 age group and 5 percent are in the 23–24 age category, you may want to combine the two groups to have 16 percent in the 18–24 age group.

A Frequency Printout

Interpreting the Table

Once the data have been "cleaned" and recoded as necessary, you are ready to run a final, clean frequency table. Figure 7.9 displays the frequency table for V60, one of the variables in the final frequency run. Remember that the master codebook had translated the original Question 43 to the computer readable variable, V60, which was then used to produce the frequency table in Figure 7.9. The variable label at the top describes the data in the printout for V60. The first column specifies whether the data are valid or missing. Usually data are missing because a contingency question was asked of only those who qualified for the question. In this example, because the question for V60 was a contingency question, only respondents who had rules for children under 18 were asked this question.

The second column lists the numerical codes, 1, 2, 3, 4, and the names for the numerical codes, "never," "rarely," "sometimes," and "often." The column labeled "Frequency" provides a raw count for each value. For example, thirty-seven of the respondents said they never use the ratings. In the next column, labeled "Percent," the raw counts have been

FIGURE 7.9   *Reading a Frequency Table*

V60   Frequency of Using Movie Ratings for Children's Viewing

		Frequency	Percent	Valid Percent	Cum Percent
Valid	1 Never	37	8.0	24.5	24.5
	2 Rarely	8	1.7	5.3	29.8
	3 Sometimes	21	4.6	13.9	43.7
	4 Often	85	18.4	56.3	100.0
	Total	151	32.8	100.0	
Missing	0	310	67.2		
	Total	310	67.2		
Total		461	100.0		

translated into a percentage of the total. Any missing data are also included in this percentage total. That's why this column is usually ignored and the next column, labeled "Valid Percent," is used for the analysis.

The Valid Percent Column Is Important

The Valid Percent column represents a recalculation of the percentages without the missing data. The Valid Percent is much more meaningful because it reports the percentage of those who answered the question. Notice that 24 percent of those who answered the question, said they never use the ratings. Remember that if every respondent is asked the question and there is no missing data, the Valid Percent column will be the same as the Percent column in the printout.

The last column, "Cum Percent," reports the cumulative percentage. At the bottom of the table, the total number of cases and number of missing cases are reported. The total for valid cases represents the number of people who answered the question. The sum of valid cases and missing cases equals the total number of people surveyed.

SUGGESTED RESEARCH ACTIVITIES

1. The following responses were obtained by asking the open-ended question: "People have different reasons for listening to talk radio. In general, what is the main reason that you listen to talk radio?"

    News
    To listen to Rush Limbaugh's opinions on
        issues
    Entertainment
    To hear opinions of others
    For entertainment
    To find out what other people think about
        issues
    No response
    Politics
    To see what's going on and learn about other
        people's opinions
    To learn about city politics

    Set up the response codes and numerical codes that could be included in the codebook to code the responses for all the questionnaires.

2. As a class activity, select one of the class questionnaires developed from the research activities in Chapter 4. Make copies of the questionnaire and interview one student randomly selected from the student directory. Using the codebook in Appendix B as a guide, create a codebook. Code the completed questionnaire on a coding grid according to the codebook instructions.

3. Have a partner code your questionnaire. Compare the coding to see how well the coding matches. Discuss any discrepancies in the coding. Finally, together agree on the most appropriate code for the coding disagreements.

4. Locate a survey data computer program and find out about two or three of its major features. Using the sample of friends, family, and classmates that you developed in Chapter 5's research activity, produce a frequency printout based on the gender of each individual in the sample. In the computer program, enter the code "1" for male and "2" for female and instruct the program to tabulate the results and produce a frequency printout. Interpret your results.

RECOMMENDED READING

For more perspectives on coding and processing data, see:

R. C. ADAMS, *Social Survey Methods for Mass Media Research*. Hillsdale, NJ: Lawrence Erlbaum, 1989.

To learn more about software programs designed for processing and analyzing survey data, see:

The most recent editions of manuals for SPSS, Statistical Package for the Social Sciences; SAS, Statistical Analysis System, etc.

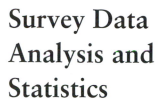

CHAPTER 8

Survey Data Analysis and Statistics

- How are survey data analyzed?
- Which statistics are appropriate for analyzing survey data?
- What is the correct way to read a cross-tabulation table?
- How is the response rate related to the overall quality of the survey results?
- How well do the sample statistics match the population?
- What is the purpose of weighting?
- How are ethical standards applied to analyzing data?

Statistics as a Tool for Understanding

Once the research expert has processed the data and produced a valid frequency printout that represents the survey results, he or she can focus on exploring the data. Statistics serve as an important tool in this exploration. The research expert may choose to use statistics to describe the data or make inferences from the survey results. Descriptive statistics are used to summarize large amounts of data or to show how responses are distributed and ordered. Inferential statistics, on the other hand, are used to make generalizations about the population. Both types of statistics can help you understand the meaning and significance of your data.

This chapter approaches statistics as a tool for understanding and interpreting data—not as mathematical theories, formulas, and calculations. If you are interested in the theories and calculations behind the statistical concepts, we recommend that you consult the statistics books listed at the end of the chapter. In these books and in this chapter you'll quickly notice that there are many statistics to choose from when analyzing data. Our goals are to introduce you to these statistics, provide guidance on selecting the right statistic for your data, and make sure you know how to correctly interpret its meaning.

Many Statistics Are Available for Analyzing Data

Statistical and analytical techniques that can be used to describe and interpret data include measures of central tendency, frequency distributions, cross-tabulations, correlations, and many more. These statistics and analytical techniques are quickly and easily computed by programs

FIGURE 8.1   *Some Categories of Statistical Techniques*

Measures of Central Tendency
Measures of Dispersion
Frequency Distribution
Rank Order

Cross-Tabulation
Measures of Association
Measures of Differences

Techniques for Prediction
Techniques for Data Reduction

that specialize in survey data analysis, such as SPSS, Statistical Package for the Social Sciences, and SAS, Statistical Analysis System. Although the research expert may not have the expertise of a trained statistician, he or she needs to understand the appropriate statistics to use in analyzing data. Statistics are tools that help the research expert describe and interpret the data, find significant relationships, and make predictions.

How do you know which statistic to use in analyzing data? One criterion that dictates which statistic or analytical technique to select is the number of variables being analyzed. Are you analyzing one, two, or three or more variables? Another criterion for deciding the type of statistical analysis is the level of measurement of the variable or question asked. For example, nominal level scales require one type of statistic, ordinal another, and ratio yet another. The purpose of the research study also determines the type of statistic or analytical technique that should be selected. Are you summarizing large amounts of data? Are you sorting out relationships between variables? Are you predicting which variables have an impact on a dependent variable? Figure 8.1 displays some categories of statistical techniques that may be used in exploring survey data. We'll examine some of the statistics that are included in the different categories and their appropriate use.

Statistics for Analyzing One Variable

Measures of Central Tendency

Perhaps the most well-known descriptive statistic is the mean. The mean is one of three measures of central tendency that report the average of the data. The *mean* tells the arithmetic average, that is, the sum of cases divided by the total number of cases. The *mode* tells the most frequent score, and the *median* reports the midpoint or middle score, that is, the point where half of the numbers are above and half are below.

Although we talk about the mean cost of a commercial during the Super Bowl, the median income of recent journalism graduates in the United States, or the modal test score on the midterm exam, practically speaking, all of these measures of central tendency are not appropriate for analyzing *all* types of survey data. For example, you can have a modal gender but *not* a mean gender. Or you can have a mean, median, and modal age but *not* a mean marital status. The level of measurement of the question dictates the appropriate measure of central tendency as well as other statistics. A glance through a typical survey questionnaire shows that most of the questions are at the nominal or ordinal levels, which means that the measures of central tendency used must be appropriate for that level of measurement.

As discussed in Chapter 3, nominal scales simply classify data, but do not place them in order. Ordinal scales classify and order data; there is no real zero point and the distances between points on the scale are not equal. Interval scales have the properties of nominal and ordinal levels plus the distance between points on the scale is equal. But there is no absolute zero in interval-level measurements. Ratio levels of measurement have the same properties as nominal, ordinal, and interval levels of measurement plus an additional property. Ratio measurements classify and order data plus they have equal distances between points and a real zero point.

Although demographic questions on age or income can be written at the ratio level of measurement, they are usually written at the ordinal level in survey questionnaires with age or income groups such as 18 to 24 years old, 25 to 29 years old, etc. or $50,000 to $69,000, $70,000 and above, etc. Consequently the modal age or income category would be the most appropriate measure of central tendency to use. Certainly, if age or income is written at the ratio level of measurement, all three measures of central tendency would be appropriate to use. Nominal levels of measurement such as marital status or political party would use the mode as a measure of central tendency.

Why wouldn't you calculate a mean on ordinal data? Remember that, for ordinal scales, the intervals between points cannot be assumed to be equal. How, for example, would you calculate a mean number of videos rented per month when the measurement scale included: none, 1 or 2, 3 to 5, 6 to 10, and more than 10? With one interval representing 1 or 2 videos and another representing more than 10, the intervals are clearly not equal and the mean would not accurately describe the average number of videos rented during the month. It would have been better to have asked an open-ended question and let the respondent supply the number of videos rented during the month. The responses would then be coded as a ratio scale, and a mean would accurately summarize the data.

To avoid potential problems of using the wrong statistic, the research expert should anticipate what analyses he or she wants to do on the data before drafting the questionnaire. If, for example, the researcher wants to report the mean number of days that news is discussed with friends or family, the question should be written as a ratio scale. Instead of providing response categories such as "never or seldom," "1 or 2 days a week," "3 or 4 days a week," etc. the response choices should be "0 days," "1 day," "2 days," "3 days," "4 days," etc.

Measures of Dispersion

Three commonly discussed measures of dispersion are the range, variance, and standard deviation. The range, which is the difference between the highest and lowest score, can be calculated on ordinal, interval, or ratio level measures. Reporting the range may be misleading because there may be an abnormally high or low score in the data, such as a billionaire who lives in a community of mostly middle-income families.

The variance and standard deviation, which require interval or ratio scales, are used to understand how much the scores or responses to a question vary or deviate from the mean. The variance, which is expressed in squared units, measures the average of the squared deviations from the mean. The standard deviation, which is the square root of the variance, is a more useful statistic because it is reported in the same units that the scores or question responses represent. If, for example, on a survey of recent communication graduates, one question asked starting salary, the variance of the salaries would be calculated as squared dollars but the standard deviation would be calculated in dollars, a measurement unit that is familiar.

To continue with the example of a survey of communication graduates, suppose you read an article entitled, "Starting Salaries of the Most Recent Communication Graduates." You quickly scan the article and learn that the mean salary of communication graduates is $26,000, and one standard deviation equals $4,000. Because your starting salary was $34,000, you begin to smile. If only the mean salary had been reported, you would have known that your salary was higher than the average salary, but because the standard deviation was *also* reported, you could easily determine that you are on the high-salary end among your peers. If your starting salary had been $22,000, you might have become depressed. By consulting one of the recommended statistics texts at the end of this chapter, you can learn more about the theoretical assumptions that are used in calculating and interpreting standard deviations.

 Frequency Distribution

Because many of the questions in survey questionnaires are at the nominal or ordinal level, the research expert uses a frequency distribution to display the percentage of responses for each value. We first looked at a frequency table in Chapter 7 when we were processing and cleaning the data for analysis. A frequency distribution is a popular method for analyzing data in business reports, newspaper and magazine articles, and television newscasts. This method of analysis simply shows what percentage of the total each response represents.

When using computer-generated frequency distributions, the research expert focuses on the Valid Percent column and ignores many of the other numbers that are printed on the output. Remember from Chapter 7 that the Valid Percent column does not include missing data when calculating the percentages. Figure 8.2 displays valid percentages from two frequency printouts.

FIGURE 8.2 *Examples of Frequency Distributions*

V37: (Ordinal Scale) Frequency of Going Downtown

	Valid Percent
Never or seldom	44.1
1–3 times a week	31.0
4–5 times a week	6.4
Almost daily or more often	18.4
Valid Cases 461	100.0

V38: (Nominal Scale) Main Reasons for Going Downtown

	Valid Percent
Restaurants	5.4
Business, Banking	20.8
Live Music & Entertainment District, Bars	16.4
Work	27.8
Shopping	5.4
No Response/No Opinion	9.8
Other	14.5
Valid Cases 317	100.0

Since the valid percent data in Figure 8.2 are from the printout in Appendix C.1, they have not been rounded yet. If these data are used in the final report, they will be rounded and dressed up in tables or charts with titles and subtitles. (Please note that if you compare V38 in Figure 8.2 with the original printout in the appendix, you'll notice that some responses have been combined or re-ordered for discussion purposes.)

Also, note that during this phase of exploring and analyzing the data, the variable numbers—not question numbers—are shown. Although these variable numbers will not be used in the tables for the final report, at this stage, they serve as a marker for the printout and codebook. How to display data in written reports will be discussed in Chapter 9 on writing research reports.

 ## Rank Ordering Data

When you're analyzing a frequency distribution of a nominal scale, the data should be rank ordered so the high, middle, and low percentages can easily be identified. Figure 8.3 shows how the nominal data for V38 would be revised from its printout form that was shown in Figure 8.2.

As a result of reordering the data from high to low, you can quickly see that the top reason for going downtown is for work and the last reasons are restaurants and shopping. The meaning of these data is now clearer.

Rank ordering can also be used when you have a series of questions with the same response choices on a similar topic. Sometimes these questions are written in a matrix format on the questionnaire; other times the questions are written separately. Picking the same response choice

FIGURE 8.3 *Frequency Distribution Rank Ordered*

V38: (Nominal Scale) Main Reasons for Going Downtown

Work	27.8
Business, Banking	20.8
Live Music & Entertainment District, Bars	16.4
Other	14.5
No Response/No Opinion	9.8
Restaurants	5.4
Shopping	5.4
Valid Cases 317	100.0

FIGURE 8.4 *Combining Every Day Responses from Multiple Questions into One Analysis*

Variables	Percents
V4, Watch local evening TV news every day	28.6
V7, Watch network evening TV news every day	16.0
V8, Read a daily newspaper every day	41.4
V9, Discuss news with friends and family every day	26.0
V11, Watch a home shopping channel every day	0.0
V15, Listen to radio every day	59.8
V17, Listen to talk radio every day	10.7

across the questions and combining them into one table can reveal a lot about the data.

Figure 8.4 displays the *every day* responses from seven questions on media behavior. Remember that if the research expert uses these data in the final report, the data will be rounded and dressed up in tables or charts. But for now, the research expert is simply exploring the data in the order that the questions were asked.

By reordering the data from the largest to smallest percentage as in Figure 8.5, you can easily see the most popular (listening to radio) to least popular (watching home shopping channel) daily media behaviors. Also, note that because the every day responses are being compared across seven different questions, the percentages do not add to 100 percent.

On the same questionnaire, a question was asked about computer use. Assigned the variable label, V22, the response choices for the computer

FIGURE 8.5 *Rank Ordering Every Day Responses from Multiple Questions*

Variables	Percents
V15, Listen to radio every day	59.8
V8, Read a daily newspaper every day	41.4
V4, Watch local evening TV news every day	28.6
V9, Discuss news with friends and family every day	26.0
V7, Watch network evening TV news every day	16.0
V17, Listen to talk radio every day	10.7
V11, Watch a home shopping channel every day	0.0

use question did not match the response choices of the media behavior questions. Instead of an "every day" response choice, the computer use question used "five or more days a week" as the top response choice. Even though the response choices differ for the computer use question, you would still want to examine how the "five or more days a week" response matches with the media behaviors.

Since 49 percent of the respondents said they use a computer "five or more days a week," the computer question fits between every day radio listening and every day newspaper reading. If these data are included in the final report, an explanation must be included to show that the questions were asked differently. Another possibility is for the research expert to combine the "nearly every day" and "every day" responses to make them more closely match the response on computer use. To combine the percentages for the two response choices, you can rerun the data with a recode command or manually add the percentages because they have the same base. This approach has been used in Figure 8.6.

Notice that in Figure 8.6 a number in parentheses has been added to the right of each percentage. This number indicates the ranking of the percentage in the list of numbers. If the rank order symbol is used in the final report, it should have a footnote to explain its presence in the table. The benefit of including this rank order symbol becomes apparent when comparing the first and second columns. For a list of four or more numbers, the rank order symbol helps you quickly identify the top and bottom ranked percentages.

Even more important, you can quickly see ranks that remain the same and ranks that change. Listening to radio, for example, remained ranked

FIGURE 8.6   *Rank Ordering* Every Day *and* Nearly Every Day *Responses*

Variables	Percents	
	Every Day	*Every Day/ Nearly Every Day*
V15, Listen to radio	59.8 (1)	73.4 (1)
V8, Read a daily newspaper	41.4 (2)	50.6 (3)
V4, Watch local evening TV news	28.6 (3)	60.3 (2)
V9, Discuss news with friends and family	26.0 (4)	45.9 (5)
V7, Watch network evening TV news	16.0 (5)	30.5 (6)
V17, Listen to talk radio	10.7 (6)	19.1 (7)
V11, Watch a home shopping channel	0.0 (7)	0.6 (8)
V22, Use a computer 5 or more days	—	48.1 (4)

number one in both columns. But watching local evening TV news edged out reading a newspaper in the second column, which combined every day and nearly every day responses. In the second column, local TV news viewing moved up to the number two spot and newspaper reading dropped to the third spot. Computer use in the second column claimed the fourth ranked spot, causing discussing the news with friends and family to drop to spot number five.

What is clear from analyzing the data using frequency distributions is that data analysis is a process of exploration. This process includes identifying the data that are relevant to the research questions that initiated the study in the first place, drafting tables that use the variable numbers for reference, ranking or combining responses to relevant questions, comparing and synthesizing responses to similar questions, recoding and recalculating in order to best understand what the data are saying.

The Analytical Technique of Cross-Tabulation

Cross-tabulation uses some of the same exploratory techniques as frequency distributions. But before you can use those exploratory techniques, you must understand the purpose of this analytical technique and know how to accurately read a cross-tab table. The purpose of a cross-tab is to examine the relationship between two or more variables by breaking down the variables into subgroups or subcategories. Often demographic or psychographic variables are examined in a cross-tab to determine their relationship to various attitudes and behaviors.

For example, the research expert might compare the demographic variable "age" with the behavior "discussing the news with friends or family" to determine if there is a relationship. Subgroups of the "age" variable would include young, middle age, and old. Frequent discussion and infrequent discussion might represent subgroups of the behavior variable "discussing the news." Age might also be compared with the attitude "comfort level in using computers." Sometimes one behavior is compared with another in a cross-tab analysis. A good example would be an examination of newspaper reading and listening to talk radio. Cross-tabulation analysis helps to better understand how subgroups are similar or different when it comes to attitudes and behaviors.

 Deciding Which Variables to Compare

To produce a cross-tab table with the help of your computer program, you must tell the computer which two variables should be compared. To help think about the relevant cross-tabs to produce, consider which vari-

ables may influence others. Demographic variables often influence behaviors. How old you are has some influence on how frequently you
read a daily newspaper. Whether you are a male or female has some
influence on what TV programs you watch. Your level of education
has some influence on what computer services you use. By influence,
we don't mean "cause." We simply mean that a relationship is being
explored.

But the concept of causation helps explain how to tell the computer
program which variables to cross-tab and how to read the table that is
produced. In scientific research and data exploration, we talk about independent and dependent variables. Independent variables influence dependent variables. We'll learn in Chapter 12 on experiments that causation can occur under controlled circumstances. But for the purposes of
survey data, we are only able to say that the independent variable is the
one that influences and the dependent variable is the one that has been
influenced. Generally the variable that occurred first in time is treated as
the independent variable. That's why demographic variables are considered as independent variables and behaviors and attitudes are treated as
dependent variables. Although it would be incorrect to say that watching network TV news has an impact on how old you are, it would be
perfectly natural to say that how old you are may influence whether or
not you watch network TV news. So as you list the cross-tab analyses
that you want to examine, think about the variables that may have an
influence on others.

Generally there are clues as to which variables may influence others.
Remember, in the second step of the research phase, that the research
expert reviewed previous studies and research literature to learn what
was already known about the topic under investigation. Previous literature would have already identified a relationship between age and newspaper reading such as that young adults read newspapers less than older
adults. The research expert would still run this cross-tab to see if he or
she confirms previous research or to determine if this trend has changed.

The cross-tabulation instruction *V21 by V87* specifies which variables
are to be compared and the placement of the variables in the table. Figure 8.7 (p. 138), which displays the relevant data from the computer printout, shows that V21, "What do you usually do when ads come on," is
treated as a dependent variable and listed down the side of the table. V87,
"Gender," is treated as an independent variable and listed across the top
of the printout table. The location of the independent variable in the table
is important to the accurate interpretation of the table. The four numbers in each cell of the printout table indicate that the research expert
instructed SPSS to include the count or raw number, row percentage,

FIGURE 8.7   *Reading a Cross-Tabulation Table*

V87 Gender of Respondent

V21 What Do You Usually Do When Ads Come On?	1 Male	2 Female	Total
1 Change Channel	44 59.5% **23.0%** 10.9%	30 40.5% **14.2%** 7.5%	74 100.0% 18.4% 18.4%
2 Don't Watch Them	29 43.9% **15.2%** 7.2%	37 56.1% **17.5%** 9.2%	66 100.0% 16.4% 16.4%
3 Turn Down Sound, Mute	17 51.5% **8.9%** 4.2%	16 48.5% **7.6%** 4.0%	33 100.0% **8.2%** 8.2%
4 Do Something Else	26 34.2% **13.6%** 6.5%	50 65.8% **23.7%** 12.4%	76 100.0% **18.9%** 18.9%
5 Watch Them	50 43.9% **26.2%** 12.4%	64 56.1% **30.3%** 15.9%	114 100.0% 28.4% 28.4%
99 Other	25 64.1% **13.1%** 6.2%	14 35.9% **6.6%** 3.5%	39 100.0% **9.7%** 9.7%
Total	191 47.5% 100.0%	211 52.5% 100.0%	402 100.0% 100.0%

	Value	df	Significance
Pearson Chi Square	15.092	5	.010

column percentage, and total percentage. Because the independent variable has been placed at the top of the table, the column percentage is the number that we'll pay the most attention to as we interpret the data.

When the Independent Variable Is at the Top

To accurately read a cross-tabulation table, you must first determine whether the independent variable is across the top of the table or down the side. Recall that the independent variable exerts influence on another variable and that the dependent variable is the one that is influenced. If the independent variable is across the top, you should compare across the column percents or the third numbers in the cell.

In the "change channel" cell for Figure 8.7, the column percentages 23.0 percent and 14.2 percent should be compared—not the row percentages 59.5 and 40.5. A correct interpretation of the table would be 23.0 percent of males and 14.2 percent of females "change channels" when ads come on the TV. Notice that the independent variable was mentioned before the dependent variable because the independent variable, gender, is viewed as influencing the dependent variable, viewers' behaviors during commercials.

Sometimes the research expert sets up the cross-tab command so that the independent variable is located down the side of the table. If the independent variable is down the side, the row percentages down the table should be compared. Regardless of where the independent variable is placed on the table, you must know how to accurately read the table to avoid incorrectly interpreting the data.

The accurate interpretation of a cross-tab table is based on the "percentaged down" rule. If the independent variable is across the top of the table and the percentages total 100 percent *down* the columns, read and compare the column percentages *across* the table. But if the independent variable is down the side of the table and the percentages total 100 percent *across* the rows, compare the row percentages going *down* (Babbie, 1995, p. 260). Just remember to compare the relevant column or row percentages in the *opposite direction*.

Once again, take a look at Figure 8.7. The column percentages for males and column percentages for females have been displayed in bold type. Add the column percentages for males: 23.0, 15.2, 8.9, 13.6, 26.2, 13.1. Because those numbers add to 100 percent, you should compare across. As a test, add the row percentages for males and you'll quickly see that the sum of the row percentages *down* is *not* 100 percent. By following the percentaged down rule, the row percentages would be the wrong numbers to use when the independent variable is across the top of the table.

Now that you know how to correctly read a cross-tab table, you can answer the question: What is the relationship, if any, between gender and behaviors when ads come on TV? The cross-tab shows that males are more likely than females to change the channel during commercials and females are more likely than males to do something else during commercials. An examination of the table shows where males and females are similar in their activities and where they are different. Although some differences are shown in the table, we won't know if these differences are real or due to chance.

Determining Significance

 ### Chi Square Can Determine Relationship between Two Variables

Real or significant differences in the data are very important, and the research expert puts the data to a statistical test to determine the significance of the results that are found. One such statistical test is chi square, which is reported at the bottom of Figure 8.7. Chi square is "used whenever we wish to evaluate whether or not frequencies which have been empirically obtained differ significantly from those which would be expected under a certain set of theoretical assumptions" (Blalock, 1972, p. 275).

To apply this statement to the cross-tab table in Figure 8.7, you would expect the same proportion of males and females to change channels when commercials are aired. If the proportions are the same, there is no relationship between gender and activities during commercials. But what we observed from the data is that males are more likely than females to change channels. The chi square test helps us interpret that this difference between what we expected and what we observed is significant or real. Notice that three numbers are reported on the cross-tab table and should be reported in the written report. The numbers are: (1) the chi square (X^2) value of 15.092; (2) degrees of freedom (d.f.) of 5; and (3) probability level of significance (p) of .010. Any of the recommended statistics texts at the end of this chapter can explain the theoretical assumptions behind these numbers.

 ### Interpreting Significance

How do we know that .010, which is reported in Figure 8.7, is significant? Three probability levels—$p < .05$, $p < .01$, and $p < .001$—are generally used to judge significance. To interpret the significance in Figure 8.7, we can say that there is a probability of less than one in one hundred that the relationship observed is due to chance and *not* gender, which are odds worth betting on.

Many statistical tests that are used to interpret data have significance levels attached to them. Generally, in the academic research journals, probability levels greater than .05 are rejected as lacking significance. The significance level in a chi square test is a guide for you to know that a relationship between two variables exists and should be paid attention to. But the significance level does not tell you the magnitude or strength of that relationship.

Although a statistical program such as SPSS will calculate and report chi square after receiving a simple command, the theoretical assumptions and step-by-step procedure for calculating chi square can be found in a comprehensive statistics book. It is important to note that chi square is most appropriate when both the independent and dependent variables are at the nominal level. Chi square can be used for variables that are at the ordinal or interval scale levels, but more powerful statistics are available to use for these higher level measurement scales and they also provide insight into the strength and direction of a relationship between two variables.

Statistical Measures of Association

Interpreting Measures of Association

Measures of association can be used to interpret the strength and direction of a relationship between two variables in cross-tabulations. In general, measures of association, which range from negative one (-1) through zero (0) to positive one ($+1$), indicate the presence or absence of a relationship between two variables. A positive ($+$) relationship indicates that as one variable increases, the other increases. A negative ($-$) relationship indicates that as one variable increases, the other decreases or vice versa. Zero (0) can be interpreted as the absence of a relationship between two variables. Note that although zero (0) would indicate the lack of a relationship between two variables, there still could be a curvilinear relationship such as the relationship between age and newspaper reading. In other words, studies have found that newspaper reading is high in the middle ages but low among younger and older adults.

Measures of association for ordinal, interval, and ratio scales indicate the strength (weak, modest, strong) and direction (positive, negative) of a relationship between two variables. But measures of association for nominal scales can only indicate the strength of a relationship. It would be inappropriate to suggest a positive or negative direction because nominal scales are not ordered. Some measures of association for nominal variables that a statistical software program would calculate include phi and Cramer's V.

Measures of Association for Nominal Data

Figure 8.8 shows how chi square, phi, and Cramer's V were used to interpret the relationship between VCRs and movies by PC owners and nonowners in an article published in *Journalism Quarterly.*

Notice that chi square is significant in the first two cross-tabulations. In the third cross-tabulation, non-significance is indicated by n.s. The phi and Cramer's V statistics indicate the magnitude of the relationship between PC ownership and VCRs and movies. Notice that phi is used when both variables are nominal and Cramer's V is used when one variable is nominal and the other is ordinal. Also, take note of the range of scores that indicate the strength of the relationship between the two variables. The phi in the first cross-tabulation is .513, which can be considered moderately strong on a scale that ranges from 0 to 1. The Cramer's V of .226 in the second cross-tabulation can be interpreted as modest, and .106 in the third cross-tabulation is weak.

Measures of Association for Ordinal Data

Some measures of association that are appropriate for data measured at the ordinal level are gamma, lambda, Kendall's tau_b and tau_c, and Spearman's rho. Although you can review the theoretical assumptions involved in selecting one of these statistics in one of the statistics books recommended at the end of this chapter, it is important to emphasize that these statistics enable the research expert to interpret the strength and direction of a relationship between two ordinal variables. All of these statistics are calculated by a computer program such as SPSS.

Let's look at an example to see how the statistic tau_b was used in a study published in *Journal of Communication.* Your authors, McCombs and Poindexter (1983), were interested in determining whether there was a significant relationship between civic attitudes—that is a duty to keep informed—and reading a newspaper. Because the measures for both variables were at the ordinal level of measurement, they used the statistic tau_b to determine the significance of the relationship. In surveys conducted in three geographic areas, they found that 82 percent of those who held strong civic attitudes read a newspaper every day, whereas only 58 percent of those with weak civic attitudes read a newspaper every day. The tau_b statistic of .169 was found to be statistically significant, indicating a definite, but perhaps modest relationship between civic atti-

FIGURE 8.8   *Statistics Used in Three Cross-Tabulations*

VCR Ownership, Movie Rentals, and Movie Going	Personal Computer	
Owns VCR	**Owners**	**Nonowners**
Yes	80%	27%
No	20	73
N = (152)	(55)	(97)
X^2 = 39.978, d.f. = 1, p <.001		
Phi = .513		
Frequency of Renting VCR Movies	**Owners**	**Nonowners**
Less than twice a month	43%	37%
Twice a month	27	25
Three times a month	16	8
Once a week	2	18
More than once a week	12	12
N = (188)	(49)	(139)
X^2 = 9.536, d.f. = 4, p < .05		
Cramer's V = .226		
Frequency of Going to Movies	**Owners**	**Nonowners**
Less than twice a month	71%	74%
Twice a month	15	14
Three times a month	2	3
Once a week	6	7
More than once a week	6	2
N = (192)	(49)	(143)
X^2 = 2.134, d.f. = 4, p = n.s.		
Cramer's V = .106		

Adapted from: "Personal Computers and Media Use" by John C. Schweitzer, *Journalism Quarterly,* vol. 68, no. 4 (Winter 1991): 696. Used with permission.

tudes and newspaper reading. Note that because ties are taken into account when calculating tau$_b$, that tau$_b$ is considered more conservative than other measures of association, such as gamma, that do not consider ties in their calculation (Weaver, 1981, p. 70).

The calculation that produces the Spearman's rho statistic is different from the other measures of association for ordinal level data because it compares *rankings* rather than the actual percentages. For example, Poindexter (1977) used a Spearman's rho to help validate the survey results that showed non-readers of newspapers ranged from 6 percent to 16 percent in six geographic areas in the northeast. To validate these survey results on non-readers, Poindexter calculated non-penetration rates, the percentage of households without newspapers, for each market. By ranking the percentage of non-readers and the non-penetration rates for each geographic area from high to low, Poindexter was able to calculate a Spearman's rho of +.77, which showed that the non-readership percentages were associated with the non-penetration figures for each geographic area.

Product-Moment Correlation (r)

For interval and ratio scales, the strength and direction of the relationship between two variables can be determined with the correlation coefficient *r*. Introduced by Karl Pearson, this statistic is called the product-moment correlation (*r*), and ranges from negative one (−1) through zero (0) to plus one (+1) as a measure of the magnitude of a linear association between two variables (Blalock, 1972, p. 376). A plus-one (+1) would indicate a perfect (very strong) positive linear relationship, and a negative-one (−1) would reveal a perfect (very strong) negative linear relationship. In a perfect positive linear relationship, as one variable increases, the other variable increases, and the rate of increase is constant. In a perfect negative linear relationship, as one variable increases, the other variable decreases at a constant rate (or vice versa). Remember, however, that a zero or low correlation value does not *necessarily* indicate a slight or non-relationship between two variables. As noted earlier, if number of days reading a newspaper is high in the middle ages but low among younger and older ages, there would still be a relationship among newspaper reading and age but not a linear relationship.

Guilford (1956, p. 145) used the following guide to interpret the strength of a Pearson *r*:

> *less than .20* = slight correlation; almost negligible relationship
> *.20 to under .40* = low correlation; definite but small relationship
> *.40 to under .70* = moderate correlation; substantial relationship
> *.70 to .90* = high correlation; marked relationship
> *more than .90* = very high correlation; very dependable relationship

Testing for Difference

Even though survey data infrequently uses ratio-level measurements, there are occasions to calculate a mean and determine if the mean differs significantly from another mean. Suppose you conducted a survey on fifty randomly selected public relations graduates and fifty randomly selected advertising graduates one year after graduation to find out their salaries. After collecting the data, you would calculate a mean salary for each group. A t-test could be used to determine if the mean salaries of public relations and advertising students differ significantly. We'll discuss the t-test in more detail in Chapter 12 on experiments because a t-test is more likely to be used for comparing means in experimental data than survey data.

Statistics and Analytical Techniques for Three or More Variables

Often the research expert's goal is to understand the relationship of three or more variables. This type of analysis requires the use of multivariate statistics or analytical techniques such as factor analysis, multiple regression, or analysis of variance (ANOVA) to name a few. The goals of these statistical techniques vary as well as the measurement scale requirements of the data analyzed.

Factor Analysis

In general, factor analysis is a technique for reducing large numbers of variables into a few, meaningful factors that can help explain the data or be used for further analysis. For example, communication researchers Stempel and Hargrove (1996) asked a national sample of over 1,000 adults about their print, broadcast, and online media behavior. Their study produced data on eleven types of media, including network TV news, local TV news, the Internet, online services, daily newspapers, news magazines, political magazines, radio news, radio talk shows, TV magazines, and grocery store tabloids. The researchers used factor analysis to sort and reduce the data into meaningful factors.

The factor analysis produced five separate factors, which contradicted conventional wisdom and previous research that consumers use more than one type of medium to be informed. The factor analysis showed that consumers were likely to use the same type of medium rather than cross over to a different type of medium. The five factors were television (network TV and local TV news), computer (the Internet and online services), print media (newspapers, news magazines, and political magazines), radio (radio news and radio talk shows), and tabloid (grocery store tabloids and television magazine shows).

Multiple Regression

Multiple regression is a tool for predicting the effects of two or more independent variables on a dependent variable. Journalism professors David Weaver and Dan Drew (1995) studied Indiana residents during the 1992 presidential election to find out the role of a variety of factors on election behavior and knowledge. The researchers used multiple regression to determine the contribution of the independent variables "age," "gender," "political party belonged to," "education," "income," "employment," and "campaign interest" in the prediction of the dependent variable "campaign issue knowledge." The researchers found that of the eight independent variables examined in the multiple regression analysis, only "campaign interest" was a significant predictor of "campaign issue knowledge."

 *ANOVA*

Unlike the t-test, which compares two means, analysis of variance, commonly called ANOVA, permits the research expert to determine if means from three or more groups or samples are significantly different. Because ratio levels of measurement are used less frequently than nominal and ordinal measures in surveys, there are fewer opportunities to calculate a mean, which would be the basis of using analysis of variance. In addition, surveys are usually conducted on one sample, whether national or local, so there is less opportunity to have three or more random samples for using analysis of variance.

In the example used earlier for calculating a t-test on salaries of random samples of public relations and advertising graduates, we could also survey journalism graduates and radio-TV-film graduates and use analysis of variance to determine if the salaries differ among the four different groups. Practically speaking, analysis of variance is mostly used for data collected from scientific experiments. We'll discuss those applications in Chapter 12.

Statistical Inferences about the Population

Rather than simply describe relationships, the research expert also uses statistical procedures to project sample results to the population. Remember from Chapter 5 on sampling that because a random sample is drawn in such a way that every member of the population has an equal chance of being picked, the research expert can predict within a confidence interval, what the results would have been if every member of the total population had been surveyed.

As a rule of thumb, the research expert uses the 95 percent confidence level to predict that if one hundred random samples had been drawn, ninety-five times out of one hundred, the real population value would fall within a specified interval of plus or minus percentage points. This confidence interval is also called the sampling error. A look back at Figure 5.2 in Chapter 5 will show the confidence interval for random sample sizes ranging from 10 to 50,000.

An example from a telephone survey will help explain how confidence interval is used in statistically inferring the random sample results to the population. In the survey, when 313 computer users were asked if they used a CD-ROM three times a week or more, 28 percent said yes and 72 percent said no. To project these random sample survey results to the total population of computer users, you could consult Figure 5.2 to find the confidence interval for a random sample of 313. According to Figure 5.2, the confidence interval is plus or minus 5.7 percentage points. Therefore, you can calculate: 28 percent plus or minus 5.7 percentage points. You would conclude that if every member of the computer user population had been interviewed, the real population value would fall within the confidence interval of 22.3 percent to 33.7 percent. In other words, between 22 percent and 34 percent of computer users use a CD-ROM at least three times a week.

Inferring the population value is the most popular statistical analysis used by journalists who write stories from survey or poll data and political strategists who manage campaigns and help politicians win elections. Political reporters use this analytical technique to predict which candidate is ahead and which is behind.

When using the results of random samples to project to the total population it is important to remember that the probability of 95 percent is essentially a bet with very good odds—ninety-five times out of one hundred the real population value will fall within the confidence interval. But like any odds, you're also betting that five times out of one hundred, the real population value will fall *outside* the confidence interval.

Even more important, it is essential when using random sample results to project to the population that the sampling error is factored into the results. If twenty-four hours before an election, a survey of a random sample of 1,200 likely voters found that 52 percent of the voters said they would vote for Candidate A and 48 percent said they planned to vote for candidate B, it would be *incorrect* to interpret the results as Candidate A is ahead in the race. Because when the sampling error for a random sample of 1,200 of plus or minus 2.8 percentage points is factored in, it becomes clear from Figure 8.9 that Candidate A may actually be *behind* Candidate B.

Remember that the confidence level and sample size determine the confidence interval or amount of sampling error. When the sampling error is factored in, Candidate A could have as low as 49.2 percent of the vote and Candidate B could have as high as 50.8 percent of the vote. Therefore, the correct way to interpret the results would be that the race is *too close to determine which candidate is ahead.*

FIGURE 8.9   *Evaluating the Impact of the Confidence Interval on the True Population Value at the 95 Percent Confidence Level*

	After Subtracting Sampling Error of 2.8 Pecentage Points	Sample Results	After Adding Sampling Error of 2.8 Percentage Points
Candidate A	49.2%	52%	54.8%
Candidate B	45.2%	48%	50.8 %

Recommendations for Appropriate Use of Statistics

As you can see from Figure 8.10, which summarizes the statistics we have discussed in this chapter, many statistical tools are available to help you correctly interpret the data and unearth important relationships between variables. Note that additional statistics and analytical techniques can be found in the academic communication journals and comprehensive statistics books. You can use the Figure 8.10 as a quick guide for selecting the right statistic or analytical technique.

Although statistical programs that specialize in analyzing survey data can easily and quickly produce statistics and report their significance, it is still your responsibility to select a statistic that is appropriate for your data. For example, it is incorrect to use statistics *only* suitable for interval or ratio levels of measurements on nominal level data. Your data must conform to the level of measurement that the statistic requires. Also, in a two-variable analysis, when one variable is at the nominal level and the other at the ordinal level of measurement, you should select a statistic that is appropriate for the variable at the *lower* level of measurement (Weaver, 1981, p. 85). Finally, because some statistics are more powerful than others, always select the most powerful statistic for the type of data that you have so that you can understand your survey results completely. If, for example, the chi square statistic is used to interpret ratio data, you will have failed to extract the full meaning from your data. Figure 8.10 and the statistics books listed at the end of the chapter can help you correctly select and use statistics to analyze data. Also, a regular reading of the communication journals provides examples of statistical analyses of data.

Evaluation of the Overall Survey Sample

Although the appropriate use of statistics is very important in understanding the data, it is also important to evaluate the quality of the over-

FIGURE 8.10   *A Guide to Selecting Appropriate Statistics and Analytical Techniques*

Level of Measurement	Analyzing One Variable
Nominal	Frequencies, mode, rank order, confidence interval
Ordinal	Frequencies, mode, median, range
Interval or ratio	Frequencies, mode, median, mean, variance, standard deviation
Level of Measurement	**Analyzing Two Variables**
Nominal	Cross-tabulation, chi square, phi, Cramer's V
Ordinal	Kendall's tau_b, Kendall's tau_c, gamma, Spearman's rho
Interval or ratio	Pearson's product-moment correlation (r), t-test
Level of Measurement	**Analyzing Three or More Variables**
Nominal	Cross-tabulation
Ordinal	Cross-tabulation
Interval or ratio	Factor analysis, analysis of variance (ANOVA), multiple regression

all sample. If the sample is poor, sophisticated statistics will not make the data better. Two methods may be used to evaluate the quality of the sample: response rate and validation of the sample characteristics.

 Response Rate

The response rate represents a percentage of respondents who completed the survey out of the total number of prospective respondents called less the nonworking, business, fax, and modem numbers. Remember from Chapter 6 that interviewers were instructed during the training session to keep a record of the numbers called and to indicate on the call record form in Figure 6.4 the reasons for not completing an interview. This information is used to evaluate the overall sample. If an unusually large number of the randomly selected respondents do not complete the interview, the sample will not be representative of the population from which it was selected.

The proliferation of real surveys, phony surveys, and telemarketing calls to the home as well as the active lives of adults makes it impossible to get a 100 percent response rate in a survey. Sometimes people refuse to participate because they were just called by another survey outfit and they don't want to be bothered. Also, even after several callbacks at different times and on different days, it is hard to reach busy people. These two factors are the main reasons that survey response rates have declined. Research expert Earl Babbie (1995, p. 262) said that a 50 percent response rate is adequate; a 60 percent response is good; a 70 percent response rate is very good. Author of *Statistical Deception at Work* John Mauro (1992, p. 83) said that a minimum response rate of 70 percent is necessary for analysis.

A minimum 70 percent response rate is ideal, but it is no longer realistic. Based on the results of an experiment conducted by The Pew Research Center for the People & the Press (1998), we, too, feel that a 50 percent response rate is adequate for analysis. In this experiment, results were compared from two telephone surveys that started on the same day, June 18, 1997, and asked the same questions. The first survey, which was referred to as the "standard survey," interviewed 1,000 adults in a five-day period. At least five attempts were made during the survey period to complete an interview. The second survey, which was called the "rigorous survey," contacted 1,201 adults and lasted eight weeks. Many of the households in the rigorous survey were sent a letter in advance of the survey announcing that an interviewer would be calling. A monetary incentive, a $2 bill, was included in the letter. An unlimited number of callbacks was made throughout the eight-week interviewing period for the rigorous survey. People who initially refused to be interviewed in the rigorous survey were contacted up to two additional times to persuade them to participate. Respondents who refused twice were sent a priority mail letter to try to persuade them to participate before contacting them a third time.

The results of the experiment showed that the length of time for surveying had an impact on response rate. The five-day standard survey produced a 42 percent response rate, and the eight-week rigorous survey produced a 71 percent response rate. But the difference in response rate did not translate into different results for the two surveys. According to the experimental study, the results of the standard and rigorous surveys were strikingly similar. Excluding time-sensitive questions on the surveys, only five of the eighty-five questions on media use, lifestyles, and political and social issues produced different results.

Validation of the Sample

Another method that is used to evaluate the quality of the survey sample is validation. The sample characteristics are compared to independent statistics to determine how well they match. For surveys of general populations, the census data are usually the basis of comparison. Figure 8.11 compares the sample statistics with available census data.

FIGURE 8.11   *A Comparison of a Random Sample and the Census*

	Austin Sample (N = 461)	1990 Austin Census
Age		
18–24	16%*	20%
25–34	23	29
35–44	28	22
45–54	16	11
55–64	8*	8
65 Plus	9*	10
Race/Ethnic Group		
White	78%	68%
Black or African American	7*	9
Hispanic or Latino	9	20
Asian American/Other	6*	3
Education		
Some High School	4%	17%
High School Graduate/Some College	48*	49
College Graduate Plus	49	36
Income		
Under $20,000	16%	36
$20,000–$49,000	38*	42
$50,000 Plus	30	22
(Refused)	15	0

*After factoring in the confidence interval of plus or minus 4.5 percentage points at the 95 percent confidence level, the sample statistic would be a good match for the census data.

The sampling error for a random sample of 461 is approximately plus or minus 4.5 percentage points. As the sample is compared to the census, the sampling error must be factored into the sample statistics to determine if the sample is a good match. According to Figure 8.11, after factoring in the sampling error, seven of the sample statistics are within one-half to one percentage point of the census statistics.

Even though many sample statistics in Figure 8.11 were good matches of the census data, it should be of concern to the researcher that in the survey, Hispanics or Latinos, adults with some high school education, and those with low incomes were significantly underrepresented. To compensate for this underrepresentation, the research expert can use the weighting procedure in SPSS to statistically increase the Hispanics or

Latinos, adults without a high school degree, and low income adults by the underrepresented amount. This weighting procedure would simultaneously statistically decrease the groups that are overrepresented such as whites and those with college and advanced degrees. The process of weighting discussed in detail in Chapter 15.

The weighting procedure may solve the problem statistically, but the fact remains that a few groups are underrepresented and some are overrepresented. The research expert should take special care in future surveys to have the correct representation for each category. The researcher also must report any statistical weighting in the final report.

Ethics and Data Analysis

During this phase in which the data are analyzed in depth, an *unethical* researcher could do what communication scholar Wayne Danielson (1981, p. 117) called "cook the data." An unethical researcher might alter the results by deleting some data or even fudging some because they do not conform to expectations. Danielson said emphatically: *Don't do it*. Cooking the data would damage your reputation and the integrity of scientific research. There are, of course, legitimate alterations that can be made to the data, such as recoding or weighting. It is imperative though that detailed records be kept on any changes to the data so they can be reported in the final report and included with the data in case others ask to use the data for a secondary analysis.

SUGGESTED RESEARCH ACTIVITIES

1. Select a frequency table from Appendix C.1. What are the significant findings from the table you selected?

2. Select a cross-tabulation table from Appendix C.2. What does the table say?

3. A scientific survey was conducted and respondents were asked about their familiarity with the term "Generation X." Those who were familiar with the term were asked the open-ended question, "When you hear or see the term 'Generation X,' what word or words come to your mind?" Use the rank order analytical technique to analyze the following results, which were taken directly from the print-

out. What else can you do with the data to make it more meaningful?

Young	26.5
20–something	6.5
30–something	.3
Generational	8.7
Age-related	5.6
MTV generation	1.6
Future-oriented	3.7
Truthseeker	.3
Free	2.8
Slacker, apathetic, lazy	9.3

Confused	3.1
Selfish	1.9
Troublemaker	5.0
Other	21.4
Don't know	3.1

Note: This survey was conducted by a graduate journalism survey class and undergraduate advertising research class at the University of Texas at Austin during Spring 1997 under the supervision of Dominic Lasorsa and Paula M. Poindexter.

4. Go to the library and look through back issues of the *New York Times,* the *Wall Street Journal, USA Today, Newsweek,* and *Time* in search of articles that reported the results of scientific surveys. Copy, read, and bring one or two articles to class. Check the reported sample size and sampling error against the table of sample sizes and sampling errors in Chapter 5. What did you find? What are the significant results of the survey?

5. Go to the library and find academic journals for your field of interest in communication. Look through issues representing the last two years of publication. What kinds of statistics are being used in the various articles? What are the levels of measurement for the data? How would you evaluate the appropriateness of the statistics used? Select one article and read it in depth. Summarize the study, methodology, data analysis, and results. Make sure you completely understand why the statistical analyses were used.

RECOMMENDED READING

For a discussion on the theoretical assumptions and mathematical calculations behind statistics and their correct use, see:

FRANK M. ANDREWS, *A Guide for Selecting Statistical Techniques for Analyzing Social Science Data.* Ann Arbor, MI: Institute for Social Research, University of Michigan, 1974.

EARL BABBIE and FRED HALLEY, *Adventures in Social Research.* Newbury Park, CA: Pine Forge Press, 1995.

HUBERT M. BLALOCK JR., *Social Statistics.* New York: McGraw-Hill, 1972.

JAMES L. BRUNING and B. L. KINTZ, *Computational Handbook of Statistics.* Glenview, IL: Scott, Foresman, 1968.

J. P. GUILFORD, *Fundamental Statistics in Psychology and Education.* New York: McGraw-Hill, 1956.

JOSEPH F. HEALEY, *Statistics: A Tool for Social Research.* Belmont, CA: Wadsworth, 1990.

STEPHEN R. LACY and DANIEL RIFFE, "Sins of Omission and Commission in Mass Communication Quantitative Research," *Journalism Quarterly,* 1993, vol. 70, no. 1, pp. 126–132.

JOHN MAURO, *Statistical Deception at Work.* Hillsdale, NJ: Lawrence Erlbaum, 1992.

LAWRENCE B. MOHR, *Understanding Significance Testing.* Newbury Park, CA: Sage, 1990.

JOHN T. ROSCOE, *Fundamental Research Statistics for the Behavioral Sciences,* 2nd ed. New York: Holt, Rinehart and Winston, 1975.

MORRIS ROSENBERG, *The Logic of Survey Analysis.* New York: Basic Books, 1968.

DAVID H. WEAVER, "Basic Statistical Tools," in *Research Methods in Mass Communication,* ed. Guido H. Stempel III and Bruce H. Westley, pp. 48–86. Englewood Cliffs, NJ: Prentice-Hall, 1981.

FREDERICK WILLIAMS, *Reasoning with Statistics: How to Read Quantitative Research,* 4th ed. Fort Worth: Harcourt Brace, 1992.

CHAPTER 9

Reporting Survey Research Results

- How are research results reported?
- What are the components of a written report?
- What are the key ingredients for writing research well?
- What is an effective oral research report?
- What ethical issues should be considered when writing the research report?

The Research Report Documents and Guides

Reporting the results of the research study to the decision maker is an essential component of the research process. In the research report, the research expert must clearly explain the findings that are relevant to the purpose of the study as well as put forward implications of the findings for future action. The research expert presents the results in both written and oral formats. The written format is a formal business report, and the oral presentation may be formal or informal, depending on the requirements of the decision maker. A poorly written research report, even if the study is well executed, will probably be ignored, but a well-written, professionally presented research report will receive wide circulation among the executives and managers of the decision maker's organization. In reporting the results, the research expert should strive to produce a lasting document that will serve as a guide for future action.

Components of the Written Report

Reporting the research results is a blend of using the correct research report format, following the rules of good writing, and knowing how to write research well. The major components of business, media, and academic research reports as listed in Figure 9.1 (p. 156) are required for a well-written, professionally packaged research report.

In this chapter, we'll primarily focus on the business research report. Some examples of media research reports can be found in Chapter 17 when applications of research are discussed. Media research reports include articles and sidebars published in newspapers, magazines, and trade journals, and stories broadcast on television or radio. Press releases, advertisements, and books that use research results are also included in the media research category. Writing academic research reports is discussed

FIGURE 9.1   *Major Components of a Written Research Report*

	Business	Media	Academic Reports
1. Cover letter	Yes	No	Yes
2. Report binder	Yes	No	No
3. Title & author page	Yes	No	Yes
4. Headline & byline	No	Varies	No
5. Table of contents	Yes	No	No
6. Executive summary	Yes	No	No
7. Abstract	No	No	Yes
8. Sidebar	No	Varies	No
9. Introduction	Yes	No	Yes
10. Lead	No	Yes	No
11. Background/Context	Yes	Varies	Yes
12. Literature review	No	No	Yes
13. Theoretical foundation	No	No	Yes
14. Description of method	Yes	Yes	Yes
15. Results	Yes	Yes	Yes
16. Discussion	Yes	Yes	Yes
17. Recommendations	Yes	Varies	Yes
18. Conclusions	Yes	Varies	Yes
19. Endnotes	Yes	No	Yes
20. References	Yes	No	Yes
21. Appendix	Yes	No	Varies

in Chapter 16. Academic research reports include journal articles, monographs, books, theses, dissertations, and conference papers.

 Cover Letter, Title Page, and Contents

An examination of Figure 9.1 shows the similarities and differences among research reports written for business, media, and academic environments. The first column indicates that the report that the research expert prepares for the business decision maker will be professionally packaged in a binder. A business cover letter, typed on letterhead stationery, will be attached to the report. As you can see in the sample cover letter displayed in Figure 9.2, the letter will briefly describe the research report and inform the decision maker when he or she should expect to be contacted to set up an appointment for an in-person discussion on the research results. The reference to an invoice in the last line of the cover letter means that the research expert was a consultant

FIGURE 9.2   *Sample Cover Letter for Research Report*

Research and Communication International, Inc.
Street Address
City, State, Zip Code
Phone, Fax, E-mail
Date

James Johnson
Senior Vice President of Marketing
Global Media Communications, Inc.
Street Address
City, State, Zip Code

Dear James:

Enclosed is a copy of the final research report, *What Do Consumers Do during TV Commercial Breaks?* Many of the results should give you ideas for developing a strategy to counteract the growing problem of consumers' avoiding commercials.

I have enjoyed working with you on this interesting and challenging study. I look forward to other research opportunities in the future.

I will call next week to schedule a convenient time to review these findings in-depth and plan for an oral presentation to your executives later in the month. Please note that I have enclosed an invoice for my services.

Sincerely,

Elizabeth T. Nelson

Elizabeth T. Nelson, Ph.D.

or research supplier who does contract research. If the vice president or director of research within the same organization as the decision maker had conducted the research study, the transmittal letter would be written in business memo format and would not have included a reference to an invoice.

The bound research report begins with a cover page that includes the title of the study, author and title, author's company or organization, and date. A table of contents, which lists each section of the report as well as the page numbers, is placed immediately following the title page.

Executive Summary

The executive summary is a key component of the research report. It is usually the first section read, and often it is the only section read by many executives of the company. Therefore, it is imperative that the executive summary be clearly and concisely written with insightful recommendations that can lead to action. Figure 9.3 displays a sample executive summary for the research report "What Do Consumers Do during TV Commercial Breaks?"

The executive summary, which is single-spaced on one to three pages, briefly states the purpose of the research study and describes how and when the information was collected. It highlights the significant findings that both confirm and differ with established knowledge about the subject, and it reports trends that appear in the data. The executive summary should conclude with the more important recommendations that come from the results, some of which may call for using the results in decision making or conducting further follow-up research.

The Report's Introduction

The main body of the research report begins with an introduction that sets the stage for the study and hooks the reader into reading the detailed report. The introduction puts the purpose of the study in context and explains why the topic is important by focusing on the benefits to be gained from the knowledge that will be learned from the research study. The introduction ends with the research question that will be answered in the remainder of the report.

Introductions in business research reports often have a sense of urgency woven through the opening words. The urgency stems from a discussion of the problem that acts as an obstacle to moving forward. The knowledge gained from the research should help solve the problem and enable the decision maker to move forward.

Background

The background section of the research report is an opportunity to let the reader know what is already known about the topic. It provides detailed context that fills in some of the gaps about what is known about the research subject. The information that is reported here may have been gleaned from internal studies, trade journals, and academic articles and conference papers.

An academic journal article may have both a background section and a separate literature review, which thoroughly examines and integrates

FIGURE 9.3   *Sample of an Executive Summary Format*

EXECUTIVE SUMMARY

What do consumers do when commercials appear on the television screen? During the spring, a telephone survey of a random sample of 461 adults in a southwestern metropolitan area helped answer that question. When asked an open-ended question, 28 percent of the respondents said they watch commercials, while 19 percent said they change the channel. Another 53 percent said they did something other than watch commercials or switch channels.

Men were significantly more likely than women to change the channel when commercials came on; women were more likely than men to "do something else." Fewer adults changed channels as they grew older. Twenty-five percent of 18- to 24-year-olds changed channels, while only 8 percent of adults 55 years and older changed to another channel.

Adults with the least amount of education were more likely to watch commercials. Forty-three percent of those with some high school or less watched commercials, while only 23 percent of those with a graduate degree watched them.

African Americans watched commercials more than any other racial or ethnic group. Forty-five percent of African Americans and 43 percent of Hispanics watched commercials, while only 26 percent of whites watched them.

The implications of these findings should be of concern to advertisers because of the enormous amount of money that is spent on advertising. It is recommended that focus groups be conducted on those who don't watch commercials to find out exactly why they are avoiding them and if they pay attention to advertising in other media.

Focus groups should also be conducted with the groups that watch commercials the most to determine what attracts them to commercials. This follow-up information will help in developing a strategy to better reach those who do not watch and retain those who do.

previous academic research results and theories. A business research report, however, has only the background section. It may include some of the academic research findings.

Well-written background sections are not simply laundry lists of what is already known about the issue but clearly written analyses that identify similarities and differences in the major body of knowledge on the topic.

 ## Description of Method

The description of method section, another important component of the research report, gives the reader a clear understanding of how, when, and where the research was executed. The type of survey should be specified as well as the population, sampling frame, method of sampling, sample size, and sampling error. When the interviews were conducted should also be reported. The types of questions asked on the questionnaire, method of coding, computer processing, and analyzing the data should be described. This section should be clearly written with enough detail that a different researcher could follow the steps, repeat the same research study, and produce similar results.

Results

The results section is the heart of the research report. It begins with a brief demographic profile of the sample of respondents, followed by text and tables that highlight the significant results of the study. The research expert also should report how well the sample matches with the latest census for the geographic area studied. This information can be included in a footnote.

The results presented in this section should have a logical flow and should point to a better understanding of the overall research question. In general, presenting the research results is like producing a video. You may start with a wide angle to present the big picture but then cut to close-ups to show how the big picture may have a different look when focused on the detail. For example, understanding what consumers do during a commercial break looks one way when examining the big picture, but the details have a different look when the focus is on consumers' gender, age, income, education, or even media use.

Figure 9.4 displays an example of how results from a frequency table should be formatted and described in a research report. Notice that the text that describes the table precedes the table. Also, notice that the table is completely labeled. If the text were lost, the reader would still be able to interpret Table 1. The tables should be integrated into the research results section and not relegated to an appendix at the back of the report.

Even though the text precedes the table in the research report, the table should be formatted before the contents are described. The table should display percentages — not raw numbers. In fact, the only raw numbers that should be included in the table are those for the total number of valid cases. Unnecessary numbers clutter up the table and make it difficult to read.

FIGURE 9.4   *Sample Text and Table Describing Research Results*

Survey participants were asked the following open-ended question about their behavior when commercials air on television: "While some people pay close attention to television commercials, others pay little attention. In general, what do you usually do when commercials come on during a TV program?" Five categories of responses were produced.

According to Table 1, more respondents *don't* watch than do watch commercials on TV. Thirty-five percent of respondents said they don't watch commercials and 28 percent said they do watch commercials when they come on during a TV program. Almost one-fifth said they "change the channel" when commercials come on.

A female respondent said she gets up during commercials or reads her book and a male respondent said that he fixes a drink or goes to the bathroom. Other activities that replaced watching commercials included: housework, getting something to eat, and talking.

Among those who watch commercials, a male respondent said he watches commercials to criticize them. And a female respondent said she enjoys commercials.

TABLE 1   *Consumer Activities during Television Commercials*

Activities	Percent
Don't watch commercials*	35
Watch commercials	28
Change channel	19
Turn down sound	9
Other	9
Total	100%
(Valid cases)	(461)

*Nineteen percent of respondents said they "do something else," and these responses were combined with the 16 percent who said they "don't watch" to produce 35 percent.

If you look at the frequency printout in the appendix for that question, labeled variable V21, you'll notice that the responses are not listed in any special order. But Table 1 has ordered the responses from most to least frequent. When you have nominal level data, always rank it from highest to lowest so that the reader can quickly and easily interpret the results. Once the table is formatted, the research expert will be able to describe the contents with ease.

The goal of the text is to clearly and succinctly describe the most important findings in the table. Although the text for Table 1 reports three different findings because they were considered important, often it is sufficient to describe the highest and lowest percentages in the text. Remember that the table displays all the findings for the variable and the reader can focus on findings that are not reported in the text. It is also desirable to point out interesting or unexpected results even if they are not the highest or lowest numbers.

The results section of the research report should include only as many tables as are necessary to convey the major results of the study. Regardless of the number of tables used, each should be numbered and include a title and subtitle for each column of information. The percentages should be rounded to the nearest whole number, and the total percentage should be shown if the table adds to 100 percent. Also, the number of cases should be included so the reader can calculate how many respondents fall into each response category. Table 1 notes valid cases. Some researchers use the terms "base" or "n" to indicate the total number of respondents who answered the question.

Make sure that the text that describes the table is not percentage heavy. Rather than say 19 percent, you may report "almost one-fifth." Generally, approximations should almost match the number being approximated. It would be somewhat misleading to say "fewer than one-third" as an approximation for 29 percent. Because the results section may have many tables, the text should reference the table. You may say, "According to Table 1..." or "(See Table 1.)"

Notice the footnote in the lower left corner that explains that two similar response categories were combined into one. Because "do something else" is slightly different from a direct statement that they "don't watch," it is better to explain that these two categories were combined. Those who think the two types of responses should not be combined can always separate them.

The text or table should include the exact wording of the question and responses. This is important because the wording can influence the answer. By including the phrasing of the question and responses, the reader is better able to interpret the results. In the case of Table 1, which presents the results from an open-ended question, it should be clearly stated that an open-ended question was used. A closed-ended question may have produced slightly different results.

In addition, whenever you have open-ended questions, you have an opportunity to enliven the text and present more meaningful information. Remember that one of the advantages of using open-ended questions is that you will have verbatim quotes from respondents. By including relevant examples of these verbatim quotes, the decision maker will have a better sense as to the meaning of the responses.

Graphically Displaying Data

Finally, note that a numerical table—not a bar chart or pie chart—has been used in Table 1. How the data are presented is a decision that the research expert makes while writing the research report. If bar charts or pie charts enhance the presentation of the results, they should be used in place of straight numerical tables. Figure 9.5 (p. 164) compares three ways to present the data for the question "Do you have cable?" The data have been displayed as a numerical table, bar chart, and pie chart. The bar and pie charts were produced as a result of simple instructions to SPSS.

Notice that Figure 9.5 does not have a line graph. A line graph would be more appropriate for displaying longitudinal data, that is, data that have been collected over time. If the same question on cable had been asked in 1965, 1975, 1985, and 1995, a line graph would graphically display changes in cable subscriptions from 1965 to 1995.

Describing Cross-Tabulations in the Written Report

In writing the research report, you will also include cross-tabulation tables. Figure 9.6 (p. 165) presents a cross-tab table that might appear in a research report. Many of the rules for describing the results of a frequency table apply to a cross-tab table. Format the table before writing the text to describe it. Always reference the table that is being referred to. Do not report every detail in the table but point out significant and interesting findings. Avoid being "percentage heavy" in describing the results. Look for appropriate opportunities to substitute proportions for actual percentages. Replace 32 percent with "almost one-third." "Over one-fourth" can be substituted for 27 percent. The major difference in reporting the results of a cross-tab table is that subgroups have to be compared and their differences highlighted.

The purpose of Table 2 in Figure 9.6 is to compare the activities of women and men during commercial breaks. The text should make this comparison by focusing on differences. Note that if female respondents and male respondents acted the same during the commercial breaks, it would be unnecessary to display a table to call attention to the differences.

When describing the major findings of a cross-tabulation in the text, refer to the independent variable *before* the dependent variable. For example, say, "Thirty percent of women and 26 percent of men said they watch commercials." Do *not* say, "Of those who watched commercials, 30 percent were women and 26 percent were men. Reporting

FIGURE 9.5   *A Comparison of Graphic Presentations of Data*

V10   **Do You Have Cable?**

Value Label	Value	Frequency	Percent	Valid Percent	Cum Percent
Yes	1	346	75.1	76.2	76.2
No	2	108	23.4	23.8	100.0
	0	7	1.5	Missing	
	Total	461	100.0	100.0	

Valid Cases   454   Missing Cases   7

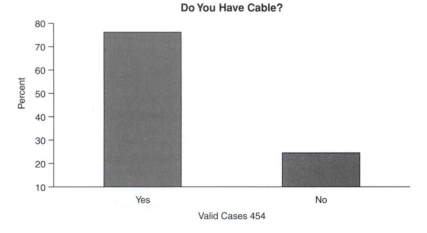

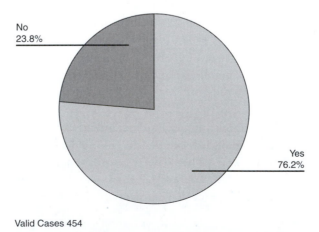

FIGURE 9.6   *Sample Text and Table Describing Results from a Cross-Tabulation*

Women are slightly more likely than men to watch TV commercials during commercial breaks. Compared to 26 percent of men, 30 percent of women said "they watch the TV commercials when they come on during a TV program." (See Table 2.) Men are significantly more likely than women to change the channel during commercial breaks. Although 23 percent of men said they "change the channel," only 14 percent of women said they switch channels.

TABLE 2   *A Comparison of Female and Male Activities during TV Commercials*

Activities	Female (%)	Male (%)
Watch commercials	30	26
Do something else	24	14
Don't watch	17	15
Change channel	14	23
Turn down sound	8	9
Other	7	13
(Valid cases)	(211)	(191)

$X^2 = 15.092$, d.f. $= 5$, $p < .05$

the independent variable first is a clearer, more active form of writing that emphasizes the influence that independent variables have on dependent variables and not the reverse.

Notice also that "do something else" and "don't watch" were not combined in the cross-tab table. Because women are more likely than men to say they "do something else," it is likely that doing something else is not exactly the same as "don't watch" and the two categories should be kept separate.

Finally, in the bottom left corner, the statistic chi square is reported. Chi square indicates that the female respondents and male respondents are significantly different in their activities during commercial breaks. In other words, the probability is less than five in one hundred that these differences are due to chance.

Figure 9.7 (p. 166) displays another example of reporting a cross-tabulation. Notice, again, that the text precedes the table that compares the relationship between age and activities during a commercial break. The table in Figure 9.7, which is completely labeled, includes the chi square statistic and the fact that it is non-significant (n.s.).

FIGURE 9.7   *Sample Text and Table Describing a Relationship between Two Variables*

Table 3 shows an inverse relationship between age and changing channels during commercial breaks. Younger adults are more likely than older adults to say they change the channel. Twenty-five percent of 18- to 24-year-olds and 8 percent of 55-plus-year-olds said they change channels during commercials. Turning down or muting the sound from commercials appears to be positively related to age. Although none of the 18- to 24-year-old respondents said they turned down the sound, 14 percent of the adults 55 and over said they muted the sound when commercials came on.

TABLE 3   *The Relationship of Age and Activities during Commercial Breaks*

Activities	Age				
	18–24 %	25–34 %	35–44 %	45–54 %	55–Plus %
Watch commercials	32	32	25	33	26
Change channels	25	21	22	10	8
Do something else	20	20	19	16	20
Don't watch them	17	15	16	21	15
Other	6	9	7	10	18
Turn down sound	0	4	11	10	14
(Valid cases)	(65)	(92)	(109)	(58)	(66)

$X^2 = 29.255$, d.f. $= 20$, p = n.s.

Even though the differences are not statistically significant in Table 3 of Figure 9.7, the research expert may decide to include the results in the report because of the relationship between age and changing channel. In an academic research article, the non-significant table would not be displayed. Although the results are not statistically significant, they are still important. The inverse relationship between age and changing the channel during the commercial break, reveals more information than a simple frequency table by showing *who* is switching channels.

Positive, negative, and curvilinear relationships are important to report because they may suggest trends for the future. Suppose, for example, that the frequency of a behavior that is being studied is low among young adults but high among older adults. The research expert would likely conclude that the low participation may increase as the young adults grow older.

Because the results section of the written report includes a lot of information for the reader to absorb, it is best to conclude this section with a brief summary that highlights the most important results. This summary can end with a transition statement that moves the reader to the next section of the report.

Discussion, Recommendations, and Conclusion Sections

After the results have been reported, the research expert discusses them. This discussion is a mixture of summary, analysis, and interpretation. In addition, previous findings that were reported in the background section of the report are placed in context. Through the discussion, the research expert is able to provide insight that comes from his or her expertise.

Recommendations should flow from the discussion section, and they should be a by-product of the results of the research. It is dishonest to make recommendations that the research results do not support. However, it is appropriate to say that there is not enough information to determine what the results mean and more specific research should be conducted.

As the introduction sets the stage for a business research report, the conclusion brings down the curtain. The conclusion, which should connect back to the introduction that established the problem that needed to be solved or the question that needed to be answered, should be a mixture of restating the most important findings and highlighting the benefits of gaining that new knowledge. Finally, the conclusion may suggest one or two ways in which the decision maker could put these results into action.

Endnotes, References, and Appendix

The research report ends with sources specifically cited, sources consulted, and material that while inappropriate to be included in the main body of the study should still be bound with the written report. The endnotes are a complete reference to any material cited in the report. The number of the endnote should correspond to the number inserted in the text for referenced sources such as verbatim and paraphrased quotes from printed materials. The reference section can list any sources consulted but not specifically cited. The endnotes and references, which should follow a consistent format such as those outlined in a stylebook, include author, title of source, publisher, city and date of publication, and page numbers used.

Stylebooks such as *The Chicago Manual of Style* describe differences among citations for books, newspapers, magazines, and journals as well as rules and guidelines for grammar, spelling, punctuation, word usage, and writing style. Writers, editors, and copyeditors regularly consult stylebooks while writing and editing copy. The appendix of the report should include the questionnaire, codebook, and any documents relevant to the study. Complete printouts and coding spreadsheets should be bound in a separate binder.

Preparing the Final Report

Once the first draft of the report is complete, it should be carefully edited and proofed. The format of a business research report is fixed, but the introduction and closing sections should be revised for better organization, flow, and clarity. In addition to setting up the research purpose, the introduction should have a sense of urgency about conducting the research. The conclusion should make the reader feel that this report, by answering the research question, removed some of the urgency associated with solving the problem.

During the editing of the research report, rework sentences that can be improved and insert transitions between paragraphs or sections that lurch from place to place. Use your computer's spell check program to check the draft, but do so carefully because the wrong word may have been used in the report. Proof all numbers in the text and tables to make sure they match the original printouts. Check to make sure that there is variety in the way that numbers are reported in the text.

Consult quality writing references such as Strunk and White's *The Elements of Style* and *Simon & Schuster Handbook for Writers* to check grammar, sentence structure, punctuation, style, and correct word usage. *The Chicago Manual of Style* also has very helpful guidelines on punctuation, spelling, and numbers. Replace jargon and technical words, delete unnecessary words, and straighten out muddled phrases. Combine unnecessarily short sentences and balance non-parallel sentences. Check overall writing for a professional and objective tone. Persuasion is permitted in the recommendations of the research report, but it should reflect the findings of the research study.

Once you think you have an excellent research report, read it aloud to identify problems that the eye didn't detect but the ear can. Write the executive summary after the final report is complete. Remember that this is the section of the report that will probably receive the widest distribution. It should be clear and succinct with a statement of the purpose, a brief description of the method, the major results, the implications, and the recommendations.

Once you're satisfied with the final draft, add the page numbers to the report and table of contents. After a final inspection of the report, have it professionally copied and bound. Attach the cover letter and invoice that itemizes services rendered to the bound report and send them to the decision maker.

The Oral Presentation of the Research Results

In business, an oral presentation of the research results is another important component of the research process. Figure 9.8 displays a checklist that can be used for preparing the presentation.

FIGURE 9.8   *Checklist for Oral Presentations of Research Results*

Preparation for the Oral Presentation
- ☐ Determine length of time for presentation and composition and size of audience.
- ☐ Determine room size, set up, lighting, and power sources.
- ☐ Determine equipment needs and request them in writing.
- ☐ Outline presentation with visuals.

Preparing Visuals and Drafting the Script
- ☐ Prepare visuals.
- ☐ Draft a script that includes a greeting, purpose, description of the method, major results, and implications and recommendations.
- ☐ Prepare a handout or leave-behind.

Rehearsing the Presentation
- ☐ Rehearse presentation.
- ☐ Anticipate questions and possible responses.
- ☐ Make sure that all materials required for the presentation have been packed.
- ☐ Dress professionally.

Delivering the Oral Presentation
- ☐ Arrive early to familiarize yourself with room and check out lights and equipment.
- ☐ Conjure up a mental image of a relaxed, professional, enthusiastic presentation.
- ☐ Once you're introduced, take a few deep breaths, make eye contact with the audience, then begin with a warm greeting.
- ☐ Make presentation, then sign off.

Preparing the Oral Presentation

Before preparation for the oral presentation begins, the research expert should determine the length of time for the presentation, composition and size of the audience, and the room size and set up. How long is the presentation time? Who will attend? Will a cross-section of senior executives attend? Or will the decision maker and his or her staff who will actually use the research results be the only ones in attendance? If representatives from across the company are in attendance, the presentation may include industry-wide background on the topic to provide context for the problem and research solution.

Will the attendees sit around a conference room table or in an auditorium? The size of the room has an impact on equipment needs, visuals used, and the formality of the presentation. Presentations in small conference rooms should be more informal, whereas larger rooms require more formality.

Overhead transparencies are usually sufficient for a smaller room, but a PowerPoint or slide presentation is more appropriate for a formal presentation in a larger room. Because PowerPoint presentations and slides are more time consuming to make than overhead transparencies, the type of visuals needs to be determined early so you have sufficient time to produce professional-level materials.

Larger rooms require microphones, so this equipment should be requested. Overheads, VCRs, and slide projectors should also be requested. If you are giving a PowerPoint presentation, verify that a power source compatible with your computer equipment is available.

Who will be responsible for dimming the lights for the visuals? Ideal lighting allows for dimming the lights without blacking out the room. Check to see what's available and plan the presentation accordingly. A dim room sometimes makes it difficult for the speaker to read the script. Check to see if a light is available for the podium.

Visuals and Script

By outlining the presentation, the research expert can determine what visuals need to be produced. It is especially important to determine if more time-consuming slides or PowerPoint visuals are necessary. The visuals should include a mixture of key words, tables, charts, graphs, and other graphics. In general, use visuals selectively. Remember that *you* are the presenter; don't let visuals dominate you. Visuals should be headlines, calling attention to important research findings, recommendations, and themes. Large type sizes and clean font styles are best for words.

Although sometimes bar charts or pie charts may best represent the major findings, often a plain, clean table will do. Thoroughly proof the visuals that will be used and produce them in the medium you have chosen.

The script has five parts: greeting, purpose of research, description of method, major results, implications and recommendations. Although the greeting usually appears to be ad-libbed, it should be planned. The greeting is an opportunity to make a brief personal connection with the audience. It may be an acknowledgment of a past association with the organization, an expression of happiness to be there, a special interest in the organization's concerns, or a recognition of any positive changes that have taken place.

The purpose of the research can be described in a statement or a question. Posing a question is often very effective because you will have answered the question by the conclusion of the presentation. Providing three or four reasons for needing to learn more about this problem makes the purpose of the research even more important and relevant. A brief summary of the research method should follow: who was surveyed, how they were selected, and during what time period.

The results should begin with an age, income, education, gender, and racial and ethnic profile of the respondents. You should disclose how well the profile matches the most recent census data. Using the visuals, you should report the major findings that are directly related to the research question. Findings that contradict the conventional wisdom should be pointed out.

The script should conclude with the implications of the findings and the recommendations for putting the results to use. After the presentation is complete, ask for questions. Before the assembly is dismissed, distribute a handout or leave-behind. This document, which should include the title, author's name, address, phone and fax numbers, and e-mail address, is similar to the executive summary in the written report. Unlike the executive summary, it can include one or two tables that represent the major findings of the study.

Rehearsing the Presentation

The script should be typed with a large, clean font, and the visuals that will be shown should be noted. During rehearsal, read the script out loud at the presentation pace to identify places that may need to be revised. During this run-through, mark the script for emphasis and pauses. The script should also be timed. Remember to allow time for a fifteen-minute question and answer session.

Rehearse the final script with visuals before a full-length mirror until the presentation runs smoothly. Words or sentences that you stumble over should receive extra practice or be revised. You should be familiar enough with the script that you only have to glance at it briefly. Also, avoid looking back at the screen to check that the correct slide is on display as this habit can be distracting to the audience. If the slides or transparencies have been placed in the correct order, there should be no reason to continually look back at the screen.

It is best to rehearse with and without a podium. A podium is more appropriate for a formal presentation. In such a presentation, the speaker may stand on the side of the podium during the question-and-answer session. In any case, you should be prepared to present with or without the podium.

The rehearsal should also include practicing answers to questions that may be asked. Anticipate questions, particularly difficult ones, and practice to achieve a clear, succinct response. It is acceptable to respond with "I don't know" to a question that is outside the parameters of the research study. Even so, you should indicate that you will find out the answer and get back to the person who asked the question.

Verify that all materials—your script, slides or transparencies, disk for a PowerPoint presentation, handouts, extra copies of the report, and other supporting documents—have been carefully packed before leaving for the presentation.

Delivering the Presentation

Make sure that you are professionally dressed and groomed before arriving at least thirty minutes early for the presentation. This should allow sufficient time to familiarize yourself with the room and check out the lights and equipment. Make sure that you've tested the volume level of the microphone and know how to turn on and focus the overhead before the presentation begins. If complicated visual equipment has to be set up, it is best to arrive even earlier.

Just before you begin, conjure up a mental image of a relaxed, professional, enthusiastic presenter with good posture. When you're introduced, take a few deep breaths, walk tall to the presentation location, make eye contact with the audience, then begin. You should have already tested the volume of the microphone if you're using one, so avoid beginning your presentation with, "Test, test . . ." or "Can you hear me?"

Once the presentation and questions have concluded, sign off by emphasizing one of the most important benefits of the research results, then return the program to the decision maker for closing comments.

Ethical Issues When Reporting Research Results

It is imperative that the written research report and oral presentation accurately reflect the results of the research study. If the data do not conform to expectations of the decision maker or contradict long-held beliefs of the organization, they should *not* be omitted from or buried in the written report. Remember that the purpose of the study is to use scientifically based research methods to produce data that accurately represent the population under study. Of course, if the data contradict previous research undertaken by the organization, this should be addressed in the report. In that case, a recommendation for further study to understand why the current research results differ from previous results would be in order.

This chapter has examined how to report the research results in both written and oral formats. Once the research expert has reported the results to the decision maker, the decision maker has the responsibility of using or ignoring the results in decisions that have to be made.

SUGGESTED RESEARCH ACTIVITIES

1. Select a frequency table from Appendix C.1. Using the guidelines for writing a research report, write the text and format the table.
2. Select a cross-tabulation table from Appendix C.2. Using the guidelines for writing a research report, write the text and format the table.
3. Look through back issues of the *New York Times,* the *Wall Street Journal, USA Today, Newsweek,* and *Time* to find several articles on survey results. Compare and discuss the various graphic presentations of the data.
4. Select one of the articles and read it carefully. Write a first draft of an executive summary of the article. Reread and revise your first draft. Now read it aloud to identify additional revisions that you should make. Finalize your executive summary copy.
5. Make an oral presentation on the article. Include the purpose of the study, description of the survey, and major findings. What tables, if any, would you include in your oral presentation?

RECOMMENDED READING

For an extended example of a research report written for newspaper executives, see:

LEO BOGART, *Press and Public: Who Reads What, When, Where and Why in American Newspapers,* 2nd ed. Hillsdale, NJ: Lawrence Erlbaum, 1989.

For books that will improve your writing clarity and style, see:

PATRICIA T. O'CONNER, *Woe Is I: The Grammarphobe's Guide to Better English in Plain English.* New York: Putnam's, 1996.

BILL STOTT, *Write to the Point.* New York: Columbia University Press, 1991.

WILLIAM STRUNK JR. and E. B. WHITE, *The Elements of Style,* 3rd ed. New York: Macmillan, 1979.

LYNN QUITMAN TROYKA, *Simon & Schuster Handbook for Writers.* Englewood Cliffs, NJ: Prentice-Hall, 1993.

For a discussion on how to make effective and inspirational oral presentations, see:

LISA FORTINI-CAMPBELL, "Presentations That Inspire," in *Hitting the Sweet Spot,* pp. 149–153. Chicago: The Copy Workshop, 1992.

JOHN H. MURPHY and ISABELLA C. M. CUNNINGHAM, "How to Develop and Deliver Effective Advertising Presentations," in *Advertising and Marketing Communication,* pp. 10–19. Fort Worth: The Dryden Press, 1993.

GRANVILLE N. TOOGOOD, *The Articulate Executive: Learn to Look, Act, and Sound Like a Leader.* New York: McGraw-Hill, 1996.

For a guide to creating PowerPoint presentations, see:

Microsoft Corporation, *User's Guide, Microsoft PowerPoint,* 1994.

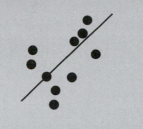

CHAPTER 10

The Post-Research Phase and the Decision Maker

- What is the post-research phase of the research process?
- Who is responsible for the post-research phase?
- What are the activities in this phase of the research process?
- What is the next step after the post-research phase?

The Post-Research Phase Begins with the Research Report

Once the decision maker learns the results of the research study, the post-research phase of the research process begins. In this phase, the decision maker carefully considers the results and their implications and how this information will factor into decisions that have to be made. The steps in the post-research phase are listed in Figure 10.1.

Although many will read only the executive summary of the research report, it is important for the decision maker to read the complete study from front to back as indicated in Step 1 of Figure 10.1.

By immersing him or herself in the report, the decision maker gains insight that will not be available to those who scan the results reported in the executive summary. The decision maker then becomes the expert on the results, which is useful if others must be persuaded to implement some of the decisions based on the results of the study.

The decision maker must also sort through the recommendations of the research expert and decide which, if any, can be used in the decision making. A careful reading of the results puts the decision maker in a better position when evaluating the research expert's recommendations.

Finally, a careful examination of the results may also reveal to the decision maker information that may be related to a similar topic of significance in the company. Only a thorough inspection of the report's detail may provide this insight.

Once the decision maker is satisfied that the obligations of the research expert have been met, he or she should process the research expert's invoice as listed in Step 2. Of course, if the research was conducted by an internal researcher such as the vice president or director of research, there would be no invoice to process. It is good etiquette for the decision maker to send a letter with the check that points out one or two benefits received from the research study or research expert's expertise.

FIGURE 10.1   *Steps in the Post-Research Phase*

Step 1. Read the report, paying careful attention to the results and recommendations in the research study.

Step 2. If applicable, process the check for the research expert and send it with a cover letter thanking him or her for research services. Personalize the cover letter by including one or two items that were especially valuable during the research process.

Step 3. Evaluate the results and recommendations, looking for trends, confirmations of previous information, inconsistencies, surprises, possible opportunities, potential problems, and completely new and useful information.

Step 4. Discuss your evaluations with the research expert to take advantage of the research expert's further insight.

Step 5. Decide which data can be used in decisions that have to be made and which data need further information to better understand what's happening.

Step 6. Consult with the research expert about developing criteria for measuring the impact of the decisions that are made based on the research results.

Step 7. Implement the decisions based on the research results.

Step 8. Evaluate the impact of the decisions.

Step 9. Decide the next step.

Step 10. Create a file for this research study that includes the report, relevant documents, correspondence, and an assessment of how well the research expert satisfied your research needs.

If the research expert is within the organization, a memo to the vice president of research specifying the value received from the research and the intended use of the results is both helpful and appreciated.

Evaluation and Decision Making

 Evaluating Results and Recommendations

In Step 3, the decision maker evaluates the results and recommendations. Because the decision maker is the real expert on the research needs, he or she should sort the results into categories like those listed in Figure 10.2 (p. 178).

FIGURE 10.2   *Categories for Evaluating Research Results*

1. Trends
2. Confirmation of already known information or conventional wisdom
3. Inconsistencies
4. Surprises
5. Possible opportunities
6. Potential problems
7. Completely new information

By sorting the research results into these seven categories, the decision maker can quickly identify areas of concern and areas of opportunity. Some research results may actually fit into two categories. For example, if the decision maker learns that readers are becoming increasingly negative about the layout of the TV section of the newspaper, that finding would be placed in the "trend" category and the "potential problem" category. Although the decision maker uses the research results mostly to identify possible opportunities, surprises and potential problems should not be ignored.

After evaluating the information, the decision maker should have a follow-up meeting with the research expert to take advantage of his or her expertise on these categories. During this discussion, which is Step 4, the decision maker, who is usually not an expert on research methods and analysis, will be able to confirm the accuracy of the interpretation.

 Prioritizing Research Results

During this meeting, the research expert can also help the decision maker prioritize the significance of the findings. Some of the findings, of course, are more significant than others, and the research expert can help sort this out. The significance of the findings should play a role in the decision to use the results or conduct more research to really figure out what is going on.

Deciding Which Results to Use

In Step 5, the decision maker decides which of the results will be used, which results require more information, and which should be ignored. For example, if the research results indicate that readers are becoming negative toward the layout of the TV section, it does not mean that the decision maker should immediately change the newspaper's TV section. That finding does suggest, however, that the decision maker may want to conduct new research that focuses specifically on what readers like and dislike about the TV section.

Before implementing decisions based on the results, the decision maker should consult with the research expert to inform him or her about the decisions that will be implemented and the reasons why. This disclosure is not required, but it can be helpful in building a relationship with a valued research expert. More important, the decision maker can ask the research expert for ideas on evaluating the implementation of the decisions based on the research results as listed in Step 6. The decision maker may also discuss the results that need further information and ask the research expert for a proposal for another study.

Implementing Decisions and Evaluating Their Impact

 Implementation of Decisions Will Vary

In Step 7, the decisions are implemented. The culture of the organization influences how implementation takes place. The decision maker may delegate the implementation or have to persuade others higher up or below him or her. Regardless of the implementation process, the decision maker should write a memo specifying the decisions and explaining the research results that played a role in the decision making. This written memo is important in Step 8 in which the impact of the decisions based on the research results is evaluated.

Evaluation of the Decision Is Important

The research results may have been used in making decisions about a new advertising or public relations campaign. The data may have been the foundation for decisions about revamping the layout of the front page of the newspaper, dropping a regular comic strip in the newspaper, launching a new magazine, or making a TV commercial in black and white. Regardless of what decisions are made, the impact of the decisions needs to be evaluated as listed in Step 8.

The criteria for evaluating decisions based on the research results may be another survey, a focus group, circulation or sales figures, ratings, or even telephone calls and letters. The evaluation must be a valid measure of the impact of the decisions that were made based on the research results. For example, if the editor of the newspaper drops a comic strip because the survey results showed only one-third of readers read it, a valid evaluation of this decision might be the number of telephone calls and letters that the newspaper receives.

The results of the evaluation study will influence the decision maker's next step as indicated in Step 9. For example, if the newspaper receives very few letters or phone calls about dropping the comic strip, the editor will conclude that the right decision was made. But if letters and phone calls flood the newspaper complaining about the loss of the comic strip, the editor will likely conclude that a bad decision was made. More research may need to be done to find out which readers are complaining and why. Ultimately the editor may have to decide to bring the comic strip back.

Now that a research cycle has been completed from the pre-research phase through the research phase to the post-research phase, the decision maker should create a file on the research project before proceeding, as indicated in Step 10. A final summary evaluation memo is an important record that can be used as a reference as further research is conducted, decisions are implemented, or the subject is revisited in the future. Suppose in two years a decision needs to be made about what comics to drop. Referring to the previous research, decisions, and results will be very helpful in planning further research for decision making.

This chapter examined the post-research phase of the survey when the results of the research are put into action. In this phase, decisions are made based on research results and the consequences of those decisions are evaluated. The post-research phase is also important in the research methods that are discussed in upcoming chapters in which you will learn how to conduct content analysis studies, experiments, focus groups, and many other types of research.

SUGGESTED RESEARCH ACTIVITIES

1. Select a communication company of interest to you. Contact a senior executive of the organization and ask if you can interview him or her about research that is conducted in their organization. Find out how the executive may have used survey research to make decisions about a new opportunity, problem, issue, or campaign. Find out why the executive decided to conduct research in the first place. Inquire about the outcome of using the research results and how that was evaluated.

2. Find out from the executive if the company has ever conducted research but then decided not to use it. Find out the reasons for not using the research results.

3. Write a paper that describes the executive you interviewed, his or her background, and what you learned, or summarize the results of your interview in an oral presentation.

RECOMMENDED READING

For a detailed look at the newspaper industry's multimillion dollar, six-year Newspaper Readership Project, see:

LEO BOGART, *Preserving the Press: How Daily Newspapers Mobilized to Keep Their Readers.* New York: Columbia University Press, 1991.

For an insider's view on the post-research phase for the prototype research on *USA Today,* see:

PETER PRICHARD, *The Making of McPaper.* Kansas City, MO: Andrews, McNeel & Parker, 1987.

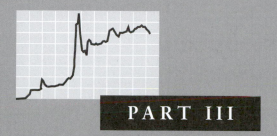

PART III

Content Analysis,

Experiments,

Focus Groups, and

Other Quantitative

and Qualitative

Research Methods

Content Analysis

- What is content analysis?
- What are the steps in conducting a content analysis study?
- What is manifest content and why is it analyzed?
- What is inter-coder reliability and how is it computed?
- What are the advantages and disadvantages of using a computer to analyze content?
- What are the ethical standards in conducting content analysis research?

Content Analysis Focuses on the Message

In 1965, *Time* magazine's news coverage was analyzed to identify biasing techniques it used to report on three U.S. Presidents — Truman, Eisenhower, and Kennedy (Merrill, 1965). This study is a classic example of how the research technique of content analysis systematically examines the words and pictures that are published, broadcast, or spoken. These words and pictures may be found in a newspaper, magazine, book, play, newsletter, house organ, or on TV, cable, or a Web site. Words may also be found in a letter, memo, speech, debate, press conference, song, or e-mail.

The *Time* magazine study content-analyzed ten consecutive issues representing three presidential administrations. The researcher attempted to determine whether or not biased reporting was employed in attribution, adjectives, and adverbs. In addition, the researcher examined articles for contextual bias and the inclusion of outright opinion. Finally, the author examined photographs and their cutlines, or captions, to determine how the presidents were pictured. Each variable was coded as favorable, neutral, or unfavorable.

The first variable examined in the study, attribution, refers to what words were used to attribute a quote to the president. Examples of quotes attributed to Truman were: "said curtly," "said coldly," "barked Harry S. Truman." These attributions were coded as negative.

When Eisenhower was quoted, attributions used included "said with a happy grin," "said warmly," and "calm and confident." These attributions were coded as positive.

Quotes attributed to Kennedy were often coded as neutral: "President Kennedy said," " President Kennedy announced," and "Concluded the President."

These examples of attributions were representative of the study's overall conclusions that the majority of *Time* magazine's reporting on Eisenhower was positive and the majority on Truman was negative. As it turned out, *Time* magazine's coverage of Kennedy was twice as likely to be positive than negative.

Applications of the content analysis research technique can be found throughout the communication literature and from time-to-time in the popular and trade press. One academic study content-analyzed newspaper and magazine articles to study the use of the term "spin doctor," which has come to represent election campaign managers and public relations professionals who attempt to manipulate media content. Communication scholars used Nexis current and archival files to search on the term, "spin doctor" over time as well as the positive or negative evaluation of it (Tankard & Sumpter, 1993). The researchers found that the term first appeared in a 1984 editorial on the Reagan-Mondale presidential debates, and in 1992, the term was used in 1,553 articles. In stories on politics and government, the term "spin doctor" was used in a pejorative context, but in stories on economic activity, the term was not used disparagingly.

Content analysis has also been used to study creative elements used in advertising. A 1994 study content-analyzed commercials that were broadcast on programs targeted to young adults to identify what Generation X elements were used to appeal to this age group (Zwarun, 1994). The top three elements were slang, Generation X music, and cynicism.

A 1991 content analysis examined the use of nostalgia as a creative element in television commercials (Unger et al., 1991). The top two methods of using nostalgia in commercials were period-oriented symbolism and period-oriented music. The researchers defined period-oriented symbolism as imagery from the 1930s, 1940s, 1950s, and 1960s as well as references to earlier symbols or icons in art, religion, education, fashion, and medical practices. Period-oriented music included golden oldies and popular music from the 1950s and 1960s. The authors also found that food commercials used nostalgia as a creative element more than any other product category.

Journalists have also used content analysis in reporting stories. The *New York Times* content-analyzed President George Bush's speeches during the 1992 election when he campaigned for a second term (Rosenthal, 1992). The study found that Bush spoke of "change" or "reform" 188 times and "revolution" 17 times. The results of this content analysis were considered newsworthy because it was ironic that Bush who had been president or vice president for the previous twelve years was talking about change, reform, and revolution.

Interest and advocacy groups often content-analyze the media to applaud or deplore media content. The results of these content analyses are often picked up and reported by the media. The National Council of La Raza, which is an umbrella group for almost 200 Hispanic organizations, conducted a content analysis to determine the representation of Hispanics in network and syndicated entertainment programs (Harlan, 1996). They found that only 18 of 139 television series featured a Hispanic in a continuing role. Fox had the highest percentage of Hispanic roles with 8 percent, and CBS had the lowest with 1 percent.

Definition of Content Analysis

In content analysis, communication content is examined independently of those who produced it. Communication professionals are not queried about their attitudes, opinions, and motivations in the production of the content. Content analysis limits itself to the produced content alone and draws conclusions based on what is there.

Content analysis is simply a "research technique for the objective, systematic, and quantitative description of the manifest content of communication" (Berelson, 1952). Written by one of the pioneers of communication research, this classic definition clearly states that content analysis uses scientific procedures to examine the apparent—not latent or hidden—communication content. The focus on manifest communication content is essential to producing scientifically valid results. By analyzing the obvious meaning, the researcher can produce objective results. But if the content analysis focuses on the meaning buried beneath the surface, the results may vary according to who is interpreting the communication content.

Ole Holsti was more general when he defined content analysis as a "multipurpose research method developed specifically for investigating any problem in which the content of communication serves as the basis of inference" (Holsti, 1969, p. 2). Content analysis can be used to describe the attributes of messages, and those attributes can be compared over time to identify trends or across sources to detect differences and similarities. Content analysis can also be used to examine the form or style, that is, the *how* of the communication content (Holsti, 1969, p. 59). Just like scientific surveys, content analysis uses numbers, percentages, and statistics to describe results and make inferences about the overall content.

The Decision Maker Identifies a Need for Content Analysis during the Pre-Research Phase

According to Figure 11.1, the pre-research phase of content analysis is similar to that for surveys. In Steps 1 and 2, the decision maker monitors the environment and literature to identify a problem, trend, opportunity, issue, phenomenon, or theory that needs to be examined in depth.

The decision maker may examine the content of the competition to better understand why they are doing a better job of reaching the target market or public. The decision maker may also conduct a self-evaluation of the content that his or her organization publishes or broadcasts to have a clearer picture as to why one segment of the target audience is indifferent or turned off. Content analysis is an opportunity to systematically monitor the content in order to better understand what's going on.

As an example for Step 3, suppose that the news director of a local TV station examines the latest ratings and a market-wide survey and finds that African Americans and Hispanics are watching the other TV stations for news. Anxious to have viewers watching from all racial and ethnic groups, the news director decides to conduct follow-up research to better understand why viewership of his or her station is much lower in these groups.

One aspect of this follow-up research includes conducting a content analysis of the news of his or her station and the other stations to find out what the African American and Hispanic viewer segments are being exposed to. The news director then formulates the research question: To what extent are African Americans and Latinos represented in news stories on the local newscasts?

FIGURE 11.1   *Pre-Research Phase of Content Analysis and the Decision Maker*

Step 1. Monitor environment and literature.

Step 2. Identify problem, trend, opportunity, issue, phenomenon, and theory.

Step 3. Specify content analysis topic in research question form or hypothesis.

Step 4. Choose type of content to be analyzed and period in which content was written, spoken, published, or broadcast.

Step 5. Choose content analysis method (human, computer, database search).

Step 6. Establish budget and timetable.

Step 7. Determine who will conduct content analysis.

In Step 4, the decision maker decides to examine news stories broadcast during the 6:00 P.M. news for all network-affiliated stations. By content-analyzing all stories for a month, the decision maker is choosing to conduct a census. If the decision maker had wanted to examine stories representing the year, he or she could have randomly sampled days to be content-analyzed and projected the results to all news stories.

Because the content analysis must be conducted on news stories that have been recorded while being broadcast, the decision to conduct human—not computer—content analysis is easy. If the content analysis had been of newspaper or magazine articles in which key words were counted, the decision maker may have opted for a computer to categorize the content.

Computer Content Analysis

Historically, computers have been used in content analysis studies to count the presence of a word, name, symbol, or even several words linked together in the text. In the past, specially designed programs identified and counted the presence of certain words or symbols in the text (Holsti, 1969, pp. 153–160). Today, with Nexis available for searching databases of recent and archived newspapers and magazines, the content analyst has a tool that makes computer content analysis fast and efficient, although limited. Also, many computer programs have been developed specifically for examining messages for a content analysis study (Popping, 1997, p. 209).

Although a computer can quickly identify the presence of words or names in volumes of text, it would be less useful in evaluating whether the words or names were used in a positive or negative context. That's why when the content analysis research question addresses the evaluation of the message, the content analyst generally turns to the human coder to evaluate the text. The decision on whether to use human or computer coding is addressed in Step 5.

Establishing a Budget and Timetable

In Step 6 of the pre-research phase, a budget and timetable are established. Content analysis studies are significantly less expensive than telephone surveys, which often require a large staff of interviewers. Assuming that the material is available for coding, the primary expenses for a content analysis study are for the services of the research expert and a few content analysis coders. The timetable, of course, is dependent on when the decision maker needs the content analysis results and the amount of material that has to be examined and coded. Once the research expert has been selected to conduct the study, he or she can help the decision maker establish a realistic timetable.

As is the case for surveys, the research expert should be experienced in conducting content analysis studies. The decision maker should select a research expert who understands the significance of selecting an appropriate unit of analysis, setting up valid coding categories, and testing inter-coder reliability.

Initial Steps of the Research Phase

Step 1 of the research phase, which is listed in Figure 11.2, is familiar because it follows the procedures that are used in surveys. The research expert consults with the decision maker on the purpose, background,

FIGURE 11.2 *The Research Phase of Content Analysis and the Research Expert*

Step 1. Consult with decision maker on content analysis purpose, research question, background on the topic, time period, whether to use a census or sample in selection of content to be analyzed, unit of analysis, codebook, budget, and ethical standards.

Step 2. Conduct in-depth literature review and background search and locate materials to be content-analyzed.

Step 3. Draft codebook with numerical codes.

Step 4. Consult with decision maker on draft codebook and make revisions as necessary.

Step 5. Hire and train content analysis coders, emphasizing ethical standards.

Step 6. Pretest codebook on small sample of content.

Step 7. Calculate inter-coder reliability. If inter-coder reliability is below 80 percent, revise codebook and retrain coders to improve inter-coder reliability.

Step 8. Test revised codebook on new sample of content and calculate new inter-coder reliability. Once inter-coder reliability reaches 80 percent or higher, consult with decision maker on latest revisions. Finalize codebook and make copies of the guide for coders to use as coding sheets.

Step 9. Code all materials.

Step 10. Process data.

Step 11. Analyze data using appropriate statistics and ethical standards.

Step 12. Write report and prepare oral presentation using ethical standards.

Step 13. Share results with decision maker.

and timetable of the research project. During this consultation, the research expert also discusses the appropriateness of analyzing all the content, which would be a census, or a random sample, which would represent the entire population of communication content.

Sampling issues that were addressed for surveys also apply to content analysis. In general, a census is more appropriate for studies that cover a shorter period of time or those in which the incidence of the unit of analysis to be coded may be infrequent. For sweeping content analysis studies that cover years, a random sample is both more appropriate and feasible.

During the consultation in Step 1, it is important for the research expert and decision maker to discuss and agree on the unit of analysis for the content analysis study because it determines how the codebook will be designed. The unit of analysis is the communication component that is actually coded for analysis. Its selection should be appropriate for the type of study being conducted.

A television news story, newspaper article, magazine ad, TV commercial, press release, editorial, opinion column, or company magazine article would be appropriate units of analysis for content analysis studies. A content analysis study might also use a word, a headline, an act of violence, an individual such as a news reporter, actor in prime-time TV, model in a commercial, subject of a news article, or even a narrator's voice as the analysis unit.

The Codebook Is Key to Producing Valid Results

The Content Analysis Codebook Is Similar to the Survey Codebook

The purpose of the content analysis study and the unit of analysis dictate the categories that are developed for coding. The research expert should discuss these coding categories with the decision maker before developing the codebook, the content analysis document that includes instructions and coding definitions.

After the consultation, the research expert proceeds to Step 2 in which a literature review is conducted to identify any published articles on the topic. This literature search adds to the background information supplied by the decision maker. Also, when the research expert finds similar studies, he or she is able to examine the categories, codes, and definitions to find any ones that may be useful in developing the codebook. Simultaneously while conducting the literature review, the research expert locates the materials that will be content-analyzed.

If back copies of the *Los Angeles Times* are being content-analyzed, the research expert wants to make sure that there is access to the materials. Access is usually not a problem for major newspapers in the United States or around the globe; however, locating specialized foreign publications or weekly and minority newspapers may be difficult.

If the content analysis study is on network TV news, transcripts of the newscasts are available through the *Vanderbilt Television News Index and Abstracts*. However, for local TV news, tapes may have to be purchased or the researcher will have to tape the newscasts him or herself. A comparison of three or more channels would make three TVs with VCRs necessary. These issues must be addressed early so that the content is available for coding as soon as possible.

In Step 3, the research expert drafts a codebook with numerical codes. A sample content analysis codebook, which is displayed in Figure 11.3 (pp. 194–198), was developed to answer the content analysis research question: To what extent are African Americans and Latinos represented in local TV news? Notice the similarities between the codebook for a content analysis and that for processing survey data. Even though the order is different, both include variable numbers, columns, and numerical precodes. The category names on a content analysis codebook would be equivalent to the questions in a survey codebook. The description column, which is unique to a content analysis codebook, instructs the content analysis coder on assigning the content to the correct categories. For coding categories that require a lot of description because judgments have to be made, the research expert should prepare a separate document that has detailed descriptions and examples that the coders can use as a reference throughout the coding process. For example, V12, evaluation of story, would be listed in the reference document with examples and explanations for coding decisions.

The categories that are developed for the codebook should reflect the purpose of the content analysis study. Notice in Figure 11.3 that the first three variables, V1, V2, and V3, are used to track each news story coded by indicating the TV station on which the story aired, assigning a unique identification number to the story, and recording the date the story aired. V4 categorizes the story according to its placement in the newscast, which signals the importance of a news story. The first story broadcast is equivalent to being the lead story on the front page of a newspaper. Notice that seven choices can be coded: first story, second story, third story, fourth story, after the fourth but before the final story, final story before credits, and other.

The story that runs in the final story slot before the credits is called a closer, or kicker. This is a prestige slot in the newscast. Generally the

FIGURE 11.3   *Sample Codebook for a Content Analysis of the Representation of African Americans and Latinos in Local TV News*

(Complete one codesheet on each news story during the local evening news.)

Variable Number	Column	Category Names and Codes	Description
V1	1	TV News Station 1. KABC (ABC) (Channel 7) 2. KNBC (NBC) (Channel 4) 3. KCBS (CBS) (Channel 2) 4. KTTV (FOX) (Channel 11)	
V2	2–4	I.D. Number	Beginning with 001, assign unique 3–digit number to each news story coded.
V3	5–10	Date	Code month, date, and last two numbers of year. For example, March 5, 1999 would be coded 030599.
V4	11	Placement of Story 1. First Story 2. Second Story 3. Third Story 4. Fourth Story 5. After Fourth and before Final 6. Final Story before Credits 7. Other	
V5	12	Reporter's Race/Ethnic Group 1. White 2. African American 3. Latino/Hispanic 4. Asian American 5. Native American 6. Unable to Determine 7. Other	

Variable Number	Column	Category Names and Codes
V6	13	Geographic Coverage of Story
		1. Los Angeles County
		2. Orange County
		3. Southern California not including Los Angeles and Orange counties
		4. Northern California
		5. National
		6. International
		7. Other
V7	14–15	Local Geographic Coverage
		01. Downtown
		02. Westside
		03. The Valley
		04. Pasadena area
		05. South Bay
		06. South Central
		07. East L.A.
		08. Orange County
		09. Surrounding Counties
		10. Other
V8	16	Primary Race/Ethnic Group of Subject(s) in the News
		1. White
		2. African American
		3. Latino/Hispanic
		4. Asian American
		5. Native American
		6. No Primary Race/Ethnic Group
		7. Other
		8. Unable to Determine
V9	17–18	Focus of Story
		01. Individual
		02. Two or More Individuals
		03. Celebrity or Well-Known Figure
		04. Organization
		05. Company
		06. Educational Institution
		07. Government Agency
		08. Geographic Community
		09. Issue
		10. Event
		11. Other

(continued)

FIGURE 11.3   *(continued)*

Variable Number	Column	Category Names and Codes
V10	19	Age of Individual(s) in Story
		1. Children Under 6
		2. Approximately 6 to 12
		3. Teens13 to 17
		4. Young Adults 18 to 29
		5. Adults 30 to 65
		6. Adults Over 65
		7. No Predominant Age
		8. Unable to Determine
		9. Other
V11	20–21	Topic of Story (Code the dominant topic of the story.)
		01. Accident
		02. Art and Culture
		03. Books
		04. Business and Industry
		05. Careers
		06. Central and South America
		07. Community Activities
		08. Consumer Information and Issues
		09. Cost of Living
		10. Crime (Not including gangs)
		11. Domestic Violence
		12. Drugs (Not including crime)
		13. Economy
		14. Education, Pre-School through 12th Grade
		15. Education, College, or Above
		16. Employment
		17. Entertainment and Films
		18. Environment
		19. Family Issues
		20. Fire
		21. Gangs
		22. Gay and Lesbian Issues
		23. Governance (City, County, State, National)
		24. Governor
		25. Health Care
		26. Higher Education Administration
		27. History
		28. Homelessness
		29. Immigration
		30. Judicial System

Variable Number	Column	Category Names and Codes
V11	20–21	31. Law Enforcement
		32. Legislature and Legislation
		33. Media and Communication
		34. Mexico
		35. Military
		36. Politics and Elections
		37. Poverty (Not including welfare)
		38. Racial Issues—General
		39. Affirmative Action
		40. Discrimination
		41. Diversity
		42. Interracial Problems and Conflicts
		43. Quotas
		44. Reverse Discrimination
		45. Religion
		46. Science, Medicine, and Health
		47. School Board and Public School Administration
		48. Sports (Professional)
		49. Sports (College)
		50. Sports (High School)
		51. Sports (Not including professional, college, high school)
		52. Taxes
		53. Technology
		54. Trade Issues
		55. Travel
		56. Unemployment
		57. Weather and Storms
		58. Welfare
		59. Women's Issues
		60. Other

Summarize story:

_____

_____

_____

Variable Number	Column	Category Names and Codes
V12	22	Evaluation of Story
		1. Positive
		2. Neutral
		3. Negative

(continued)

FIGURE 11.3 *(continued)*

Variable Number	Column	Category Names and Codes
V13	23	**Number of Expert/Official Sources** 1. None (Skip to V17.) 2. One 3. Two 4. Three 5. Four or More
V14	24	**Race or Ethnic Group of First Expert/Official Source** 1. White 2. African American 3. Latino/Hispanic 4. Asian American 5. Native American 6. Other 7. Unable to Determine
V15	25	**Race or Ethnic Group of Second Expert/Official Source** 1. White 2. African American 3. Latino/Hispanic 4. Asian American 5. Native American 6. Other 7. Unable to Determine
V16	26	**Race or Ethnic Group of Third Expert/Official Source** 1. White 2. African American 3. Latino/Hispanic 4. Asian American 5. Native American 6. Other 7. Unable to Determine
V17	27–29	**Length of Story** _____ (Write in number of seconds.)

story is a human interest feature that makes special note of interesting people, places, or events. Although news directors, anchors, and reporters understand the purpose of this story is to leave the audience with something uplifting, viewers do not necessarily understand the prestige associated with this slot in the newscast. The last slot may be perceived as a negative.

Coding Categories Must Have Validity and Reliability

When establishing coding categories, the research expert must adhere to the same rules as when writing survey questions. Just as survey questions must have validity and reliability, content analysis categories must, too. Validity asks the question: Is the category an accurate representation of the content to be coded? Remember that reliability addresses the issue of consistency. If two coders coded the same content, would they assign the content to the same categories? When coders fail to agree in their coding decisions, the reliability of the content analysis study is diminished.

Evaluating Categories Requires Special Attention

By clearly describing what should and should not be included in the categories, the research expert should be able to achieve a high level of agreement between coders. But even so, the more judgments that must be made about classifying the content, the harder it will be to achieve high reliability. It should be relatively easy for coders to code V14, whether the expert source is white, black, or Latino, but it is not so easy to decide whether the treatment of the topic in the story should be classified as positive, negative, or neutral as indicated by V12 in the sample codebook. Only explicit descriptions of the coding categories; thorough training of the coders with examples of positive, negative, and neutral stories; and inter-coder reliability tests on samples of the coding will help to achieve a high degree of reliability for that variable and the study as a whole.

To better understand the more difficult coding task of deciding whether a story is positive, neutral, or negative, let's use an example. Suppose a news story reported that the new state government computer that was designed to process child support payments collected from non-custodial parents had been late in sending out child support checks to custodial parents. As a result of these late payments, custodial parents did not have the child support supplement required to cover expenses for their children. Suppose the news story also reported that, in one case, the State had indeed collected child support from the non-custodial father, but because the computer had not sent the money to the custodial mother, the father had been arrested for non-payment of child support.

This news story would obviously be coded as negative because of the harm the computer caused. For a story that is not as obvious, the following questions might help in deciding whether the story should be coded positive, neutral, or negative:

1. Who or what was responsible for the action or activity? (Individual, group, or institution)
2. Was the action good, bad, or neutral?
3. Who or what was the recipient of the action? (Individual, group, or institution)
4. Was the recipient helped, harmed, or neither helped nor harmed by the action or activity?

As a rule of thumb, bad actions that cause harm would be evaluated as negative and good actions that help would be evaluated positively. Actions that are routine that neither help nor hurt would be coded as neutral. If, for example, the story had reported that as a result of the new computer, child support payments collected by the State were being mailed out one week *earlier* than before, it would have received a positive evaluation. Or if the announcement was simply that the State was using a new computer to process child support payments, the story would have been coded as neutral.

As you'll recall, survey question response choices are required to be mutually exclusive and exhaustive and the same is true for coding categories for content analysis. The categories must not overlap, and all possible categories must be included. The category "other" helps the content analysis research expert fulfill the requirement of being exhaustive.

 ### Coding Categories Reflect Different Levels of Measurement

Coding categories for content analysis studies also conform to the measurement scale that was discussed in Chapter 3. For example, in the sample codebook, V11, topic of the story, is a nominal level measurement in which the news stories can be labeled and sorted into mutually exclusive categories, but there is no order to the categories. V12, evaluation of the story, is an ordinal level variable in which the categories are labeled, sorted, and ordered from positive to negative. V17, length of story, would be treated as a ratio measure because exact seconds are coded. In addition to the attributes of the nominal level measure, seconds are ordered, have a real zero point, and the distance between points is equal.

Once the codebook has been drafted, the research expert consults with the decision maker in Step 4 in Figure 11.2 to confirm that it reflects the issues of concern and the descriptions are representative of the categories to be coded. After incorporating any revisions into the codebook, the research expert uses it for training the coders.

Reliable Coding Is Required for Valid Results

Hiring and Training Content Analysis Coders

Unlike surveys, which may have twenty-five to eighty interviewers or more, content analysis studies generally use only two or three coders. As specified in Step 5, the research expert hires and trains the coders. If only a few coders make decisions about the coding of content, there will be fewer discrepancies in the actual coding.

It is unnecessary for content analysis coders to have graduate educations, but they should have at least some college education with some knowledge about the type of content that is being coded. In the case of coding TV news, coders who generally pay attention to the news on TV and in newspapers tend to make more reliable coding decisions than those who ignore the news.

The training session familiarizes coders with the purpose of the content analysis study, the content that will be coded, and the codebook that will be used. The research expert reviews the two types of decisions—routine and judgmental—that will have to be made. Even though routine coding does not require the coder to judge or evaluate the information before coding, the coder must pay attention in order to accurately record the necessary information. If the coder codes "08" to represent the month of September, the coding is inaccurate because he or she was inattentive or careless.

Judgment is used when the coder must decide in which category to place the subject of the story. Determining whether a story is an economic or educational story is easier than deciding whether it is positive, neutral, or negative. These judgments—both agreements and discrepancies—must be discussed in order to ensure high inter-coder reliability. During the training, the coders practice coding several examples of the content and the research expert evaluates the reliability of the coding before pretesting the codebook on a larger sample of content.

Ethical standards of content analysis research are also emphasized in the training session. Coders must be informed that they must be honest in their coding, coding all material that is expected and using the guidelines set by the research expert. Coders are not to falsify or fail to code some content because they dislike or disagree with what they are finding in the content or they are frustrated with the tedious process of coding.

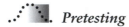 *Pretesting the Content Analysis Codebook*

After training the newly hired coders, the research expert uses them to pretest the content analysis codebook. By using the trained coders, the research expert provides the coders with more practice opportunities and involves them in the process of revising the codebook for increased reliability.

A pretest should be conducted on a sample of the content that represents the various types of issues that will be encountered. For example, having coders practice code different subjects that are positive, neutral, and negative helps increase the reliability of the coding. Pretesting the codebook is also an opportunity to see how well it works on real content and to determine the reliability of coding decisions. The pretest helps to identify coding categories that are clear, comprehensive, and do not overlap other categories as well as those that are deficient and must be developed further. By calculating an inter-coder reliability, the research expert gains an independent assessment of the validity and reliability of the coding.

Calculating Inter-Coder Reliability

Inter-coder reliability measures the consistency of coders in coding the content. Ideally coders will code content exactly the same, producing 100 percent agreement, or a coefficient of reliability of 100 percent. In reality, the more judgments that are made about the correct code to assign, the greater the chance of disagreement between coders. By calculating consistency of agreement between pairs of coders, the research expert can evaluate the reliability of the coding. Although there are a variety of formulas for calculating inter-coder reliability, one widely used formula computes a coefficient of reliability by stating the ratio of decisions that coders agreed on to the total number of decisions made by each coder (Holsti, 1969, pp. 140–141). Figure 11.4 displays both this formula and a sample calculation.

C.R. is reported as a percentage. To determine the M, or the number of decisions that coders agree on, the pretest coding must be compared code by code. Any discrepancies that are found should be flagged for follow-up discussion. The number of coding decisions that match will be used in the formula. Although M represents the number of decisions that the coders agree on, the formula doubles this number to represent the agreed upon decisions of two coders. In the denominator, the total number of decisions, N, made by each coder is summed. In the example, two coders matched on 180 coding decisions. Each coder made 240 coding

FIGURE 11.4 *Formula for Calculating the Coefficient of Reliability to Evaluate Reliability of Content Analysis Coders*

$$\text{C.R.} = \frac{2M}{N_1 + N_2}$$

C.R. = Coefficient of Reliability
M = Number of Coding Decisions Agreed On
N = Total Number of Coding Decisions Made by Each Coder

Example of Calculating Inter-Coder Reliability

$$\text{C.R.} = \frac{2\,(180)}{240 + 240}$$

$$\text{C.R.} = \frac{360}{480}$$

$$\text{C.R.} = 75\%$$

M = 180 (Number of Coding Decisions Agreed On)
N = 240 (Total Number of Coding Decisions Made by Each Coder)

decisions. By doubling the numerator, M, and summing the denominator, N, a coefficient of reliability of 75 percent is calculated.

A rule of thumb for an acceptable coefficient of reliability is 80 percent or above. Because the coefficient of reliability in Figure 11.4 is below 80 percent, the research expert should increase it before proceeding with the content analysis coding.

Improving Inter-Coder Reliability

Regardless of whether the coefficient of reliability is 95 percent or 65 percent, the research expert should discuss the discrepancies in coding with the coders. Some of the discrepancies will be due to routine or clerical errors and some will be due to differences in opinion as to how to categorize the content. The research expert should pay attention to both types of discrepancies as well as to the coder who is making both types of errors. If one coder is making lots of routine or clerical errors, it may be due to carelessness. Because the research project will suffer in the long run if coders are careless, the research expert should consider replacing careless coders before the full-scale content analysis begins.

There is no substitute for discussing discrepancies in coders' judgments. This discussion helps the research expert learn which categories in the coding guide are causing problems because they aren't mutually exclusive or because the descriptions are inadequate. This information can be used to revise the codebook. The coders also have the benefit of further training by learning the context for making decisions and judgments.

Once the codebook has been revised, the research expert instructs the coders to code another sample of content, then conducts another intercoder reliability test. This additional effort should increase the coefficient of reliability to 80 percent or above.

Some researchers have criticized the coefficient of reliability formula in Figure 11.4 because it does not adjust for the amount of coder agreement that would occur by chance. An index of reliability, pi, adjusts for the coder agreement that would occur by chance. Figure 11.5 shows how pi would be calculated (Holsti, 1969, p. 140).

FIGURE 11.5   *Formula for Calculating an Index of Reliability*

$$pi = \frac{\% \text{ observed agreement} - \% \text{ expected agreement}}{1 - \% \text{ expected agreement}}$$

where:

% observed agreement = percentage of coding decisions agreed on
% expected agreement = proportion of items falling into each category of a variable and summing the square of those proportions.

Before you can calculate pi, you must calculate % of expected agreement. Let's say for V12, evaluation of story, in our content analysis example, 80 stories are coded for one TV station, and the frequency and proportion for positive, neutral, and negative are:

Category	Frequency	Proportion
Positive	10	.12
Neutral	40	.50
Negative	30	.38

To calculate the % of expected agreement, insert the proportions into the formula:

$$(.12)^2 + (.50)^2 + (.38)^2 =$$
$$.01 + .25 + .14 = .40$$

The formula shows that % of expected agreement is .40. Let's say the % of observed agreement from the inter-coder reliability formula in Figure 11.4 was found to be 85%. To calculate pi, insert % of observed agreement and % of expected agreement into the formula:

$$pi = \frac{.85 - .40}{1 - .40}$$
$$= .75$$

Notice that when the formula takes into consideration that a percentage of agreement by coders will occur by chance, the observed agreement of .85 is reduced to .75. Does this mean the reliability is no longer at an acceptable level? No, not necessarily. But it does help to explain why the inter-coder reliability of observed agreement should be as high as possible. If some of the coding agreements are by chance, it gives a false sense of security to think that all of the content analysis coding is due to meticulous attention to detail and thoughtful judgments.

Although both formulas provide guidance on the overall quality of the coding, remember that the most important thing for the research expert to pay attention to is disagreement between coders when judgment is required. Good coder training and valid coding categories with explicit descriptions will help improve coder agreement. The research expert would be wise to calculate inter-coder reliability tests on the coding that requires judgments to be made.

According to Step 8 in Figure 11.2 of the content analysis research phase, once the inter-coder reliability reaches an acceptable level, the research expert can discuss the final content analysis codebook with the decision maker. Once approvals have been secured on the final version of the codebook, the research expert can make copies for the coders.

In Step 9, coders follow the codebook to code the news stories in the hypothetical content analysis. Coders can code each story directly onto a coding spreadsheet, or individual codesheets can be copied from the codebook and coders can code the variables on these forms. When individual codesheets are used for coding, they are treated somewhat like survey questionnaires. In other words, just as a survey questionnaire is used to capture information about an individual respondent, an individual codesheet would be used to capture information about an individual news story. If, for example, 400 news stories are to be coded, there will be 400 corresponding codesheets. Each codesheet will have a unique identification number representing one local TV news story.

The Final Steps of the Content Analysis Research Phase Are Similar to Those of a Survey

Processing Content Analysis Data

The same procedure that is used for processing survey data as discussed in Chapter 7 is used for processing content analysis data. In Step 10 of the research phase, the codes from each codesheet are transferred to the corresponding columns on a coding spreadsheet. The seventeen variables

FIGURE 11.6   *A Partial Content Analysis Coding Spreadsheet*

```
100101259911101607719312881 02
100201259921103202214231121 10
```

in the sample codebook displayed in Figure 11.3 will produce one line of twenty-nine columns of codes. The finished coding spreadsheet will have the same number of lines as the number of TV news stories coded.

An examination of the partial coding spreadsheet displayed in Figure 11.6 reveals that the content analysis coding spreadsheet looks like a coding spreadsheet for a telephone survey. The first line of the content analysis spreadsheet, which indicates the TV station coded and an identification number of 001, is the sample news story about the computer that was late processing and sending out child support payments that we discussed earlier. The second line of the spreadsheet represents the second story on the same TV station. In this example, fourth-, fifth-, and sixth-grade children were asked their opinion about social promotion, a school policy in which children are promoted to the next grade even though they have not satisfactorily completed the academic work in their current grade. Elected officials and education experts have been calling for an end to this practice.

Analyzing Content Analysis Data

According to Step 11 of the content analysis research phase in Figure 11.2, the research expert analyzes the data using appropriate statistics and ethical standards. This step uses the same procedures for analyzing survey data that we discussed in Chapters 7 and 8. A statistical package such as SPSS, Statistical Package for the Social Sciences, can be used to produce frequencies, cross-tabulations, and appropriate statistics.

Before focusing on the specific research question, the research expert would run a frequency printout to produce frequency distributions of all variables. The research expert would verify that the variables are being read in the correct columns and then check for and clean any dirty data or out-of-range codes.

Once the research expert feels that the data are clean, the focus can turn to answering the research question. Using the sample content analysis study, he or she would examine V8, the variable for racial/ethnic group of news subject across local TV stations. Through cross-tabulation analysis, the research expert would be able to compare the percentage of subjects of local TV news stories that were white, African American, Latino,

Asian American, and Native American, for every station in the market. An additional cross-tabulation analysis would sort out whether the news stories were positive, neutral, or negative for each news station.

By instructing SPSS to run the appropriate statistics, the research expert would also be able to determine if the differences were real or significant. However, it's important to remember that when content analysis studies analyze *all* the content and not a random sample of the content, the differences that are found are *real,* which makes it unnecessary to run statistics that report significant differences or project to the population. Many statistics that were discussed in Chapter 8 would be appropriate for content analysis data. A mean statistic could be calculated on V17, length of the story. For content analysis studies that use randomly selected content, chi square could be calculated on nominal variables to determine if the differences between categories are significant. Statistics that are appropriate for ordinal level data could be used to determine if there is a correlation between whether a story is positive or negative and the length of time it is broadcast.

Throughout the process of analyzing the data from the content analysis study, the research expert must adhere to ethical standards. All data, even data that contradict expectations, must be included in the analysis.

Writing the Content Analysis Report

Once the data have been analyzed in the context of the research question, the research expert is ready to draft the written report, as listed in Step 12 of Figure 11.2. The components of the research report for content analysis are virtually the same as those for a survey research report described in detail in Chapter 9: cover letter, report binder, title and author page, table of contents, executive summary, introduction, background/context, methodology, results, discussion, recommendations, conclusions, footnotes, references, and appendix.

The advice for writing a quality survey research report applies to a written content analysis report. Check the draft for organization and transitions as well as correct grammar, sentence structure, and punctuation. The tone should be professional and objective. Persuasion is permitted in the recommendations section only. Proof all numbers in the text and tables to make sure they match the original printouts. The format of the text and tables for content analysis reports is the same as that for survey research reports as discussed in detail in Chapter 9. And, of course, ethical standards must also be used when writing a content analysis research report. Data should not be omitted or buried because they do not conform to expectations.

FIGURE 11.7   *Text and Frequency Table from a Published Content Analysis Study on the Use of Nostalgia in Television Advertising*

As shown in Table 2, period-oriented symbols and music were the most common nostalgic elements used, appearing in 30 percent and 28 percent of the ads, respectively. References to old brands and patriotism were least likely to be found in the television advertising. Eight percent of the ads referred to old brands and 3 percent mentioned patriotism.

TABLE 2   *Frequency and Combination of Nostalgic Elements*

Type of Nostalgia	Percent
Period-oriented symbolism	30
Period-oriented music	28
References to "olden days"	18
References to past family experiences	13
References to old brands	8
Patriotism	3
	100%
(Base)	(158)

Copyright AEJMC. Used with permission.

To show an example of how content analysis results are reported, let's look at excerpts from two reports. Figure 11.7 displays the text and table adapted from a published content analysis article, "The Use of Nostalgia in Television Advertising: A Content Analysis." This study content-analyzed 1,031 spot and network television commercials during a two-week period to determine whether six elements of nostalgia were used in commercials (Unger, McConacho, & Faier, 1991). The nostalgic elements that were found in 158 commercials included:

1. Reflections on past experiences with family and friends
2. Olden days
3. Period symbolism (imagery from 1930s, 1940s, 1950s, 1960s, references to earlier symbols or icons in art, religion, education, fashion, medical practices)
4. Period music (golden oldies, popular music from 1950s and 1960s)
5. Old brands (use of old brand names, brand characters/spokespersons, old ads or clips)
6. Patriotism (buy American, celebration of American heritage)

FIGURE 11.8   *Text and Cross-Tab Table from a Content Analysis Study That Examined the Use of the Term "Spin Doctor"*

Whether statements about spin doctors were pejorative or not was also related to the source of the statement, with 41 percent of the statements by journalists being pejorative and 73 percent of the statements by news sources being pejorative. (See Table 6.)

TABLE 6   *Kind of Statement about Spin Doctors by Source*

	Journalist	News Source
Pejorative	41	73
Not pejorative	59	27
	100%	100%

Chi square = 5.31, d.f. = 1, $p < .05$

Used with permission from the authors.

Another content analysis study, which we mentioned earlier, used current and archival Nexis files to search published news articles to determine how the term "spin doctor" has been used in the mass media since its first appearance in 1984 (Tankard & Sumpter, 1993). Spin doctors were described in the study as engaging in spin control, a process of providing certain interpretations of events in hopes that journalists will include the interpretations in the stories they write and report. Twenty articles were selected from a stratified random sample representing each year between 1988 and 1992. A cross-tab table with the chi square statistic is displayed in Figure 11.8. It compares whether or not the term "spin doctor" was used in a pejorative or disparaging manner by journalists or the news source.

Including examples of the content that were analyzed in the appendix section of the report will enhance the study. Copies of newspaper or magazine articles or advertisements or transcripts of broadcast news stories or entertainment programs will illustrate the types of content that were examined. These content illustrations can be used effectively in the oral presentation on the content analysis results.

Once the written report is finalized, it should be professionally copied and bound. According to Step 13 of Figure 11.2, after attaching a cover letter and invoice that itemizes services, the report should be shipped to the decision maker.

 *Presenting the Content Analysis Orally*

Preparation for the oral presentation of a content analysis study should follow the checklist for preparing a survey research oral presentation because the steps are the same. Using the checklist developed in Figure 9.8 in Chapter 9, the research expert determines the length of presentation time, room set up, and composition and size of the audience before outlining the oral presentation and visuals that will be used. From the outline, the research expert drafts a script that includes a greeting, purpose, description of the content analysis method, major results, implications, and recommendations. As discussed in Chapter 9, the research expert should rehearse the presentation to ensure that the purpose, method, and results are clear; the implications are insightful; and the recommendations persuasive.

Visuals can enhance an oral presentation of the content analysis results. For content analyses of TV news stories or prime-time entertainment TV, video excerpts can be shown during the presentation to illustrate the predominant findings in the research study. For content analysis studies of print media, slides of newspaper and magazine news articles or ads can be shown to represent some of the significant results of the study.

As discussed in the Chapter 9 checklist for an oral presentation on survey results, the research expert should prepare a written handout or leave-behind for those who attend the oral presentation. The oral presentation should conclude with questions from the audience.

The Role of the Decision Maker during the Content Analysis Post-Research Phase

After the decision maker receives the results from the research expert, the post-research phase of the content analysis study begins. Notice from Figure 11.9 that the post-research phase of a content analysis research study is the same as the post-research phase of surveys.

After reading the written report carefully and, if applicable, processing the check for research services as listed in the first two steps, the decision maker can turn his or her attention to Steps 3, 4, and 5, evaluating the results and recommendations, discussing them with the research expert, and deciding whether or not to use the results in decision making.

Let's use the hypothetical content analysis study on the representation of racial and ethnic groups in local TV news as an example of how the post-research phase might proceed. Remember in that example that the decision maker's problem was that African Americans and Hispanics were watching the *other* local TV stations at a higher rate. Consequently

FIGURE 11.9   *The Post-Research Phase of Content Analysis and the Decision Maker*

Step 1. Read the report, paying careful attention to the results and recommendations in the research study.

Step 2. If applicable, process the check for the research expert and send it with a cover letter thanking him or her for research services. Personalize the cover letter by including one or two items that were especially valuable during the research process.

Step 3. Evaluate the research results and recommendations, looking for trends, confirmations of previous information, inconsistencies, surprises, possible opportunities, potential problems, and completely new and useful information.

Step 4. Discuss your evaluations with the research expert to take advantage of the research expert's further insight.

Step 5. Decide which data can be used in decisions that have to be made and which data need further information to better understand what's happening.

Step 6. Consult with the research expert about developing criteria for measuring the impact of decisions that are made based on the research results.

Step 7. Implement the decisions based on the research results.

Step 8. Evaluate the impact of the decisions.

Step 9. Decide the next step.

Step 10. Create a file for this research study that includes the report, relevant documents, correspondence, and an assessment of how well the research expert satisfied your research needs.

the news director decided to have a content analysis of the news coverage of *all* local TV news stations to gather data that would show how the different TV stations in the market were covering African Americans and Hispanics.

Suppose the content analysis results showed that the other TV stations not only carried more stories on African Americans and Hispanics, but that more of these stories were positive or neutral. These results also mean that the TV news director had fewer stories on African Americans and Hispanics and the stories were significantly more negative than the coverage on other stations.

Results Offer Several Options for Decision Making

How should the decision maker proceed with this new information? The decision maker has several options for decision making. The news director can decide to ignore the data. The decision maker can decide to call for a content analysis study that covers a longer time period to determine if the results are different or the same. The decision maker can also decide to act on the results of the content analysis study. Of course, calling for a different research expert to review the study and results is also an option. But we'll assume that the decision maker feels that the data are valid because of the researcher's expertise. And, of course, the data offer a plausible explanation for the lower viewing among African Americans and Hispanics. The decision maker decides to act on the data.

How to act on the data will *not* be answered directly by the content analysis results. The content analysis will not say: "Do this." Remember a content analysis study only provides information about the amount and types of content. But in that information are some clues as to how the news director might proceed.

As a first step of action, the decision maker can look at the competition's stories that were coded neutral and positive as well as his or her own stories that were coded negative to have a better sense of the different types of coverage that African Americans and Hispanics are being exposed to. As a second step, the decision maker can monitor the available news for a week to ten days, then observe which stories are actually getting reported on the air by the different stations. The news director can then determine if a greater emphasis is placed on negative stories from the available pool.

Finally, the news director can call a staff meeting of producers and reporters to present the overall results of the content analysis and his or her own observations from monitoring the competition as well as his or her own station. If the news director wants to have more balance in the coverage of African Americans and Hispanics, he or she will then tell the staff to make sure that negative stories are balanced with neutral and positive ones. Without this effort, the decision maker may have to tell the staff that their station will continue to have a problem with African American and Hispanic viewers' choosing the other stations for their news.

 ## Experience and Goals of the Decision Maker Influence How the Results Are Used

The experience and goals of the news director dictate how he or she uses the data in decision making. Of course, if the goal is to increase viewership among African Americans and Hispanics, the decisions and actions in the content analysis example are plausible responses to the findings and will likely produce positive results.

The Impact of the Decisions Should Be Evaluated

In Step 6 of the post-research phase, the decision maker should consult with the research expert again about developing evaluation research that will measure the impact of the decision that was made based on the research results. Evaluating the decision's impact is very important to the overall research process. This evaluation stage helps the decision maker make better short- and long-term decisions about the issue, problem, or opportunity that initiated the research in the first place.

In Step 7, the decision maker takes action by implementing decisions based on the research results, and six months later, he or she is ready for Step 8, evaluating the impact of the decisions. Suppose the evaluation research shows that viewing by African Americans and Hispanics has increased slightly. At this stage, Step 9, the decision maker decides the next step. The news director may want to conduct another content analysis as well as conduct focus groups among African American and Hispanic viewers to gauge their perceptions of the news coverage. Focus groups are discussed in Chapter 13.

Finally, in Step 10 of the post-research phase, the decision maker should create a file for the research study that includes the report, relevant documents, correspondence, and an assessment of the overall process as well as the research expert. This file, which should be stored for easy retrieval, is a basis for follow-up research.

This chapter examined content analysis, a research method that examines the content of communication. Even though there are limitations as to what can be learned, content analysis still provides an opportunity for the systematic and objective examination of messages that are communicated.

SUGGESTED RESEARCH ACTIVITIES

1. Review the content analysis codebook in Figure 11.3. What other coding categories might you add? Why?

2. Record three days of local TV news. Use the codebook to content analyze the newscasts. Calculate an inter-coder reliability using the formula in Figure 11.4. Discuss any discrepancies in coding. What are your primary findings for this sample of newscasts?

3. Develop a content analysis codebook for the World Wide Web addresses that are displayed at the conclusion of commercials. Discuss the variables that you included in your codebook and why.

4. Develop a content analysis codebook for the TV ratings that are displayed at the beginning of TV programs. Discuss the variables that you included and why.

5. Look through back issues of communication journals for the past two years. Find a content analysis study of interest. Read it carefully. How were the data analyzed? Write a summary of the study's purpose, method, and results. If you were to conduct this study, what, if anything, would you do differently?

RECOMMENDED READING

For additional insight into conducting content analysis studies, see:

DANIEL RIFFE, STEPHEN LACY, and FREDERICK G. FICO, *Analyzing Media Messages: Using Quantitative Content Analysis in Research.* Mahwah, NJ: Lawrence Erlbaum, 1998.

For research studies that have used content analysis to examine a variety of topics including the treatment of violence, sex, race and ethnicity, gender, children, political candidates, the environment, diseases, and controversial issues in advertising, news, or prime-time television, see:

Past issues of *Journalism and Mass Communication Quarterly.*

For a discussion of the quantitative vs. qualitative debate in content analysis, see:

GUIDO H. STEMPEL III, "Content Analysis," in *Research Methods in Mass Communication*, ed. Guido H. Stempel III and Bruce H. Westley, pp. 119–131. Englewood Cliffs, NJ: Prentice-Hall, 1981.

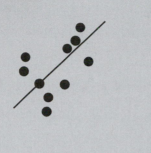

CHAPTER 12

Experiments

- What is an experiment?
- What are the benefits of conducting experiments?
- How are experiments conducted?
- What are the threats to the validity of experiments?
- How are experimental results analyzed?
- What are the ethical issues that surround experimental research?

Experiments Can Determine What Causes What

In 1963, a laboratory experiment conducted at Stanford University became influential in the national debate on the effects of television violence on children. Psychologist Albert Bandura and his colleagues designed an experiment using forty-eight boys and forty-eight girls at Stanford University Nursery School to determine if the children would learn and perform aggressive behavior portrayed on television (Bandura et al., 1963). This experiment assigned the children to one of three experimental conditions—real-life aggression, human film aggression, or cartoon film-mediated aggression—or a control group not exposed to aggression.

One by one, the children were taken into a room that contained toys to play with, plus a five-foot inflated Bobo doll and mallet. Depending on the experimental condition, the children observed a live, human, or cartoon film model perform aggressive behavior toward the large plastic Bobo doll. These aggressive behaviors included sitting on the Bobo doll and punching it in the nose, striking it on the head with the mallet, throwing it up in the air and kicking it around the room, and saying the words: "Sock him in the nose . . . , Hit him down . . . , Throw him in the air . . . , and Pow."

The results of this famous experiment showed that the filmed human violence had the most influence on the children. The children in this experimental condition exhibited more aggressive behavior than those in the control group, who were not exposed to the aggression toward the Bobo doll. A comparison of boys and girls showed that boys displayed significantly more aggressive behavior than girls. According to the study, girls were more likely than boys to sit on the Bobo doll, even though they did not punch it.

Why were these researchers able to conclude that children exposed to filmed violence were more aggressive? They were able to draw that conclusion because they used one of the most powerful scientific research methods—the experiment.

Definition of an Experiment

Experiments date back to the thirteenth century, when French scholar Pèlerin de Maricourt, also known by his Latin name Petrus Peregrinus de Maricourt, conducted scientific experiments that led to the discovery of magnetic poles. Galileo, though, is credited with being the founder of experimental science because of his experiments on moving bodies that were conducted in the sixteenth century (Asimov, 1994).

An experiment, a methodology that cuts across the physical, biological, social, and communication sciences, is a research method in which an independent variable is manipulated and its effects on the dependent variable are observed. When an experiment is conducted scientifically, the researcher is able to attribute any change in the dependent variable directly to the independent variable and not to extraneous variables or factors unrelated to the study. In other words, the independent variable is said to have caused changes in the dependent variable. In fact, the controlled experiment has been called the most powerful method available for finding out what causes what (Westley, 1981, p. 196).

The Experiment's Pre-Research Phase

How do the three phases of the research process apply to experiments? We'll use a hypothetical example to see how the experimental process works. Imagine Steps 1 and 2 of the pre-research phase in Figure 12.1 (p. 218) in which the chairman and chief executive officer (CEO) of a major family-owned communication conglomerate monitors the environment and notices news stories about the problem of preteen and teen smoking. Anxious to do something about this problem, the chairman announces that he will make available free space in his newspapers and choice time on his radio and TV stations for public service announcements (PSAs) that will discourage preteens or teens from smoking.

The chairman of the media company then invites journalism, advertising, radio-TV-film, and public relations professors to develop an effective non-smoking public service campaign that will discourage preteen or teen smoking and promises to underwrite any expenses associated with the campaign and research. The CEO poses the research question,

FIGURE 12.1   *Pre-Research Phase of Experiment*

> **Step 1.** Monitor environment and literature.
> **Step 2.** Identify problem, trend, opportunity, issue, phenomenon, or theory.
> **Step 3.** Specify research question.

according to Step 3 in the pre-research phase as shown in Figure 12.1: What type of public service announcement will discourage preteens or teens from smoking cigarettes?

A public relations professor reads about the CEO's announcement in the newspaper and decides to develop a campaign to discourage preteen smoking as well as an experiment to test the effectiveness of the public service announcement. The public relations professor will submit the campaign and supporting research documentation to the CEO after the research is completed.

Applying the Research Phase to the Experiment

Figure 12.2 displays the steps involved in the research phase of an experiment. After completing Step 1, in which the research literature and background articles on preteen and teen smoking (including work on the reasons why some start as well as the reasons that some *never* start smoking) are reviewed, the professor identifies a variable that may be significant in a public service campaign and whose effects can be tested in an experiment.

In Step 2, the researcher specifies the hypothesis, a statement that predicts the relationship between two or more variables, that will be used in conducting an experiment on the effectiveness of the PSA. In the hypothetical example, the researcher will test the following hypothesis:

H_1: *Preteens who view a PSA that says smoking is **stupid** are less likely to plan to smoke when they grow up.*

Often a research study has more than one research hypothesis to test and each has a subscript (H_2, H_3, H_4, . . .) to indicate its number.

Experimental Concepts, Designs, and Symbols

 Experimental Validity

In Step 3, the researcher designs the experiment using ethical standards and specifies the setting, subject population, and how the independent

FIGURE 12.2   *Research Phase of Experiment*

Step   1. Conduct in-depth literature review and background search.
Step   2. Specify hypothesis.
Step   3. Design experiment using ethical standards. Specify setting, operationalization of independent and dependent variables, manipulation of independent variable, and subject population and size. Address internal and external validity issues.
Step   4. Prepare sample independent and dependent variables and develop experimental procedures.
Step   5. Identify best source for subjects and recruit them for the pretest and actual experiment.
Step   6. Conduct pretest of experiment and check validity of manipulation of independent variable.
Step   7. Evaluate pretest results and make necessary adjustments to the procedures and independent and dependent variables.
Step   8. Conduct experiment using ethical standards.
Step   9. Process and analyze data using appropriate statistics and ethical standards.
Step 10. Write report.
Step 11. Share results.

variable will be operationalized and manipulated. In addition, the researcher spells out how the dependent variable will be operationalized and measured. The researcher designs the experiment to ensure internal validity, which answers the question: Did the independent variable cause the change in the dependent variable?

External validity is also important when designing an experiment. It addresses the question: Can the results be generalized to a larger population beyond the actual participants in the experiment?

Experimental Designs

The design of the experiment specifies the framework for how the study will be conducted. Experimental research scholars Donald T. Campbell and Julian C. Stanley (1963, p. 1) identified sixteen such frameworks that have been used for conducting experiments. Figure 12.3 (p. 220) describes four of these experimental designs that are likely to be encountered in the research literature. Notice that the internal validity of these experimental designs varies from weak to strong.

FIGURE 12.3 *Four Experimental Designs*

Description	Random Assign-ment	Pretest	Condition	Posttest	Internal Validity
1. One-Group Pretest-Posttest Design		O	X	O	Weak
2. Pretest-Posttest Control Group Design	R R	O O	X	O O	Strong
3. Solomon Four-Group Design	R R R R	O O	X X	O O O O	Strong
4. Posttest-Only Control Group Design	R R		X	O O	Strong

Symbols: X = Independent Variable
O = Dependent Variable
R = Random Assignment

Experimental Symbols

To interpret an experimental design, it is first necessary to understand the symbols X, O, and R that are displayed in Figure 12.3. By knowing how to read this experimental shorthand, you can interpret the type of design used to conduct an experiment. In addition to knowing that X represents the independent variable, O stands for the dependent variable, and R is for random assignment of subjects to the experimental condition and control group, you must also know how to interpret the placement of the X's and O's.

For example, when O is placed before the X, it means that the dependent variable has been measured before manipulation of the independent variable. In other words, there has been a pretest. When O is placed after the X, the dependent variable has been measured after the manipulation of the independent variable. There has been a posttest.

The placement of the symbols also reveals whether or not a control group, the condition that was not exposed to the manipulated independent variable, was used. Whenever an O in the posttest condition is *not* preceded by an X, it means that condition represents the control group.

According to Figure 12.3, the internal validity of the first design, One-Group Pretest-Posttest Design, is weak because there is no control group. An experimental design with strong internal validity has a control group and attempts to ensure at the outset of the experiment that the experimental and control groups are equal. That is the reason for randomly assigning subjects to the experimental and control groups. If the two groups are equal at the outset, the researcher can reasonably assume that the only variable accounting for a difference in the dependent variable at the conclusion of the experiment is that one group is exposed to X, the experimental manipulation, and the other group is not.

 ## The Control Group

Awareness of the importance of a control group in an experimental design dates back to the early 1920s, when a series of studies on worker productivity was conducted at the Hawthorne plant of the Western Electric Corporation (Kerlinger, 1973, p. 155). In these experimental studies, working conditions in the plant were manipulated to determine the effect on worker productivity. Researchers found that worker productivity increased when working conditions became more favorable. More favorable working conditions included change in payment, more frequent rest periods, and shorter work days. But worker productivity *also* increased when working conditions became *less* favorable. Because a control group was not a part of the experimental design, researchers did not recognize that productivity was increasing because of the attention being paid to workers—not because of a change in working conditions.

The term "Hawthorne effect" has come to symbolize experimental designs without control groups in which subjects change because of the attention they receive from participating in an experiment (Kerlinger, 1973, p. 345). Without control groups, it is impossible to separate the change that is due to the increased attention and the change that is due to the manipulation of the independent variable.

Threats to Internal Validity

Researchers Campbell and Stanley (1963, p. 5) called problems like the Hawthorne effect threats to internal validity because the experimenter's ability to attribute the effect on the dependent variable to the independent variable is significantly reduced. Let's examine how some of these threats, which are listed in Figure 12.4 (p. 222), could affect our hypothetical experiment.

To illustrate the internal validity threat of history, imagine that the hypothetical experiment is conducted on middle school children, those

FIGURE 12.4 *Threats to an Experiment's Internal Validity*

1. History: any events that occur between the pretest and posttest measurements.
2. Maturation: any changes that occur in the subjects between the pretest and posttest. Changes might include becoming older, more knowledgeable, more confident, etc.
3. Testing: any effects of taking the pretest on the scores of the posttest.
4. Instrumentation: any effects resulting from changing the measuring instruments from the pretest to the posttest.
5. Statistical Regression: when subjects are selected on the basis of extreme scores, the posttest scores tend to regress toward the mean of the distribution of scores.
6. Differential Selection of Subjects: when subjects in the experimental group differ significantly from subjects in the control group.
7. Experimental Mortality: when subject drop-out from pretest to posttest in the experimental and control groups is not equal.

in grades six through eight, and the experimental design includes both a pretest and posttest. Suppose that the researcher thinks a baseline measurement on smoking attitudes and intentions would be helpful, so he or she decides to conduct a pretest on Monday with plans to administer a posttest on the following Wednesday. But what if, on Tuesday, the middle school principal announces on the school public address system that any student caught smoking at any school activity will be expelled. Imagine the impact of this announcement on attitudes about smoking. This event intervening between the pretest and posttest could have a chilling effect on students' honest expression of opinions on smoking.

The maturation threat can be illustrated in a similar manner. Again, imagine that a pretest is conducted on Monday and on Tuesday the American Cancer Society sponsors a schoolwide program on the health risks of cigarette smoking. The fact that the children have become more knowledgeable about the deadly effects of cigarette smoking can also have a significant impact on how they respond to the posttest questionnaire.

Testing can threaten internal validity because the process of taking a pretest can familiarize subjects with the test. This familiarity might help the experimental subjects answer questions better or differently during the posttest. The instrumentation effect on internal validity also relates to the pretest and posttest. The major difference, though, is that instrumentation refers to the use of *different* tests for the pretest and posttest. Of course, if you don't ask the same questions or use the same instrument during both the pretest and posttest, you will not be able to attribute any changes to the experimental manipulation.

Statistical regression can occur when the pretest is used to select subjects who have extremely high or low scores for the follow-up posttest. When the posttest is administered, the extreme scores have been found to regress toward the mean or average score of the distribution.

When subjects in the experimental group differ significantly from subjects in the control group, the internal validity of the experiment is also threatened. Suppose the experimental group is filled with children who have smokers as parents and the control group has children with non-smoking parents. This differential selection of subjects makes the effect of the experimental manipulation difficult to sort out.

The last threat to an experiment's internal validity as listed in Figure 12.4 is experimental mortality. Suppose again that a pretest is conducted on Monday and the posttest is administered on Wednesday. It turns out that on Wednesday half of the subjects in the control group have to attend a special assembly. A great number miss the posttest. Now the experimental and control groups are no longer equal, which can negatively affect internal validity.

An addition of a control group to the experimental design will minimize most of the threats to internal validity. For example, because history and maturation affect both the experimental and control groups equally between the pretests and posttests, any changes in the dependent variable can still be attributed to the independent variable. Although random assignment of subjects is important to the experimental design to minimize any threats to internal validity, it is particularly important for the sixth internal validity threat, differential selection of subjects. Through random assignment, the experimenter is assured that the two groups are equal.

The importance of having equal groups is due to the role that *variance* plays in scientifically based research. Experimental design scholar Fred N. Kerlinger (1973, pp. 71–84) said that there are two types of variance, systematic and error. Systematic variance, which is produced by known or unknown natural or man-made influences, causes the scores to lean in one direction or another. For example, children who learn in a classroom with computers and Internet access will likely have better computer skills than those who learn in a classroom without that technology. In this example, the variance in computer skills among children is a function of the type of classroom.

Experimental, also called between-groups variance, is a type of systematic variance. For experimental variance, the researcher manipulates an independent variable to cause a difference between groups. To attribute any difference between groups to the independent variable, the researcher must make the groups equal by randomly assigning subjects to them. Without this random assignment, one group might be loaded with one type of subject and the other loaded with another type and you wouldn't be able to determine whether or not the independent variable had an effect. Random assignment would distribute the subjects equally to the groups.

Error, the other type of variance, is due to chance. In other words, this type of error, which is random, is the variance that is left over after the systematic variance has been accounted for.

Sometimes it is impossible to randomly assign subjects to the experimental and control groups to make them equal. When that happens, the researcher must rely on matching subjects based on relevant criteria to the experiment. In the Bobo doll experiment discussed earlier, nursery school subjects were rated on an aggression scale, then matched by their level of aggression when assigned to the experimental and control group.

Without matching the nursery school children, highly aggressive children may have all been assigned to the experimental group and children low on the aggression scale assigned to the control group. With unequal groups at the beginning of the experiment, the internal validity would have been affected negatively and the experimental outcome would have been erroneous.

Threats to External Validity

In addition to internal validity threats, there are threats to the experimenter's ability to generalize to the population. Known as threats to external validity, three primary risks are in this category: pretesting, subject selection, and experimental setting (Campbell & Stanley, 1963). The experimental design that includes a pretest cannot be generalized beyond the experimental group because the larger population to which the subjects belong has not experienced the effects of the pretest.

The selection of subjects can also threaten external validity because experiments are often conducted among subjects, such as college students, who are not representative of the population as a whole.

The third threat relates to the artificiality of the experimental setting. Many experiments are conducted in a classroom that serves as a laboratory rather than the real world. When an experiment is conducted in a laboratory, the experimenter has the undivided attention of the subjects, but in a natural environment, the experimenter competes with all the other elements in the environment for the subjects' attention. When it is feasible to conduct the experiment in a natural environment, the experimenter can eliminate this threat to external validity. Experiments conducted in a natural environment are called field experiments.

Despite these threats to external validity, experiments are the best methodology for establishing internal validity. Ultimately we need information in both areas.

How do all of these design and validity issues apply to our hypothetical experiment on non-smoking PSAs? The researcher considers all of these design and validity issues before deciding to conduct the experiment using the fourth design, posttest-only control group design, which is displayed in Figure 12.5.

The researcher feels this design will provide the most valid and efficient test of the effectiveness of the non-smoking PSA. According to experimental design experts Campbell and Stanley, as long as subjects are randomly assigned to experimental and control groups to make the groups equal, it is unnecessary to include pretests, which will require more subjects, a larger budget, and more time.

Even though the researcher has settled on the posttest-only control group design for the experiment, important questions still must be answered before the experiment can be conducted. How should the researcher operationalize the independent variable? How should the dependent variable be measured? Given the operationalizations of the independent and dependent variables, the researcher must address: What is the ideal setting? Who are the appropriate subjects? What procedures should be used? To address these questions, the researcher draws on scientific tradition, creativity, media and marketing savvy, and basic common sense.

FIGURE 12.5 *Posttest-Only Control Group Design*

	(Independent Variable)	
R	X	O_1
R		O_2 (Control Group)
(Random Assignment)		(Dependent Variable)

The Hypothetical Experiment's Design

The Independent Variable

According to Step 4 of the research phase, the researcher prepares the independent and dependent variables and develops procedures that are appropriate for the experimental design, setting, and subjects. For the hypothetical experiment, the researcher decides to create a public service announcement that uses preteen models who speak the language of middle school children. The PSA copy, described in Figure 12.6, will say "Smoking is stupid. Don't smoke." The experimental group will be exposed to this PSA. To disguise the purpose of the experiment, the researcher will place the PSA in a magazine that will be described as a new publication that is being created for preteens. The control group will see the same magazine, but it will not contain the non-smoking PSA.

The prototype magazine will be named *Almost Teens,* and it will contain three short articles of interest to preteens plus three ads. In addition to the PSA on non-smoking, the magazine will contain a backpack ad, a jeans ad, and an ad for a new movie appropriate for that age group. The dependent variable, future intentions to smoke, will be measured with a short questionnaire.

Experimental Setting

In addition to operationalizing the independent variable to be manipulated, the researcher will have to decide whether or not to conduct the

FIGURE 12.6 *Experimental and Control Groups*

Experimental Group	Control Group
PSA	No PSA

Smoking is stupid.

Don't smoke.

(Artwork will consist of one group of five
sixth graders waiting together at the school bus stop.
The sixth graders are dressed in cool clothes,
carrying cool backpacks, and chatting happily.
Standing alone away from the group is an unkempt
middle school kid. His tattered backpack is open and
tossed on the ground. He is frowning as he smokes a cigarette.)

experiment in the artificial environment of a laboratory or a realistic environment in the field. Experimental expert Kerlinger said that in the laboratory experiment, by isolating the research in a controlled physical situation apart from ordinary living, the researcher can keep the variance of all or nearly all of the possible influential independent variables not relevant to the investigation to a minimum. On the other hand, the field experiment is conducted in a realistic situation, which more readily generalizes to real life. Still, the experimenter tries to control as many variables as the situation will permit—but the field experiment does not provide the control that can be found in a laboratory setting (Kerlinger, 1973, pp. 398–401).

The researcher decides to conduct the hypothetical experiment in the school auditorium, which will serve as a laboratory. The environment will certainly be artificial when the students are exposed to the PSA. Generally, when consumers are looking at ads, they're thumbing through a newspaper or magazine, perhaps, talking, listening, or having many activities competing for their attention. In the controlled environment of a school auditorium or classroom, the researcher will be able to get the subjects to focus their full attention on the PSA. This can be characterized as measuring the maximum impact of the independent variable.

 ## *Experimental Subjects*

The decision on the appropriate subjects for the experiment is made in Step 3, and in Step 5 the research expert identifies the best subject pool for recruitment. Because preteens are the target age group, the researcher will have to obtain permission from a middle school or Girl Scout or Boy Scout troop to get children of the right age. Unlike a survey, which may have 400 to 1,200 respondents to minimize sampling error, an experiment may have as few as fifty to one hundred subjects in the experimental and control groups. A survey uses random selection to ensure that every individual in the population has an equal chance of being selected; an experiment uses random assignment of subjects to the experimental and control groups to ensure that the two groups are equal.

As the researcher considers the best source for recruiting experimental subjects, the researcher is mindful of the external validity problems that are introduced when the subjects don't match the population. As discussed earlier, external validity addresses the question: Can the results be generalized to the population? An experiment conducted among subjects who do not match the population cannot be generalized. Using subjects from a middle school would better meet the external validity requirements of an experiment than using subjects from a Girl Scout or Boy Scout Troop because children in the middle school grades represent the population that the experiment is designed for. The researcher recruits two groups of middle school children. A practice run of the experiment will be conducted with one group. A second group will be used for the actual experiment.

 ### *The Dependent Variable*

The dependent variable is also developed in Step 4 of the research phase. The experimental design calls for a posttest measure in both the experimental and control groups to assess the effects of the independent variable on the dependent variable. A review of the experimental literature shows that experiments have used a variety of methods to measure dependent variables. Subjects have been surveyed by telephone and rated by independent observers. TV ratings and product sales have also been used to measure the dependent variable. The researcher decides to use a self-administered questionnaire to determine future smoking intentions as a measure of the dependent variable.

In developing the self-administered questionnaire, the researcher follows the guidelines that were used in developing survey questions and the survey questionnaire, discussed in Chapters 3 and 4. Questions must have validity and reliability. Questions can be open-ended or closed-ended. Closed-ended response choices must be exhaustive and mutually exclusive.

As the researcher prepares the dependent variable measure, attention is paid to the potential problem of making the measure so obvious that the subjects will be able to guess the purpose of the experiment. To camouflage the purpose, the researcher includes an introduction that explains that the magazine is a new publication for preteens that he or she would like to receive feedback on. In addition, the researcher includes questions on the self-administered questionnaire about the other articles and ads in the magazine.

Finally, the researcher includes several questions about future intentions of several types of behavior. The smoking question is included in the list. These questions are listed in Figure 12.7.

Translating the Design to Experimental Procedures

 ### *A Practice Run Precedes the Actual Experiment*

How the experiment is actually carried out depends on the purpose of the study and how the independent and dependent variables are mea-

FIGURE 12.7   *Questions That Measure Various Future Intentions and the Dependent Variable, Future Smoking Intentions*

1. When you grow up, do you plan to buy whatever you want?
   1. Definitely Yes
   2. Probably Yes
   3. Unsure
   4. Probably No
   5. Definitely No
2. When you grow up, how many hours of TV do you plan to watch a day? Please write in number of hours:

   _____

3. When you grow up, do you plan to eat as much candy as you want?
   1. Definitely Yes
   2. Probably Yes
   3. Unsure
   4. Probably No
   5. Definitely No
4. When you grow up, how many cigarettes do you plan to smoke a day? Please write in number of cigarettes:

   _____

sured. According to Steps 6 and 7 of the research phase, the researcher conducts a pretest or practice run of the experimental procedures and evaluates the results. Figure 12.8 (p. 230) describes the experimental procedures in detail. The practice run to pretest the experimental procedures is conducted on subjects who are similar to the subjects who will be used in the actual experiment. The practice experiment enables the researcher to identify and fix any problems in the procedures or independent and dependent variable measures before conducting the real experiment.

The researcher must prepare all materials before the procedures are pretested. The articles, ads, and PSA must be included in the prototype magazine. Half the magazines will contain the PSA, and the other half will not. The self-administered questionnaire will include instructions on proceeding through the materials. The question to check the validity of the independent variable will be printed on the last page of the self-administered questionnaire.

The researcher begins the experiment by explaining that the purpose is to solicit feedback on a new magazine, *Almost Teens*. It is important in these introductory remarks that the researcher *not* explain the true

FIGURE 12.8   *Procedures for Non-Smoking PSA Experiment*

1. Prepare materials. Half of the copies of the prototype magazine will include the PSA; half will not have a non-smoking PSA. The two versions of the magazines should be alternated in the stack of materials to be distributed. Self-administered questionnaires will contain the questions to measure the dependent variable. One question will be used as a validity check on the independent variable.
2. Begin experiment by explaining the purpose of study is to solicit feedback on a new magazine, *Almost Teens.*
3. Distribute materials.
    a. The prototype magazine, alternating the two versions of the magazine.
    b. The self-administered questionnaire that measures the dependent variable and includes the following question as a manipulation check:

Describe the contents of the magazine.

_____

_____

Describe something you liked in the magazine.

_____

_____

4. Instruct experimental subjects.
5. Collect materials.
6. Debrief subjects.

purpose of the study. The researcher distributes the materials, which consist of the magazine and questionnaire.

The subjects are told to keep the materials closed until instructed to open them. Once all materials have been distributed, the researcher instructs the subjects to open the magazine, read it, then close it and turn it over. The experimenter should time the length of time it takes to read the magazine. This information will be used for the full-scale experiment. Once everyone has read the magazine, the experimenter asks them to open the questionnaire and answer it. The experimenter should remind the subjects that once a page has been turned in the questionnaire, they cannot return to it.

After all materials have been completed, the experimenter collects them. Finally, the experimenter should debrief the subjects and explain the real purpose of the study. Since this experiment was only conducted for practice, the experimenter may explain the purpose in broad terms until the actual experiment has been conducted.

After the practice or experimental pretest, the researcher evaluates the procedures to decide which, if any, changes need to be incorporated into the real experiment. The researcher evaluates the time required for pretest subjects to read through the magazine. In the actual experiment, the researcher will specify the amount of time subjects are allotted to read the magazine. This time period should be based on a median time period determined during the pretest.

The researcher examines the responses to the questions in the questionnaire, paying special attention to the questions that measured the dependent variable and the manipulation check of the independent variable. The question that asked subjects to describe the contents of the magazine was a manipulation check to determine if the non-smoking PSA was noticed. If the researcher finds that the independent variable, the non-smoking PSA, was noticed, he or she should proceed with the actual experiment. If the results fail to show the independent variable was noticed, the researcher needs to develop new materials to better represent the independent variable.

Once the researcher is satisfied with the pretest procedures and results, he or she conducts the experiment on a new group of middle school children as listed in Step 8 of the research phase in Figure 12.2. At the conclusion of the experiment, the researcher debriefs the subjects, explaining that the magazine was fictional and he or she was really interested in their responses to the non-smoking PSA.

Ethical Standards Guide the Experimental Procedures

Because it is possible to conduct an experiment without the knowledge of the experimental participants and because it is necessary to conceal the purpose of the experiment until the experiment has been conducted, ethical requirements for experiments with human subjects are more stringent than any other research method. In addition to informing participants and securing written permission, the experimental researcher must not deceive, mislead, purposely influence research participants, or cause physical, mental, or emotional harm. At the conclusion of the experiment, the experimental researcher must debrief participants, explaining the true purpose of the study.

The experimental researcher must treat participants with dignity and respect, regardless of race, ethnicity, religion, national origin, age, education, income, or sexual orientation, during the course of conducting the research. As we have discussed before, an ethical researcher promises confidentiality and honors that promise to all participants in the study.

Usually experiments that are conducted by employees of institutions that receive federal funding have to submit their experimental procedures to human subjects review committees for approval. These committees are responsible for reviewing proposals for research that will be conducted on human subjects. They ensure that the experiment will not harm the subjects and the researcher has received informed consent. In our example, the research expert must secure permission from the principal and parents of the middle school children. The research expert prepares a letter that describes the study and requests permission. Permission slips for parents to sign, date, and return to the researcher are also prepared. To avoid influencing the results of the experiment, the study's description should be general.

Processing and Analyzing Experimental Data

In Step 9 of the research phase, the researcher processes the results from the questionnaire that measured the dependent variable in the same manner that the survey questionnaire was processed. A codebook, which specifies variables and columns as well as codes for the open-ended questions, would be developed.

After assigning a unique ID number to each questionnaire and specifying codes to indicate which questionnaire corresponds with the magazine that contained the PSA, the researcher sets up a special coding for the question that measures the dependent variable. According to Figure 12.9, this coding indicates how many cigarettes the middle school children plan to smoke when they grow up.

If a student responded two, the response would be coded as *02* in columns eight and nine. A response of eleven cigarettes would be coded as *11*.

Figure 12.9 *Excerpt from Codebook for Non-Smoking PSA Experiment*

Variables		Columns
V4	4. When you grow up, how many cigarettes do you plan to smoke a day?	8–9

Now the researcher codes the questionnaires on a coding spreadsheet. After the coding is complete, the researcher runs the data using a statistical program such as SPSS, the Statistical Package for the Social Sciences. A frequency printout is used to check that codes are being read in the correct columns and to search for dirty data. Dirty data is cleaned before proceeding with the SPSS analysis.

The relevant analysis for the experiment is a comparison of the responses on the future smoking intention question for subjects who were in the experimental group and those in the control group. Means are calculated and compared for the experimental group that saw the PSA and the control group that didn't see it.

 ## The t-Test

A t-test, a significance test that is often used in two-group comparisons, is used to determine whether or not the mean in the experimental group is significantly different from the mean in the control group. If you use the t-test formula, you can calculate a t-value from the scores of the experimental group and control group. Of course, a statistical package such as SPSS will also calculate a t-value and determine its significance. When the t-value that is calculated from the data from the experiment is compared to the t-value at the appropriate degrees of freedom and significance level in a t-distribution table, you can determine whether the independent variable had an effect on the dependent variable. The t-test formula and a t-distribution table can be found in one of the statistics books recommended at the end of Chapter 8.

Now, how does this apply to our hypothetical experiment? The results of the question asking how many cigarettes the preteens planned to smoke in the future were used to calculate a t-value. Both the experimental group, which saw the "smoking is stupid" PSA, and the control group, which didn't see the PSA, had sixty preteens. The mean number of cigarettes that the experimental group planned to smoke in the future was one. The mean number for the control group was 4.86. The question is: Is the difference between these two means statistically significant?

The t-value calculated was 8.57. This t-value was compared with a t-value in a t-distribution table. The t-value for 118 degrees of freedom, a number based on the number of cases minus 2, in the table was 3.73 at the .001 significance level. Since the t-value of 8.57 is larger than the t-value of 3.73, it can be said that the means for the experimental and control groups are significantly different. In other words, the preteens who were exposed to the "smoking is stupid" PSA planned to smoke significantly *fewer* cigarettes in the future than the preteens who didn't see the PSA.

It is important to emphasize that ethical standards must be used when analyzing the data. The data must accurately represent the data collected even if the results are not statistically significant.

Analysis of Variance

In the hypothetical experiment, we used a t-test, a statistic appropriate for comparing the means from two groups such as an experimental and control group or a sample and population. But often in the research environment, more than two groups are studied and compared. When more than two means are compared, analysis of variance, also known as ANOVA, can be used, and a statistical computer program such as SPSS will do the multivariate analysis.

For example, the multivariate statistic ANOVA was used by communication scholar Melvin DeFleur and his colleagues to compare four groups in an experiment that tried to determine which of four types of news story presentations was most effective in recall (DeFleur et al., 1992). The experiment, which was conducted among college students, compared a newspaper version, television version, radio version, and computer version of the same news story. The independent variable was the version of the news story, and the dependent variable was recall. Analysis of variance was used to analyze between-group and within-group variance to determine if different presentations contributed to significantly different levels of recall among the experimental subjects.

Kerlinger (1973, p. 216) emphasized that analysis of variance is not a statistic but an approach—a way of thinking (Kerlinger, 1973, p. 216). Analysis of variance calculates a ratio of variance between groups and variance within groups. The resulting ratio is called the F-ratio. The F-ratio is compared to an F-ratio that can be found in an F table in a comprehensive statistics text to determine if the results are statistically significant (Kerlinger, 1973, p. 222).

In the experiment that compared four types of news story presentations, the analysis of variance produced a significant F-ratio. The experimental researchers also used t-tests to compare each version of the news story directly with another version. The t-test results showed that the newspaper and computer screen presentations had a significantly higher recall than the same news stories in TV and radio versions. Although recall of the print versions of the news story was significantly different from recall of the broadcast presentations, there was no significant difference between recalling the newspaper and computer versions of the news story.

The Written Report for an Experiment

 The Description of the Method Section Is Unique

Once the researcher has completed the data analysis for the hypothetical experiment on the non-smoking PSA, he or she is ready to draft the written report as listed in Step 10 of the research phase. Many of the issues that were addressed in Chapter 9 are relevant to writing the experimental research report. But there are two major differences: how the research method is described and how the results are reported. Figure 12.10 lists the components of the section of the written report that describes the experimental method.

In the section of the report that describes the experimental method used, the researcher specifies the type of design using descriptive words as well as experimental symbols, X, O, and R. The subjects and how they were recruited and assigned to the experimental and control groups as well as the setting are also described. The independent variable and how it was manipulated in the experiment are discussed along with the procedures for the experiment and measurement of the dependent variable. If a questionnaire was used, relevant questions and response choices should be included in this section. Finally, the procedures for coding, processing, and analyzing the data for the dependent variable are summarized.

The Results Section Emphasizes Differences in Means

The results section of a written report on an experiment also differs from a survey or content analysis because the focus is on whether or not the means of the experimental and control groups differ statistically. For example, the table for the hypothetical experiment would display the means and standard deviation of the experimental and control groups as well as the t-value, degrees of freedom, and significance of the t-test results. This information can be gleaned from the printout once a statistical program such as SPSS is instructed to make the calculation.

FIGURE 12.10 *Components of the Method Section for a Written Report on an Experiment*

1. Description of experimental design, including subjects, setting, and independent and dependent variable measures
2. Description of procedures
3. Description of data processing and analysis

Once the report is complete, the researcher writes an executive summary highlighting the major findings of the experiment and a cover letter to the CEO describing the overall non-smoking PSA experiment. In the cover letter, the public relations professor requests a meeting to discuss the study and its impact. According to Step 11, the last step of the research phase, the research expert sends the cover letter and report to the chairman of the media conglomerate.

Making Decisions during the Post-Research Phase

In the post-research phase of the hypothetical experiment, which is displayed in Figure 12.11, the decision maker (in this case, the chairman and chief executive officer of a media conglomerate) reads the research report and reviews the prototype non-smoking PSA according to Step 1. In Step 2, the chairman invites the public relations professor to his office to discuss the PSA and research results in depth.

In Step 3, the decision maker decides that the experimental results warrant developing a campaign based on the PSA. In Step 4, the deci-

FIGURE 12.11 *Steps in the Post-Research Phase of the Experiment*

Step 1. Read the report, paying careful attention to the experimental procedures, results and recommendations in the research study.

Step 2. Discuss the experimental procedures, results, and recommendations with the research expert to take advantage of the research expert's further insight.

Step 3. Decide whether the results warrant developing a campaign based on the non-smoking PSA or if further information is needed.

Step 4. If a campaign is to be developed, consult with the research expert about developing criteria for measuring the impact of the campaign.

Step 5. Produce and run the PSA in the relevant media.

Step 6. Evaluate the impact of the PSA.

Step 7. Decide the next step.

Step 8. Create a file for this research study that includes the report, relevant documents, correspondence, and an assessment of how effectively the public relations professor answered the initial research question: What type of public service announcement will discourage preteens or teens from smoking cigarettes?

sion maker consults with the research expert about a procedure for evaluating the effectiveness of the PSA.

After producing and running the PSA as described in Step 5, the impact of the PSA would be measured in Step 6. One form of evaluation research could be a survey. For example, a follow-up survey could be conducted to determine the middle school children's awareness of and reactions to the PSA.

The decision maker might also ask the public relations professor to conduct an experiment outside of a laboratory environment. When a field experiment moves into a natural environment, external validity may increase at the expense of the experiment's internal validity. The experimental researcher cannot control many of the variables in a natural environment.

For the field experiment to be successful, one of the more complex issues to be addressed is how to expose the PSA to middle school children. How can the "smoking is stupid" PSA be exposed to the experimental group only? Using radio and TV would not be effective because these media broadcast to the total market, which would expose the control group to the PSA. Newspapers also would not be very effective because this age group usually does not read newspapers.

Perhaps the PSA can be enlarged and produced as a poster that can be hung on the walls of a school. A matching school, which would serve as a control group, would not have the posters. Schools can be matched on variables such as size, socio-economic characteristics, and academic performance. With permissions from the principal and school district, the PSA posters could be hung on the walls of one school for a specified period of time. At the conclusion of the experiment, the children in the experimental school and the matching control group school would be administered a posttest to measure future non-smoking intentions of middle school children.

The field experiment data would be processed and analyzed in the same manner as laboratory experimental data. By calculating and comparing the means, the researcher would be able to determine if the independent variable had an effect on future non-smoking intentions in a natural environment.

Once the non-smoking PSA campaign has run and the evaluation research results are examined, the decision maker decides the next step as listed in Step 7. If the evaluation research suggests that the non-smoking PSA is effective, the decision maker may decide to continue — or even expand — the campaign. Finally, in Step 8 of the post-research phase, a file of the experiment, the campaign, and the research expert's contribution is created.

SUGGESTED RESEARCH ACTIVITIES

1. Review the procedures for the hypothetical experiment using a non-smoking PSA. Working with a classmate, develop an experiment to test the effectiveness of a non-smoking PSA on TV. Describe your experimental design, independent and dependent variables, and procedures.

2. Look through back issues of the communication research journals and find a research study that conducted an experiment. Read the article carefully. Describe the purpose of the experiment, hypothesis, independent and dependent variables, procedures, and results. What statistical procedures were used to analyze the data?

3. Find and read the article, "An Experiment in Austin: Making TV Coverage Fit the Crime: A Texas TV Station Tries to Resist the Allure of Mayhem" by Joe Holley in *Columbia Journalism Review,* May/June 1996, pages 27–32.

   The article reports that the ABC-affiliated TV station in Austin, Texas, implemented new guidelines for reporting crime that changed the way the station covered crime just *before* the February ratings period. These new guidelines were promoted on the air and in the newspaper.

   The new guidelines specified that a crime could be reported on the air only if the reporter could answer in the affirmative to one or more of five questions: (1) Does action need to be taken? (2) Is there an immediate threat to safety? (3) Is there a threat to children? (4) Does the crime have significant community impact? (5) Does the story lend itself to a crime-prevention effort?

   When the ratings were taken again in May, the TV station's ratings were the highest in ten years. What is your opinion of this field experiment and why?

4. Reread the description of Bandura's experiment using nursery school children at the beginning of the chapter. What ethical issues are raised in the study? What specific actions would you have taken to ensure that the experiment was conducted with high ethical standards?

RECOMMENDED READING

For further information on experimental research, see:

DONALD T. CAMPBELL and JULIAN C. STANLEY, *Experimental and Quasi-Experimental Designs for Research.* Chicago: Rand McNally, 1963.

FRED N. KERLINGER, *Foundations of Behavioral Research,* 2nd ed. New York: Holt, Rinehart and Winston, 1973.

BRUCE H. WESTLEY, "The Controlled Experiment," in *Research Methods in Mass Communication,* ed. GUIDO H. STEMPEL III and BRUCE H. WESTLEY, pp. 196–216. Englewood Cliffs, NJ: Prentice-Hall, 1981.

For an example of an experiment, including the independent and dependent variables and the procedures for conducting the experiment, see:

DIXIE LEE SHIPP EVATT, "The Influence of Emotion-Evoking Content of News on Issue Salience," Ph.D. dissertation, The University of Texas at Austin, 1997.

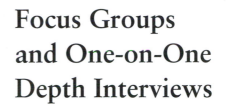

CHAPTER 13

Focus Groups and One-on-One Depth Interviews

- What are focus groups?

- How should focus groups be used?

- What are the steps in conducting focus groups?

- How does focus group data analysis differ from surveys?

- What are one-on-one depth interviews?

- How are one-on-one interviews similar to focus groups?

- What ethical standards are used in conducting focus groups and depth interviews?

Definition and Purpose of a Focus Group

Results of a focus group of twelve voters conducted several months before the 1996 presidential election and several weeks before the Republican and Democratic National Conventions revealed that participants were unable to identify any accomplishments of President Clinton and expressed concern about the age of seventy-three-year-old Senator Bob Dole (Anderson, 1996). This focus group, which was conducted by the nonpartisan Campaign for America and pollster Peter Hart, is an example of a popular method of research that differs significantly from the survey method of asking questions, selecting participants, and analyzing and reporting results.

Unlike a survey, which is a quantitative method of research that relies on numbers, percentages, and statistics for describing results and making inferences about the population, a focus group is a qualitative research method that uses open-ended, follow-up, and probing questions to scratch below the surface of a small group of participants' attitudes, opinions, and behaviors to understand motivations, feelings, and reactions. Focus groups rely on participants' words to provide insight, fill in the texture, capture the nuance, and explain why participants behave and respond the way they do.

A focus group is a small group discussion on a specific topic that is led by a moderator. Eight to twelve people who possess attributes that are relevant to the focus group topic are recruited to respond to the open-ended questions that the moderator asks. Focus group discussions generally last one and a half to two hours, and participants are paid for their time.

When used appropriately, a focus group can be an effective research tool and a useful device for generating new ideas. It can be a helpful first step in developing a survey questionnaire to explore a new topic and an effective approach to following up on specific survey results. This qualitative method can be a beneficial way of soliciting consumer reactions to concepts, campaigns, creative products, and images. Focus groups can be a powerful means of learning *how* consumers talk about issues, candidates, products, commercials, celebrities, news anchors, TV programs, companies—and the reasons why.

Pre-Research Activities of a Focus Group

Even though the purpose of a focus group differs from that of a survey, Figure 13.1 shows that its pre-research phase is similar to that of a survey. In Steps 1 and 2, the ever vigilant decision maker monitors the environment and literature to identify potential problems, trends, opportunities, issues, phenomena, and theories that demand reliable data to better understand what's going on.

As always, the nature of the problem or opportunity to be researched should dictate the research method used. In Step 3, the decision maker should consider whether a focus group will best serve his or her research needs. If the decision maker seeks to generalize the results to the general population, he or she should use a survey and not a focus group. Even though results from a focus group cannot be generalized to the population at large, they do provide a type of data that helps the decision maker understand what's happening in the hearts and minds of consumers.

FIGURE 13.1   *Pre-Research Phase of Focus Group and the Decision Maker*

Step 1. Monitor environment and literature.
Step 2. Identify problem, trend, opportunity, issue, phenomenon, or theory.
Step 3. Decide if a focus group is the most effective method for understanding the problem, trend, opportunity, issue, phenomenon, or theory.
Step 4. Specify focus group topic in research question form.
Step 5. Design focus group study using ethical standards.
Step 6. Decide type of focus group participants to recruit.
Step 7. Establish budget and timetable.
Step 8. Determine who will conduct focus group.

A focus group is invaluable for generating a list of issues or ideas that should be considered for a full-scale survey and for determining how to frame or phrase questions for a survey. Because of the face-to-face interaction with consumers, a focus group provides an opportunity to get verbal and nonverbal reactions to concepts, campaigns, candidates, products, and companies. Even more important, a focus group can provide the language that consumers use to discuss concepts, campaigns, candidates, and products. By using language that consumers use, campaigns to promote products, issues, companies, and candidates will be "in touch" rather than "out of touch."

Examples of research topics that might be specified in Step 4 are: How do voters perceive the candidates for the upcoming presidential election? What are reactions of consumers to World Wide Web addresses that are displayed at the conclusion of commercials? How do young adults feel about the way they are portrayed by the news media and advertising professionals?

Step 5 states that focus groups are designed with ethical standards. It is unethical to select focus group participants because they are already favorable toward the topic that is being researched. Likewise, it is unethical to recruit participants because they hold negative views toward the focus group topic and will express negative opinions. It is also unethical to ask questions that will elicit only desired responses. Finally, it is unethical if, during the focus group, participants are only allowed to express opinions desired by the decision maker.

Ethical standards also specify that participation in focus groups is voluntary and participants will not be harmed. Because focus group participants are usually offered a cash incentive for participation in the group discussion, ethical standards require that participants receive the incentive at the conclusion of the focus group. It would be unethical to lure participants to a focus group with an offer of a cash incentive, then tell them at the end of the discussion that a check will be mailed at a later date.

Just as survey respondents are promised confidentiality, so are focus group participants. The decision maker, moderator, and others associated with the research project must honor this promise.

In Step 6, the decision maker has to determine the type of participants to be recruited for the focus group. Unlike a scientific survey in which respondents are randomly selected from the population of interest, focus group participants are recruited because they possess certain characteristics that are relevant to the focus group topic.

In the first research question example discussed in Step 4, likely voters would be recruited for the focus group, but unregistered voters would not. For the second research question, viewers who have seen Internet addresses displayed at the conclusion of commercials and understand their purpose would be appropriate for the focus group. In the final research question example, young adults in their twenties and early thirties would be recruited to participate in a focus group discussion on how they're portrayed by media and marketing professionals.

The decision maker establishes a budget and timetable in Step 7. The budget includes fees for the research expert, expenses for recruiting and paying focus group participants, costs for renting a focus group facility and recording equipment, and refreshments. (A sample focus group budget can be found in Appendix D.3.)

The timetable that's established in Step 7 doesn't require much time. Because only eight to twelve people who possess the relevant attributes are needed, focus groups can be organized in a week or less. Even so, it's better to allow more time to ensure sufficient opportunity for recruiting focus group participants. Plus, as we'll discuss later, at least two or three focus groups are usually conducted to fully understand the issue that is being studied, which, of course, requires additional time.

The Moderator Is Key to a Successful Focus Group

Step 8 is, perhaps, the most important for the decision maker in the pre-research phase. In this step, the decision maker hires the best experienced focus group research expert to plan and organize the focus groups, develop the discussion guide, moderate the groups, analyze the data, write the report, and present the results. Figure 13.2 (p. 244) lists many of the essential characteristics of an effective focus group moderator.

Unlike the survey research expert who usually has a master's or Ph.D. degree, specific academic credentials are not required for moderating focus groups. In fact, the list of characteristics of a good focus group moderator shows that people skills and confidence are more important than academic achievements. Figure 13.2 also indicates that the focus group moderator does more than moderate the small group discussion. Moderators are also responsible for organizing the focus groups and analyzing and reporting the results.

Focus group moderators must be able to manage the discussion among different personalities, income groups, educational levels, ages, and racial and ethnic groups. Because they can deviate from the prepared discussion guide to add questions during the course of the focus group, moderators must actively listen to the comments of the participants, injecting follow-up questions when appropriate. Moderators who are thoroughly briefed

FIGURE 13.2 *Some Characteristics of a Focus Group Moderator*

1. Experienced in organizing and conducting focus groups and analyzing and reporting focus groups results.
2. Thoroughly briefed on the background of the focus group topic.
3. Confident.
4. Able to establish rapport and control group dynamics with eight to twelve people.
5. Able to establish a relaxed, comfortable environment so people will feel at ease about sharing their opinions and feelings.
6. Able to manage different personalities in a discussion and make sure each person participates.
7. Active listener who can ask appropriate, unscripted follow-up questions.
8. Flexible, quick thinker who is able to respond confidently to unexpected events.
9. Respectful of individual differences, nonjudgmental and objective.
10. Professional and ethical.

on the focus group topic are more prepared to ask relevant follow-up questions.

Moderators are professionals who are guided by ethical standards. They must be respectful of different individuals as well as nonjudgmental and objective while listening to diverse opinions. Moderators must *not* influence the focus group participants' answers in any way.

Research Phase of Focus Group

 ### The Research Expert Consults with the Decision Maker

Figure 13.3 lists the steps of the research phase of the focus group. During the first step, the moderator consults with the decision maker about the research purpose and the details necessary to set up and conduct the focus group.

 ### Number of Focus Groups

Focus group experts agree that two or three focus groups are generally sufficient to explore a research topic. In fact, experts say that little new

FIGURE 13.3 *Research Phase of Focus Group and the Research Expert*

Step 1. Consult with decision maker on:

- Focus group purpose, research question, and background on topic
- Number and size of focus groups
- Moderator's outline and discussion guide
- Waiting room or background questionnaire
- Criteria for focus group participants, recruitment method, cash incentives
- Budget, research timetable, focus group dates
- Recording needs and focus group observers

Emphasize ethical standards during discussion.

Step 2. Conduct in-depth literature review and background search.

Step 3. Reserve focus group facility with adjacent viewing room and equipment; schedule an assistant to greet participants; order refreshments. If focus group is held in a hotel, verify that meeting rooms in close proximity do not have loud activities.

Step 4A. Recruit more focus group participants than needed. Send letter of confirmation.

Step 4B. Draft moderator's outline and discussion guide and waiting room or background questionnaire.

Step 4C. Prepare visual stimuli.

Step 4D. Interview moderators if additional moderators are needed.

Step 5. Consult with decision maker and secure approval of moderator's outline and discussion guide, background questionnaire, visual stimuli, and additional moderators. Discuss handling of cash incentives with decision maker.

Step 6. Several days prior to the focus group, fax a re-minder to the decision maker about the cash incentives.

Step 7A. Forty-eight hours before the focus group, reconfirm participants by telephone. Prepare list of confirmed participants.

Step 7B. Prepare cash incentives, receipts, and 12-inch 3 ×6-inch name cards. Gather fourteen pencils and markers.

Step 8. Arrive at least one hour before focus group to make sure that room, recording equipment, and refreshments are correctly set up. Place a blank name card, marker, and background questionnaire at each seat.

(continued)

FIGURE 13.3 *(continued)*

> **Step 9.** Brief observers on the focus group. Ask decision maker and observers to write down any questions that they think of during the focus group.
>
> **Step 10.** Conduct and record focus group using ethical standards.
>
> **Step 11.** Analyze focus group results using ethical standards.
>
> **Step 12.** Write focus group report and prepare oral presen-tation using ethical standards.
>
> **Step 13.** Share results with decision maker.

information is learned after three focus groups (Greenbaum, 1988, pp. 116–117; Qualitative Research Council, 1985, p. 9). There are exceptions to this two-to-three rule for number of focus groups. When gender, race or ethnic group, age, or even geographic region may vary on the topic, two to three groups of each category should be conducted. For example, in the 1996 presidential election, there was a gender gap in which males and females evaluated the presidential candidates differently. A wise strategy would have been to conduct two to three focus groups among males and the same number among females for a total of four to six. This would have helped one to really understand the issues and concerns that explained the difference between men and women on the candidates.

 Number of Participants

How many should participate in a focus group? The Qualitative Research Council of the Advertising Research Foundation (1985, pp. 8–9) recommends eight to ten participants per focus group to take advantage of group dynamics while maintaining the control that comes with smaller groups. Although some focus group experts prefer twelve participants, the larger size, while doable, slows the pace of the focus group discussion. This can cause participants to lose interest because it takes longer to share their opinions.

During the consultation step with the decision maker, the research expert is also thoroughly briefed on the background of the research topic. The research expert adds to this background information by reviewing trade publications, academic journals, and relevant magazines and newspapers as well as searching the Internet.

A Location Must Be Determined before Recruiting Can Begin

Because the focus group location must be confirmed before participants can be recruited, the research expert needs to rent a facility for a specific date and time. Because two focus groups can be scheduled in one evening, the focus group expert can rent a facility from 4:30 P.M. to 10:30 P.M., allowing time for set up, conducting the focus groups at 6:00 P.M. and 8:00 P.M., then cleaning up and packing materials after the groups have concluded.

Many medium to large cities have professional focus group facilities that can be rented, or the focus group research expert can reserve a hotel meeting room. Professional focus group facilities are set up with one-way mirrors so the decision maker and colleagues can observe the discussion. An observation room can be created in a hotel by installing a video camera in the discussion room and wiring it to a closed-circuit TV in an adjacent room. One hotel meeting room can be used for the discussion and the other for observation. When using a hotel, the research expert must specify that the room should be set up with a conference table and separate refreshment table.

To avoid distracting noises that may intrude on the focus group discussion in a hotel, the research expert should find out what activities are scheduled for adjacent or nearby meeting rooms. If a party or loud motivational meeting is scheduled in the next room, the research expert should consider changing to a quieter location or different hotel.

Whether using a professional focus group facility or a hotel room, the research expert needs to rent video and audio recording equipment and order refreshments. At the minimum, cookies, cold beverages, and coffee and tea should be ordered for the participants. Focus groups that are held during the dinner hour can provide sandwiches for participants to eat.

The research expert must also schedule a focus group assistant to greet and seat participants and to handle paperwork and the payment of cash incentives at the conclusion of the discussion. Having an assistant allows the moderator to concentrate on the discussion.

 Recruiting Focus Group Participants

Unlike survey respondents who are randomly selected, focus group participants are recruited because they possess characteristics that are directly related to the purpose of the study. A focus group on attitudes toward presidential candidates requires registered voters who are likely to vote. For a focus group on attitudes about zip drives, the focus group moderator would recruit computer users who store lots of data on their machines. A focus group to determine receptivity to a new jazz radio station would recruit radio listeners who like jazz. To understand reactions to the V-chip, the focus group moderator would recruit parents of children who are under eighteen. To gauge reactions to a revamping of the business section of the newspaper, the focus group moderator would recruit newspaper readers who read the business page.

Focus group participants can be recruited from a variety of sources. In general, the focus group moderator hires a professional focus group firm to recruit participants based on specific criteria. The research expert should specify if he or she wants the recruitment firm to call numbers randomly from the phone book or a list of plus-one numbers in order to gain access to unlisted numbers. Without this specification, the recruiter may rely on names compiled from intercept surveys at the mall, lists of previous participants, membership lists from various organizations, or mailing lists compiled by companies or nonprofit organizations. It is also possible to recruit focus group participants through newspaper advertisements or postings in high traffic areas. The recruiter may have to use a variety of sources to find participants who meet the specifications of the focus group.

It is important for the recruiter to screen out professional focus group participants, people who frequently participate in focus group discussions. Using lists from previous focus groups increases the chances of recruiting people who often give their opinions in focus group sessions. Caution should also be used when recruiting participants at the mall. To get more of a cross-section of prospective focus group participants, it would be better to recruit from several malls in different parts of town rather than relying on one geographic area.

The professional focus group recruiter would use a questionnaire similar to the one in Figure 13.4 to screen prospective participants and determine if they qualify for the focus group. Notice that the introduction to the recruitment questionnaire specifies that focus group participants will receive a cash incentive. Participants who qualify are then asked to participate in the focus group. For a focus group on reactions of young adults to the term "Generation X," a phrase used to describe the post-baby boomer generation born during the years 1965 through 1978, the key qualifying variable is whether or not the participants are familiar with the term. If the term is unfamiliar, they would not be asked to participate because they would not contribute to a substantive discussion about the term.

Notice that the screener questionnaire also indicates how many to recruit of each group. By setting a quota in advance on age, gender, and media use, the focus group moderator can have a discussion among diverse participants who still meet the criteria. This diversity will aid the discussion on the topic of interest to the decision maker.

FIGURE 13.4   *Recruitment/Screener Questionnaire*

Name and Phone Number Called: _____

　Hello, my name is _____ and I'm calling from PMP Research and Communications, Inc. We're looking for people to participate in a discussion of issues of interest to your age group. The discussion will last one hour and 45 minutes and participants will receive $50 cash for taking the time to come and share in the discussion. I have just a few questions to verify your participation. First of all . . .

(Age: Recruit one-third 21–24, one-third 25–29, one-third 30–34)
1. How old are you? _____ *(Terminate if not between 21–34.)*

(Occupation: Recruit maximum three students.)
2. What is your full-time occupation? _____

(Media Use: Recruit minimum three participants who read a newspaper and watch TV news.)
3. Do you read a daily newspaper at least one day a week?
_____

4. Do you watch television news at least one day a week?
_____

5. Do you have cable? _____

6. Do you pay at least some attention to TV commercials?
_____

7. Have you ever used the Internet to find information? _____

8. Are you familiar with the term "Generation X"? _____
(Terminate if not familiar with term "Generation X.")

(Gender: Recruit half male and half female.)

9. Do not ask but indicate whether person is male or female:
_____

(Recruit 14 for each focus group time.)

The group discussion is being held on Monday, September 30, at the Downtown Hilton. Will you be able to attend at:

　　1. _____ 6:00 P.M.

　　2. _____ 8:00 P.M.

　With introductions and the completion of a little paperwork, the group will last about one hour and 45 minutes. You will be discussing media and issues of interest to 21- to 34-year-olds. Refreshments will be served and you will be compensated $50 for your time and opinions. Since we will be sending you a letter confirming the time, date, and location of the discussion, I will need your name, address, and phone number.

(continued)

FIGURE 13.4   *(continued)*

Name: (CHECK SPELLING!!)_____

Address: _____ Apt No. _____

City _____ Zip Code: _____

Home Phone _____ Work Phone _____

We will also call to remind you about the group discussion. Is it better to call you at work or home?

     1. Work
     2. Home

In general, what is the best time to call?

_____

Thank you very much for agreeing to participate. We look forward to hearing your opinions about media and issues of interest to your age group.

 How Many to Recruit

Notice in the questionnaire that the recruitment expert is to recruit fourteen for a focus group of ten. Always recruit more participants than you need to ensure that you have an adequate number for the focus group discussion. Even though it is unlikely that all fourteen participants will show up for the focus group, the moderator can send the extra participants home after paying them the incentive for their time.

Once the recruitment specialist determines that the person qualifies, he or she asks the person to participate in the focus group. The focus group specialist requests an address from the participants to send a follow-up confirmation letter. If the focus group is being held in a location that is not well known, the recruitment specialist should enclose a map for the participant. A sample confirmation letter is included in Figure 13.5.

Discussion Guide, Background Questionnaire, and Visuals

Moderator's Outline and Discussion Guide

While the recruiting specialist recruits participants, the research expert drafts the moderator's outline and discussion guide that will be used during the focus group. In the sample outline and discussion guide displayed in Figure 13.6 (pp. 252–254), the research expert lists what the partici-

FIGURE 13.5 *Confirmation Letter*

PMP Research and Communications, Inc.
Street Address
City, State, Zip Code
Phone, Fax, E-mail

Date

Sandi Johnson
Street Address
City, State, Zip Code

Dear Sandi:

We would like to thank you very much for agreeing to participate in our upcoming group discussion. This is a special research project in which you will be joining nine other 21- to 34-year-olds discussing a variety of topics of interest to your age group. The discussion will be led by Dr. Paula Poindexter, and the information will be used for research purposes only.

As a reminder, the discussion will be held on Monday, September 30, at 6:00 P.M. and will last about one hour and 45 minutes. It will take place at the Downtown Hilton.

Refreshments will be served, and you will receive $50 cash for taking the time to share your opinions. Please arrive 15 minutes early so the discussion can begin promptly at 6:00 P.M.

IT IS EXTREMELY IMPORTANT THAT YOU ATTEND! Very few people have been asked to participate and any cancellation means we run the risk of not having valid research results. Again, thank you for coming and we'll see you Monday, September 30.

Sincerely,

Alexandra Wilson

Alexandra Wilson
Focus Group Coordinator

pants should do when they arrive, the welcome and ground rules, participant introductions, questions, and the closing and payment of the cash incentives. By including each important segment of the focus group on the outline and discussion guide, the moderator should not forget anything during the hour and forty-five minute session.

FIGURE 13.6   *Sample Focus Group Moderator's Outline and Discussion Guide*

I. Arrival of Participants.

Have participants write first name on name card with black marker, then complete background questionnaire.

II. Welcome, Purpose, and Ground Rules.

Good evening. I'm Paula Poindexter. Thank you for taking time from your busy schedule to share your opinions this evening. You were asked to participate in this evening's discussion because you are between the ages of 21 and 34 and have opinions about issues that are of interest to your age group.

I have a series of questions to ask you about the media and your age group. There are no right or wrong answers to my questions. I'm simply interested in your honest opinions, whether positive or negative. Everything that you say or write will remain confidential and will not be associated with you as an individual.

Let me share a few of the ground rules so that I can make sure I get in all of my questions and hear what each of you thinks.

First, each person's individual opinion is important. It's important for one person to speak at a time so I can hear what each person has to say.

Second, some people naturally talk more than others. It will be my job to make sure that each person gets to comment on each question.

Third, as you can see, we're videotaping and audiotaping our discussion so I'll have a record of your comments to refer to later. Also, some of my colleagues are observing the discussion because they're interested in what you have to say. Please ignore the observers and camera and just talk naturally.

Fourth, feel free to enjoy the cookies and soft drinks while we're talking.

Fifth, I'll save time at the end of our discussion for any questions you have for me.

Finally, before you leave, I'll distribute your incentive of $50.

III. Participant Introductions.

Let's begin by going around the room for introductions. I'd like for you to tell me your name and an activity that you like to do most in your free time.

IV. Questions.

   A. I'd like you to think about any products, services, TV programs, articles, films, or commercials that are trying to reach 21- to 34-year-olds. As I call your name, please name one product, service,

TV program, article, film, or commercial and say why you think it is trying to reach your age group.

B. I'd now like for you to look at a product, a commercial, a weekly section of the newspaper, and a segment of a television program. After you've taken a look, I'd like for you to tell me what age group it appeals to and why. We will take a look and discuss one at a time.

1. Rollerblades™
2. Michael Jordan commercial
3. Entertainment section of the newspaper
4. Segment of *X-Files*

C. I'm going to show you a headline from the newspaper.

Headline:

'Generation X' plugged in and purchasing
Technology—and plenty of it—is rallying point for 'screenagers'

D. What is your reaction when you see the term "Generation X"?

1. Probe to find out how participants *feel* about the term.
2. Probe to find out whether the term makes them feel good, bad, or indifferent.

E. Where did you first learn the term "Generation X"?

F. If you were asked to think of one word that comes to mind when the term "Generation X" is used, what would that one word be? I'd like for you to write that one word on the back of the questionnaire that you filled in when you first arrived. (Allow 10 to 15 seconds for them to write down a word.) Now, let's go around the room so you can tell us what that word is and why that word comes to mind.

G. What other terms have you heard used to describe your age group?

H. What term would you like media and marketing professionals to use when describing your age group and why do you select that term? I'd like for you to write that term on the back of the questionnaire, also. Just draw a line and write the term that you would like for media and marketing professionals to use when describing your age group. Now, let's go around the room, again. Please tell us the term and why you would like for that term to be used to describe your age group.

V. **Additional or follow-up questions not included on the outline.**
Check to see if observers have questions that need to be asked.

(continued)

FIGURE 13.6 *(continued)*

VI. Questions from Participants.

    I'd said at the beginning that I'd leave a few minutes at the end of our discussion in case you had questions for me. Are there any questions?

VII. Closing.

    Thank you very much for your time. Your comments have been very helpful. I'm now going to distribute your $50. Please sign the form that states you received $50 for participating this evening.

    That concludes our evening. Again, thank you for your help.

As listed on the sample discussion guide, when participants arrive, the moderator has them write their first names on blank name cards and complete background questionnaires. Both of these items will already be at the participants' seats. The name cards help make the discussion friendlier and more relaxed because the moderator will be able to call participants by their first names. The background questionnaire, which is sometimes completed while participants wait for the focus group to start, includes some questions that were listed on the screener as well as relevant demographic questions. The background questionnaire is discussed in detail later in the chapter.

In the second section of the discussion guide, a welcome and description of the ground rules are included. In addition to thanking participants for attending the focus group, this section explains how the focus group discussion will proceed and emphasizes the importance of individual, honest opinions. As part of ethical standards in conducting focus groups, participants are notified that the discussion is being observed and taped but that their individual opinions are confidential. Participants are also invited to enjoy refreshments during the discussion.

The participant introductions section is actually an ice-breaker. It's an opportunity for participants to become comfortable speaking among the other participants. This ice-breaker introduction should be fun or at least interesting to get the focus group off to a good start.

Notice that the questions in the outline and discussion guide differ significantly from questions that would be found in a telephone survey questionnaire. Focus groups use open-ended questions that elicit detailed descriptions of actions, feelings, reactions, and opinions. If the focus group questions are written in such a way that the participants would respond "yes" or "no," they need to be revised. But whether written for a focus group discussion guide or a survey, both types of questions must be unbiased and should not attempt to lead participants to a desired response.

It is unethical to write focus group questions that intentionally mislead participants or try to bias their answers. It is also unethical to deliberately write focus group questions that have false information about an individual, organization, or issue in order to influence the opinions, behaviors, or votes of focus group participants.

The outline and discussion guide also includes unaided recall, as in the question:

> I'd like you to think about any products, services, TV programs, articles, films, or commercials that are trying to reach 21- to 34-year-olds. As I call your name, please name one product, service, TV program, article, film, or commercial and say why you think it is trying to reach your age group.

The discussion guide also includes visual stimuli for participants to react to. By showing a pair of Rollerblades, a commercial, a section of the newspaper, and a segment of a TV program, participants can react with their opinions and feelings on the spot. The use of the visual stimuli gives the moderator an opportunity to observe verbal and nonverbal responses.

Often a focus group is used to solicit reactions to different versions of a new commercial, redesigned newspaper layout, or soon-to-be-launched magazine. Regardless of which type of visual stimuli is shown to the focus group, care must also be taken to avoid influencing participants to produce a desired response. It is unethical to show two obviously unacceptable versions of the visual stimuli in order to get participants to respond favorably to the preferred version. All versions of the visual stimuli shown to the focus group participants must have a reasonable chance of being selected as the candidate for the latest TV commercial, redesigned layout, or new magazine.

While the discussion guide contains many questions, the most important question is Question D: What is your reaction when you see the term "Generation X"? This question is asked after participants are shown a newspaper headline that uses the term "Generation X." It is better in a focus group to lead up to the most important question and not spring it at the beginning. A review of the preceding questions shows that the participants have been primed for the Generation X question once it is asked.

Question F asks participants to associate the term "Generation X" with a word and write that word on the back of their background questionnaire. This technique of making participants commit before the discussion helps to eliminate a "me, too" syndrome in which participants may be tempted to say what the person before them said.

Question H uses a similar technique when it asks participants: What term would you like the media and marketing professionals to use when describing your age group? The moderator asks the participants to write their answer on the back of the questionnaire.

Section V of the discussion guide gives the moderator an opportunity to ask questions that were not initially listed on the guide. Ideas for new questions often surface during the discussion, and the moderator should make a note to ask these questions at the end. Although some moderators may be tempted to ask these questions when they come up, the moderator should make sure that all planned questions have been asked first before starting in on unplanned questions. The focus group would be judged a failure if all of the carefully thought out questions were not asked but spur-of-the-moment questions were.

The decision maker may also think of new questions while listening to the comments of the focus group participants. To get any questions to the moderator, either the moderator can plan to go to the observation room to check with the decision maker regarding additional questions or the focus group assistant can bring in written questions from the decision maker. But under no circumstances should the decision maker or other observers enter the focus group discussion room and ask their questions directly. If the observers enter the discussion room, they will interrupt the flow of the discussion and may cause participants to become self-conscious or even intimidated. An intrusion by the observers would change the dynamics of the rapport that the moderator has already established with the participants and negatively affect answers to subsequent questions. Regardless of which method is used to solicit additional questions from the decision maker, the process should only take two or three minutes.

Notice that a section at the end of the moderator's discussion guide has been reserved for participants to ask questions of the moderator. There may be little time for questions, but it at least provides the moderator with an excuse for not answering questions during the course of the discussion. The moderator can always politely say that he or she has reserved a little time at the end for their questions.

Given the chance, participants will likely ask who the client is and how the information will be used. The moderator needs to be prepared either to answer the question or to politely avoid answering the question in detail. Often the decision maker prefers to remain anonymous.

The moderator's outline ends with a closing that includes a thank you and the disbursement of the cash incentives as well as a form for participants to sign that they did indeed receive cash incentives for their participation.

Background Questionnaire

As mentioned earlier, the research expert also drafts a background questionnaire to be used on the arrival of the focus group participants. Notice in Figure 13.7 that many of the questions look like survey questions

FIGURE 13.7   *Sample Background Questionnaire*

Please fill in the blank or circle the number that matches your response.

1. What is your favorite TV network?
   1. NBC
   2. ABC
   3. CBS
   4. FOX
   5. PBS
   6. Other (Please specify.) _____

2. What is your favorite TV program?

   _____

3. Do you have cable?
   1. Yes
   2. No

(If you have cable, please answer question 3a:)

3a. What do you usually watch on cable?

   _____

4. Do you read magazines at least once a month?
   1. Yes
   2. No

(If you read magazines, please answer 4a:)

4a. What is your favorite magazine?

   _____

5. How often do you read a daily newspaper?
   1. Never or seldom
   2. 1 or 2 days a week
   3. 3 or 4 days a week
   4. Nearly every day
   5. Every day

6. How often do you watch TV news?
   1. Never or seldom
   2. 1 or 2 days a week
   3. 3 or 4 days a week
   4. Nearly every day
   5. Every day

(continued)

FIGURE 13.7 *(continued)*

7. What do you usually do when commercials come on during a TV program?

_____

8. Do you have access to the Internet?
  1. Yes
  2. No

(If yes, please answer 8a:)
8a. How many days a week do you access the Internet?
    1. Never or seldom (Skip to Q. 9.)
    2. 1 or 2 days a week
    3. 3 or 4 days a week
    4. Nearly every day
    5. Every day

(If you never or seldom access the Internet, please skip 8b.)
8b. What do you usually do on the Internet?

_____

9. How old are you?

_____

10. What is the highest level of education that you've completed?
  1. Some high school or less
  2. High school graduate
  3. Some college or technical school degree
  4. College graduate
  5. Some graduate or professional school
  6. Masters, M.D., or doctorate

11. What is your full-time occupation?

_____

12. What is your race or ethnic group?
  1. Caucasian or white
  2. African American or black
  3. Hispanic or Latino
  4. Asian American
  5. Other _____

13. Approximately, what is your household income?
  1. Under $20,000
  2. $20–$29,000
  3. $30–$39,000
  4. $40–49,000
  5. $50,000 to $75,000
  6. More than $75,000

14. Are you?
  1. Male
  2. Female

Thank you. Please turn over the questionnaire after you've finished.

because of their closed-ended format. This information will be used to profile the focus group participants when the results are reported.

Preparing Visual Stimuli

Unlike a telephone survey, a focus group provides an optimum opportunity for a show and react experience. The moderator can show prototype products, mock-up magazines, competitors' products, commercials, or entertainment or news programs to participants and observe their reactions. The more realistic the stimuli, the more realistic the response to it. Concepts of products or programs do not elicit the same response as products that can be touched, viewed, or heard.

If video or audio stimuli are being used, they must be professionally recorded. Excerpts must be professionally edited and all recordings must be played using professional level equipment to avoid distracting participants from their natural reactions to the recordings. Stimuli must be prepared as early as possible to avoid producing last minute, poor quality examples. Recordings should be timed so the moderator knows how much time of the focus group discussion will be used. Shorter rather than longer segments keep the focus group discussion moving.

When the Moderator Is Other Than the Research Expert

Sometimes a person other than the research expert who designed the focus group study moderates the discussion. This can happen because multiple focus groups are being conducted with different age groups, genders, or racial or ethnic groups, and the client or research expert thinks it best to match the moderator with the composition of the group. The research expert still oversees the focus group study even though he or she may not conduct all of the focus groups. When this happens, the research expert must find an experienced moderator who fits the criteria discussed in Figure 13.2.

Consulting with the Decision Maker on the Focus Group Progress

In Step 5 of the research phase of the focus group in Figure 13.3, the research expert consults with the decision maker for the purpose of securing approval of the moderator's outline and discussion guide, background questionnaire, visual stimuli, and any additional moderator who must be hired. During this meeting, the research expert and decision maker also discuss the amount of time to allot for each segment of the outline.

During this discussion, the research expert can find out how many observers will watch the focus group so refreshments can be ordered for the observation room. The research expert should also discuss the handling of the cash incentives for the participants and inform the decision maker to expect a fax reminder about the incentives at least two days before the focus groups.

According to Step 7A, forty-eight hours before the focus group, the focus group recruitment specialist should remind and reconfirm participants by telephone. The final list of attendees should be faxed to the moderator so he or she can check in participants when they arrive. The list of participants is only one of several items that must be carried to the focus group. In Step 7B, the moderator should sort the cash incentives into envelopes. The confirmed list of focus group participants can serve as a receipt. The moderator can have participants sign next to their name to verify that they received the money. If the research expert is using a focus group facility, expect pencils, name cards, and markers to be on hand. If the research expert is conducting the focus group in a hotel, he or she will need to take these items to the discussion.

Step 8 of the focus group research phase states that on the day of the focus group, the research expert should arrive at least an hour before the discussion to verify that everything has been set up as requested. When the decision maker and other observers arrive, the research expert will have adequate time to brief them on the final list of participants and provide them with a copy of the discussion guide.

During this briefing, which is listed as Step 9, the research expert should ask the decision maker to write down any additional questions that he or she thinks of during the discussion. Just before the discussion concludes, the moderator can excuse him or herself and dash to the observation room to get the additional questions or the moderator can have the assistant bring in questions.

Conducting the Focus Group

 Starting the Focus Group on Time

In Step 10 of the research phase, the moderator follows the outline and discussion guide, which was discussed earlier, and conducts the focus group using ethical standards. Assuming all participants have arrived, the moderator should shut the discussion room door and start the focus group on time. If the quota has not been reached by the appointed hour, the moderator may want to wait a few minutes but not much longer than that. The focus group assistant should be stationed at the door to turn away latecomers and thank them for coming. The moderator is not obligated to pay a cash incentive to those who arrive too late to participate in the discussion.

But remember that the research expert had asked the focus group recruitment specialist to recruit four more participants than required in case some did not show up. If the extra recruits arrive before the focus group start time and the moderator does not need them, the moderator is obligated to pay the cash incentive even though the person does not participate in the discussion.

Establishing the Right Atmosphere for Producing Objective Results

With name cards and background questionnaires completed, the moderator can start the recording equipment and begin. A warm welcome sets the tone for a relaxed discussion on the research topic. The moderator should make sure that everyone has an opportunity to respond to each question. By calling on individuals by name, the moderator can ensure that everyone talks and pays attention. Sometimes the moderator may move clockwise around the room and sometimes counterclockwise. Varying the start point helps to keep everyone paying attention and involved. Following up questions with probes helps quieter participants talk more. And from time to time, the moderator should remind participants that their individual opinions are important and that there are no right or wrong answers.

It is imperative that the moderator not influence participants' responses to questions in any way. A head nod or smile may give the impression that the moderator likes a response. A frown may signal that the moderator dislikes a response. Whether intended or unintended, nonverbal cues may influence the focus group results as well as breach ethical requirements for conducting focus groups. The moderator should simply listen attentively to each participant, make notes for follow-up questions, and pay attention to the clock so that he or she will not run out of time before all questions have been asked.

If back-to-back focus groups have been scheduled, the moderator will have to conclude the first focus group on time, reset the room, and refresh the food and beverages before ushering in the next focus group. In addition, the moderator will need to check in with the decision maker and observers.

Analyzing Focus Group Data

Once all focus groups have been completed, the moderator is ready to review and synthesize the results and prepare to write the focus group report. Analysis of focus group data varies significantly from analysis of survey data. Within days of the completion of the focus groups, the research expert should review the videotapes and take notes on general themes and verbatim quotes. By using the discussion guide as an outline, the research expert will be able to easily pick out the more important findings.

Some research experts prefer to have the tapes transcribed, then analyze the transcripts. Not only does transcribing add to the cost of conducting focus groups, but analyzing transcripts is not a good substitute for viewing the videotapes. The tapes capture one of the main benefits of conducting focus groups. They reflect the texture, the tone, the nuances, the mood, the hearts and minds of real people and how they feel and talk about the products, services, issues, ideas, and images of concern to the decision maker. Videotapes — not typed transcripts — capture the participants' enthusiasm or lack thereof. The research expert is better able to accurately analyze all facets of the data by reviewing the videotapes and not simply relying on cold, typed transcripts of what was said.

The background questionnaires provide information that can be used to profile the participants. Even though focus group results cannot be generalized to the population, it is important to summarize the age, gender, racial or ethnic group, and education composition of the groups. Other relevant data such as media use should also be included in the summary. This summary profile of the participants helps place the results in perspective.

It is imperative that ethical standards guide the analysis of the focus group results. Because focus groups are qualitative, it would be easy to ignore or dismiss comments that do not fit with any preconceived expectations of the results. Ethical standards require that the analysis and interpretation of the results accurately reflect what the focus group participants said and *not* what the decision maker wanted to hear.

Writing the Focus Group Research Report

The major components of a focus group research report, which are listed in Figure 13.8, are essentially the same as the survey research report

FIGURE 13.8   *Components of a Focus Group Report*

1. Cover Letter
2. Report Binder
3. Title and Author Page
4. Table of Contents
5. Executive Summary
6. Introduction
7. Background/Context
8. Description of Method
9. Results
10. Discussion, Limitations, and Recommendations
11. Conclusions
12. Endnotes
13. References
14. Appendix

components discussed in Chapter 9. The major differences include how the research method is described, how the results are reported, and how the limitations of focus groups are discussed.

 ## Description of the Focus Group Method

In the section of the written report that describes the focus group method, the research expert should explain how participants were recruited (including the list or source used for recruitment), the criteria used for selecting participants, and any incentives offered for participation. This section should also briefly describe the moderator who conducted the focus groups, indicate the number of focus groups conducted, and name the place, date, and time of the discussions.

 ## The Results Section Begins with a Profile of Participants

The results section should begin with a profile of the focus group participants so the decision maker will have a sense of whose opinions and reactions are represented. This profile provides greater insight than the criteria used for recruiting participants. For example, knowing that voters were recruited to participate in focus groups on attitudes about the importance of character and issues in a presidential election is insufficient in interpreting the results. A profile of the participants should include which political parties or voter tendencies (conservative, moderate, or liberal) and age groups were represented and in what proportions. And certainly when interpreting focus group results, it would be helpful to know the sources of information relied on for information about the candidates.

The Results Section Shuns Numbers

Unlike the results section of a survey research report, which uses numbers, percentages, and statistics, focus group results avoid these mathematical tools. Also, unlike survey reports, tables and charts are used sparingly. With such small samples, it would be incorrect to say "seventy percent of ten said. . . ." But it would be appropriate to say "all or most or some or none said. . . ." By including verbatim quotes and how they were delivered during the discussion, the research expert can write the results section with a qualitative richness that cannot be found in the numbers of quantitative research.

Although a well-written focus group report captures the unique insight that focus groups can provide, it must be emphasized again that ethical standards require that the report accurately reflect the opinions and observations of the focus group participants, even if the comments fail to support the reasons the research was undertaken in the first place. Figure 13.9 shows how the results of two focus groups of young adults could be reported in the results section of a focus group report. These focus groups were conducted with public relations and advertising students to illustrate the process of this qualitative method. Students were selected based on their awareness of the term, "Generation X."

Discussion, Limitations, and Recommendations in the Report

The discussion section of the report suggests an interpretation of the results and puts the results in the context of information that is already known about the topic. The interpretation is tentative because of the limitations of this qualitative research method. The research expert must address these limitations. Because of their very small samples and non-random selection techniques, focus groups cannot be generalized to the population at large. Focus groups simply provide insight into the attitudes, feelings, and motivations of participants and suggest hypotheses and research questions.

Even though focus group results cannot be projected to the population, the research expert can make recommendations based on emerging themes. The most obvious recommendation would be to conduct a larger

FIGURE 13.9   *An Excerpt from the Results Section of a Focus Group Report*

Twenty young adults in two separate focus groups were shown the newspaper headline, "'Generation X' plugged in and purchasing," then asked their reaction to the term "Generation X." Most of the participants disliked this term that has been used to describe the generation born after the baby boomers during the years 1965 through 1978. The majority of participants preferred for their generation to be described in positive terms. They suggested such positive terms as future, independent, hopeful, diverse, visionary, and innovative.

quantitative study to determine the general awareness of and reaction to the term "Generation X." If the term is offensive or at least bothersome to this age group, then advertisers, marketers, public relations professionals, journalists, media managers and executives, political campaign managers, and politicians should rethink whether it's good business or good journalism to use the term at all. Why turn off those markets or publics, or viewers, or readers, or listeners, or voters whom you're trying to attract by using inappropriate or insensitive terminology?

The finished focus group report, which includes an executive summary, table of contents, and an appendix with the recruitment/screening questionnaire, moderator's outline and discussion guide, and background questionnaire, is bound and delivered to the decision maker. As discussed in Chapter 9, the accompanying cover letter informs the decision maker that he or she will be contacted to set up an appointment to discuss the results and the details of the oral presentation. The research expert should also attach an invoice.

Oral Presentation for Focus Group Results

The major difference between the oral presentation for a focus group and that for the survey discussed in Chapter 9 is that the focus group oral presentation can use excerpts from the focus group videotape to illustrate the presentation's themes. The research expert should pick the excerpts carefully — fewer and shorter excerpts keep the presentation moving along.

Excerpts used in the oral presentation must be professionally edited with five seconds of black leader tape at the beginning and clean visual and audio cuts. The research expert should allow at least a couple of days to guarantee professional editing. Before the presentation, cue up all video excerpts and note the verbal out-cue. Being prepared to start and stop the video excerpt enhances the professional quality of the oral presentation.

A review of the oral presentation checklist in Chapter 9 will help in preparing for the presentation. Rehearsing the starting and stopping of the VCR to show the excerpts will ensure that the presentation will run smoothly.

Activities during the Post-Research Phase of the Focus Group

Once the decision maker receives the research report, the post-research phase of the research process begins. Figure 13.10 lists the steps of the post-research phase of the focus group. Notice that most of the steps are similar to those of the post-research phase of the survey, content analysis, and experiment.

The major difference in the focus group post-research phase is Step 5, which emphasizes caution in using focus group data for decision making because of the limitations of the results. The decision maker must be

FIGURE 13.10   *Post-Research Phase of Focus Group and the Decision Maker*

Step 1. Read the report, paying careful attention to the results and recommendations in the research study.

Step 2. If applicable, process the check for the research expert and send it with a cover letter thanking him or her for research services. Personalize the cover letter by including one or two items that were especially valuable during the research process.

Step 3. Evaluate the results and recommendations looking for trends, confirmations of previous information, inconsistencies, surprises, possible opportunities, potential problems, and completely new information.

Step 4. Discuss your evaluations with the research expert to take advantage of the research expert's further insight.

Step 5. Use caution when deciding which data can be used for decision making and which data need further research such as a survey.

Step 6. Decide the next step.

Step 7. Create a file for this research study that includes the report, relevant documents, correspondence, and an assessment of how well the research expert satisfied your research needs.

careful about making major changes or launching or terminating projects or products based on focus group results only.

The decision maker must recognize that focus groups are more like a Geiger counter that picks up a signal about something that may be going on in the marketplace or among members of the audience or certain publics. If there is a faint signal, the decision maker has a responsibility to follow it by using research techniques that have greater validity and reliability and are more representative of the population of interest. Data from more reliable research techniques will give the decision maker information that can be trusted when making important decisions that will affect consumers, the audience, or publics.

For example, if the decision maker learns through focus groups that the young adult age group dislikes the label Generation X, the next step for the decision maker might be to conduct a full-scale survey to determine if this attitude is universal or simply a reflection of participants in the focus groups. If the decision in Step 6 is to conduct a survey to examine the attitudes of the young adult population toward the label Generation X, the decision maker would start the research process again, beginning with the pre-research phase of the survey.

In fact, based on the results of these focus groups, a survey was conducted to determine if widespread dissatisfaction with the Generation X label could be found. The survey results showed that among young adults, the label was considered negative (Poindexter & Lasorsa, 1999).

As the decision maker completes the post-research phase for the focus group, he or she would create a file as listed in Step 7. The decision maker and the research expert would use this file for subsequent studies on this topic.

The focus group is a useful research tool for understanding how consumers think about and talk about news, advertising, television programs, films, online services, the World Wide Web, issues, products, political candidates, elected officials, and other topics. Sometimes, however, it is impractical to bring together a group of people for a focus group discussion. An alternative to the focus group is a one-on-one depth interview.

One-on-One Depth Interviews

 ### When One-on-One Interviews Are More Effective Than Focus Groups

One-on-one depth interviews are similar to focus groups except they are individual rather than group interviews. Typically, one-on-one interviews are conducted with individuals who have access to information that average people do not have or who, because of their positions, can influence others, be receptive to novel ideas, or act as obstacles to change. One-on-one interviews are often conducted with individuals who have unique backgrounds or experiences that make them research worthy. These individuals may be opinion leaders, executives, newsmakers, university administrators, civic leaders, professional athletes, publishers, elected officials, or some other variation of decision maker.

Often, one-on-one depth interviews are conducted because it is impractical, unrealistic, or too expensive to bring opinion leaders or decision makers together as a group. Opinion leaders may be scattered across the country, or even if they reside in the same city, their hectic schedules may be impossible to coordinate. Consequently the interviewer goes to them. Ideally the interview is conducted in person, but sometimes it is conducted on the telephone. One-on-one interviews can also be conducted *within* the same organization to gauge support for or resistance to change in organizational structure; change in policies or services; the start-up of a new product, project, or program; or the modification or discontinuation of an old product, project, or program.

As an example of a situation in which one-on-one depth interviews would be conducted, let's say that a newspaper has been publishing a weekly stand-alone technology section and after three years, the section is still losing money. The executive vice president of marketing might commission one-on-one interviews with decision makers in technology companies to find out their opinions of the technology section and their future advertising intentions. Also, the publisher of the newspaper might direct a senior aide to conduct *internal* one-on-one interviews with heads of departments, including editorial, display advertising, classified advertising, circulation, production, and research and planning, to assess the advantages and disadvantages of continuing the stand-alone technology section. The results of the one-on-one interviews would be used in the decision to continue or abandon the newspaper's technology section.

 ### One-on-One Interviews Require Less Preparation Time

The pre-research and post-research phases of the one-on-one depth interview are the same as the focus group, but there are some differences in the *research* phase of the depth interview. Notice in Figure 13.11 that depth interviews require less preparation because you don't have to recruit and confirm participants, reserve a facility, order refresh-

FIGURE 13.11   *Steps of Research Phase of One-on-One Depth Interview*

Step 1. Consult with decision maker on:

- Purpose of one-on-one interviews
- Research question
- Background on topic
- Number of interviews to be conducted
- Criteria for selecting people to be interviewed
- Questions to be asked.

Use ethical standards when designing one-on-one depth interview study.

Step 2. Conduct in-depth literature review and background search.

Step 3. Schedule interviews with two to three dozen people and follow up with confirmation letters.

Step 4. Draft questions and prepare any visuals that may be used during the interview.

Step 5. Consult with decision maker and secure approval of questions.

Step 6. Conduct and record interviews using ethical standards.

Step 7. Analyze results using ethical standards.

Step 8. Write one-on-one depth interview report and prepare oral presentation using ethical standards.

Step 9. Share results with decision maker.

ments, or secure cash incentives that are paid to focus group participants. But scheduling appointments with busy people and actually conducting two to three dozen individual hour-long interviews can be very involved.

When the research expert meets with the decision maker as shown in Step 1, he or she will learn the compelling reasons for conducting one-on-one depth interviews rather than focus groups. One-on-one interviews are most beneficial as a research tool when the topic being explored involves change, novelty, or uniqueness and the people being interviewed play influential or unique roles. If the decision maker is simply interested in opinions about the topic, a focus group of ten might be better.

To decide when one-on-one interviews are more appropriate than focus groups, let's use an example. Suppose that after the impeachment trial of President Clinton, print and broadcast news media executives from around the country jointly commissioned an independent study to assess news media coverage of the White House sex scandal and impeachment of President Clinton. If one aspect of that study focused on evaluating the media coverage from the points of view of those who prosecuted or defended the President, the appropriate research method would be one-on-one interviews. The research expert would conduct one-on-one interviews with the House Managers who served as prosecutors and the White House and private attorneys who served as President Clinton's defense attorneys. Clearly the prosecutors and defense attorneys would have unique perspectives from which to evaluate news coverage. If another aspect of this evaluation of news coverage explored public opinion in a qualitative way, focus groups of people who had paid attention to news coverage of the scandal and impeachment would be the appropriate research method.

In Step 2, the research expert reviews the literature and searches background information in an attempt to find and synthesize information that is already available on the one-on-one depth interview topic.

According to Step 3, two to three dozen people who fit the requirements for the study should be scheduled for interviews. For one-on-one depth interviews conducted within an organization, telephone scheduling may be sufficient; for interviews with opinion leaders from different organizations, an introductory letter with a follow-up phone call may be required to schedule appointments.

In Steps 4 and 5, the research expert drafts relevant open-ended questions and discusses them with the decision maker. When the interviews are conducted in Step 6, the interviewer should listen attentively and be prepared to follow up with probing questions. If the interviewee grants permission, the research expert may record the interview on audio tape. If the research expert finds that the tape recorder is inhibiting, however, he or she should turn it off and simply take notes.

As listed in Step 7, one-on-one interview data are analyzed in the same manner as focus group results. Because of the qualitative nature of this data, numbers, percentages, and statistics are avoided and the research expert discusses the results in terms of general impressions and themes. The research phase of the one-on-one depth interview concludes in the same mode as the focus group research phase. According to Steps 8 and 9, the research expert writes a report and makes a presentation, including the same components that were used for the focus group report.

A review of the steps listed in Figure 13.11 reveals that ethical standards are an essential part of a one-on-one depth interview study. Such interviews must be designed and conducted using ethical standards, and ethical standards must be the foundation of the analysis and reporting of the interview results.

Both one-on-one interviews and focus groups are qualitative research methods that provide texture and context that can't be gleaned from surveys. Ideally, focus groups of regular consumers, viewers, readers, publics, and voters are used concurrently with one-on-one depth interviews of opinion leaders to produce a more revealing picture of what's going on. By starting with qualitative results from focus groups and one-on-one depth interviews, then following up with a survey to project to the population of interest, the decision maker will have solid evidence to support any decisions that may be made.

SUGGESTED RESEARCH ACTIVITIES

1. You have been asked to conduct a focus group study on volunteerism as part of a national initiative to encourage people to volunteer. The data that you gather will be used in planning a campaign on volunteerism. Decide what group you will target for the focus group, then do the following:

A. Develop a screening/recruitment questionnaire.

B. Develop a moderator's outline and discussion guide.

C. Develop a background questionnaire.

D. Describe the kinds of visual stimuli that you could use in the focus group.

2. You have been commissioned to conduct a one-on-one depth interview study on the impact of the Internet on your field during the twenty-first century. Who would you interview and why? What questions would you ask?

RECOMMENDED READING

For more perspectives and examples of focus group studies, see:

ADVERTISING RESEARCH FOUNDATION, *Qualitative Research Council. Focus Groups: Issues and Approaches.* New York: Advertising Research Foundation, 1985.

RUTH CLARK, *Changing Needs of Changing Readers: A Qualitative Study of the New Social Contract between Newspaper Editors and Readers.* Yankelovich, Skelly & White, May 1979. (Commissioned by The American Society of Newspaper Editors as a part of The Newspaper Readership Project).

ROBERT FERGUSON, "Focus Groups May Provide Unfocused Marketing Direction: Too Many Marketers Use Them as Cure-All," *Advertising Age,* June 12, 1995.

THOMAS L. GREENBAUM, *The Practical Handbook and Guide to Focus Group Research.* Lexington, MA: D.C. Heath, 1988.

ELIZABETH KOLBERT, "Test-Marketing a President: How Focus Groups Pervade Campaign

Politics," *The New York Times Magazine,* 18+, August 30, 1992.

WARREN MITOFSKY, "Focus Groups: Uses, Abuses, and Misuses," *The Harvard International Journal of Press/Politics,* 1996, vol. 1, no. 2, pp. 111–115.

For an example of one-on-one depth interviews with ordinary citizens, see:

DORIS GRABER, *Processing the News,* 2nd ed. New York: Longman, 1988.

CHAPTER 14

More Research Methods

- What other research methods are used in the communication field?

- What similarities, if any, do these other research methods have with surveys, content analyses, experiments, and focus groups?

- When is it appropriate to use these other methods?

Overview of Other Quantitative and Qualitative Research Methods

Our earlier focus on surveys, content analyses, experiments, focus groups, and one-on-one depth interviews does not mean that there aren't many other research methods that communication professionals and academics use. Some of them such as intercepts and exit polls use many of the same principles as surveys; others that we'll touch on in this chapter such as unobtrusive observation and case studies are completely different. Figure 14.1 shows the range of other research methods used in the field of communication.

FIGURE 14.1 *Some Other Research Methods Used in the Communication Field*

Intercept Surveys

High-Tech Surveys

Tracking Studies

Exit Polls

Secondary Data Analysis

Syndicated Research

Copy Testing and Other Testing Methods

Perceptual Mapping

Evaluation Research

Unobtrusive Observation

Case Studies

Ethnography and Other Academic Qualitative Methods

Multiple Methods

Intercept Surveys

The intercept survey, which is popular among marketing researchers, has come to replace the face-to-face or door-to-door scientific survey even though it lacks the scientific method of random sampling. Although intercept surveys are often conducted in a mall, they can also be conducted in front of grocery stores, movie theaters, or any high-traffic area that is relevant to the purpose of the survey. A respondent is stopped, informed that a brief survey is being conducted, and asked for his or her participation. Often the interview is conducted immediately on the spot as soon as the respondent grants permission, but sometimes the intercept interviewer asks the respondent to follow him or her to a nearby permanent research facility to complete the questionnaire. In these cases, the interviewer may have visuals to show or a new product to taste or test.

The process of conducting intercept and telephone surveys during the pre- and post-research phases of the research process is the same, but several differences are apparent in the research phase. Figure 14.2 (p. 276) highlights the distinct differences between these two methods of surveying in bold italicized lettering.

Steps 1 and 2 show that telephone surveys and intercepts both require consultation with the decision maker and a literature review and background search. In addition to discussing the purpose, questionnaire, and sample during the initial consultation, the research expert also discusses any visual stimuli that may be shown to respondents when they are intercepted. In Step 3A, a questionnaire is drafted for both a telephone and an intercept survey, and both types of questionnaires promise confidentiality. Whereas a telephone survey might last up to twenty minutes, an intercept questionnaire should be very short, lasting only a few minutes. If you're stopping people in the mall or in front of a movie theater, remember that they will have very little time, if any, to give to you. Keeping the questionnaire as brief as possible may increase the percentage of respondents who agree to participate.

An example of an intercept questionnaire that focused on older mall walkers can be found in Appendix A.3. This questionnaire used twenty-three questions to find out why mall walkers exercised in the mall. After interviewing thirty-nine senior citizens who mall walked, the researcher found that the main reasons for mall walking were: safety, convenience, and lack of interference by weather (Taylor, 1995). This questionnaire, which took only a few minutes to conduct, was written to make it easy for the interviewer to walk along side the mall walkers while asking questions and recording answers. If the intercept questionnaire *must* be

FIGURE 14.2 *A Comparison of Telephone Survey and Intercept Steps during the Research Phase*

	Steps	Survey	Intercept
Step 1.	Consult with decision maker.	Yes	Yes
Step 2.	Conduct literature review and background search.	Yes	Yes
Step 3A.	Draft questionnaire using ethical standards.	Yes	Yes
	Prepare visual stimuli.	*No*	*Yes*
Step 3B.	***Identify most current sampling frame and draw random sample.***	***Yes***	***No***
Step 3C.	***Identify locations for intercepts, secure permissions, develop intercepting strategy.***	***No***	***Yes***
Step 3D.	Recruit and hire interviewers.	Yes	Yes
Step 4.	Consult with decision maker on pretest questionnaire.	Yes	Yes
	Consult with decision maker on visuals.	***No***	***Yes***
Step 5.	Pretest questionnaire and revise.	Yes	Yes
	Pretest visual stimuli and revise.	*No*	*Yes*
Step 6.	Secure final approvals from decision maker.	Yes	Yes
Step 7.	Duplicate questionnaires, etc.	Yes	Yes
Step 8.	***Train interviewers for telephone interviewing.***	***Yes***	***No***
	Train interviewers for intercept interviewing and discuss appropriate dress.	***No***	***Yes***
Step 9.	Conduct interviews. Supervise fieldwork.	Yes	Yes
Step 10.	Code and process data.	Yes	Yes
Step 11.	Analyze data using appropriate statistics.	Yes	Yes
Step 11A.	***Generalize results to the population within sampling error.***	***Yes***	***No***
Step 12.	Write report and prepare oral presentation.	Yes	Yes
Step 13.	Share results with decision maker.	Yes	Yes

longer than a few minutes, monetary incentives should be offered to increase respondent participation.

Because an intercept survey, unlike a telephone survey, offers an opportunity to show a respondent some type of visual, whether a print ad, commercial, product, or brochure, you need to prepare the materials and incorporate the relevant questions into the questionnaire. The visual stimuli preparation is listed as part of Step 3A.

As discussed in Chapter 5, the scientific survey interviews respondents who have been randomly selected from the most current sampling frame to guarantee that the results will be representative of the population under study. An intercept, though, does not use random sampling. The interviewer simply stops and attempts to interview consumers who are in a mall or entering or exiting a supermarket.

Securing Permission to Conduct Intercept

Any time that intercept interviews are conducted at the mall or in front of a supermarket or movie theater, the research expert must secure permission from the owners or managers to conduct interviews on their property. According to Step 3C, permission must be secured well in advance of the planned fieldwork to make sure that the intercept interviewing can be done. If permission is not granted, the research expert will have time to seek permission to conduct interviews at another location before the interviewing is scheduled to begin.

Intercepting Strategy

Even though the intercept lacks the scientific validity of a random sample, intercept interviewers should still strive to vary the participants to be intercepted as much as possible. Days of the week, times of the day, entrances and exits, and even locations where respondents are intercepted can be varied to try to get as much of a cross-section of consumers as possible, given the non-random sampling procedures.

Developing strategy for interviewers to follow is included in Step 3C. In addition to varying days, times, and locations, this intercepting strategy should specify that every third, tenth, etc. person during the hour is intercepted. Using this strategy, the interviewer will not be able to avoid certain types of people to interview. The interviewer should intercept respondents regardless of their age, gender, race, or ethnic group, or even how they are dressed or whether or not they look friendly or approachable. Unfriendly looking people should also have a chance to be intercepted and interviewed for the study.

According to Step 4 in Figure 14.2, the visual stimuli that have been prepared for pretesting must be shown to the decision maker prior to pretesting, and in Step 5, the visuals are actually pretested with a small sample of respondents. Once the pretests and revisions of the visuals as well as the intercept questionnaire have been completed and the decision maker's approvals have been secured, the research expert must train the interviewers. The intercept survey training session is similar to the telephone interviewing training session that was discussed in Chapter 6. In both types of training sessions, the purpose of the study, the record-keeping procedures, and the interviewer's protocol are reviewed. In addition to demonstrating and practicing the questionnaire, the importance of promising and honoring confidentiality is emphasized. But Step 8 indicates that there are a few noteworthy differences between training interviewers for an intercept survey as compared to a telephone survey.

 Training the Intercept Interviewer

Unlike the telephone survey interviewer, the intercept interviewer does not have to worry about phone numbers or callbacks. The interviewer, though, must keep a record of respondents who refuse to participate. A high refusal rate is one of the disadvantages of the intercept survey because people are often busy and don't have time to stop to answer questions. By keeping a record of the number of refusals, the research expert can monitor the quality of the intercept sample as well as the work of the interviewer. A high refusal rate could really mean that the intercept interviewer is ineffective, and the research expert should consider replacing that person.

The interviewer should fasten the questionnaire to a clip board to facilitate recording responses. Appropriate dress is a relevant issue for the intercept interviewer because he or she, unlike a telephone interviewer, is having face-to-face contact with a prospective respondent. A professional, clean, and groomed interviewer is ideal when interacting with the public. Inappropriate dress and lack of grooming should not be the reasons that a prospective respondent refuses to be interviewed.

How the interviewer approaches the respondent is also important in intercept interviewing. It is important for the interviewer to be pleasant, polite, and professional when asking for the intercepted person to participate in the interview. A too aggressive, rude, and unprofessional interviewer will cause respondents to hurry away. And every time a respondent refuses to participate in the intercept survey, the results become less representative of those who passed by the interviewer in the mall.

Processing, Analyzing, and Reporting Intercept Data

The data in an intercept study are processed, analyzed, and reported using the same procedures for a telephone survey that were discussed in

Chapters 7 and 8. The primary difference, according to Step 11A in Figure 14.2, is that the research expert is prevented from generalizing the intercept survey results to the population or even to all people who visit the mall during the week. Without random sampling, the research expert cannot project the results within a certain sampling error. This limitation plus the high refusal rate diminish the intercept survey's scientific value. But with the opportunity to intercept 100 or more respondents and show them visual stimuli to respond to, the research expert could certainly gain more data than would be available in a focus group of ten. By comparing the intercept sample with census data, the research expert will have a sense of how well the sample matches with or deviates from the real population.

High-Tech Surveys

 Issues That Affect Validity

It was inevitable that the development of the microprocessor, the revolution in and accelerated adoption of personal computers, and consumer acceptance of electronic mail, fax machines, and the Internet and World Wide Web would converge to one day revolutionize how scientific surveys are conducted. A closer look at these surveys with high-tech names shows that they are perhaps closest to the traditional mail survey that the respondent self-administers. For these high-tech surveys, the pre- and post-research phases remain the same, and the rules for writing valid questionnaires have not changed. The major differences are the availability and quality of a sampling frame or list, the way in which respondents are selected, and the response rate. These three issues affect the validity of the survey results and the ability to generalize to the population of interest.

Just like the telephone survey, high-tech surveys must have access to or compile an up-to-date, comprehensive list of potential respondents. For an organization that uses electronic mail to communicate routine announcements, memos, comments, and questions and answers such as the editorial department of the *Los Angeles Times,* access to a current list of electronic mail addresses is easy because the organization updates a directory at least annually. An online service such as America Online would certainly compile a directory of its current subscribers. There are even professional firms that compile and sell e-mail addresses for marketing research. Fax numbers can also be found in organizational or professional directories because they are compiled as routinely as mail addresses and phone numbers.

Any of these sources may serve as a sampling frame from which to select a random sample, but the research expert must be sensitive to their limitations. Just because a respondent has an e-mail address does not mean the respondent checks his or her e-mail. Also, because a cost is often associated with returning a fax survey, the respondent may be less likely to return it. Recall that, in a mail survey, the research expert encloses a return self-addressed, stamped envelope and there is no cost to the respondent. All of these issues may reduce the response rate, which negatively affects the validity of the survey results.

You have probably already noticed that it is not unusual to dial into an online service such as America Online or surf the Net, drop in on a Web site, and find a questionnaire waiting to be answered. Although these online and Internet surveys provide some information about those who are stopping by, the validity of the results is limited. The respondents are self-selected, not randomly selected. Their responses cannot be generalized to the whole population of Web site visitors.

For disk-by-mail surveys, which actually send the questionnaire on disk and ask the respondent to complete and return the questionnaire on disk, the research expert is confronted with the issue of a current and comprehensive sampling frame as well as a format issue. Should the questionnaire be formatted on a PC or Mac disk? Currently, Mac computers can read PC disks, but Mac formatted disks must be converted to be read by a PC computer. Does the respondent really want to be bothered with all of this extra effort? Such issues can certainly suppress the response rate.

 ## Recommendations for High-Tech Surveys

With computer, fax, e-mail, and Internet use increasing, e-mail, fax, online, and Internet surveys are here to stay. The following recommendations may help you to better use these methods:

1. Don't get carried away by the high-tech bells and whistles if the results will be useless. In other words, if a more traditional survey method such as telephone or mail will produce more valid results, go with the traditional.
2. Keep the questionnaire short and simple enough to encourage participation.
3. Build in follow-up reminders and incentives like those used for mail surveys to encourage higher response rates.
4. Try to avoid surveys in which participants are self-selected because these surveys will not be representative of the population of interest.
5. If self-selected surveys are the only possible vehicle for reaching users on the Internet, interpret the results conservatively.

6. Experiment with these high-tech surveys and read the current literature. When the market and method become viable for surveying, you will be prepared to conduct a survey that produces valid results.

Surveys That Monitor Consumers and Voters

 ## Tracking Studies

Tracking studies use the survey method to monitor the behavior of consumers, readers, viewers, listeners, or voters over a period of time. Newspapers conduct surveys to monitor which features are being read in the newspaper. Advertisers conduct surveys to track perceptions toward products, advertising, and the competition. Political campaign strategists conduct polls to monitor voter reactions to candidates and issues. News organizations poll voters to determine their likes and dislikes as well as preferred candidates and most important issues.

For tracking polls to be able to detect changes in behavior, opinions, or attitudes of readers, viewers, listeners, consumers, and voters, the research expert must use the *same* sampling frame and method of selecting respondents as well as the same phrasing of questions from survey to survey. If there is any change in the methodology, the research expert or decision maker cannot attribute any change in the results to the respondents. In these cases, change is likely due to the new methodology or questions.

As discussed in Chapter 2, if the research expert tracks the *same* respondent, this longitudinal study is considered a panel. If *different* consumers are surveyed for these tracking studies, the study is called a trend study. These tracking studies can be conducted monthly, semi-annually, annually, or even every day as they are during presidential elections.

Exit Polls

Exit polls are another type of scientific survey. These face-to-face surveys follow most of the steps in the pre-research, research, and post-research phases except for the sampling procedures, which involve sampling voter precincts, and intercepting voters as they leave the voting booths. Exit polls are usually conducted by news organizations to predict the election outcome and learn more about the voters' profiles, preferences, and the reasons they voted as they did.

Around 1990, the major broadcast and print news organizations merged their exit polling units to create Voter News Service, VNS, to conduct exit polls during major national elections (Goodfellow, 1996).

During the 1996 presidential election, VNS surveyed voters when they were leaving the polls in 1,500 precincts that had been selected from 188,000 precincts nationwide. In addition, 300 voters were randomly selected nationally for the remaining interviews. Over the course of the day, exit pollsters interviewed over 12,000 voters, then called the data into processing stations from the precincts three times during the day. These results were relayed to the networks and broadcast during the evening hours and reported in the next day's newspapers along with the election results.

Secondary and Syndicated Research

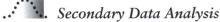 ### Secondary Data Analysis

Secondary data analysis has been defined by communication scholar Lee Becker (1981) as the "reuse of social science data after they have been put aside by the researcher who gathered them." This research data can be reused by the original researcher or by someone else not associated with the project. After securing permission and access to the data and codebook from the primary researcher, the research expert can re-analyze the data according to his or her interests. Secondary data analysis is less expensive and faster than collecting primary research. In fact, many of the steps in the research phase, including sampling, questionnaire writing, and hiring and training interviewers, can be skipped in this type of research.

Secondary data analysis does not mean that the standards for scientific research are any less stringent. The responsibility for thoroughly checking out the quality of the data and methods for collecting the data rests on the shoulders of the secondary data analysis researcher. Even though the secondary data analyst is stuck with the original question phrasing, sampling frame and procedures, if the overall quality of the work is acceptable, the researcher can proceed with the analysis.

Sources of data that might be available for further analysis include communication scholars, media organizations, academic and professional polling organizations, and the census. In fact, the census is a secondary data analysis researcher's gold mine. News reporters and academic researchers rely on the census as an important source of data for carrying out this research procedure. For example, a secondary analysis of census data enabled the *New York Times* to report that for the first time since the Census Bureau began keeping track, the quality of life for many of the 33.5 million African Americans is up (Holmes, 1996).

Syndicated Research

Media managers and executives, advertisers, and ad agencies pay a subscription fee to syndicated research services to have access to data collected. Syndicated research services use a variety of research methods to provide national, regional, and local data on television viewers, radio listeners, newspaper and magazine readers, and consumers. Probably the most famous of these syndicated research services is Nielsen because it collects and reports data on what television viewers watch. Nielsen data can determine the fate of a television program as well as how much advertisers must pay to air their commercials during a specific time slot. Certainly, advertisers carefully studied Nielsen data before agreeing to pay $2 million for a thirty-second commercial during the final episode of *Seinfeld* (Ross, 1998). This commercial rate exceeded the record $1.6 million paid for a thirty-second spot during the 1999 Super Bowl.

Although most syndicated research services use some type of random sampling method to select respondents in order to ensure that the results will represent the population at large, the actual data collection techniques vary from service to service. Nielsen Television uses in-person or telephone interviews as well as people meters, automatic recording devices that are attached to the television sets, to measure television viewing and estimate the audience for a TV program in terms of ratings. TVQ uses mail questionnaires to gather attitude data about various TV programs.

Arbitron uses diaries to collect data on radio listeners. Simmons Market Research conducts personal interviews to learn what magazines consumers read and what they pay attention to while reading the magazines. Starch uses face-to-face interviews to gather data on readership of magazine advertisements. Audit Bureau of Circulation (ABC) audits newspapers to measure newspaper circulation, the number of newspapers sold in a market. Gallup & Robinson's In-View service conducts telephone interviews to measure attitudes toward television commercials.

Syndicated services such as SRI International's Values and Lifestyles (VALS) Program use surveys to gather data, then segment the results into distinct lifestyle groups. This type of analysis is also known as psychographics. Psychographics go beyond standard demographics because they represent a composite of a person's "attitudes, beliefs, opinions, hopes, fears, prejudices, needs, desires, and aspirations" (Townsend, 1988, p. 60).

For example, you could do a psychographic segmentation of viewers and nonviewers of the Super Bowl. Rather than just analyzing whether or not consumers watched or didn't watch this annual mega-TV event, you could analyze them by a variety of characteristics that represented their attitude toward football; their attitude toward the Super Bowl itself; motivations for watching or not watching the Super Bowl; whether or not they liked to attend a Super Bowl party; whether or not they liked to host a Super Bowl party; what they liked best about Super Bowl parties; whether they were sports spectators or participants; whether their peer group consisted of football enthusiasts; their favorite sport; and their gender and age. This psychographic analysis could produce distinct Super Bowl viewing segments such as: Football Fans; Super Bowl Party Goers, Super Bowl Party Hosts, Independents, and the Anti-Super Bowl crowd. These Super Bowl lifestyle groups could then be used to predict amount of attention paid to Super Bowl commercials as well as the creative elements that were appealing.

Because these syndicated research services provide data that all media outlets and advertisers use, subscribing to them is required. Even so, it is imperative to monitor the sampling techniques, data collection methods, phrasing of the questions in the questionnaire, non-response rates, and data analyses in order to have confidence in the results.

It is also important to monitor the results from syndicated study to syndicated study. Because changes in consumer behavior and attitudes are often incremental rather than dramatic, any significant changes in results should be examined carefully to make sure that the shifts can be attributed to consumers and not to changes in methodology or the quality of the data collection.

Research Designs for Testing Consumer Response and Perceptions

Copy Testing

A variety of research tests—copy, concept, trial, market—have been used to gauge consumer reactions to messages, products, brands, and services. Copy testing is conducted to measure whether the consumer noticed, understood, recalled, and responded to an ad in the way the advertiser intended. Advertising that runs on TV or in newspapers and magazines can be tested. Sometimes the tested advertising is a finished product; sometimes it is rough or just a storyboard, a step-by-step description of what will take place in the ad. Copy test validity increases when the advertisement tested with consumers is most like the finished product.

Focus groups, one-on-one depth interviews, surveys, intercepts, and laboratory and field experiments have been used to assess unaided and aided recall of advertisements, comprehension, and reactions to ads, products, and brands. Reactions might include positive or negative attitudes to the advertisement's copy, headline, layout, illustration, organization, and product as well as intentions to purchase the brand.

In a focus group, participants would be shown rough or finished ads and asked questions about them. Focus group participants might be asked to describe a word that they associate with the brand or to project thoughts and feelings about the brand onto someone else. Surveys might be conducted the day after an advertisement runs on television to measure recall, both unaided and aided. A field experiment might be conducted by splitting the placement of the ads and placing one version of an ad in half of the newspapers or magazines and a different version in the other half. This split-run would be followed by a survey to obtain recall, comprehension, and attitude data. The data from the two versions would be compared to determine which version of the ad was more effective.

Consumers might also be invited to a theater to watch a new TV program with the commercials to be tested embedded in the program. Follow-up interviews with the consumers would measure recall and reactions to the commercials. Reactions may include positive or negative attitudes as well as intentions to buy the product advertised.

Advertising copy and the total format can be tested in the concept stages of the campaign to allow consumer input in the process. The copy may also be tested after the campaign has begun. Regardless of which method is used for testing copy, the steps of the different research methods should still be followed to develop valid research that represents consumers' recall, attitudes, behavior, and behavioral intentions.

Professional research firms offer these copy testing services for a fee. Some copy testing services include Gallup & Robinson's InTeleTest and ASI's Recall Plus, which test television commercials, and Starch, which tests magazine ads.

In addition to questionnaires and focus group discussion guides that are used to gather data, mechanical devices have been used to measure everything from changes in the size of a pupil to movements of the eye to physiological responses of the body. These mechanical devices can measure what part of an ad attracts or arouses a consumer.

 ## Trial and Concept Research

Another type of testing is trial research, which may be used to assess consumer interest and attitudes before new products and services are launched in the marketplace. In this type of research, consumers actually use the new product or service for a specified period of time, and the researcher collects data on consumer use and reactions to various aspects of the product or service. Because consumers are actually trying out a new product or service, trial research provides a better indicator of consumer reaction than concept research, which describes the concept of a new product or service and then asks consumers their opinions about the idea and whether or not they would buy or use the proposed product or service.

A prototype of a concept can also be developed for testing. For example, a prototype of a new magazine or section of a newspaper can be shown to focus group participants for their reactions. If research suggests that reaction to the concept or prototype of a new product, service, or advertisement is positive, it might be tested in a specified geographic area. This market test evaluates consumer reaction in the real world.

Perceptual Mapping

Perceptual mapping is an analytical technique that uses survey data to visually represent consumer perceptions of a product, brand, or company in two or more dimensions. In her book, *Hitting the Sweet Spot,* Lisa Fortini-Campbell (1992, p. 119) said that perceptual mapping gives insight into consumers by letting you "position one brand relative to others with respect to the dimensions that consumers use to distinguish them."

For example, you might conduct a survey of consumers to learn their attitudes toward soft drinks and juice drinks. Consumers might be asked to rate soft drinks and juice drinks on several dimensions, including how they feel about serving them to their friends and whether the beverages are for kids or Generation X.

The results of the survey of consumer perceptions about soft drinks and juice drinks would be analyzed using multivariate statistical techniques such as factor analysis, then visually displayed as a perceptual map. An examination of the quadrants on the perceptual map would show the following relationships of soft drinks and juice drinks:

1. To each other
2. To the dimension of "fun beverage to serve friends"
3. To the dimension that it's associated with being a drink for kids or a beverage that Generation X drinks.

This simple hypothetical example in Figure 14.3 shows that some respondents perceive juice drink products as kid drinks that are not fun to serve to friends and soft drinks as a Generation X beverage that's fun to serve to friends. To capture some of the Generation X market, the perceptual map suggests that the juice drink marketer and advertiser may want to try to reposition juice drinks as more of a Generation X beverage that's fun to serve to friends.

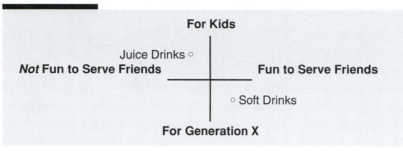

FIGURE 14.3 *An Example of a Perceptual Map*

Evaluation Research

In the public relations field, evaluation research has been described as offering "quantitative support to the argument that the public relations campaign was effective" (Stacks, 1994). One of the basic methods of evaluation research in public relations is the "clip file," which cuts out articles from newspapers and magazines and records news stories that have been generated by a press release, pitch letter, media advisory, or press conference. The articles and videos can be content-analyzed for accuracy, comprehensiveness, context, and positive, neutral, or negative messages about the client. Inquiries that result from news stories can also be counted and analyzed by question and source.

Field experiments designed with pre- and posttest surveys or focus groups have been conducted before and after a new campaign or program was launched to evaluate change in awareness or attitudes. As discussed in Chapter 12 on experimental design, control groups should be included in the design in order to have confidence that the change in awareness or shift in attitudes was due to the public relations campaign and not due to some unknown factors.

To produce valid research data, these surveys and focus groups should follow the steps that have been outlined for the pre-research, research, and post-research phases. A review of the steps in the three phases of the research process is a reminder that evaluation research must be incorporated into the planning of the public relations campaign for it to be most effective.

Unobtrusive Observation

A very different type of research in which neither the questionnaire nor the interview is used has been called unobtrusive observation (Webb et al.,

1966, p. 1). The developers of this research method said that three types of data are appropriate for unobtrusive observation: physical traces, archives, and observation.

 ## Physical Traces

An example of unobtrusive observation that relies on physical traces might be an early morning walk down randomly selected streets to count the circulation of newspapers in a neighborhood. A subsequent stroll through the neighborhood on recycling day might indicate how many people who subscribed to newspapers actually *read* them. For example, newspapers that are still in plastic bags or rolled up and secured with some type of fastener might be counted as unread. Newspapers that have been opened with sections somewhat askew might be counted as looked at or read. Thus it is not necessary to conduct a survey or focus group to learn about newspaper reading habits. By simply observing unobtrusively, the researcher can predict newspaper circulation and readership in the neighborhood. Of course, a follow-up survey of the neighborhood that asked readers if they read the newspaper would independently validate the conclusions from the unobtrusive observations.

Unobtrusive observation could also have been used to measure the reaction of the United Kingdom and the world to the death of Diana, Princess of Wales, in Paris during August 1997. The vast number of flower bouquets, hand-written notes, and teddy bears left at Windsor and Kensington Palaces during the days following Princess Diana's death were expressions of immense grief and love for the thirty-six year-old princess who was killed in a car accident.

 ## Archives

Another type of unobtrusive observation analyzes archival data such as birth, marriage, property tax, and death records to sketch a portrait of a community. Analyses of the archival sets of a daily newspaper can fill in the details in a community portrait. In fact, John Naisbitt (1982) content-analyzed newspapers and identified ten significant social trends that were shaping the United States. He called these social trends megatrends and wrote a bestselling book about them in 1982. One of the most explosive trends that Naisbitt was able to identify from the content analysis was the transformation of the United States from an industrial to an information society. The content analysis of the newspapers also revealed the shift from a national to a global economy as well as a population shift from the North and East to the South and West.

Observation

The third type of data that's appropriate for unobtrusive observation is simply called observation. One type of observation is without any recording devices, and the other uses hidden recording devices. Even though they were not social scientists, Presidents Lyndon Johnson and Richard Nixon used hidden tape recorders in the White House to unobtrusively record conversations for the historical record. The content of former President Nixon's hidden tape recordings became a major part of the Watergate scandal, eventually forcing him to resign. The recorded conversations of both presidents have provided historians, legal experts, journalists, and filmmakers with a wealth of information about the personalities and actions of the leaders of the land as well as those who visited them.

Another type of observation that uses a mechanical device is one that we all encounter regularly—the supermarket scanner. The scanner provides consumers with an itemized receipt of purchases during a trip to the grocery store, but more important, scanners provide supermarkets with a record of which items were bought that day. The supermarket can use that information to monitor items bought, the use of coupons, and the effectiveness of advertisements and special sales promotions.

Case Studies

Case studies can be thought of as a study of a sample of one. Case studies can be used to study an individual, institution, organization, event, issue, or some type of phenomenon. The case study researcher examines his or her subject in depth, conducting hundreds of interviews and reviewing hundreds of contemporary and historical records in order to understand everything about the research topic. The pre- and post-research phases would be used in case studies, but the research phase would differ. Rather than sampling and questionnaire design, the researcher would identify the relevant people to interview and appropriate documents to examine. The snowball method of identifying subjects to interview is usually used in case studies. As subjects are interviewed, the researcher asks who else would be relevant to talk to. After interviewing that person, the researcher asks for additional recommendations of people to interview. Often case study results are written and published as a book. David Halberstam (1979) combined three case studies of *Time* magazine, CBS, and the *Los Angeles Times* in *The Powers That Be*. Nan Robertson (1992) examined the role and treatment of women at the *New York Times* in *The Girls in the Balcony: Women, Men, and The New York Times. The Making of Mc-Paper: The Inside Story of USA Today* by Peter Prichard (1987) was a case study on the development and launching of what became the highest circulated newspaper in the United States.

Rather than examine an institution, Anthony Smith (1980) studied a phenomenon, the effect of computers on the newspaper industry in *Goodbye Gutenberg: The Newspaper Revolution of the 1980s.* The creation and duration of the advertising campaign for Absolut vodka, the Swedish liquor that has become the nation's best-selling vodka, is examined in *Absolut Book* by Richard W. Lewis (1996).

All case studies are not books. Hadley Cantril (1974) conducted a case study to understand the panic caused by Orson Welles's 1938 Halloween radio broadcast of a fictional invasion of Martians. Albert H. Hastorf and Hadley Cantril (1974) tried to understand the psychological processes of perception in a case study of a 1951 football game between Dartmouth and Princeton. One thing to remember about the case study method is that because a sample of one is studied, the case study results, although they can provide insight into that one subject, cannot be generalized to other cases. Each case would have to be examined individually.

Ethnography and Other Academic Qualitative Methods

Academic qualitative research differs from most of the other research methods we have examined because it is grounded in the humanities—not science. Academic qualitative research is characterized by interpretation rather than measurement, statistical assumptions, and analysis. Even though W. James Potter (1996) identified seven qualitative methods, four are most applicable to research in mass communication. Generally used on the academic side of communication, these four qualitative methods include ethnography, cultural studies, reception study, and textual analysis. Focus groups and one-on-one depth interviews, which were examined in Chapter 13, would also be characterized as qualitative, but these research methods are usually used in the media and communication industry rather than in an academic setting.

 Ethnography

The qualitative research method of ethnography, which some academics also call participant observation, differs significantly from surveys, focus groups, content analysis, and experiments. Ethnography relies on observation and interviews to examine one phenomenon, community, culture, or program over time. The ethnographic researcher goes to live in the environment that is under observation for several weeks, months, or even years to understand the everyday lives of the people being studied. As a research method that has its roots in anthropology, the data collection takes place on the turf of those who are being observed.

The researcher collects data by observing and interviewing relevant informants and respondents in the research environment. Following the observations and interviews, the researcher records the data in a notebook or on a tape recorder. The researcher then analyzes the notes and recordings from the observation study, identifying relevant themes about the subject under observation that will be reported in a written research report, academic journal, or book.

In an effort to better understand consumers who may have difficulty articulating their attitudes and opinions in focus groups and surveys, advertisers are turning to ethnography as a means of gathering data by observing what consumers do with products or services in their own environments, whether at home, in the car, or going shopping or out to eat (Fortini-Campbell, 1992; Kaufman, 1997).

Cultural Studies, Reception, and Textual Analysis

Cultural studies researchers differ from ethnographers because they gather their data from television programs, films, commercials, or newspaper and magazine articles. Cultural studies researchers use the content from these various media sources to interpret or criticize society or culture as an influencer of the media content or text.

Reception study researchers also examine media content or text. In addition, they study the individuals who read the text to determine how the ideas in the text are brought to life in the reader's imagination.

Textual analysis, the final qualitative method that is applicable to academic communication research, has its roots in literary criticism. In this research approach, television programs, films, and commercials are interpreted from a literary point of view. Textual analysis seeks to use these interpretations to define the culture that produced this communication content.

Multiple Methods

As the name suggests, the multiple methods approach uses more than one research method to answer a research question. Surveys might be combined with focus groups or content analysis studies. Experiments might be combined with one-on-one depth interviews. The research design might include secondary data analysis with unobtrusive observation or case studies. The combinations may be endless, but the real purpose of the multiple method approach is to strengthen the design and increase the validity of the results.

This chapter has examined the many research methods beyond surveys, content analysis studies, experiments, and focus groups. Some of these studies actually use the basic research methods but under a different name. Tracking studies, for example, are really surveys conducted over time. Exit polls are surveys that are conducted as voters exit the voting booths. One type of unobtrusive observation relies on content analysis of documents.

Regardless of these additional research methods, the three-phase research process still applies. From monitoring the environment in which a problem, opportunity, issue, or theory is identified in the pre-research phase through designing, conducting, and reporting the results of the study according to the requirements of each of the various methods in the research phase, to deciding the next step in the post-research phase, all of the components of the research process are relevant to the various research methods discussed in this chapter. And just as we discussed ethical issues for surveys, content analyses, experiments, and focus groups, ethical standards must also be an integral part of these other methods.

SUGGESTED RESEARCH ACTIVITIES

1. Working with one other student, contact a local advertising agency to determine if you can interview them about copy testing that they may have conducted. Make an oral presentation to the class on what you learn.

2. Working with another student, contact the publisher of the local newspaper or the general manager of a local TV or radio station. Ask if you can interview him or her about the syndicated research that the company subscribes to and how the company uses it in planning and decision making.

3. Working with another student, contact a local research firm that may be located in one of the malls in your city. Ask if you can interview the staff about intercept research, how they conduct it, and some of the problems they encounter.

4. Browse the World Wide Web for several days in search of surveys that are being conducted online. Print a copy of a questionnaire that you find. Critique the questionnaire and bring it to class to discuss. Who is likely to complete the questionnaire? Are they representative of the population?

5. Search past issues of newspapers, magazines, trade journals, and academic journals in the communication field. Find an example of an exit poll, secondary data analysis, or study using multiple research methods. Read it carefully. Summarize the purpose, method, and major findings.

6. Find a qualitative study that has been published in the academic communication journals. Read it carefully. Summarize the purpose, description of the method, and results. How is the study similar to or different from a survey or content analysis study?

RECOMMENDED READING

For an in-depth treatment of syndicated research services and research information sources, see:

ALAN D. FLETCHER and THOMAS A. BOWERS, *Fundamentals of Advertising Research,* 4th ed., pp. 201–310, 354–359. Belmont, CA: Wadsworth, 1991.

For a critique of the Nielsen ratings, see:

ELIZABETH JENSEN, "Meet the Nielsens," *Brill's Content,* March 1999, pp. 87–91.

For a comprehensive list of organizations that conduct polls and surveys, see:

JEAN WARD and KATHLEEN A. HANSEN, *Search Strategies in Mass Communication,* 3rd ed., pp. 255–262. New York: Longman, 1997.

For studies that address fax surveys, e-mail surveys, and response rates of online surveys, see:

JOHN P. DICKSON and DOUGLAS L. MACLACHLAN, "Fax Surveys: Return Patterns and Comparison with Mail Surveys," *Journal of Marketing Research,* February 1996, pp. 108–113.

AILEEN CROWLEY, "E-Mail Surveys Elicit Fast Response, Cut Costs," *PC Week,* January 30, 1995.

The Pew Research Center For the People & the Press, "A Survey Methods Comparison: Online Polling Offers Mixed Results," January 27, 1999.

For more perspectives on advertising research methods and issues, see:

JOEL AXELROD, *Choosing the Best Advertising Alternative: A Management Guide to Identifying the Most Effective Copy Testing Technique,* rev. ed. New York: Association of National Advertisers, 1986.

PHILIP WARD BURTON and SCOTT C. PURVIS, *Which Ad Pulled Best? 50 Case Histories on How to Write Ads That Work,* 5th ed. Lincolnwood, IL: NTC Business Books, 1987.

FIONA CHEW, "Electronic Media Audience Measurement," in *How Advertising Works: The Role of Research,* ed. John Philip Jones, pp. 180–202. Thousand Oaks, CA: Sage, 1998.

RUSSELL HALEY and ALLAN BALDINGER, "The ARF Copy Research Validity Project," *Journal of Advertising Research,* April/May 1991, pp. 11–32.

JOHN PHILIP JONES, "Perceptual Mapping," in *How Advertising Works: The Role of Research,* ed. John Philip Jones, pp. 136–138. Thousand Oaks, CA: Sage, 1998.

JAN S. SLATER, "Qualitative Research in Advertising," in *How Advertising Works: The Role of Research,* ed. John Philip Jones, pp. 121–135. Thousand Oaks, CA: Sage, 1998.

JON STEEL, *Truth, Lies & Advertising: The Art of Account Planning.* New York: Wiley, 1998.

DAVID STEWART, "Measures, Methods, and Models in Advertising Research," *Journal of Advertising Research,* June/July 1989, pp. 54–60.

For a discussion on qualitative research in an academic environment, see:

CLIFFORD G. CHRISTIANS and JAMES W. CAREY, "The Logic and Aims of Qualitative Research," in *Research Methods in Mass Communication,* ed. GUIDO H. STEMPEL III and BRUCE H. WESTLEY, pp. 342–362. Englewood Cliffs, NJ: Prentice-Hall, 1981.

THOMAS R. LINDLOF, *Qualitative Communication Research Methods.* Thousand Oaks, CA: Sage, 1995.

MICHAEL QUINN PATTON, *Qualitative Evaluation and Research Methods,* 2nd ed. Newbury Park, CA: Sage, 1990.

W. JAMES POTTER, *An Analysis of Thinking and Research about Qualitative Methods.* Mahwah, NJ: Lawrence Erlbaum, 1996.

For a discussion on the problems with trial research, see:

A. MICHAEL NOLL, "Pitfalls of Trials," in *Highway of Dreams: A Critical View along the Information Superhighway.* Mahwah, NJ: Lawrence Erlbaum, 1997.

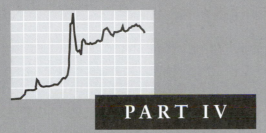

PART IV

Research Issues,

Applications,

Ethics, and the

Future

CHAPTER 15

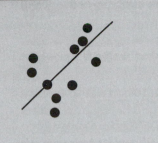

Researching Racial and Ethnic Minorities

- Why is it necessary to address the methodological issues involved in researching racial and ethnic minorities?

- What can be done to improve the sampling frame when researching minorities?

- What validity issues should the researcher be concerned about when developing the survey questionnaire?

- How does the race of an interviewer have an impact on survey results and how can the impact be minimized?

- What issues should be considered when analyzing survey results?

- What are the methodological issues when conducting focus groups, one-on-one depth interviews, intercepts, and content analysis studies on minorities?

Race and Ethnicity Can Influence the Validity of Research Studies

During the O. J. Simpson criminal trial, national polls revealed that blacks and whites were divided on the former football star's guilt in the murder of his ex-wife, Nicole Brown Simpson, and her friend, Ron Goldman. Blacks and whites were also divided in a local survey we conducted several months after the criminal trial began. When 383 respondents who were familiar with the murder case were asked their opinion about O. J. Simpson's guilt, whites were almost twice as likely as blacks to say Simpson was guilty: 66 percent of whites and 35 percent of African Americans said O. J. Simpson was definitely or probably guilty of killing his ex-wife and her friend.

Because the difference between blacks and whites is too great to attribute to sampling error, we must conclude that the difference in opinion is related to the race of the respondents. But do other factors related to how the study was conducted explain some of the difference in opinion on O. J. Simpson's guilt? It is likely that some of the difference may be due to the topic, the sample, and even the interviewers. Results of opinion polls on the O. J. Simpson trial illustrate the importance of paying special attention to each step of the research process to ensure that information collected from different racial and ethnic groups is accurate and not a consequence of the way the study was conducted.

In this chapter, we address issues that must be considered when designing and conducting general population research studies as well as studies that focus specifically on African Americans, Hispanics or Latinos, Asian Americans, and Native Americans. If, for example, Latinos are underrepresented in the survey sample, the results will not represent the total population. If African Americans do not voice honest opinions on race sensitive topics to white interviewers, the results will not be accurate. These issues, and many more, can make the results of a research study invalid. The potential problems that we identify and the solutions that we propose will help the research expert avoid pitfalls that can produce invalid data. If the research expert is aware of potential problems and incorporates solutions into the research design, he or she should be able to produce valid results for important decision making.

Each research method—surveys, intercepts, focus groups, content analysis studies, etc.—has its own unique set of issues that must be addressed to ensure that the research results accurately reflect the racial and ethnic groups that are represented in the total population. We'll explore these unique issues and the solutions as they relate to each research method.

Issues That May Affect Telephone Survey Results

It is probably fair to say that biased results from surveys have the potential to cause more damage than any other research method we've discussed. Because we have confidence that scientific surveys can produce results that accurately represent the *total* population, we accept the results as fact. We use survey results to predict presidential elections, make multi-million dollar decisions, write front page newspaper stories, and track voters' concerns. If the survey results are inaccurate, we could be wrong in our election prediction, which would damage our reputation. If we make a business decision based on inaccurate information, we could lose millions of dollars. If we're wrong in a news report, we would damage our credibility and prestige with our readers and journalistic peers. If we are wrong on the issues that voters care about, we could be seen as out of touch and ultimately voted out of office. The stakes can be quite high when relying on results from surveys.

Because the process of conducting surveys involves multiple components and many steps, things can go awry and inaccurate results can be produced in several areas. When it comes to ensuring that racial and ethnic groups are accurately represented in a survey, the potential for pitfalls and missteps is especially acute. The pitfalls that can affect the validity of the survey results can occur with the sample, interviewers, questionnaire, and analysis. To ensure that a survey is representative of the total population under study, each component must be examined for how racial and ethnic groups will be treated.

Sampling Frame Issues

Because a survey is only as good as the sampling frame that it selects respondents from, the critical question to ask is: Does the sampling frame include an accurate listing of members of racial and ethnic groups? Remember from earlier discussions that random samples can be assumed to represent the population if each individual in the population had an equal chance of being selected. If certain individuals are not included on the sampling frame or list, they do not have an equal chance of being picked to participate in the survey. In national telephone polls, for example, all African American homes do not have an equal chance of being selected for the study. According to a 1995 Census Bureau report on the African American population, 13 percent of African American homes (about 1.3 million) had no telephone. What this means for national telephone surveys is that before the first phone numbers are randomly picked for the sample, 1.3 million African Americans do not have an equal chance of being selected.

Another issue that can affect the representation of racial and ethnic groups is how the sampling frame is compiled. In general, research experts may use a combination of census tracts, telephone exchanges, street addresses, and zip codes to ensure a comprehensive and up-to-date sampling frame. This strategy certainly identifies minorities who live in neighborhoods that have high concentrations of African Americans, Latinos or Hispanics, Asian Americans, and Native Americans. But this strategy will not necessarily identify racial and ethnic minorities who live in predominantly white neighborhoods.

On one hand, it can be said that minorities who do *not* live in minority neighborhoods will have the same chance of being picked for the survey as the general population. But they do not have an equal chance of being selected as other members of their racial or ethnic group. When predominantly minority areas are included in the sampling frame, minorities who live in mostly minority neighborhoods have a greater chance of being selected than minorities who do not. Does this make the survey results less valid? It certainly biases the survey results in favor of minorities who live in predominantly minority neighborhoods.

If minorities who live in predominantly minority neighborhoods have different experiences with city government, the schools, city services, property taxes, crime, the police, the courts, environmental issues, and even the media, than those who don't live in minority neighborhoods, the survey results will not be representative of the experiences of *all* minorities. The survey will only represent those who live in minority neighborhoods.

Improving the Sampling Frame

How then can a research expert find a sampling frame that represents the entire minority population of the survey area? The researcher must compile a more representative list by gaining access to membership lists and subscription lists, and monitoring mainstream and minority media. This compiled sampling frame can then be used with the traditional sampling frame in the random selection of the survey sample.

Membership Lists

Several sources can be used in compiling the sampling frame, but to gain access to this information, the research expert has to persuade those who control the information that their participation in the development of a compiled list is important. Membership lists of minority community organizations and churches as well as subscription lists of minority newspapers can be excellent sources for compiled sampling frames. Minority community organizations might include the NAACP, the Urban League, Jack & Jill, Delta Sigma Theta Sorority, Alpha Phi Alpha Fraternity, the Links, the National Association of Black Journalists, the National Association of Hispanic Journalists, LULAC, MALDEF, the Hispanic Chamber of Commerce, the Asian American Chamber of Commerce, and many more. These organizations represent local chapters of national organizations, so there are also national membership lists. Other national organizations such as associations of black doctors, lawyers, engineers, and MBAs also have members who reside in local areas around the country.

Church membership directories also can be excellent sources for compiling a minority sampling frame. On the surface, it may appear that churches that are in minority neighborhoods will only have members from the surrounding neighborhood. But that is not necessarily true: minorities who live in predominantly white neighborhoods may drive across town to attend church in a minority neighborhood.

Although the various membership lists contain the names and addresses of minorities who live within and outside of minority neighborhoods, the sampling frame should be compiled from those who live *outside* minority neighborhoods. Remember that the traditional sampling reaches those who live in high minority population areas. Using census tracts and the Cole Directory, a listing of street addresses and telephone exchanges assigned to each census tract, the research expert can identify the streets that represent minority neighborhoods in order to eliminate those streets from the supplemental minority sampling frame.

Getting access to membership lists of organizations and churches is not always easy. The research expert often has to meet with presidents of organizations, boards of directors, and ministers to explain the importance of having comprehensive lists of all minorities so that everyone has an opportunity to be randomly selected for the survey. It is important to stress that their members will not be sold anything and that just because someone is on the list, does not mean that that person will be called.

What should be emphasized is that if their members are *not* on any list, they have less of a chance than those who are on the list of being called and having their opinions represented. And having opinions from every segment of the community is important to the well-being of the total community. Newspapers and television stations base stories on survey data and the data should be representative. City and county officials make decisions based on survey data and everyone should be included. Most important, it should be stressed that the goal is to avoid undercounting or underrepresenting anyone in surveys, which are the basis for so many decisions that affect everyone.

 Subscription Lists

A different tack must be used to get access to subscription lists of minority publishers. Even though most of their circulation is in the surrounding minority neighborhood, it is also likely that minority newspapers have subscribers outside of the minority area who receive the newspaper through the mail. Like most publishers, minority publishers may make their subscription lists available for a fee. Of course, offering to provide survey results to the publishers for publication in their newspapers may also increase the likelihood of their sharing a list.

National magazines such as *Ebony, Essence, Black Enterprise, Hispanic Magazine, Latina,* and *A, the Asian-American Magazine* would also serve as sources for names and addresses. The databases of these publications would certainly have subscribers in the survey area, and some of these addresses may be in areas outside of predominantly minority neighborhoods.

Monitoring the Media

Another source of names would be the news and editorial pages of minority newspapers and community radio and television programs. Regular monitoring of these publications and programs can produce names that should be added to the list. Of course, extra research must be done to find out whether the person lives within or outside of a minority neighborhood. The local mainstream newspaper and TV newscasts can also be useful for identifying minority opinion leaders who are covered in the news.

Drawing a Sample from the Compiled List

Having compiled the list of minorities who live outside of minority neighborhoods, the research expert needs to determine the number of names that should be selected randomly. Using census data, a ratio of those who live in minority neighborhoods compared with those who don't is calculated. Separate ratios are calculated for African Americans, Latinos or Hispanics, Asian Americans, and Native Americans.

If, for example, a random sample survey of 1,000 is being conducted in a city that is 30 percent minority, and an analysis of census data shows that 75 percent of the minority population lives in a minority neighborhood, the research expert would expect a valid sample to have 300 questionnaires completed with racial and ethnic minorities. But that's only part of the picture.

If the census data show that three-fourths of minorities live in minority neighborhoods and one-fourth do not, 225 of the 300 interviews should be conducted with minorities who live in minority neighborhoods and 75 should be with those who don't. Of course, these interviews would have to be further broken down to represent racial or ethnic groups. In addition, the research expert must ask for a zip code on the questionnaire to verify whether the respondent's home is in a minority or non-minority neighborhood.

As discussed in Chapter 5, by using random sampling methods, the sample should have representation according to minority neighborhood residence, but in reality that may not be the case. If a street has twenty homes, for example, and a black family lives in one of them, their chance of being selected is one in twenty. But if another street has twenty homes and all are occupied by a black families, there is no question that a black family will be selected for the survey.

Even without the extra effort of compiling a list of addresses that represents minorities who live outside minority neighborhoods, the percentage of blacks will certainly match the percentage in the population. However, unless there is some type of stratification based on the racial-ethnic composition of a neighborhood, the minority home addresses in non-minority neighborhoods will have a significantly smaller chance of getting picked, and the overall validity of the sample will have been compromised.

The process of compiling and updating the sampling frame of minorities who do *not* live in minority neighborhoods should be an ongoing enterprise. It is also important to initially code and analyze the compiled list separately from the primary random sample. The research expert should validate the composition of the primary random sample before combining it with the sample based on the compiled list. With an analysis of zip codes, the research expert can determine the percentage of minority and non-minority neighborhood respondents represented in the primary sample. Then the research expert should be able to add the randomly selected non-minority neighborhood minority respondents to the primary sample according to their representation in the population.

Some researchers may argue that the supplemental sample of minorities who live outside predominantly minority neighborhoods jeopardizes the assumptions behind random selection. We feel that randomly selecting minorities from this supplemental sampling frame increases the likelihood of producing a more representative sample. However, when randomly selecting a sample from this supplemental sampling frame, you should compare the results with the most current census data to determine if the overall sample results of minorities are more representative of the minority population.

An alternative to all this is weighting, a statistical procedure that is discussed in more detail later in this chapter. The research expert can simply instruct a statistical computer software program such as SPSS to weight the sample according to the ratio of minority neighborhood and non-minority neighborhood representation. Of course, the ratio must be based on census data.

Weighting may initially solve the problem, but ultimately the research expert must develop a long-term solution such as compiling a sampling frame of minorities who live in predominantly white neighborhoods. This representation issue is at the heart of surveying in an ever-increasing diverse society in which minorities are no longer confined to specific areas of a community.

The Questionnaire

Another component of the research process that must be addressed for potential problems is the questionnaire. In addition to making sure that the rules for questions and questionnaires as outlined in Chapters 3 and 4 are followed, the research expert must take care in the phrasing of the question to identify the respondent's racial or ethnic group, make sure that translations of the questionnaire are accurate, and include information that will help in the analysis of the sampling frame and compiled list.

 ## Name for Racial or Ethnic Group

What is the best way to ask for a respondent's racial or ethnic group? This question, which the Census Bureau grappled with when it planned the 2000 census, involves several issues. First, and foremost, the researcher must not use phrasing that would offend a respondent and cause the respondent to terminate the interview. Today it would be inappropriate to use the term "Negro" — although questionnaires did just thirty-five years ago. Forty years ago, it would have been offensive to use the term "black" in the question for race. Only ten years ago, the term "African Americans" in the questionnaire would have offended some.

Today, should "black" or "African American" be used in the race-ethnic group question? With both terms enjoying wide use across the country, it would be best for now to say: Black or African American. In the future, "African American" may be the only term necessary to use when phrasing the question on race.

Which term is appropriate to describe those of Mexican or Latin American heritage? Is the preferred term "Hispanic," "Latino," or some other term? Again, a valid term should elicit a valid response as well as not offend respondents. In three focus groups of Hispanics that were conducted in Texas, a state with a large Latino population, participants were asked what name they preferred to be called. In these focus groups, which were developed by the first author at the request of a TV station, there was no consensus among participants. Some said Hispanic; others said Latino. Quite a few said they preferred being called Mexican American. A few said Chicano.

The recommendation of communication researcher Gonzalo Soruco in his book, *Cubans and the Mass Media in South Florida* (1996, pp. 30, 33) is consistent with the diversity of opinion in the three focus groups. Soruco said to let respondents define themselves as Mexican, Mexican American, Chicano, Puerto Rican, Cuban, other Spanish/Hispanic and non-Hispanic. He also emphasized that mixing race and ethnicity must be avoided because it leads to confusion — Hispanics can be white, black, and even Asian.

To sort out the best way to ask about race and ethnicity among Hispanics or Latinos may require some experimentation. This could include asking the race question separately from the ethnic group question as well as exploring the effects of the order in which the question is asked. If ethnic origin is asked before the race question, will the results differ from asking ethnic origin *after* the race question? The Census Bureau tested the effect of the order of asking ethnic origin and race and found that order does make a difference (Goldberg, 1996; Smith, 1996). It concluded that when ethnic origin was asked after a race question, including "white," "black," "Native American," or "other" as options, Hispanic or Latino respondents picked "other," specified where their parents or grandparents came from, and skipped the follow-up question on ethnic group because they thought they had already answered the question.

Another option is for the research expert to leave the question open-ended, asking: What is your race or ethnic group? By providing respondents with the opportunity to self-identify rather than force them into closed-ended response choices, the researcher could categorize the responses according to the respondents' definitions.

An open-ended question option would also apply for Asian Americans who can be of Japanese, Chinese, Korean, Taiwanese, or Vietnamese descent to name a few. Even though a geographic part of the world binds these groups, their cultures, histories, politics, and languages differ, and a valid question should be sensitive to that distinction.

Perhaps the best approach is to periodically conduct focus groups to determine the preferred label. Even including a question on a questionnaire that asks directly about a preferred term could help avoid confusing and offending those whom you're trying to study. An example of a question that could be asked of everyone is:

> As you know, individuals representing different racial and ethnic groups live in the United States. Many prefer to be identified by certain names when describing them in research studies such as this. What name would you prefer for us to use in describing your racial or ethnic group?

Practically speaking, if the researcher finds that there are only a few of each group, he or she will need to collapse the data to have a large enough sub-sample for analysis. At least by initially identifying individual differences among Latinos or Hispanics and Asian Americans, the researcher would be able to analyze how these subgroups differ and what they have in common. We discuss collapsing small groups to create larger groups for analysis later in the chapter.

Translating the Questionnaire for Respondents Who Speak Other Languages

We have focused on a few specific questions in the questionnaire to enhance the validity of the study, but the questionnaire as a whole becomes an issue when it requires translation for Spanish-speaking respondents. Gonzalo Soruco (1996, p. 32) said that translations can cause validity problems because some words and scales that are commonly used in English-language questionnaires do not have Spanish-language equivalents.

To avoid validity and reliability problems, Soruco recommended reverse translation. For example, a translator would translate an English-language questionnaire from English to Spanish. A second translator would re-translate the questionnaire from Spanish to English. The two versions would then be compared for similarities and differences in concepts. Of course, these translation issues would also be relevant for those who speak Chinese, Korean, Japanese, or any other language.

Zip Code as a Standard Variable

As a rule, zip codes should be routinely included on a questionnaire just like gender, age, and racial or ethnic group. Zip code information enables you to analyze the sample's composition and determine what percentage of racial and ethnic minorities drawn from the traditional sampling frame live in predominantly white neighborhoods and what percentage live in predominantly minority neighborhoods.

Interviewing Issues

Does the race of the interviewer matter when interviewing minority respondents? A 1971 study found that white interviewers had an effect on lower socioeconomic blacks when questions were asked on race-sensitive issues (Schuman & Converse, 1989). In addition, white interviewers had a higher refusal rate (12 percent) than black interviewers (6 percent) when interviewing black respondents.

Should researchers be concerned about interviewer effects today? Yes, when the interviewers are asking questions on race-sensitive issues. Although on the surface the O. J. Simpson trial was a murder trial, in reality it became a trial about race. How many of the responses to the many surveys that were conducted during the time of the trial were influenced by the race of the interviewer?

Because the majority of the interviewers were white in the survey that we conducted which asked about O. J. Simpson's guilt, it is unknown whether or not some percentage of the responses of blacks would have been different if the interviewers had been black. With three-quarters of blacks and whites in a 1995 Gallup Poll saying that the O. J. Simpson trial has hurt race relations in this country, it would *not* be surprising to find that blacks respond differently depending on whether the questions are asked by white or black interviewers. What then should researchers do? To ensure that results are valid, special attention should be given to hiring, training, callbacks, and monitoring fieldwork.

 ### Hiring and Training

On questionnaires that include race-sensitive questions, hire interviewers who match the respondent's race or ethnic group. If that is not feasible, extra emphasis must be placed in the training on the potential effects of whites interviewing racial and ethnic minorities on race-sensitive issues. The research expert needs to emphasize that interviewers are merely recorders who should not respond positively or negatively to responses that minority respondents give on questions that may be perceived as racially sensitive. During the interviewing training, the research expert should demonstrate questionnaires with race-sensitive questions, then have interviewers role play interviewing those of different races or ethnic groups on race-sensitive issues. Through the practicing, the researcher should be able to identify any potential problems that could cause minority respondents to terminate the interview before its conclusion or give less than candid responses.

 ### Bilingual Interviewers

It is also imperative for the research expert to hire interviewers who speak Spanish or any other languages spoken in the survey area. If the respondent does not speak English and the research expert does not have trained interviewers on staff who speak the same language, the non-response will negatively affect the validity of the survey. Of course in areas like Los Angeles where over eighty-four different languages are spoken in the schools, the research expert must decide which languages are needed among interviewers.

If most of the non-English-speaking respondents speak Spanish, the research expert needs to hire and train Spanish-speaking interviewers. An analysis of the survey call record forms that were discussed in Chapters 6 and 8 tells the researcher how many survey questionnaires were not completed because the interviewer did not speak the language necessary for completing the interview.

Number of Callbacks

Because the response rate of a survey is directly related to the validity of the results, one of the goals of a survey is to have as high a response rate as possible. It is especially important for the researcher to complete questionnaires with minorities who have been selected for the sample. Sometimes it may be necessary to do more than two or three callbacks to connect with selected minority respondents. If the researcher is able to determine in advance which respondents are racial and ethnic minorities, he or she should make more callbacks than normal to these respondents to ensure a high response rate. Analyses of census tracts, street addresses, or telephone exchanges may provide clues as to which respondents in the primary sample might be African Americans, Latinos, or Asian Americans. And, of course, the compiled sample is a list of racial and ethnic minorities.

Monitoring Fieldwork

The research expert should carefully monitor the fieldwork to identify refusals and terminations before interviews with minority respondents have been completed. The refusals and terminations should be reassigned to specially trained minority interviewers to convert them to completed interviews. With special training and a unique job description, these interviewers should be paid a higher wage than those who are conducting regular interviews. Converting even a few refusals or terminations increases the response rate and overall validity of the study.

Analysis of Data

Once the data have been collected, coded, and processed, five issues should be of concern in the analysis:

1. Validation of the sample
2. Comparison of minorities from the compiled sampling frame versus the traditional sampling frame used for random selection
3. Analysis of nonresponse among minorities from both the compiled and regular sampling frame
4. How to treat minorities when the numbers are small
5. Determining whether differences are real

Validation of Sample

As soon as the survey data have been processed and the frequency table run, the research expert should compare the survey results on the question for racial or ethnic group with the most recent census data for the survey area to determine how well the sample and census match. Remember that the results from a random sample should be within the sampling error for that size sample. Discrepancies should be reported in the final report, and the research expert should identify ways to correct the problem in future surveys. For example, Figure 15.1 compares race or ethnic group with census data. As discussed in Chapter 8, the comparison shows that discrepancies exist between the random sample and the census data that *cannot* be attributed to sampling error.

Because the sampling error for a random sample of 476 is plus or minus 4.5 percentage points, it is clear that the sub-sample of whites and Hispanics or Latinos does not match the census statistics. Whites are overrepresented, and Hispanics or Latinos are underrepresented. The research expert should report the discrepancies as well as seek to find explanations for them in order to make corrections in future surveys. In this survey, Spanish-speaking interviewers were not used, thereby ruling out the participation of respondents who only spoke Spanish. To fully correct this problem, the survey needed both Spanish-speaking interviewers and reverse-translated questionnaires. Reverse translation ensures that the Spanish-language questionnaire is comparable to the English-language one.

The underrepresentation of Hispanics or Latinos might also be due to confusion caused by the wording of the question on race and ethnic group discussed earlier. Some Hispanics or Latinos may have reported their racial group rather than ethnic group, which may partially explain why whites were overrepresented in the survey.

FIGURE 15.1 *A Comparison of Race/Ethnic Group with Census Data*

Race/Ethnic Group	Sample (N=476)	1990 Census
White	78%	68%
Black or African American	7%	9%
Hispanic or Latino	9%	20%
Asian American/Other	6%	3%

Analyzing the Compiled Sampling Frame

As discussed earlier, the demographics of the minorities selected from the compiled sampling frame of those who live in predominantly white neighborhoods should be compared with those who were drawn from the regular sampling frame before combining the two groups. It is important to identify any educational, income, and media use differences to better understand the data. If the differences are pronounced, the researcher may decide to keep the two groups separate in the analysis because the distinctions would be lost by combining the two groups.

With an eye toward the next survey, the research expert should also analyze the non-response among minorities from both compiled and regular sampling frames. Is the non-response due to refusals, not-at-homes, or language barriers? For refusals, the research expert should examine the race and gender of the interviewer to identify any race or gender effects on response rate. Although the research expert can only report any problems for this study, the next survey can certainly be designed to avoid these possible problems.

Deciding Whether to Weight the Results

Depending on the number of minorities in the sample, the research expert must decide about weighting and combining subgroups of minorities. If, after matching the sample results, the researcher finds that a group is underrepresented, he or she can use the SPSS weighting command to statistically increase the percentage of minorities until it matches the percentage it should represent in the population. To do this, the research expert needs to calculate the ratio by which the sample group should be adjusted.

For example, in the results in Figure 15.1, the adjustment ratio is: $9 \times X = 20$, or $X = 2.2$. By multiplying the 9 percent by 2.2, the percentage of Hispanics or Latinos would increase to 20 percent, which matches the census data. The researcher also must adjust the white group down so it matches its representation in the population. In this case, $79 \times X = 68$, or $X = .86$. Multiplying 79 percent by the adjustment ratio of .86 would reduce the sample percentage to 68 percent, thereby matching the census number.

Weighting the data should be done with care. If the sample of Hispanics had been only 2 percent and the researcher wanted to increase the number statistically to 20 percent, weighting isn't a solution. The problem would be in the actual survey. In such a drastic example, whatever suppressed the response rate cannot be fixed by employing the statistical procedure of weighting.

Handling Small Numbers

When numbers are very small because there is in fact small representation in the population, the researcher should consider recoding the data into an "other" category. In doing so, however, the researcher should recognize that there is a problem with such a category because very different people may have been grouped analytically but should not be grouped in any other way. When this happens, the "other" category is usually ignored during the analysis because it is unclear what it stands for. In some areas, where there are very few minorities, the researcher may combine African American, Hispanic, and Asian into one category, calling it "minority." This combination is a problem because minority groups are quite distinct historically, socially, culturally, and in language. The researcher should avoid combining groups that shouldn't be combined if valid results are sought.

Determining Whether Racial Differences Are Real

One other issue that relates to analysis is the issue of determining whether or not racial or ethnic group distinctions are, in fact, real. Through the appropriate analysis, the researcher can determine if the distinctions are due to education or income rather than race. This should always be checked before differences that are not there are seen as real.

For example, until the early 1990s, survey data usually showed that a larger percentage of whites than blacks read daily newspapers. But when education was examined, it was learned that differences in newspaper reading between whites and blacks disappeared. In other words, newspaper reading was found to be a function of level of education and not race. Research has consistently shown that those with higher educational levels read newspapers more than those with less education. So if you compared whites and blacks with the same levels of education, newspaper reading was the same.

Handling Race-Ethnic Group Issues in Focus Groups

Even though focus groups are not representative of the total population, they can be a valuable tool for understanding how consumers and voters think about issues, products, campaigns, institutions, and individuals. Two aspects of focus group research require special attention when conducting research on racial and ethnic groups: recruitment and the moderator.

Recruitment

Focus group participants are selected because they possess characteristics relevant to the research topic. A political strategist, for example, might commission focus groups to find out how voters perceive his or her presidential candidate and the issues. The political strategist may also want to determine how different racial and ethnic groups perceive the candidate. How participants are recruited is important to the outcome of the research study. If a professional recruiter is hired, the research expert should ask the recruiter what source was used to compile the names for focus group recruitment. If the names were compiled from people who shop at a mall that is frequented by mostly non-minorities, the recruiter will have difficulty recruiting minorities. If the topic of the focus group requires minority participants, it is especially important that the recruitment list comprise diverse minority groups, including those who live in predominantly minority neighborhoods and those who don't.

The problem of representation can be solved in a way similar to the technique used with the survey sampling frame. The recruiter can identify census tracts that have significant minority populations, then use the Cole Directory to identify streets in the minority census tracts and phone numbers. Households can be randomly selected for focus group participation. In addition, the recruiter can use the compiled sampling frame of minorities who do not live in minority neighborhoods as a source of recruitment. The breakdown of minorities who live in minority neighborhoods and those who don't should determine the representation in the focus group.

 The Moderator

Should the focus group moderator's race or ethnic group match the race or ethnic group of focus group participants? If you use the guidelines for matching survey interviewers with respondents for surveys that address race-sensitive issues, the answer is yes. The moderator and participants should match for focus groups on race-sensitive topics and cultural specific subjects. For non-race-sensitive and non-cultural focus groups, the race of the moderator should not matter.

What constitutes a race-sensitive topic is probably more obvious than what might constitute a cultural topic. A cultural topic might include music, food, family rituals, celebrations, art, books, films, community organizations, or historical figures and events. Suppose a focus group is being conducted among African Americans and the moderator asks the participants to recall family occasions that conjured up pleasant memories and one participant mentions Kwanza. If the focus group moderator is unfamiliar with this holiday that is celebrated by some African Americans during the Christmas season, the focus group moderator would not be able to respond appropriately or even be able to interpret the focus group participant's comments. References to Juneteenth, the National Council of La Raza, *The Joy Luck Club,* or Wounded Knee would be other cultural examples. (Juneteenth commemorates the day that slaves in Texas were notified of their freedom, which was two years after the 1863 Emancipation Proclamation. The National Council of La Raza is an umbrella group representing more than 100 Hispanic community organizations. *The Joy Luck Club* is Amy Tan's best-selling book about Chinese American women. Wounded Knee refers to the 1973 takeover of the Wounded Knee settlement on the Sioux Reservation in South Dakota by supporters of the American Indian Movement. Wounded Knee was symbolic because in 1890, the U.S. Seventh Cavalry massacred 300 Indians at the site.)

Regardless of the color or ethnic group of the focus group moderator, the research expert should make sure that the moderator is comfortable with all minority focus group participants. If the moderator is uncomfortable, and the participants sense the discomfort, the answers will probably be less candid and certainly less valid.

One-on-One Depth Interviews

Issues that represent potential problems in focus groups should also be of concern when conducting one-on-one depth interviews. To avoid the potential of less than candid responses on race-sensitive questions, the research expert should match the interviewers who are conducting the interviews with those who are being interviewed.

One example of matching the interviewer with the respondents was in a study conducted by Terry A. Wilson (1993). Wilson conducted one-on-one, face-to-face interviews with African American opinion leaders around the state of Texas to find out their perceptions of the largest university in the state, The University of Texas at Austin. Participants in the one-on-one depth interview study were candid in their comments, expressing negative opinions about the flagship university. Would a non-African American interviewer have been able to elicit such candid responses? Probably not. The interviews revealed that the perception of the university's image among African American opinion leaders was still grounded in its history of segregation and discrimination and did not match some of the university's efforts to recruit and support African American students. The match of the interviewer with the respondent probably made a difference in the candor of the responses and the overall validity of the results. The results of the study helped the university develop a plan to correct its image in the African American community.

One-on-one depth interviews can also be conducted by telephone when respondents live in different parts of the country. The challenge, though, is identifying individuals who should be interviewed. Without a master list to identify appropriate respondents, the researcher must rely on a snowball sampling technique. Kristin Kehl (1996) used snowball sampling in a national study of minority advertising professionals. After completing one-on-one telephone interviews with Latino, African American, and Asian American advertising professionals, Kehl asked respondents to recommend people in other advertising agencies who could be interviewed.

This method worked for developing a list of names and also provided an entree when trying to set up an interview. Kehl could simply say that a respondent who had already been interviewed recommended them. Although questions in the depth interview study were asked about minority status, they would not be classified as race sensitive. Even so, Kehl promised confidentiality, saying that she would not reveal the names or agencies of those who participated in the study. She felt that confidentiality helped secure interviews because some respondents may have worried that their comments could be traced back to them.

In comparing the ease of confirming interviews with African American, Latino, and Asian American professionals, Kehl found that Asian Americans felt less comfortable about participating in the study. But, by sending a letter in advance of the phone call, she was able to reassure them and many participated in the one-on-one interviews. (The questionnaire and advance letter can be found in Appendix A.4.)

Intercept Surveys

What issues should be addressed when conducting intercept surveys among racial and ethnic minorities? As discussed in Chapter 14, the intercept survey, which is face-to-face, does not use random sampling techniques to ensure that everyone has an equal chance of being selected. Because there are no random sampling requirements, the interviewer is generally at liberty to select any respondent he or she wants to interview.

In this type of face-to-face interviewing, which is held in a public place, some interviewers may feel more comfortable about approaching those who are like themselves. For example, white interviewers might be more likely to seek out white respondents, African American interviewers might be more likely to seek out African American respondents, and the same may be true of Hispanic or Latino interviewers. If this happens, some groups may be overrepresented and others underrepresented.

To guard against this potential problem, the research expert must develop procedures for interviewing a cross-section of those who may be found in a mall, movie theater, or other high-traffic area. Also, by having the interviewer keep a record of the racial and ethnic groups approached as well as a record of those who completed or refused to be interviewed, the research expert can monitor the intercept fieldwork to ensure adequate representation from all racial and ethnic groups.

Because intercepts are face to face, the research expert must emphasize the importance of interviewing a cross-section of every group during the training session. In addition, the research expert must emphasize the importance of being professional and polite and treating all prospective respondents with respect.

By keeping track of each interviewer's refusals, the research expert can also determine if any interviewers have a significant number of refusals from minority respondents. For example, one white interviewer may have a significant number of refusals from African Americans. An African American interviewer may have a significant number of refusals from Hispanics. A Latino interviewer may have a disproportionate number of refusals from Asian American and Native American respondents.

If a disproportionate number of refusals is found to be associated with one interviewer, the research expert should observe that interviewer's interactions with respondents from other racial or ethnic groups to pinpoint any problems. If necessary, the research expert should provide additional training to ensure that the intercept survey results have a cross-section of representation from all racial and ethnic groups. If the problem persists, the research expert may have to replace the interviewer.

Issues That Affect Content Analysis Studies

When researching minorities through content analysis fewer issues of concern arise perhaps because there is no human interaction between researcher and subject. But even with fewer issues, the researcher must still pay special attention to how the coding categories are defined, availability of minority publications, and the hiring and training of content analysis coders.

 ### Categories for Coding

As long as the content analysis codebook is a valid representation of what is being analyzed, the reliability of the coding should be high. Caution, though, should be taken when setting up categories that reflect different minority groups. If newspaper stories are being analyzed, it would not be sufficient to set up a category that allows only for Hispanic being mentioned in the headline. The category should encompass Hispanic, Latino, Mexican American, and so on. A content analysis of Latino stories in the *Los Angeles Times* used the following definition: An item qualified as a Latino story if the story (1) had a Spanish surname; (2) mentioned Hispanic culture, customs, language, habits, art, heritage; (3) referred to issues, problems and information relating to Latinos as a minority in the United States; (4) mentioned a Hispanic country (Poindexter, 1982).

For content analysis studies of television programs and print and broadcast advertising, it is also important to code for prominence of role to have an accurate portrayal of minorities in communication content. For example, if only the primary role is examined, the fact that many minority groups are used in secondary and even less significant background roles will not be included in the content analysis results.

 ## Availability of Minority Publications

Sometimes the problem in conducting a content analysis study is the difficulty in getting access to minority publications. If neither the university nor public library subscribes to minority newspapers or magazines, the content analysis researcher may not have the material to conduct the study. One of the very first things to check when developing a content analysis study on minority publications is the availability of newpapers or magazines. If the publications are unavailable through the library, the researcher may have to buy past issues directly from the publisher or redesign the study and subscribe to the publication in order to analyze just-published newspapers.

Coders

Regardless of the subject, coders must be appropriate for the study and specially trained. In a content analysis of Latino news coverage for the *Los Angeles Times,* coders had to be bilingual and knowledgeable about the Latino community in Los Angeles as well as Mexico and Central and South America. In addition to analyzing content in the *Los Angeles Times,* the study also examined content in *La Opinion,* a Spanish-language daily newspaper.

Similarly, for a content analysis of news coverage of African Americans, coders would need to have in-depth knowledge of the African American community, including neighborhoods, schools, issues, opinion and community leaders, cultural activities and traditions, institutions, events, and history.

When minority representation is being analyzed in network television programs or commercials, special attention must be paid in the training to coding different minority groups. In some cases, the racial or ethnic group is obvious because of skin color, but in other cases, you may have to rely on language or cultural symbols to identify the racial or ethnic group. A category of "unable to determine race or ethnic group" would be better than incorrectly coding an actor or model as African American, Latino or Hispanic, Asian American, or Native American.

Which Method Is Best for Gathering Valid Data on Racial and Ethnic Groups?

The purpose of the research study should determine which method is best for researching racial and ethnic groups. For example, qualitative research consultant Roberta Maso-Fleischman (1996, p. 6) wrote that ethnographic research is better than focus groups when researching Hispanics or Latinos for an advertising campaign. She said elements that make a general market campaign effective may offend if directed at the Hispanic community. She said by conducting ethnographic research, the researcher can learn what elements can be included and what elements should be avoided.

According to Maso-Fleischman, ethnography, a qualitative research method discussed in Chapter 14, provides an opportunity to learn how a brand or product fits into the lives of Hispanic families; what behaviors, values, beliefs, and attitudes are associated with the brand or product; and what emotional language is used to refer to it. Maso-Fleischman added that conducting ethnographic research means going to a Hispanic community and a respondent's home to fully understand the Hispanic consumer.

Overall we believe that trend studies that use a combination of quantitative and qualitative research methods are best for gathering reliable data on racial and ethnic minorities. Trend studies that track racial and ethnic groups over time through surveys and focus groups will provide both broad strokes and close-up details on the values, attitudes, opinions, behaviors, and language of African Americans, Latinos or Hispanics, Asian Americans, and Native Americans.

This chapter has examined important issues that must be addressed in order to ensure an accurate representation of racial and ethnic minorities in research studies that are conducted. Ensuring that racial and ethnic minority groups are represented in research results is essential because decision makers rely on research data to make decisions that affect so many

areas, including local, state, and federal government policies and laws, marketing and political strategies, budgeting and disbursement of funds, primary, secondary, and higher education, consumer products and employment, economic and health concerns, and media content and campaigns.

Perhaps most important, we should *not* take it for granted that data on racial and ethnic minorities are valid. But if careful attention is paid to how the data are collected and analyzed, decision makers should have confidence in the results.

SUGGESTED RESEARCH ACTIVITIES

1. Using *Communications Abstracts* in the library, find an abstract for a survey on African Americans, Latinos or Hispanics, Asian Americans, or Native Americans. Using the citation, locate the complete study in the academic research journal. Read the study carefully, paying close attention to the purpose, method, results, and discussion. How were the racial or ethnic groups defined? What suggestions, if any, do you have for improving the methodology?

2. Working with a partner, develop a codebook for content-analyzing African Americans, Latinos or Hispanics, Asian Americans, and Native Americans in commercials during prime-time. Now pretest the codebook on ten commercials. Conduct an inter-coder reliability as discussed in Chapter 11, then evaluate the results. What problems, if any, did you encounter?

3. Working with a team of two other students, develop a focus group moderator's outline and discussion guide that would be used in a focus group of African Americans, Latinos, or Asian Americans to obtain opinions about local news coverage of their racial or ethnic group or a TV program or commercial with a minority as the main character.

4. Interview the publisher of a newspaper, the general manager of a radio or TV station, the CEO of an advertising or public relations agency, or a major advertiser to find out what research, if any, their organization is conducting on racial and ethnic minorities and how they are using that information. Make an oral presentation on the results of your interview.

RECOMMENDED READING

For a detailed treatment of researching Hispanics, see:

GONZALO R. SORUCO, *Cubans and the Mass Media in South Florida*. Gainesville, FL: University Press of Florida, 1996.

For articles and research studies that address race and the mass media, see:

GAIL BAKER WOODS, *Advertising and Marketing to the New Majority*, pp. 69–74. Belmont, CA: Wadsworth, 1995.

SHIRLEY BIAGI and MARILYN KERN-FOXWORTH, *Facing Difference: Race, Gender, and Mass Media*. Thousand Oaks, CA: Pine Forge Press, 1997.

VIRGINIA DODGE FIELDER and LEONARD P. TIPTON, *Minorities and Newspapers*. Washington, DC: American Society of Newspaper Editors, 1986.

CHAPTER 16

Research in the Academic Environment

- What are the distinguishing characteristics of research in an academic environment?
- What are the sources of academic scholars' ideas?
- What is the role of theory in academic research?
- How does an academic researcher advance a program of research?

Research Is a Creative Enterprise

Research is as much a creative enterprise as painting, sculpture, advertising, or journalism. There is a tendency, however, to stereotype scholars in terms of their tools, to limit their role to the narrowest definition of the research expert. This is especially true for social scientists engaged in communication research, whom professionals commonly regard as technicians with special competence in survey research, content analysis, experimental design, focus groups, or other methodologies. Every research expert is, of course, a competent technician. But so too are painters, sculptors, and other creative professionals.

Because research methods are no more than a means to an end, a set of tools to assist in achieving a goal, the preceding chapters in this book have encouraged the media decision maker to draw upon the creative talents and insights of the research expert in the pre-research phase when the details of a project are being planned and in the post-research phase in order to make the best and fullest use of the research results. Good research is simultaneously creative and well executed methodologically.

The Academic Researcher as Decision Maker

This chapter puts the emphasis on the research expert as the creator of original work, not as a consultant for a media decision maker. In the chapters up to this point, the research expert typically applied his or her creative talents and methodological sophistication to a situation in which the media decision maker specified the ground rules. The media professional determines which aspect of mass communication requires new research (the focus of the research), at least in general terms what kind of research will be done (the ground rules for the research expert), and, ultimately, what business and professional decisions will be made on the basis of the research.

Participation in this applied research situation where the media decision maker has the leading role can be intellectually exciting and gratifying, but many people are attracted to the academic world specifically because it allows the research expert to set his or her own ground rules and to pursue research projects that are less constrained by the needs and wants of others. Freedom from constraints does not mean freedom from discipline and order. The productive scholar works within the framework of the three phases with which you are now familiar, the pre-research, research, and post-research phases.

Pre-Research Phase

 Deciding the Focus of the Research

The basic question here is: What will the focus of the research be? That focus could be on some specific idea about communication content, how the process of communication works, or what the effects of communication are. The purpose of the research would be to test that idea. At other times, the focus is more general. There is a research question, but no specific idea about the likely answer. The purpose of the research is to map at least a portion of the array of answers to the question.

To understand how an academic scholar decides on the focus of his or her research and on the design of a specific project, first consider the three basic types of mass communication research, as listed in Figure 16.1, that define the intellectual playing field.

 *Counting*

This is by far the largest research arena in mass communication, whether measured by the number of dollars spent annually, the number of research projects and reports completed, or the sheer number of research personnel involved. Mass communication is by definition the distribution of some message—including large numbers of physical copies in

FIGURE 16.1 *Three Basic Types of Communication Research*

1. Counting
2. Decision making
3. Strategic theoretical analysis

the case of newspapers, books, magazines, and even many of the new electronic media—to a large, typically scattered, and frequently heterogeneous audience. As a result, many things need counting. Some counts, such as the circulation figures for newspapers and magazines, are available from the production process and circulation lists.

But finding out the size of the television audience for specific programs and advertisements requires large-scale, continuing research projects. The Nielsen TV ratings may be the best known of all communication research. Beyond the simple tally of total audience size, there also are counts of the various subgroups in the audiences of the mass media, including the number and proportion of men and women, and various age groups. Also, because of the plethora of messages the media distribute, there are research services that count the messages about a particular topic, person, group, or whatever might be of interest to a client.

Most of the time there is little opportunity and little intellectual excitement for the academic researcher here. The commercial services are well organized and command vast resources. Although they dominate this research arena, new questions always can be raised about what should be counted and new ideas advanced about how we should do the counting.

Decision Making

With the sheer scale of activity in mass communication and the constant need for new versions of our message products, there are many decisions to be made. These routine decisions about the ongoing process can be enhanced through research. There also is frequent innovation in mass communication, the introduction of a new service or kind of message. Newspapers add new sections or change the mix of standing features, new magazines are conceived and launched, and new TV programs are produced. With new technologies come numerous attempts at innovative communication. Because these innovations typically involve decisions about significant investments of time and money, a research component frequently is included. This kind of research is appealing because innovations in mass communication offer an opportunity for—and sometimes demand—creative research designs to test their success among their target audiences.

The downside of decision-making research for the academic is that almost always it is someone else's communication that is the focus of the research. But the limited goals of that communicator—for example, will this find a receptive audience?—do not limit the intellectual goals of the researcher. The research can be approached from a broader perspective.

One of the most famous examples comes from World War II. Turning millions of young Americans into an effective military force required considerably more than technical training, and in 1942 Army Chief of Staff General George C. Marshall turned to famous Hollywood director Frank Capra for a series of orientation films.

> Now Capra, I want to nail down with you a plan to make a series of documentary, factual information films—the first in our history—that will explain to our boys why we are fighting and the principles for which we are fighting.
>
> (Lowery & DeFleur, 1983, p. 117)

In short order, Capra produced seven fifty-minute films that were incorporated in the Army's training programs. But did these films produce the desired results?

To answer that question, the Army turned to a team of social scientists brought into the military to provide psychological expertise. This team could have defined its task narrowly and specifically. Were these films successful in conveying factual information and in influencing soldiers' perspectives on the war? But, as psychologist Carl Hovland and his associates (1949) later reported in *Experiments on Mass Communication*, the task was defined from the larger perspective of identifying key message and audience characteristics that influenced the outcome of the learning and persuasion process. For these social scientists, the films and their military audiences were convenient operational definitions of a larger communication process. Answering the specific decision-making questions that the Army asked did not preclude theoretical research applicable in a much broader arena.

In their book, *Milestones in Mass Communication Research*, Shearon Lowery and Melvin DeFleur sum up the research of Hovland and his colleagues this way:

> The researchers, drawn into the war effort from the academic world, were able to make a significant contribution to the practical problems of designing and testing orientation, teaching, and persuasive communication. But perhaps their most significant contribution was that they uncovered significant issues that would be explored by communication researchers in the decades that followed the war.
>
> (Lowery & DeFleur, 1983, p. 144)

Applied research designed to answer decision makers' immediate concerns can be cast more broadly as strategic analysis.

 ## Strategic Theoretical Analysis

The kinds of research projects designated here as counting research and decision-making research also can be described as tactical research. In contrast to tactical research, which offers short-term guidance to mass communication decision makers, strategic analysis takes the long-term view. Most frequently referred to in the academic world as theoretical research, strategic analysis aims to provide a general intellectual map of some aspect of the mass communication.

Among these general theoretical maps are uses-and-gratification theories, which map a variety of psychological variables that influence the selection of material from the mass media; agenda setting theory, which maps the influence of news coverage on the focus of public attention; and the scientific rhetoric, a theoretical map of message and audience characteristics relevant to attitude change that originated with Hovland's evaluations of the Army orientation films.

Unlike counting research, which is largely in the hands of commercial research organizations, and decision-making research with its constraints imposed by the decision maker, theoretical research is a virtually limitless domain open to the academic researcher with little competition. Mass communication is a vast frontier for scholarly inquiry, a frontier that continues to change and expand almost daily. There are maps of some aspects of the field, but even these maps present major opportunities for creative research. And there are many aspects of mass communication without theoretical maps. In the academic setting the creative scholar has virtually unlimited freedom to chart his or her own route of exploration.

Origins of Research Ideas

There can be many origins for research ideas, ranging from pure whimsy and idle curiosity to systematic efforts at explicating some aspect of mass communication. Coming full circle and pulling the poles of this continuum together is possible if whimsical ideas are subsequently explored in a disciplined way. The winner of a major prize in physics for his work on the basic nature of matter was once asked how he came up with his theoretical insight. It all began on a warm summer afternoon, he said, upon opening a bottle of beer and noting the bubbles rushing up through the brew. That bit of idle curiosity, supplemented by some very disciplined thought and research, yielded significant new knowledge on the nature of matter. Situations prompting good research ideas are all around us.

Idle curiosity and systematic theoretical explication are the polar opposites. Figure 16.2 lists several other major benchmarks in between that denote possible starting points for academic research.

For that matter, all of these benchmarks could be starting points as well for research in a professional or commercial setting, but the need to

FIGURE 16.2 *Starting Points for Academic Research Ideas*

1. Idle curiosity
2. Topics of the moment
3. Applied research
4. Transformation of research questions into programs of research
5. Elaboration and extension of existing theory

count and to produce decision-making research tends to dominate and push the research of mass communication organizations into the middle of this continuum.

Idle Curiosity

Here the creative, innovative bent of the individual is given total free rein. Although many of the research fragments resulting from this starting point remain isolated research fragments, some will prove highly productive, changing things in highly significant ways. One example, based on idle curiosity about why beer foams, already has been considered. Another classic example—which also shows that the value of such work is not always recognized at first—is the invention of the computer mouse. Today the mouse is a commonplace device, but when a Xerox research group invented it, the company gave it away as a whimsical device with no practical application. Within the mass communication arena, the value of several early studies about the influence of the news media on the images of political candidates was not fully recognized until the theory of the agenda-setting role of the mass media was systematically expanded and explicated twenty years later.

Because research originating in whimsy and idle curiosity often enough pays major dividends in the form of innovative intellectual advances, over the years major research operations such as Bell Laboratories, IBM, the Rand Corporation, and Xerox have instructed many of their researchers to follow their whims. For many academics, one of the great attractions of the university is a similar freedom.

Topics of the Moment

Mass communication is a lively arena these days. Long-established media, such as daily newspapers and network television, are caught up in major changes that began a decade ago or more. There are changes in their content, declines in the size of their audiences, and new roles for them in the corporate world. New media—or plans for new media services—dominate the horizon. The Internet, for example, sometimes seems to be everywhere and about everything. But in this evolving multimedia environment, few, if any, have a clear vision of its future. Opportunities and needs for research abound.

Furthermore, the impact of these media on the public and the implications of all these changes for society generate a steady stream of controversy. Among the recurring topics of the moment are the professional ethics and implications for public perceptions and opinions of docudramas—George Wallace recently, John F. Kennedy a few years ago; that centuries-old staple of journalism, crime reporting—O. J. Simpson and a concurrent, but nonexistent crime wave a few years ago; the perennial efficacy and possible bias of political reporting that surfaces every four years for the presidential campaign; and a continuing discussion of what the Internet means for journalism and for society. In short, numerous topics of the moment are of direct relevance to professional communicators. Any of these could be the focus of a research project.

But is this kind of research a good investment of academic time and resources? Much of the research on topics of the moment is descriptive, simple compilations of who is doing what or, more often, who is saying what, promising what, or prophesying what. Although these descriptive overviews are helpful in current professional discussions, they also quickly become dated. In most cases, the short life span of this research results from the lack of any original intellectual contribution that advances our understanding of the topic. The research is simple description, not actual analysis that adds an intellectual dimension to the compilation. Of course, this does not have to be the case.

Current topics are often the latest manifestation of phenomena with long histories in the evolution of mass communication. In his book *MediaMorphis* (1997), technology expert Roger Fidler views the current evolution of new communication technologies as a later phase in the third mediamorphosis in human communication. Placing topics of the moment in a theoretical context can yield insight into the present situation and a rich opportunity for present research to build creatively on the previous work of other scholars. To use a venerable cliché, placing the present in a larger theoretical context expands our perspective from the handful of contemporary trees that are so fascinating to the ongoing history of the forest.

Applied Research

For faculty members or students in a university's professional program in advertising, journalism, or public relations, numerous practical questions exist whose answers can be systematically pursued. Sometimes this pragmatic research is decision-making research funded by a media organization. This was the case in a research project conducted by one of the authors of this book that produced a decision model for editors to use in evaluating the standing features in newspapers.

The origin of this decision model was the practical question of an editor at a mid-size newspaper in upstate New York who wanted to add new material to his newspaper. But to do so, he needed to delete some of the existing columns and features. The ensuing research project gave the editor the specific information that he needed to revamp the newspaper. The project also yielded a general model for decision making by editors that has been applied across the country by many researchers, including a national research firm that helped a West Coast daily redesign its entire newspaper. There also is a theoretical contribution in this body of research to our knowledge of how people read the newspaper.

Sometimes applied research is based on a general, pragmatic question rather than an immediate decision-making situation. At the outset, that question could be very broad, such as "Why do people read newspapers?" In other words, the origins of a research project could be a creative mixture of pragmatism, curiosity, and a desire to advance our theoretical knowledge of mass communication.

Over the years, the authors of this book have completed a wide variety of research on newspaper audiences, much of it in pursuit of answers to that broad, basic question of why people do, or do not, read a daily newspaper regularly. The origins of one project were in that axiom of democratic theory: "A good citizen is an informed citizen." One implication of this assertion is that each individual in a democratic society has a civic obligation to keep up with the news by reading a daily newspaper, watching the news on TV, or by some other strategy of information seeking. The key to turning this idea into a research project was to devise a measure for the strength of this normative belief that there is a duty to keep up with the news. Once it was possible to measure individual differences in the strength of this belief, those individual differences could be compared to individual differences in the frequency of exposure to various news media.

The first task, the construction of an attitude scale, was completed during a series of newspaper audience surveys at four sites across the

United States. Using data on exposure to news media from the same surveys, McCombs and Poindexter also established the predictive validity of their civic attitude scale. Responses to a series of attitude items, such as "It is important to be informed about news and current events," were very good predictors of exposure to the news, especially readership of newspapers. For example, among persons with low scores on the civic attitude scale, only 58 percent were frequent newspaper readers. Among persons with high scores on the civic attitude scale, 82 percent were frequent newspaper readers (McCombs & Poindexter, 1983).

Interestingly, this research was nested within a project that basically was counting research. But the pursuit of intellectual curiosity about one possible answer to a broad, but pragmatic, professional question quickly resulted in widespread practical applications. The concept of civic attitudes was used in applied research projects ranging from national surveys in the United States by the Newspaper Advertising Bureau and in Europe by the Swedish press association to market research in individual cities such as Chicago (Newspaper Research Journal, 1983). Idle curiosity harnessed to theoretical and methodological discipline can yield both practical applications in the mass communication arena and theoretical contributions.

Transformation of Research Questions into Programs of Research

Many research projects begin with a question whose generic form is "What are the effects of . . . ?" or "What is the relationship between . . . and . . . ?" One of the major assets of the academic world is the opportunity to read widely about mass communication and to teach a variety of courses. Both the preparation for teaching and the actual classroom experience produce numerous questions about mass communication. From this stream of questions come numerous queries that can be the origins of research projects.

One criterion for winnowing out the best questions to be pursued in empirical research is to consider which ones are sufficiently significant and insightful to warrant a program of research. In other words, which questions warrant a commitment to pursue the question and its implications across a number of research settings and several specific research projects?

One illustration of this benchmark is a series of studies on newspaper competition and its presumed benefits to the public. This program of research also provides a smooth transition from the previous benchmark, applied research, to this intellectual setting, a program of research. There are few matters more practical than a newspaper's defense against government charges of monopoly and restraint of trade. The opening phase in this program of research, an extensive series of content analyses of newspapers in Montreal and Winnipeg, was part of Thomson Newspapers' defense against charges brought by the Canadian government following a series of transactions that ended newspaper competition between Thomson and Southam Inc. in Montreal, Winnipeg, Ottawa, and Vancouver. At the time, the two companies together accounted for about two-thirds of Canada's daily newspaper circulation.

With both the immediate application and the larger social and theoretical implications in mind, two research questions were asked:

1. Does economic competition among daily newspapers create diversity in news content?
2. Will the disappearance of daily competition in a city result in negative changes in the surviving newspaper?

Comparisons of the competing newspapers in both Winnipeg and Montreal two years prior to the disappearance of daily competition yielded a portrait of "rivals in conformity." Only minor differences existed in each pair of rivals. And, in response to the second question, McCombs (1987) noted in a *Journalism Quarterly* article, "Only a few changes from before to after the end of competition were found, and all of these were positive changes in the quality of the editorial product."

Although the same patterns were found in Montreal and Winnipeg, the guiding questions in that research deserved broader inquiry. An individual study, no matter how well conceived, examines only one or, at best, a few outcroppings of a more general phenomenon. This general topic, the increasing concentration of newspapers in North America, has been the focus of hundreds of books and articles. Rather than empirical investigations of the key research questions pursued in Canada these books and articles were primarily philosophical. So the research begun in Canada was continued in an American setting, where the suspension of the Cleveland *Press* in June 1982 left that city with a single daily newspaper voice. In line with the findings from the Canadian project, few differences were found in the competing Cleveland dailies in the preceding years; and after the suspension of the *Press*, the surviving *Plain Dealer* remained essentially the same newspaper.

The empirical conclusions of these projects also advanced the broader theoretical perspective that the increasing professionalization and bureaucratization of journalism "exerts a centripetal force on news gathering and editing that works against diversity" (McCombs, 1987, p. 744).

This perspective is applicable to a very broad range of research settings and an extensive program of research.

Elaboration and Extension of Existing Theory

Many research projects originate in a question about some aspect of mass communication. If the question is sufficiently interesting and significant, several different researchers are likely to pursue an answer, or a single researcher, perhaps with colleagues, will conduct studies across various settings to answer the question. The research on newspaper competition in Canada and its extension to Cleveland is a simple example of the accumulation of knowledge beyond the specific circumstances of one or two settings. The result, as McCombs noted, was a general theoretical proposition that news norms enhance homogeneity, not diversity. More specifically, the research questions about competition and diversity and performance in the absence of competition that guided the research in Montreal, Winnipeg, and Cleveland are now transformed into research hypotheses. With evidence in hand from three sites, it is now reasonable to hypothesize what the specific effects of competition will be on diversity and what the specific outcome will be in the absence of competition. Future research can do considerably more than answer a question. It can test specific hypotheses about competition and take the first steps toward an elaboration of a theory about the impact of competition on news organizations.

Sometimes, as we have just seen, hypotheses and the beginnings of theory arise from the accumulation of empirical research on a topic. Other times, hypotheses and the initial elaboration of a theory are forged from the merger of several previously unrelated theory fragments. In this situation, the hypotheses have added strength because of their origins in a variety of empirical and conceptual settings.

As more research tests these hypotheses, typically new concepts are added to the theory or the domain of the theory is enlarged. Either way, the result is an extension of the theory with a larger number of hypotheses to test and more opportunities for researchers to explore that aspect of mass communication. Historically this was true for agenda-setting theory, which began with the simple assertion that the prominence of public issues in news coverage would influence the salience of those issues among voters. Extensions of the theory identified a variety of conditions under which this influence would be enhanced or reduced. Further extension of the theory began with a question: Who sets the media's agenda? The question rapidly spawned a large set of hypotheses about influences shaping the media agenda. The more recent extension of agenda-setting theory to include the idea of an agenda of attributes—the way that public issues, political candidates, or other topics on the news agenda are framed—has created a vast new set of hypotheses that researchers are just beginning to test.

In the social sciences, the term "theory" covers a diverse variety of situations. Some theories are little more than loose perspectives with ambiguous hypotheses at best. Other theories are narrowly discrete statements about some aspect of mass communication. They are theoretical fragments. Other theories are also fragments in the sense that they deal with a rather limited portion of mass communication, but for that sector there are detailed sets of related hypotheses. Yet other theories cover major portions of mass communication and contain numerous hypotheses. What all these theories have in common are testable hypotheses to guide the design of new research projects that will, in turn, contribute to the continued elaboration and growth of the theory.

Intertwined Benchmarks

Although presented in an orderly manner here as a continuum that ranges from whimsical thoughts to disciplined reasoning, we saw at the outset that the five origins of research projects are intertwined benchmarks. It is possible, of course, for just one of these benchmarks in isolation to be the starting point for a new research project, and one of the great assets of an academic career is the freedom to begin an intellectual journey at any of these points. But, as we already have seen in numerous examples, the best research projects—which is to say, those most likely to make significant contributions and to be noticed by peers—draw together several of these starting points. At the outset, we considered examples of how projects originating in a casual observation about beer or with a series of films that had a very specific applied goal were strengthened by the application of existing theory.

To organize a general strategy for designing good communication research, these five points of origin can be divided into two groups. In the first group are idle curiosity, topics of the moment, and applied research. In the second group are transformation of research questions into programs of research and the elaboration and extension of existing theory. Applying the strategy is easy: Select at least one point of origin from each group. Essentially any combination works, and, of course, you can add more elements as you proceed. That is part of the creativity of the research process.

Intersection of Benchmarks and Intellectual Tools of the Scientific Method

To simplify the strategy even more, Figure 16.3 shows that in terms of scientific method, these points of origin are grounded to varying degrees on four intellectual tools.

 Operational Definitions

All five benchmarks involve operational definitions. An operational definition is the specific sets of circumstances that represent a concept in a particular study, and many projects arising from the first group of three starting points are devoid of any explicit concepts. But even without an explicit concept, the specific communication, measures, historic setting, and so forth that define a particular piece of research are all present. Of course, the contribution of such research is limited to the situation at hand and adds little to our accumulated knowledge of mass communication that can be applied in new situations. Because the academic perspective favors theoretical research with long-range value, few academic projects fail to place the work in the context of established communication concepts. Most academic work also goes beyond descriptive research on isolated concepts and at least asks questions about the relationships among concepts. For much of the research, the goal is to contribute to theory, and the starting point for the research is a hypothesis or a set of related hypotheses that constitute a theory (or some portion of a theory) about mass communication.

 Concepts, Hypotheses, and Theories

Philosopher of science Carl Hempel (1965) has compared these four intellectual elements of the scientific method to a spider web. The strands of the web connecting it to a wall or the ground are the operational definitions linking concepts to some specific aspect of reality that is the focus of a particular study's observations. The knots in the web, those points where two strands connect, are the abstract concepts the researcher uses to organize his or her observations and ideas. Typical concepts in mass communication research range from simple demographics to complex psychological concepts such as attitude or need for orientation. The strands in the web linking one knot to another are the hypotheses, explicitly stated relationships among the concepts. The entire web, which is composed of concepts, hypotheses, and operational definitions, is the

FIGURE 16.3   *Four Intellectual Tools in Academic Research*

1. Operational definitions
2. Concepts
3. Hypotheses
4. Theory

theory as it exists at any moment in its evolution. Like spider webs, good theories continue to grow and expand.

Doing the research that makes the theory grow and expand is a core value in the academic world. This emphasis on theoretical contributions exerts major influence in the pre-research phase on the series of decisions about which specific new project to undertake. The pre-research phase for planning new research can start with any point in the web, even the entire web. But central to the set of decisions that focus the research—that put a fence around the specific operational definitions, concepts, and/or hypotheses to be included in the study—is the criterion of fruitfulness and long-range productivity.

A young field of research like mass communication research offers many opportunities to add to our theoretical knowledge. Books detailing our knowledge of mass communication typically discuss dozens of concepts and theories. Some of these intellectual webs contain only a few strands. They easily can be expanded or connected to other webs. Even the larger, more fully developed webs have many gaps that can be filled in. Coming up with a new research project that adds to one of these theoretical webs is easy. However, the objective is not just to fill in one more strand. The creative aspect of theoretical research is to identify a particular strand or to define a new concept whose addition to some existing web creates a set of new insights and opportunities for research.

In some fields of research, the value of any particular study—or on a larger plane, the professional contribution of a particular researcher—is measured by the number of subsequent research reports and articles that cite a particular study or researcher. When we describe a study as fruitful, we mean that it has stimulated other researchers' work in that area and led to significant additions to the theoretical web. Defining a study with high potential for fruitfulness is the creative, intellectual challenge in the pre-research phase. The academic setting affords tremendous freedom in selecting research topics and planning a specific research project, but this freedom should not be squandered in haphazard decisions at the pre-research phase.

Translating Goals into Research Methods

Once the intellectual goals of the research are set, the next step is to translate these goals into specific research methodologies. Whether the goals of the research have an academic or professional origin, the researcher now decides how to gather evidence pertinent to these goals. Sometimes the methodological decision is obvious. If, for example, the goal is detailed information about some message or set of messages — books, TV newscasts, or advertisements — content analysis is an obvious answer. But sometimes the answer is not so obvious, as, for example, when the goal is to learn something about audience reaction. In this case, the options include focus groups, survey research, and both field and laboratory experiments. Because the academic researcher working on his or her personal research is under fewer constraints than most researchers working on professional projects, the choices sometimes seem perplexing. In too many cases, the methodological decision is based on personal whim and convenience.

In the case of audience research, there is a compelling logic in selecting the research methodology based on a simple question: How much do we know about the research topic? Or, in terms of Hempel's metaphor of social science theory as a spider web: How much of the web exists? The logic based on this question is a cumulative sequence of methods for studying audiences, a sequence that extends from the situation in which we know little or nothing about a topic to one in which our knowledge of the audience is highly detailed. The sequence of methods is displayed in Figure 16.4.

As you know, the focus group is a good way to find out how people think about and talk about some aspect of mass communication. It is a useful opening gambit in our quest for mapping audience response to mass communication. On the basis of focus group findings, previous research, and/or previous experience, the researcher then can move forward in the sequence and formulate a survey questionnaire. (*Warning:* Previous professional experience and "common sense" are often poor guides for questionnaire construction because of their many hidden assumptions. The explicit knowledge obtained in prior research, such as focus groups, is a far better guide for questionnaire construction.)

FIGURE 16.4 *Sequence of Research Methods*

Focus group $\longrightarrow$ Survey $\longrightarrow$ Field experiment $\longrightarrow$ Laboratory experiment

Compared to the focus group, the survey has the advantages of external validity and a tremendous capacity to systematically gather comparative data from large samples on dozens of variables. These also are its advantages over experiments, which must focus narrowly on how a handful of individuals respond to one or two variables. The survey enables the researcher to canvass the audience on dozens of potentially relevant variables and, in the analysis of that data, to identify the variables that are central to the audience's responses. It is this scope of the research, plus the added precision, that places survey research second in the sequence of methods.

The findings at this stage enable the researcher to move forward to the experiment and to employ the rigor of the experiment to examine in close, precise detail those few variables that are central to the audience's behavior. Premature use of experiments risks missing relevant variables and learning a great deal about minimally useful topics. Field experiments have been listed between survey research and laboratory experiments because they have some characteristics of both methods. In any event, they almost always lack the precision of the laboratory experiment with its close control of the communication environment and its compelling evidence of causality.

This sequences of methods for audience research spans the two roles played by researchers, explorers, and surveyors. For new and unfamiliar topics, the researcher is an explorer whose best methodological tools are the focus group and survey. As the surveys become increasingly sophisticated and detailed, the researcher's role evolves into that of the surveyor, who has the task of taking precise measures and making detailed maps. The surveyor's task often can be greatly enhanced through the use of experiments with their precise controls.

Executing the Research Plan during the Research Phase

The core of the research phase is the systematic and creative application of research methodology to achieve the goals of the project. This is the tactical execution of the research plan prepared in the pre-research phase. Little in this phase distinguishes the behavior of the academic as researcher from the academic as consultant or contractor to the decision maker. Whether the purposes of the research are academic or professional, the researcher executes the appropriate methodological steps to secure the data needed to meet the project's goals. In this phase of research, the methodological requirements detailed in the earlier chapters of this book are identical, regardless of the origins of the project.

Two of the major journals of our field, *Public Opinion Quarterly* and the *International Journal of Public Opinion Research,* publish both academic and professional research on mass communication and public opinion. There is a single standard for publication. All research should be methodologically rigorous and meet the highest possible standards.

The research phase concludes with the preparation of a written report and the reporting of the results to the relevant audience. Figure 16.5, which compares the written academic and business reports, shows that most of the core requirements are the same. The differences charted in Figure 16.5 primarily result from the difference in the relevant audience. Typically the audience for the business report is the decision maker and possibly a few of his or her colleagues who are focused on a particular professional or commercial situation. Typically the audience for the academic research report is a more diffuse group of scholars, persons who are interested in the topic and may use the information in their teaching or subsequent research.

These audience differences account, for example, for the absence of a literature review and discussion of the theoretical foundations in the business report, but for their presence in the academic report. But the core information makes the two kinds of reports essentially identical. According to Figure 16.5, both types of reports detail: how the research

FIGURE 16.5 *Comparison of Academic and Business Research Reports*

	Academic Report	Business Report
1. Cover Letter	Yes	Yes
2. Report Binder	**No**	**Yes**
3. Title and Author Page	Yes	Yes
4. Table of Contents	**No**	**Yes**
5. Executive Summary	**No**	**Yes**
6. Abstract	**Yes**	**No**
7. Introduction	Yes	Yes
8. Background/Context	Yes	Yes
9. Literature Review	**Yes**	**No**
10. Theoretical Foundation	**Yes**	**No**
11. Description of Method	Yes	Yes
12. Results	Yes	Yes
13. Discussion	Yes	Yes
14. Recommendations	Yes	Yes
15. Conclusions	Yes	Yes
16. Endnotes/Footnotes	Yes	Yes
17. References	Yes	Yes
18. Appendix	**Varies**	**Yes**

was done (#11 Method); what it found (#12 Results); what the larger meaning of these results are, either for the specific professional situation or for future academic research, and what specific conclusions can be drawn from this empirical investigation (#13 Discussion, #14 Recommendations, and #15 Conclusions); the sources and background for statements made in the report (#16 Endnotes/Footnotes and #17 References). A business report usually includes an appendix (#18) to display the questionnaire or other measurement instrument. Although an academic journal article might ocassionally include an appendix, a master's thesis or doctoral dissertation always includes this section. Effective communication requires shaping the report to your audience. Effective academic research reporting also requires covering the basics listed in Figure 16.5.

Activities during the Post-Research Phase

The research project is now completed and a written report prepared and disseminated to the pertinent audience. In the case of counting research or decision-making research, this almost always means that the research is at an end. The desired answer is in hand, and media professionals will go about their tasks with this additional information in mind. However, in the case of theoretically oriented strategic analysis, the completion of a project is far from the last word. Any single project is just one step along the trail of creative exploration and intellectual mapping.

> Scientists know that questions are not settled; rather, they are given provisional answers for which it is contingent upon the imagination of followers to find more illuminating solutions. Practitioners of science are different from artists in that they give primacy to logic and evidence, but the most fundamental progress in science is achieved through hunch, analogy, insight, and creativity.
>
> (Baltimore, 1997)

Noted sociologist Robert K. Merton has described these tandem roles of logic and evidence on the one hand and creativity on the other in terms of a spiral in which the work of the academic oscillates between theory and empirical research. As we saw in the discussion on the origins of research, the starting point can be highly empirical, the collection of data relevant to some topic of the moment or to some specific goal of a media professional. At other times, the starting point is theoretical. Regardless of the starting point, or the mix of starting points, the emphasis in the academic world is on research that has value beyond the situation of the moment. A key academic goal is the production of fruitful research that advances the explication of the mass communication process. To unfold the fuller professional and social meaning of mass communication, to make clear and explicit just what mass communication is about, involves both theory and empirical research.

Theory, by which we mean here concepts, hypotheses, and the theories that they define, guides empirical research. What should the researcher observe? Too many surveys, for example, are filled with questions that, at the time, are interesting to ask, but that add little to our cumulative knowledge and insight. Theory imposes discipline on empirical observations. In turn, the findings of the empirical observations put the theory to the test and open the door to its advancement. On some occasions, the findings contradict or, at least, fail to fully support the theory. Changes and modifications must be made in the theory. But the findings also can yield new insights and advance the development and expansion of the theory. Over time, if the area is a fruitful and productive one for research, the spiral continues as theory spawns empirical research and empirical research expands the theory in an ongoing cycle.

Advancing the Program of Research

Deductive Reasoning

In this ongoing cycle, both deductive and inductive reasoning are at work. Deductive reasoning is moving from the general to the specific. Or, to put it another way, deductive reasoning is tracing out the consequences of a general perspective or statement in detail. Although frequently termed "deductive logic," which would seem to imply an inevitable, sure path from the general to the particular, deductive reasoning in any field of research involves a considerable element of creativity.

> It is impossible to follow the march of one of the great theories of physics, to see it unroll majestically its regular deductions starting from initial hypotheses, to see its consequences represent a multitude of experimental laws, down to the smallest detail, without being charmed by the beauty of such a construction, without feeling keenly that such a creation of the human mind is truly a work of art.
>
> (Duhem, 1954)

On a less grand scale and more familiar to most Americans is the use of deductive reasoning by Sherlock Holmes, perhaps the most famous of all fictional detectives. A typical Holmes adventure involves the same spiral of empirical observation and theorizing described by Robert Merton in scholarly research. Almost always for Holmes the cycle begins with the gathering of empirical data, followed by the formulation of a theory that explains the events at hand. With a theory in mind, Holmes then pursues a mental "if . . . then . . ." game in which he deduces the consequences of the theory (the general picture) for additional empirical particulars (the specifics). For example, *if* the perpetrator of the crime is a stranger to the household, *then* there should be footprints outside the window. This is an empirically testable hypothesis that logically flows from the general theory of the crime and leads the investigator to new empirical observations. From theory, Holmes returns to empirical observation that puts the theory to test. In the adventures of Sherlock Holmes, the theories nearly always result in empirical observations that support the theory. Real-life investigators of mass communication are not always so lucky.

 ## Inductive Reasoning

Inductive reasoning is the opposite process: reasoning from the particular to the general in an effort to find a general pattern from the empirical particulars. In this regard, it is the creative process exemplified by Sherlock Holmes or by academics who formulate theories about physics or mass communication or any other topic.

The limitations of both inductive and deductive reasoning are the inherent limitations of the scope of our empirical evidence. General theories aim at universal or near-universal statements that will hold across most, if not all, settings in time and space. But our empirical evidence can never have this scope. In the face of this dilemma, deductive reasoning generally has the superior position. Typically the theory that results from inductive reasoning is limited in scope—a simple spider web in terms of Hempel's metaphor—whose structure rests almost wholly on a limited set of empirical observations. The theory is an effort to spin a theoretical web from limited empirical evidence. In contrast, theories that lend themselves to deductive reasoning frequently are more complex webs of theoretical relationships. Under these circumstances, the strength of theory lies not just in the empirical evidence relevant to the hypothesis at hand, but also in the web of logical relationships and the body of evidence supporting other portions of the theory.

Both deductive and inductive reasoning can be significant paths of advancement in our explication of mass communication. To repeat the opening sentence of this chapter: "Research is as much a creative enterprise as painting, sculpture, advertising, or journalism." Harnessing this creativity to research methodology for specific projects is the key to successful and intellectually satisfying research.

SUGGESTED RESEARCH ACTIVITIES

1. Identify a professor who is conducting interesting research. Interview the professor about his or her program of research, how he or she became interested in the research area, the process used to conduct the research, and future research interests. Describe what you learned from your interview in a three- to five-page paper.

2. Read one of the published articles from the person you interviewed. Summarize the study's purpose, method, and major findings.

3. Review academic journals such as *Journalism & Mass Communication Quarterly* to find an article of interest. Read the article, paying careful attention to its organization. Summarize the article, including the purpose, method of research, and major results. Which type of academic research starting point, as described in Figure 16.2, best describes the study and why?

RECOMMENDED READING

For perspectives on reporting academic research studies, see:

JEAN FOLKERTS, "An Editorial Comment," *Journalism & Mass Communication Quarterly*, 1996, vol. 32, no. 2, pp. 280–281.

MICHAEL RYAN, "Pitfalls to Avoid in Conducting and Describing Scholarly Research," *Journalism & Mass Communication Educator*, 1998, vol. 52, no. 4, pp. 72–79.

 **CHAPTER 17**

Research Applications, Ethics, and the Future of Communication Research

- How has research been used in creative, marketing, planning, and management decisions?
- How has research been used to generate news stories?
- How has research been used as a reporting tool?
- What are the ethical issues that should be of concern to researchers?
- What issues will affect the future of research?

Research Is Behind Large and Small Decisions

In the movie *Up Close and Personal,* starring Michelle Pfeiffer and Robert Redford, a young woman who dreams of becoming a famous television reporter, even though she has no TV reporting experience, gets her first break. Warren Justice, a former network television White House correspondent, who is now the news director in Miami, hires Sally Atwater—not as a reporter—but as a news desk assistant. Warren teaches the aspiring reporter good journalism, and he eventually promotes her to on-air reporter while changing her name from Sally to Tally.

After succeeding in Miami, the now experienced Tally gets hired by the news director at the network-owned television station in Philadelphia, a much larger market. After watching Tally report on the air, the news director, ever mindful of ratings, tells the marketing people to conduct focus groups to gauge viewers' reactions to the new on-air reporter.

The focus group participants hate Tally. They especially dislike her blond hair. One woman describes Tally as "nobody from nowhere." After reviewing the focus groups, the news director decides to make over Tally's appearance. He starts by ordering Tally to change her hair color from blonde to brunette.

Although this use of focus groups was in a fictional movie, it is not very far from reality in the real world of research applications. In the movie, television, newspaper, radio, cable, magazine, and advertising industries, research is conducted to help make decisions. And sometimes research is conducted to validate decisions that have already been made. In academic institutions that offer degrees in the communication fields, research is conducted to understand social and human behavior and its relationship to media, communication, and society. This understanding can lead to building models and constructing theories about how communication works, including how messages are produced, and how they are used and received by the audience.

Many research studies conducted in universities also have practical applications for industry as well as government. Often industry and government will commission studies from academic researchers because they have expertise in the methodology and knowledge of the literature on the issue to be studied.

Industry uses research to plan, create, and evaluate campaigns; launch new programs, products, and features; and drop old ones. News editors and producers use research to generate poll stories that tell about the communities or the country. Government uses research to make funding decisions and write or change policies. Lawmakers use research to write laws and politicians use research to identify issues that resonate with the voters so they can get elected. The research applications are endless.

Research Applications for Marketing, Promotion, and Advertising

What have been some specific uses of research? The domestic marketing division of the 20th Century Fox Film Corporation used research to create trailers for the hit movie, "Home Alone" that would "encourage kids to come back even more by humorously suggesting they see the film a million times" (Elliott, 1991).

According to senior vice president of research and marketing for the Fox Broadcasting Company, audience research helped them identify market opportunities among young adult viewers who were turning off the three major networks. Fox Broadcasting was able to target this youthful market segment with programs like "21 Jump Street" and "Beverly Hills 90210" (Elliott, 1991).

Research also helped Foote, Cone & Belding, San Francisco, the advertising agency for Levi Strauss & Company's Dockers' casual clothes for men, in the creation of the Dockers campaign that showed Dockers-clad men feeling comfortable in a Dockers world (Elliott, 1991).

ScrippsHealth, a managed healthcare organization in San Diego County used Kenneth C. Smith Advertising to develop a campaign that would help them better reach consumers who were signing up for a health and medical provider. The agency conducted focus groups to learn consumer perceptions of ScrippsHealth, which is a joint venture of the renowned Scripps Clinic and Research Foundation and Scripps Memorial Hospitals (Pickard, 1996).

From the focus groups, the agency and client learned that the Scripps name was highly respected in the field of medical research. Focus group participants thought it was the place to go if you were rich and had an exotic disease, but they didn't feel it was a good choice for a cold. As a result of what was learned during the focus groups, the agency humanized Scripps by creating a humorous campaign that showed how real people with ordinary medical problems should turn to Scripps when they need medical attention (Pickard, 1996).

Research was not used in the creation of a Nissan advertising campaign, but it was used after the campaign was launched. According to the *New York Times,* a $200 million image campaign for Nissan Motor Corporation U.S.A. by creative director and copywriter Rob Siltanen of TBWA Chiat/Day started with the idea of remote control toy cars (Barboza, 1996). The spot, which used the tag line "Life is a Journey. Enjoy the Ride," was chosen by *Adweek* as one of the best of September 1996. Even though the creative director did not take advantage of research to create the campaign, research was used after the campaign was launched to measure the impact of the advertising. The focus groups and surveys found that consumers liked the spots a great deal.

According to *Newsweek,* when Warner-Lambert wanted to find out how consumers used mouthwash, it hired a company to conduct some ethnographic research (Kaufman, 1997). Thirty-seven families were paid to set up cameras in their bathrooms that would videotape how they used Scope and Listerine's new mint-flavored mouthwash, Fresh Burst Listerine, which was designed to compete with Scope. The taping showed that Scope users swished the mouthwash around and immediately spit it out, whereas users of the new mint-flavored Listerine held the mouthwash in their mouths longer. According to *Newsweek,* the results suggested that Listerine was still associated with medicines.

Ethnographic research was also used to help develop an advertising campaign for Pioneer Stereo (Kaufman, 1997). Before developing the campaign, BBDO West ad agency sent the Pioneer Stereo account executive to Austin, Texas, to drive around with the type of consumers who might buy their product. The agency wanted to find out how consumers talked about their car stereos. According to *Newsweek,* consumers' verbatim quotes such as "My car is my holy temple," were incorporated into the ad campaign, which helped Pioneer Stereo surge ahead of its chief rival, Sony.

The lead creative advertising agency for McDonald's, DDB Needham Chicago, which regained that role from Chicago-based Leo Burnett in July 1997, also conducted research in developing a new campaign (Kane, 1997). They conducted twenty-six focus groups in seven or eight cities around the country to test the tag line for its new campaign, "Did somebody say McDonald's?" According to the *New York Times,* focus group participants responded positively to the new theme, and the new advertising campaign was launched in October 1997.

Interested in expanding its share of the African American market, Kraft General Foods' Stove Top Stuffing brand hired Chicago-based Burrell Communications to create a campaign to reach the African American consumer (Burrell, 1997; Woods, 1995). Brainstorming, focus group research, and taste tests preceded the development of an advertising campaign. One important issue that needed to be addressed in research was attitudes toward the term "stuffing." In the African American community, the term "dressing" rather than "stuffing" is used to refer to the bread or cornbread side dish that is traditionally served with turkey during the Thanksgiving and Christmas holidays.

After the focus group research confirmed that "dressing" was still the preferred term among focus group participants, the advertising campaign incorporated the word "dressing" into the new ads that were created. The tag line said, "The box says stuffing. The taste says dressing."

Research is also used by Mad Dogs and Englishmen, a New York–based creative advertising agency. According to Chairman Nick Cohen (1997), the agency conducts research in every project to ask consumers how they feel. For example, when developing an advertising campaign for dx.com Internet Business Center, an internet consulting firm, the agency conducted focus groups that revealed the fears and anxieties people had about both using the Internet and being left behind if they didn't know how to use the Internet.

As a result of the focus groups, the agency created ads that first expressed consumers' anxieties, then offered a solution to the anxieties. Copy from three of the print ads said:

> **Are the geeks taking over the world?** *Am I the last person on earth who hasn't been on the net?* Relax. Take an hour off work this week and come down to dx.com Internet Business Center. Let our very human staff sit you down on the very latest equipment, take a deep breath and test drive the net until it all makes sense.

> **Damn, the Internet!** *It comes barging into my life while I'm still figuring out how to set the clock on my VCR.* Relax. Take an hour off work this week and come down to dx.com Internet Business Center. Let our very human staff sit you down on the very latest equipment, take a deep breath and test drive the net until it all makes sense.

> **Will the net steal my job?** *Will I blow millions on the wrong equipment? If I don't have a web site, will I be ostracized by society?* Calm down. Take an hour off work this week and come down to dx.com Internet Business Center. Let our very human staff sit you down on the very latest equipment, take a deep breath and test drive the net until it all makes sense.

Before proposing ideas for a campaign for California's Division of Recycling, the California-based advertising agency Muse Cordero Chen analyzed secondary research and conducted intercept interviews to better understand recycling behavior in California (Wilson, 1998). Specifically the agency wanted to know why consumers recycled and why they were less likely to recycle large plastic bottles. The information from this research would be used to develop an advertising and public relations campaign to increase recycling in general and large plastic bottle recycling in particular.

A secondary analysis of the research that had already been conducted by the Division of Recycling suggested that people with higher educations were more likely to recycle for environmental reasons, whereas people with less education recycled for economic reasons. In addition, newly arrived immigrants also often recycled for the money they would receive for recycling various products.

The intercept interviews, which were conducted at several recycling centers around Los Angeles, tried to find out why the 32-ounce plastic bottles were not a popular item to recycle. The research suggested that plastic bottles were recycled less than other items because they were inconvenient, cumbersome, and more of a hassle. In addition, the research revealed that consumers were not even aware that the large plastic bottles could be recycled.

As a result of the research, Muse Cordero Chen recognized that they needed to develop separate messages for the recycling campaign. One message would target those who recycled for environmental reasons; a separate message would target those who recycled for economic reasons. The research results also helped the agency realize the importance of educating consumers about recycling large plastic bottles. The message also needed to teach consumers efficient methods for recycling the cumbersome plastic bottles and educate them about the valuable products produced from recycled plastic bottles.

The Economist used research to increase its circulation (Elliott, September 1997). Interested in increasing circulation in North America, the weekly British magazine conducted research and found that in North America, people who should know and understand what *The Economist* is, don't. Research among professional-managerial households with incomes of $100,000 or more found that respondents were unaware of the weekly magazine or incorrectly thought it was a journal of economics. As a result of this research, the New York advertising agency Weiss, Whitten, Stagliano developed a campaign to emphasize *The Economist*'s international business and news coverage.

Research caused BMW of North America to revamp its advertising strategy (Elliott, August 1997). Research conducted by its advertising agency, Minneapolis-based Fallon McElligott, revealed that Lexus, Acura, and Mercedes owners bought their cars because they were "fun to drive." Because the luxury car maker was surprised and disappointed that BMWs weren't included in the "fun to drive" group, they decided to conduct more research to help them revise their advertising strategy.

To better understand how luxury car owners talked about their cars, research participants were given disposable cameras to take pictures of their cars. Mercedes and Lexus owners parked their cars in front of their houses and took pictures from far away. But BMW owners took close-up pictures of the parts of their cars such as wheels, engines, and gearshifts. The photographs "inspired the campaign's concentration on car parts."

Research Applications for Public Relations

 To Evaluate Impact

Ketchum Public Relations has conducted a significant amount of research for clients. Almost half of the sixty-four research studies conducted in 1992 were to measure and evaluate PR impact. About one-fourth of the studies were for planning purposes, and the remainder were for promotional or publicity activities for clients (Lindenmann, 1993).

One Ketchum research study used a classic experimental design to assess a public education campaign's effectiveness in reducing public exposure to a herbicide. In a different research study, Ketchum content-analyzed press coverage in the United States and Europe after simultaneous press conferences in New York and Paris. News coverage was analyzed for mentions of Ketchum's client, the competitor, and which media carried the story.

Another content analysis for a different client examined 427 newspaper, magazine, radio, and television stories that referred to the client and its product for themes and copypoints. Ketchum also used surveys in a crisis communication situation and intercepts at the mall to assess awareness of a campaign.

Research was used when Cathay Pacific Airways was launching its inaugural non-stop service from Los Angeles to Hong Kong in 1990. Rather than rely solely on advertising, the British-owned, Hong Kong–based airline wanted to use an educational program to help create awareness. The airline asked the *Los Angeles Times in Education* program to help them develop an educational program that would make Southern Californians aware of the new nonstop service. Your first author, who was then *Los Angeles Times* special projects manager directing the *Times in Education Program,* and the Cathay Pacific Airways marketing manager created an academic competition for ninth and tenth graders with prizes that included a free one-week educational trip to Hong Kong for up to thirty student winners and their teachers. The educational program was called "Ambassadors to Asia."

To participate in the competition, students, working in teams of up to six, had to write an essay on the past, present, and future of Hong Kong and one other Asian country. Winning essay teams would participate in an oral competition that asked questions on Asian culture, geography, current events, and much more. The *Los Angeles Times* newspaper was one of several sources that students used for the essays and oral competition. Twenty-seven students representing the different regions of Southern California won and received an expense-paid trip to Hong Kong (Quintanilla, 1990).

While in Hong Kong, your first author drafted a self-administered evaluation questionnaire for the students to complete on the return flight from Hong Kong. These evaluations supplemented the survey questionnaires that were sent to all teachers and students who had submitted essays for the competition. Evaluations of the "Ambassadors to Asia" program were very favorable and were subsequently used by Lufthansa, the German airline, to develop a similar academic competition to take Southern California students and their teachers to Germany for a week-long, expense-paid educational trip. Lufthansa was interested in creating awareness of its thirty years of service to California. That competition, which was expanded to include eleventh and twelfth graders, was called "Ambassadors to Europe."

 ## To Enhance Image

Research has also been used to enhance the images of institutions, organizations, and individuals. Image enhancement in the African American community became one of the goals of the University of Texas at Austin after one-on-one depth interviews were conducted by then consultant Terry A. Wilson (1993). The one-on-one interviews revealed that many African American opinion leaders in Texas associated the University with its segregationist past and not with its present efforts to recruit and support African American students.

Based on the data from the study, Wilson recommended that the University of Texas increase awareness in the African American community by running image ads in the black press. These ads were designed to tell the story of African American graduates of the University of Texas who had become successful.

Political candidates also use research to mold their image. In the 1992 presidential campaign, then presidential candidate Bill Clinton used focus groups extensively to shape his image and message, according to *The New York Times Magazine* (Kolbert, 1992). As a result of focus group research, Clinton started revealing his personal background more. Focus group results showed that participants thought Clinton had grown up with many advantages. Focus group participants were unaware that Clinton's father had been killed in a car accident before he was born or that his stepfather was an alcoholic who sometimes physically abused his mother.

Focus group results also encouraged the Clintons to expose their daughter, Chelsea, to the public more. Focus groups revealed that participants thought the Clintons didn't have children. Bill Clinton even changed his hair style because of focus groups. Focus group participants said his hair looked too blow-dried.

To Generate News

Another research application in public relations is releasing new survey results in a press release for the purpose of generating news. This technique has been used by the U.S. Census Bureau, the Pew Research Center for the People & the Press, and many more. To show how data can be used to generate news, a sample press release, displayed in Figure 17.1 (p. 352), was written from the survey that we have used throughout the book.

Research Applications in the News Media

Newspapers have used research to generate news stories based on poll results and focus groups; understand reader interest in and reaction to the editorial content, design, and features of the newspaper; and better service subscribers and advertisers. When the news media use scientific survey research methods to gather data for a news story, Phil Meyer (1991) said that's called precision journalism. These poll stories, which can cover almost any topic and are ongoing during an election season, provide a way for the public to systematically speak out. Reporters and editors may develop the topics and questions, but the opinions represent the community—not just official sources. Major national news organizations that publish or broadcast polls regularly include ABC/*Washington Post,* CBS/*New York Times, Los Angeles Times,* NBC/*Wall Street Journal,* and CNN/*USA Today.*

FIGURE 17.1 *Sample Press Release Using Survey Data to Generate News*

Downtown Business Association
Street Address
Austin, Texas 78701

Contact: Peggy Roberts
Terry A. Wilson
Telephone: (512) xxx–xxxx

FOR IMMEDIATE RELEASE

MORE SPARK AND PLACES TO PARK COULD ATTRACT AUSTINITES TO DOWNTOWN

AUSTIN, Texas—The results of a survey, commissioned by the Downtown Business Association, were released today indicating that shopping, varied entertainment, and improved parking would encourage Austinites to frequent the downtown area.

The survey, conducted by Dr. Paula Poindexter, a University of Texas at Austin Journalism and Advertising Professor, and a group of UT graduate and undergraduate students, randomly selected 476 Austin-area adults to respond to a variety of questions concerning the downtown area.

Nearly one-fifth of the survey respondents said they travel to Austin's downtown daily and one-fourth cited work as the main reason. Only 15 percent viewed shopping and restaurants as a reason to frequent downtown.

"To identify what would encourage Austinites to go downtown, our survey asked participants questions concerning improved parking, more shopping, and varied entertainment," Poindexter said.

Nearly 60 percent of the respondents indicated accessible parking as a significant factor as to whether they would consider traveling downtown more often. More available shopping and varied entertainment would attract almost 50 percent of the participants.

"These results will greatly assist us in understanding what improvements are needed to attract visitors to downtown Austin," said Stuart Williams, president of the Downtown Austin Business Association.

Respondents were also asked about the future use of Robert Mueller Airport, which will be replaced by a new airport. Nearly one-half of the respondents had no opinion or didn't know. Utilizing the old airport for housing or park land and as a recreation area were the more popular suggestions.

—30—

The *Austin American-Statesman* (1995) used results from a Texas Poll on computers to write a front page story for the TechMonday section. Because results of the statewide poll revealed that 78 percent of Texas households with incomes exceeding $60,000 own a computer, they were able to write the following lead:

> For some Texans, a computer is becoming as common a home fixture as a television set, according to a survey conducted by the Harte-Hanks Texas Poll.

The poll, which is now sponsored by Scripps-Howard, also found that 41 percent of all homes had computers and 12 percent had Internet access. A follow-up or longitudinal poll would likely reveal that the numbers had increased significantly.

Graphics Are Used to Make Poll Stories Interesting

Figure 17.2 (p. 354) is an example of how poll stories that are reported in the news use attractive graphics to visually enhance a story. This national trend study compared attitudes and opinions of adults at the beginning of Bill Clinton's first term as President of the United States in January 1993 and the start of his second term in January 1997 (*New York Times*, 1997). Pie charts and rank order tables illustrated changes in attitudes toward the economy and the most important problems facing the United States. In a four-year period, the percentage of those who thought the economy was "very good or fairly good" had more than doubled from 35 percent to 71 percent.

A bar chart compared presidential approval ratings at the beginning of the second term for Presidents Clinton, Reagan, and Nixon. Three-fifths approved of Presidents Clinton and Reagan as they started their second terms, but only half approved of then President Nixon. A line graph was also used to compare changes in outlooks for the future from 1979 to 1997.

Sidebars Are Used to Describe Poll's Method

As mentioned in Chapter 9 on writing research results, sidebars are sometimes included with poll stories published in newspapers and magazines. The sidebar that accompanied the trend story comparing the start of the first and second terms of President Clinton can be seen in Figure 17.3 (p. 355) (*New York Times*, 1997). Often a sidebar describes the methodology of the study in detail, emphasizing how survey participants were selected, how many were interviewed, and what the sampling error was. Any weighting of the data is usually included in this sidebar.

FIGURE 17.2 *Graphics Used to Display Data in the* New York Times/CBS News Poll, *"Public's Assessment of Presidents and Problems"*

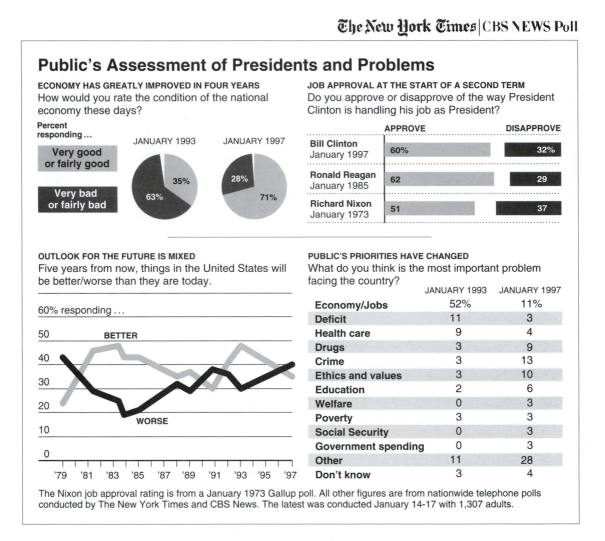

Polling Standards Dictate What Information Should Be Disclosed in a Sidebar

Whether the information on how a survey was conducted is included in the main story or a sidebar, professional polling standards require that this

FIGURE 17.3   *Sidebar for the* New York Times/CBS News Poll, *"Public's Assessment of Presidents and Problems"*

How the Poll Was Conducted

The latest *New York Times*/CBS News Poll is based on telephone interviews conducted from Tuesday through Friday with 1,307 adults throughout the United States.

The sample of telephone exchanges called was randomly selected by a computer from a complete list of more than 36,000 active residential exchanges in the country.

Within each exchange, random digits were added to form a complete telephone number, thus permitting access to both listed and unlisted numbers. Within each household, one adult was designated by a random procedure to be the respondent for the survey.

The results have been weighted to take account of household size and number of telephone lines into the residence and to adjust for variations in the sample relating to geographic region, race, sex, age, and education.

In theory, in 19 cases out of 20, the results based on such samples will differ by no more than three percentage points in either direction from what would have been obtained by seeking out all American adults.

For the question that asked respondents to rate on a scale of 1 to 10 the way things are going in the United States at the present time, the margin of sampling error was plus or minus 0.10; that is, in 19 cases out of 20, a mean rating by the poll's respondents of 5.64 on that scale would be no lower than 5.54 and no higher than 5.74 if all adults had been sought out.

In addition to sampling error, the practical difficulties of conducting any survey of public opinion may introduce other sources of error. Variations in question wording or the order of questions, for instance, can lead to somewhat different results.

Source: The *New York Times*, January 20, 1997. Copyright © 1997 by The New York Times Company. Reprinted by permission.

information be disclosed. In fact, in May 1997, the American Association for Public Opinion Research (AAPOR) published standards for disclosing all methods associated with conducting a poll in order to permit evaluation and replication. The AAPOR list includes standards previously issued by the Council of American Survey Research Organizations (CASRO) and the National Council on Public Polls' (NCPP) "Twenty Questions a Journalist Should Ask About Poll Results." These standards, which are displayed in Figure 17.4 (p. 356), enable a reader to judge a poll's validity.

Whimsical Graphics Can Be Used to Illustrate Social Data

Graphic displays of survey data can be serious and straightfoward like the one displayed in Figure 17.2 or whimsical and fun, depending on the

FIGURE 17.4   *AAPOR Standards for Disclosure of Survey's Methods*

The following information should be disclosed with poll results:

1. Who sponsored the survey, and who conducted it;
2. The purpose of the study, including specific objectives;
3. The questionnaire and/or the exact, full wording of all questions asked, including any visual exhibits and the text of any preceding instruction or explanation to the interviewer or respondents that might reasonably be expected to affect the response;
4. A definition of the universe — the population under study — which the survey is intended to represent, and a description of the sampling frame used to identify this population (including its source and likely bias);
5. A description of the sample design, including cluster size, number of callbacks, information on eligibility criteria and screening procedures, method of selecting sample elements, mode of data collection, and other pertinent information;
6. A description of the sample selection procedure, giving a clear indication of the methods by which respondents were selected by the researcher, or whether the respondents were entirely self-selected, and other details of how the sample was drawn in sufficient detail to permit fairly exact replication;
7. Size of samples and sample disposition — the results of sample implementation, including a full accounting of the final outcome of all sample cases: e.g., total number of sample elements contacted, those not assigned or reached, refusals, terminations, non-eligibles, and completed interviews or questionnaires.
8. Documentation and a full description, if applicable, of any response or completion rates cited (for quota designs, the number of refusals), and (whenever available) information on how nonrespondents differ from respondents;
9. A description of any special scoring, editing, data adjustment or indexing procedures used;
10. A discussion of the precision of findings, including, if appropriate, estimates of sampling error — with references to other possible sources of error so that a misleading impression of accuracy or precision is not conveyed — and a description of estimating procedures used;
11. A description of all percentages on which conclusions are based;
12. A clear delineation of which results are based on parts of the sample, rather than on the total sample;
13. Method(s), location(s), and dates of interviews, fieldwork, or data collection;
14. Interviewer characteristics;

15. Copies of interviewer instructions or manuals, validation results, codebooks, and other important working papers; and

16. Any other information that a layperson would need to make a reasonable assessment of the reported findings.

poll's topic. The pie chart in Figure 17.5 is an example of a fun way to display the results of a survey. In this *Time* (1997) magazine graphic, Gen Xers were asked: "If you were stranded on a deserted island, what would you most like to have with you?" Twenty-nine percent responded, "my parents."

FIGURE 17.5 *A Fun Graphic to Display Data*

PIE CHART

Gen Xers were asked: "If you were stranded on a deserted island, what would you most like to have with you?"

TV
Books
MY PARENTS
10%
15%
29%
21%
24%
A computer
Music
Due to rounding, numbers do not equal 100%
Source: BMG Entertainment TIME Graphic by S. Hart

Source: *Time,* June 30, 1997. Reprinted by permission.

Content Analysis Can Generate News Stories

Content analysis has also been used as a source for news stories. *Washington Post* media critic Howard Kurtz (1997) reported on the results of a four-year content analysis of the nightly newscasts of ABC, CBS, and NBC that was conducted by the Center for Media and Public Affairs. According to the news article, from 1990 to 1992, crime coverage of murders ranked sixth on the news, but after 1992, murder stories ranked number one on the network evening news. Nineteen percent of the 7,448 crime stories over four years involved O. J. Simpson. The article also said the emphasis on news coverage of murder does not match homicide statistics. From 1993 through 1996, the United States homicide rate decreased by 20 percent.

The content analysis of the network news also showed the following rankings of various types of news stories reported on the evening news: health (ranked 2nd), economy and business (ranked 3rd), Bosnia (ranked 4th), 1996 presidential campaign (ranked 5th), Russia (ranked 6th), the Middle East (ranked 7th), the federal budget (ranked 8th), entertainment (ranked 9th), and Haiti (ranked 10th). The content analysis also found that news about Hollywood gets more coverage than education, the environment, or Japan.

Public and Computer-Assisted Journalism Rely on Research Methods

Another method of using research to gather story ideas has been called public journalism by New York University journalism professor Jay Rosen who served as director of the Project on Public Life and the Press. Richard Oppel (1996), editor of the *Austin American-Statesman* and former editor of the *Charlotte Observer,* which launched a public journalism project during the 1992 presidential election, described public journalism as surveying voters *before* the election to identify the most important issues, then interviewing respondents in-depth and writing about the issues in special reports.

Computers and content analysis techniques have made it possible for large and small newspapers to do computer-assisted investigative reporting. In her book, *Computer-Assisted Investigative Journalism,* Margaret DeFleur described a 1990 *Newsday* story that examined the safety and crash records of 140 airlines around the world for a twenty-year period. The computer-assisted investigative report showed that the chances of dying on foreign carriers were significantly higher than on U.S. airlines (DeFleur, 1997, p. 87).

A *Los Angeles Times* computer-assisted investigative report was also described in the book. In this investigation, *Los Angeles Times* journalists examined the records of over 18,000 adults who had undergone heart bypass surgery in California during 1986 and concluded that death rates were highest in hospitals that did few bypass operations and lowest in hospitals that performed the most bypass surgeries (DeFleur, 1997, p. 86).

To do computer-assisted investigative reporting, reporters obtain public documents from federal, state, or local agencies in the form of electronic records on magnetic tape. Unlike content analysis, the reporter does not have to code the data because the information has already been coded and stored in a database. To analyze the data, the reporter does need to have a codebook that explains how the data were coded and stored. Once the reporter understands how the data were input, he or she can use a computer to identify and analyze the variables of interest, including trends over time, background for events in the news, and the performance of government institutions or officials (DeFleur, 1997, pp. 217–279).

 ### *Editorial Management Decisions Rely on Research*

Research has also been used in newspapers to make decisions about what to keep and what to drop in the editorial pages. For example, the Vancouver (Washington) *Columbia* planned to drop a year-end special section on the top news stories. However, the new researcher for the paper surveyed 350 readers and advertisers and learned that the special section was very popular. After the research results were shared with the editorial staff, the special section was continued (Veronis, 1989).

Research Applications When Launching New Programs and Products

Launching a New Program

In the early 1980s, the *Los Angeles Times* was the only major newspaper in the United States without a newspaper-in-education program, which newspaper professionals call NIE. In fact, many small newspapers in the country had newspaper-in-education programs. The newspaper industry viewed such programs as a way to introduce newspapers to kids in the classroom with hopes that by the time they became adults, they would be hooked on newspapers and make them a regular part of their media world. The idea of "growing" newspaper readers was important to the industry because, according to newspaper industry statistics, there was a significant drop-off in readership among young adults.

Senior executives of the *Los Angeles Times* decided to commit resources to starting a newspaper-in-education program as part of a long-range goal to increase newspaper readers, but that was only the beginning. Teachers throughout Los Angeles also had to be persuaded that the *Los Angeles Times* would be a viable teaching tool or current "textbook" to add to their already full curriculum. To persuade teachers, the first author, who was then special projects manager at the *Los Angeles Times* in charge of starting up the program, and her staff designed an experiment as a pilot study to measure the effectiveness of the newspaper in the classroom (Poindexter, 1986).

Teachers were trained how to use the newspaper as a teaching tool and provided teaching guides. Those teachers taught the experimental group of 2,000 kindergarten through twelfth grade students who received the newspaper once or twice a week. A matched control group of 500 students did not receive the newspaper in the classroom.

Teachers and students completed questionnaires before and after the pilot study to gauge their attitudes about newspapers in the classroom. After ten weeks, both experimental and control groups of students were administered a twenty-five-question test to assess their reading comprehension and their knowledge of people, places, and vocabulary in the news.

Overall, students who received the newspaper for the ten-week period scored higher on questions about people, places, and vocabulary. For example, 50 percent of the students who received the newspaper knew the meaning of "apartheid," but only 35 percent of those who did not receive the newspaper knew it. Before apartheid was dismantled, the term was used frequently to describe the legal separation of blacks and whites in South Africa.

Even though teachers in the control group were not asked their opinions on the newspaper in the classroom, favorable attitudes of teachers participating in the pilot study almost doubled from 32 percent before the pilot to 62 percent after it. The controlled pilot experiment and the favorable ratings of teachers and students persuaded the Los Angeles Unified School District superintendent to approve bringing the newspaper-in-education program into the schools and funding the newspapers.

The pilot research results had other applications. The research results were announced in an advertisement that was published in the *Times* introducing the new newspaper-in-education program. The research results were also included in a brochure that was used to promote the new program aimed at future newspaper readers. And, when the newspaper industry publication *Editor & Publisher* (1988, p. 33) wrote an article on the status of newspaper-in-education programs around the country, the experimental study was featured as an innovative approach to developing a successful newspaper-in-education program.

Launching a National Newspaper

Research was also used in the unprecedented start-up of a national daily newspaper. At least two years before *USA Today* was launched, Al Neuharth's vision for a national newspaper was clear, according to Peter Prichard's (1987) inside account of the making of *USA Today*. According to the book, the then chairman of the Gannett Company, the nation's largest newspaper chain, envisioned a broadsheet—not a tabloid. Neuharth wanted color in every section and an emphasis on sports results and weather. And he wanted a regular feature to be a roundup of top stories from every state.

After testing the concept of a national newspaper, the newspaper company chairman ordered prototypes for field testing with readers and advertisers. Media critics and analysts were negative about the concept of a national newspaper. Prototypes, accompanied by a postage-paid reply postcard, were mailed to 4,500 opinion leaders, including publishers, editors, advertisers, and business, government, education, and sports leaders.

The postcards asked respondents to check one of the two responses: 1. "I hope you start publishing *USA Today* regularly." 2. "I hope you forget about the idea." Even though media critics were negative toward the prototypes, 74 percent of the opinion leaders responded, "I hope you start publishing *USA Today* regularly."

Neuharth said the decision whether or not to launch *USA Today* would hinge on what readers thought, and reader reaction would be determined by scientific surveys. Two thousand personal interviews were conducted with readers who had read the prototypes in twenty-four of the largest markets. Louis Harris and Associates, a research firm owned by Gannett, conducted these interviews. Twenty-one percent of the respondents said they were likely to buy the newspaper.

An independent research firm, Simmons Market Research Bureau, conducted another 1,150 personal interviews with single-copy buyers and heavy readers of national news in the eight largest markets. Twenty-seven percent said they would buy *USA Today*.

The favorable research results from readers were factored into the decision making by Al Neuharth, his executives, and board of directors. Of course, the financial risk and potential for failure weighed heavily on the decision, too. The board unanimously approved going ahead with *USA Today*, and it was launched September 15, 1982. Today, *USA Today* is the largest circulation newspaper in the country.

Research Can Tell You When It's Time to Shut Down a Business

Although the launching of the *Los Angeles Times in Education Program* and *USA Today* are examples of how research helped decision makers start a new program or product, research also helps decision makers shut down a new business. Research was used to decide the fate of videotex a decade and a half ago, before computers entered homes in great numbers and America Online, the Internet, and the World Wide Web became available for consumer use.

In the late 1970s, Knight-Ridder Newspapers, parent company of the *Miami Herald, Philadelphia Enquirer,* and *San Jose Mercury News,* teamed up with AT&T to develop a videotex service in Coral Gables, Florida, and test consumer reaction to it. Videotex, a precursor to the Internet and the World Wide Web, was a communication medium for sending and receiving information, including news, entertainment and games, travel, advertising, financial and shopping transactions, and inter-personal communication, over a telephone line or cable between a large central computer and a dedicated terminal hooked up to a television-like monitor or personal computer. Similar interactive computer-based information services had already been launched or were in the developmental stages in Great Britain, France, and other countries in Europe and Asia.

During the videotex trial, researchers tracked how consumers spent their time on the novel interactive service. For example, by using the large central computer to record how much time each consumer spent on the online newspaper versus games, the researchers could determine which features on the videotex service attracted the attention of consumers. In addition to this unobtrusive observation of consumer time on the videotex service, surveys and focus groups were conducted to gauge consumers' positive and negative reactions to the service.

Based on the research gathered from the trial, Knight-Ridder concluded that consumers did not especially want the service and shut it down in 1985. According to A. Michael Noll (1997, p. 160) who designed the trial for AT&T, Knight-Ridder lost $50 million dollars on this new service and he estimated that AT&T lost twice as much.

Shortly after Knight-Ridder began developing its videotex service, Times Mirror, the parent company of the *Los Angeles Times,* developed a similar videotex service and conducted a market trial in Orange County, California, with a Canadian partner, Infomart. After letting consumers use the computer-based interactive information service, which included an electronic version of the *Los Angeles Times,* for a period of time and conducting unobtrusive observation studies, surveys, and focus groups, Times Mirror shut its service down, concluding that consumer reaction to the videotex service was insufficient to warrant full-scale development of videotex as an ongoing business (Link Resources Corp., 1986).

Summary of Research Applications

As you can see from the examples in this chapter, there are many applications of research in the field of media and communication. Research has been used for creative and business decision making in marketing, promotion, advertising, and public relations. It has been used to enhance images and generate news. Finally, research has been used to write news stories and launch new projects and programs.

Even though all of these examples focused on advertising, marketing, public relations, and journalism, there would be as many examples or more in politics and policy. Some of the policy research that communication scholars have often conducted has addressed the effects of television violence and advertising on children. Recently policy research has begun to examine the awareness and effects of the TV ratings that now appear in the top left corner of the screen when a TV program starts.

Research is the foundation of the academic arena in all disciplines across the country and around the world. Every research method examined in this text is being used in an academic setting. These methods are used to conduct research about practical and theoretical issues in the field of media and communication, and the results are taught to you through lectures, textbooks, and various projects and assignments.

Conducting Ethical Research

Clearly in the research applications discussed in this chapter, research results were used to make decisions because they were trusted. They were considered credible because of the expertise and ethical standards of the research expert. As discussed throughout the book, it is not enough to be systematic and objective in conducting research; the highest ethical standards must be used from the pre-research through the post-research phase of the process.

Ethical standards demand that research be conducted with integrity. Research must not deceive, mislead, purposely try to influence, or bring harm to those who participate. Throughout the discussions of the various research methods, we've emphasized the role of ethical standards in the research process. This section summarizes and reviews those ethical standards as they relate to four areas, regardless of the type of research that is being conducted:

1. Designing the research study
2. Treatment of research participants
3. Collecting, processing, and analyzing data
4. Reporting research procedures and results

 Designing the Research Using Ethical Standards

Perhaps the most well-known example of ethical misconduct in conducting research was the Tuskegee Syphilis Study. In this federal government study, which began in the 1930s and lasted for forty years, 399 poor African American men who lived in rural southern Alabama were used as human guinea pigs without their knowledge (Jones, 1981). The men, who volunteered to receive medical care for what the researchers called bad blood, were not informed that they had syphilis. The medical researchers withheld treatment for the venereal disease so they could observe the effects of this fatal disease on the bodies of the infected men. Many of the men died as a result of not receiving treatment.

The *Washington Star* exposed the unethical experiment on July 25, 1972. That initial story on the Tuskegee syphilis experiment caused a series of follow-up news reports and editorials, a Congressional hearing, a class action lawsuit, the adoption of tough new regulations for human experimentation, and guidelines for research projects involving human subjects. Twenty-five years after the experiment was disclosed to the public, President Bill Clinton apologized to the three remaining survivors of the experiment and the families of all the men who were a part of the unethical study (Mitchell, 1997, p. A9).

 ## Inform and Respect Participants

Even though the Tuskegee Syphilis Study was medical research and not communication research, it is an example of how ethical guidelines must be incorporated into the research design from the beginning. It is also an extreme example of the failure to secure informed consent, an important ethical standard when conducting research with humans. In the Tuskegee study, because the subjects were not informed that they were participating in an experiment, they certainly could not have agreed to be a part of it.

In research methods that ask respondents questions, whether in surveys or focus groups, participants are informed of the study and its purpose at the beginning and given an opportunity to decline to participate.

In experimental research, though, it is possible to conduct an experiment without the individual's knowledge, as was done in the Tuskegee experiment. That's why ethical research means informing and securing written permission before proceeding. Informed consent is defined as "the knowing consent of an individual or his legally authorized representative, so situated as to be able to exercise free power of choice without undue inducement or any element of force, fraud, deceit, duress, or other form of constraint or coercions" (Bower & de Gasparis, 1978, p. 8).

Institutional review boards (IRBs), which have been established at universities and other agencies that receive federal money, are responsible for reviewing and approving research proposals for studies that will be conducted on human subjects. University institutional review boards, which are composed of faculty, also make sure that the informed consent requirement is not disregarded. Many social science and communication studies are generally exempt from these review boards because they are considered of minimum risk. Asking about a TV program or newspaper article would be considered harmless to the participants in the research study (Babbie, 1995, p. 455; Rudestam & Newton, 1992, pp. 196–205).

An ethical dilemma arises, however, when experimental studies are conducted. In communication research, a valid experiment means that the independent variable being tested must be concealed until the data have been collected. How can an experimental subject be informed and give informed consent if the true purpose of the experiment must be withheld? The only solution is to debrief experimental subjects, explaining the true purpose of the study and the variables tested, immediately after the experiment is over.

In addition to informing and securing permission, the research expert follows other ethical standards in the treatment of participants. First and foremost, the research participants must be treated at all times with dignity and respect regardless of race, ethnicity, gender, religion, sexual orientation, national origin, age, education, or income. An ethical researcher also promises confidentiality and honors that promise to participating respondents. This means that the researcher never reveals the identities and answers of individual respondents. The data are reported in aggregate form.

An ethical researcher does not deceive, mislead, purposely influence research participants, or cause physical, mental, or emotional harm. Clearly the Tuskegee Syphilis Study deceived and harmed the participants. One type of research that has been used to influence participants is called a push poll, a type of survey used in political campaigns. Instead of asking voters objective questions about the candidates and issues, these surveys are designed to feed voters negative information about the opposing candidate in order to influence voters and the outcome of the election (Sabato & Simpson, 1996, p. 245). AAPOR, the American Association for Public Opinion Research (1997, pp. 8–9) specifically condemns this practice.

Collect, Process, and Analyze Data Using Ethical Standards

Ethical standards must also be applied when data are collected, processed, analyzed, and reported. Focus group participants must be informed when they are being taped or observed. Data must represent what real research participants said, what phenomena were actually observed, or what elements were actually contained in content that was examined. Data must never be falsified.

Ethical standards also require that the processing and analysis of data accurately reflect *all* of the data gathered for a specific study. Do not omit data that do not conform to your research expectations. The data that do not appear to fit an otherwise neat pattern must be included in the results because they are part of the overall picture.

Report Results Using Ethical Standards

Finally, ethical standards require that the research report accurately represent the procedures used to conduct the study and analyze the results. Do not exclude information about the procedures that may have some impact on the results or their interpretation. Do not misrepresent non-random polls as scientifically valid. The wording of questions, sample size, response rate, and any weighting and recoding of the data must be explained. For research studies released to the media or reported by the media, the sponsor of the study must be disclosed. Finally, do not slant the report to reflect what you or others would like the results to be. The report must be an accurate representation of the process and results. From research design to final report of the procedures and results, ethical standards must guide the entire research process.

Figure 17.6 summarizes the ethical do's and don'ts in the world of scientific research.

FIGURE 17.6 *Ethical Standards When Conducting Scientific Research*

RESEARCH DESIGN

- Design the research study using ethical standards.
- Do not skew the design or slant the questions to elicit a certain response.

TREATMENT OF RESEARCH PARTICIPANTS

- Do not coerce participation in the research study.
- Promise and honor confidentiality to research participants.
- Treat participants with dignity and respect.
- Secure written permission from experimental subjects and debrief them at the conclusion of the experiment.
- Do not misuse research techniques to influence respondents.
- Push polling is unethical and should not be done.

DATA COLLECTION, PROCESSING, AND ANALYSIS

- Disclose when focus group participants are being taped or observed in any way during the discussion.
- Do not falsify or misrepresent data in collection, processing, or analysis.

REPORTING

- Do not represent phone-in, write-in, fax-in, or e-mail-in research results as if they were produced by valid, scientific survey methods and represented the population.
- Disclose question wording, including any filter questions that may have influenced responses, sampling method, sample size and sampling error, response rate, weighting, or any recoding of data when releasing them.
- Disclose the sponsorship of research results when releasing them.
- Do not let others influence you to misuse research methods and analytical techniques, or misrepresent research results.
- Report the results of research accurately and fairly.

Professional associations that conduct research are equally concerned about ethical conduct. Standards such as those summarized in Figure 17.6 have been established as codes of ethical conduct by organizations such as American Association for Public Opinion Research (AAPOR), American Statistical Association (ASA), Research Industry Coalition (RIC), American Psychological Association (APA), American Marketing Association (AMA), and Council of American Survey Research Organizations (CASRO).

The Future of Research

The use of research in all phases of mass communication has increased dramatically in recent decades. Although mass communication in the United States is almost 170 years old, dating from the appearance of the penny press in the 1830s, social science research on mass communication did not appear until a hundred years later.

By the midpoint of the twentieth century, the primary research methods—surveys, content analysis, and experiments—had been developed and applied in the fields of journalism, advertising, public relations, broadcasting, film, politics, and public policy. Three-quarters into the twentieth century, scientific and non-scientific variations of these primary research methods plus new methods such as focus groups, one-on-one depth interviews, ethnography and other methods of observation had been developed or borrowed from other disciplines and applied to communication issues.

As the first act of a new millennium opens, it is a fact that not one of the research methods developed during the twentieth century can be considered best for understanding the multifaceted relationship of communication and the consumer, reader, viewer, listener, Internet or online user, public, or voter. It is clear though that answers to future communication questions can be found by relying on a combination of research methods that are systematically used to unearth answers to complex questions about the audience and its relationship to media in society.

It is predicted that the professional side of communication will rely more on the academic research model to gain insight into the target audience. With the increasing difficulty in attracting the attention of consumers; declines in audiences for print and broadcast news; fierce competition for consumers' time and money; the availability of more and more choices for information and entertainment; changes in household, labor force, racial, and ethnic composition; the aging of the baby boom generation; the proliferation of personal communication technology; and the expansion of communication networks and markets globally, the professional side of communication needs to try the academic research model that uses appropriate research methods to construct theories about the consumer, reader, viewer, listener, voter, or public and the world of communication.

Likewise it is predicted that the academic communication world will become more proficient in translating what is sometimes dismissed as ivory tower mumbo jumbo to professional communicators. In other words, academic researchers need to explain in clear language how research is used in theory building and why theory construction is relevant to professionals' understanding of their target audiences.

As we look ahead, we feel confident in predicting that the use of research and the application of the results will accelerate in the fields of journalism, advertising, public relations, broadcasting, film, politics, and government policy. It is only hoped that scientifically based research methods and the appropriate analysis and use of the research results will be at the forefront of this research trend.

As we anticipate the next 100 years, we also foresee that those communication professionals, executives, managers, creative directors, and academics who do not understand the value of scientifically based research, the appropriate method or methods for understanding communication issues, or how research is conducted, analyzed, communicated, or appropriately applied will be left behind like pointless props on a darkened stage.

Although we could argue that the development and refinement of random sampling between the 1930s and 1960s was one of the most important developments in research during the twentieth century, we envision that the explosive growth in consumer-oriented technology and software that have had such a profound influence on research during the last quarter of the twentieth century will continue.

The telephone, answer machine, tape recorder, microprocessor, computer, computer software, videocamera, videocassette recorder, fax machine, videoconferencing technology, Internet, e-mail, World Wide Web, and caller ID have had positive and negative effects on research. Much of the technology has made conducting, processing, analyzing, and reporting research easier, cheaper, and faster, and in many cases, more reliable and more valid.

Combining a computer with a telephone has produced computer-assisted telephone interviewing, which speeds up the recording, processing, and analysis of survey data. Bringing statistical software such as SPSS to the personal computer has made analyzing data easier and faster. Video-cameras have enhanced the focus group experience by recording focus group participants' verbal comments and non-verbal expressions. Video-cameras have also made it possible to observe consumers in their own environments for ethnographic studies. Videocassette recorders have made it easy to show visual stimuli such as commercials to focus group, intercept, and one-on-one depth interview participants. Videoconferencing has enabled researchers to conduct focus groups in which the moderator and participants are in different locations.

Unfortunately these technologies have also contributed to a proliferation of research with questionable validity. Telephones, the Internet, World Wide Web, online services, e-mail, and fax machines have also made self-selected surveys that lack scientific validity easy, fast, and cheap to conduct. Some technologies such as computer interviewers, answer machines, and caller ID have become barriers to high survey response rates. Non-human computer interviewers can annoy respondents and cause them to hang up before the interview is started. Answer machines and caller IDs, which can be used to screen callers, can screen out survey interviewers.

It is anticipated that fax, e-mail, and the World Wide Web will be used more often in conducting research in the future. It is hoped that the emphasis will be on valid applications of these technologies rather than the current use of self-selection.

Another trend of the final quarter of the twentieth century was the development of surveys or polls as a reporting tool. In fact, every major news organization either has its own polling unit or subscribes to a service that conducts polls. Poll stories have mostly been used to report political, election, and public policy stories, but we envision the use of this reporter's tool for a variety of stories in the future. Because we expect even more poll stories, we predict that there will be more emphasis on training reporters on how poll stories are conducted and evaluated. Future reporters will know the difference between fake and real polls.

In many ways, public perception of research is central to the future of research. Without the cooperation of the public, most of the research methods that we've discussed, could not be conducted. Because surveys, experiments, intercepts, and focus groups require the participation of the public, it is imperative that the public understand the importance of their participation. This is particularly true with scientific surveys, which represent the voice of the people. It is, indeed, in the best interests of the public to participate in a scientific survey when the telephone rings. Refusing to participate increases the chances that the survey results will be biased in favor of those who recognize the importance of having their voices heard through a poll.

Herbert Asher (1988, p. 2) viewed public opinion polls as "instruments of democracy since they allow everyone's views to be represented." Asher added that "polls today have become a major way in which Americans learn what their fellow citizens are thinking." Consequently citizens can compare their own opinions with other citizens.

It is hoped then that in the future more attention will be paid to educating the public about research, especially scientific polls. The public must understand that scientific polls are representative of the population within a known amount of error, even when only 1,200 randomly selected people are queried about their opinions. The public must understand that politicians, government officials, corporate executives, policy makers, advertisers, studio heads, filmmakers, publishers, and network TV executives use scientific survey results to make decisions that affect us all. What television programs or films are seen, what new products or programs are available to purchase or participate in, what newspaper and magazine features are added or dropped, what new policies are implemented, even which political candidates receive financial backing are decisions that are often based on the results of scientific polls.

Polls also played a role in deciding the fate of the President of the United States. After the year-long White House sex scandal, the release of the Starr Report, and the House of Representatives' impeachment of President Clinton, polls were a factor in the Senate's vote to acquit the President on two articles of impeachment. Senators who voted to acquit the President on charges of perjury and obstruction of justice consistently cited the President's high standings in the polls as a referendum on impeachment. Throughout the Senate impeachment trial, job approval ratings for President Clinton were 65 percent to 69 percent (*New York Times*, 1999, p. A9). And according to a February 8, 1999 *Newsweek* poll, 72 percent of the American people said they did *not* want the President removed from office (Thomas & Hosenball, 1993, p. 24).

It is equally important that the public understand the difference between valid and invalid polls. Valid polls should be participated in; invalid polls should be avoided and complained about. As more and more journalists have been trained how to spot an unscientific poll, so should every student be taught the basics of valid scientific polls. This knowledge will help students develop into more knowledgeable consumers, citizens, voters, and even more savvy readers, viewers, listeners, and users of news, entertainment, and information.

Some of the responsibility for educating the public rests with professional and academic researchers as well as journalists who report research results as part of the news. Professional and academic researchers and journalists must become effective advocates for survey results. They must explain the importance of participation and how influential individuals can be through their participation in scientific polls. Academic and professional researchers must also become advocates for including understanding valid and invalid surveys in the curriculum just as computers and, now, the Internet are included in the curriculum. Academic and professional researchers must publicly condemn poor research practices and unethical research. They must condemn marketers who pretend they are conducting research but are really trying to make a sale and unethical political strategists who conduct push polls to influence voters. These practices give valid research a bad name and diminish the public's trust. Practices that annoy, offend, or alienate the public must also be discontinued if more people are to participate in research in the future.

Looking at the demographic shifts that are predicted for the U.S. population during the twenty-first century, we can see the importance of emphasizing how to conduct valid research on racial and ethnic minorities. The Bureau of the Census (1996, p. 13) predicts that by the year 2010, the U.S. population will be 68 percent non-Hispanic white, 14 percent Hispanic, 13 percent African American, 5 percent Asian, and 1 percent American Indian. By the year 2050, the percentage of non-Hispanic whites will have dropped to 52 percent, Hispanics will have increased to 25 percent, and blacks will have inched upward to 14 percent of the population.

These demographic changes mean that in the twenty-first century, Hispanics, African Americans, and Asian Americans will become major segments of the regular audience for news, entertainment, information, and advertising on TV, cable, and in newspapers and magazines. In addition, these groups will become a significant segment of Internet, World Wide Web, and online information service users, movie-goers, and the overall consumer buying public. In her book *Advertising and Marketing to the New Majority,* Gail Baker Woods (1995, p. 4) said "Marketers will not be able to survive unless they can tap this major economic force." And understanding how to conduct valid research on these racial and ethnic groups in order to better understand their media and consumer behaviors, attitudes, demographics and lifestyles will be key to tapping this major economic force in the future.

We began *Research in Mass Communication* by emphasizing the relevance of research in your future communication career. Today, few important decisions are made without data that have been conducted through primary and secondary research methods. Although we have focused on scientifically valid research methods, scientifically valid research methods will *not* guarantee results that are appropriate for good decision making if the overall research design is flawed.

For example, marketing scholar Robert F. Hartley (1995) said that marketing research failed in Coca-Cola's 1985 attempt to replace its well-known coke with a sweeter formula, called New Coke, because it was losing market share to Pepsi. Loyal Coke consumers revolted, and Coca-Cola had to bring back the old formula, which it renamed Classic Coke.

Coke spent $4 million in research over a two-year period, conducting interviews and focus groups on the concept of a new Coke soft drink. In addition, taste tests were conducted with over 190,000 people in thirteen cities. According to the author of this case study, the research design failed to inform the research participants that the New Coke formula would actually replace the old Coke formula. Without the knowledge that the old Coke formula would disappear included in the research design, the soft drink company was unable to measure the intense feelings of loyal Coke drinkers. In addition, some of the strong negative reaction that appeared in the research results seemingly was ignored by the decision makers.

Although it is unknown at what stage the researchers became involved in the planning of the research on New Coke, this case study does suggest something important for the three-phase research model that was introduced in Chapter 1. Rather than wait until it is time to start the research, the decision maker should involve the research expert as soon as a problem, issue, or opportunity has been identified. And the research expert should *remain* involved throughout the three-phase research model process. The earlier and longer the research expert is involved, the better.

American advertising agencies, following Great Britain's lead, have expanded the role of research experts, given them the name of account planners, and involved them at an earlier stage of the research process. Account planners, who rely on a variety of research methods, including ethnography, act as advocates for consumers and their insights. The *New York Times* says account planning "reflects a refocusing of agencies' attentions from consumer attitudes to consumer behavior, which is examined with methods not unlike those used by detectives or anthropologists" (Elliott, 1998).

When Lisa Fortini-Campbell (1992) described the responsibility and history of account planning, a research expert role unique to advertising agencies, she also provided evidence for why the research expert should be a full partner with the decision maker in phase one and phase three of the three-phase research process. As you'll recall from Chapter 1, phase one includes monitoring the environment to recognize the need to conduct research to understand an issue, problem, or opportunity and specifying the appropriate research method and population to study. In phase three, decisions are made about how to effectively and creatively use the research results in decision making.

For the research expert to assume the role of full partner in the three-phase research process, he or she must be knowledgeable about much more than designing, executing, analyzing, and reporting scientifically valid research. The research expert must also be knowledgeable about all aspects of the communications terrain that he or she operates in as well as knowledgeable about the business, economic, political, legal, social, educational, technological, demographic, cultural, global, and marketing issues and trends that may influence newspaper and magazine readers, television and cable viewers, radio listeners, movie-goers, consumers, Internet and online users, and the communication business as a whole. The research expert must know his or her own business as well as the business of competitors. As the decision maker monitors the environment to know what's going on, so must the research expert. And the research expert must be able to translate the research process and results into the language of the decision maker. The research expert must be able to put forth recommendations that are relevant to the issue, problem, or opportunity that is of priority concern to the decision maker if a full partnership in the overall research process is to be developed.

We predict that in the twenty-first century, a new model of the research process will emerge. In this new model, the research expert will become a full partner with the decision maker from phase one through phase three. With the anticipated increased reliance on data produced from scientifically valid research, the decision maker can only benefit from a full partnership with the research expert, the one who through research studies is closest to and most knowledgeable about those who read, listen to, and pay attention to the product produced in the world of communication and media.

SUGGESTED RESEARCH ACTIVITIES

1. Write a proposal for a study that examines a public relations, journalism, advertising, marketing, or communication issue using one of the research methods presented in this book. A proposal, which is a document that describes the plans for a project, should include the purpose and rationale for the study, background on the topic, a detailed description of the research method to be used, your data collection instrument, plans for analysis, and an explanation of how you intend to report and use the results of the study.

2. Working in groups of five, discuss the various research proposals. Select one of the five proposals and carry out the research study. As a group, consult with your professor on the details of your research design, the measurement instrument, the data collection process (which will vary according to the research method used), and the processing, analysis, and reporting of the data. Present your results in a written report and an oral presentation to the class.

3. Using a standard business memo format, write a memo to your professor describing your experience in carrying out this research study.

RECOMMENDED READING

For a list of news media, professional, and academic polls and their addresses, see:

JEAN WARD and KATHLEEN A. HANSEN, *Search Strategies in Mass Communication*, pp. 259–262. New York: Longman, 1997.

For a look at how research has been used in the newspaper industry, see:

LEO BOGART, *Preserving the Press: How Daily Newspapers Mobilized to Keep Their Readers*. New York: Columbia University Press, 1991.

CHRISTINE REID VERONIS, "Special Report: Research Moves to Center Stage: Its Importance Soars as Newspapers Reach Out to Readers and Advertisers, But Some of It Still Collects Dust," *Presstime*, November 1989, pp. 20–26.

"Newspapers Turn to Research to Sell NIE Programs," *Editor & Publisher*, May 14, 1988, p. 33.

PETER PRICHARD, *The Making of McPaper: The Inside Story of USA Today*. Kansas City, MO: Andrews, McNeel & Parker, 1987.

For an insider's look at research in the advertising industry and the latest trends in the marketing research industry, see:

JON STEEL, *Truth, Lies & Advertising: The Art of Account Planning*. New York: John Wiley, 1998.

DAVID OGILVY, *Ogilvy on Advertising*. New York: Vintage Books, 1985.

MELANIE WELLS, "New Ways to Get Into Our Heads: Marketers Ditch Old Focus Groups for Video Cameras, Beepers, Chats Over Coffee," *USA Today*, March 2, 1999, 1B+.

"Business Report on the Marketing Research Industry," *Marketing News*, June 7, 1999, H1–H39.

For guidelines on using research to evaluate the effectiveness of public relations, see:

The Institute for Public Relations Research & Education, *Guidelines and Standards for Measuring and Evaluating PR Effectiveness*, 1997. <www.instituteforpr.com>

For an examination of how research has been used in presidential campaigns, see:

ELIZABETH KOLBERT, "Test-Marketing a President: How Focus Groups Pervade Campaign Politics," *The New York Times Magazine*, August 30, 1992, 18+.

DICK MORRIS, *Behind the Oval Office: Winning the Presidency in the Nineties*. New York: Random House, 1997.

For insight and guidelines on polling for journalists, see:

SHELDON R. GAWISER and G. EVANS WITT, *A Journalist's Guide to Public Opinion Polls*. Westport, CT: Praeger, 1994.

National Council on Public Polls, *Twenty Questions a Journalist Should Ask about Poll Results*.

For a discussion of ethical and unethical research practices, see:

American Association for Public Opinion Research, *Best Practices for Survey and Public Opinion Research and Survey Practices AAPOR Condemns*, May 1997.

For an in-depth discussion of Institutional Review Board (IRB) standards on human experimentation research, see:

ROBERT T. BOWER and PRISCILLA DE GASPARIS, *Ethics in Social Research: Protecting the Interests of Human Subjects.* New York: Praeger, 1978.

For new research applications and issues and technology and techniques that will affect research in the future, see current issues of:

The *New York Times* business section, the *Wall Street Journal, Advertising Age, Marketing News, American Demographics,* etc.

APPENDIXES

377

Appendix A.1

What's Wrong with This Questionnaire?

Introduction: Hello, my name is _____ . I'm calling to ask your opinions on several subjects.

My first question is:

1. How much money do you make?

   _____

2. How many days a week do you surf the Internet?

1 day	2 days
3 days	4 days
5 days	6 days
7 days	

3. Have you ever noticed advertising on the Internet?

   Yes

   No

3. Don't you agree that the term "Generation X" is negative?

   Agree strongly

   Agree a little

   Disagree

4. How satisfied are you with shopping on the Internet?

   Very satisfied

   Satisfied

   Somewhat satisfied

   Not satisfied

5. Do you watch commercials and buy the products advertised?

   Yes

   No

5. Do you not like the ratings that are shown at the beginning of TV programs?

   Yes

   No

7. Do you use the ratings to screen programs for your children?

   Yes

   No

8. Don't you think it is bad for advertisers to advertise on programs rated TV 14?

   Yes

   No

9. How often do you read a daily newspaper?

   1 or 2 days a week

   3 or 4 days a week

   4 or 5 days a week

   6 or 7 days a week

10. What is the most important problem facing people in the United States today?
    Economy
    Environment
    Social Security
    Health care
    Crime
    Education
    Drugs
    Poverty
    Deficit
    Jobs
    Welfare
    Government spending

Those are all of my questions. Good-bye.

Appendix A.2

Telephone Survey Questionnaire

Media Use Survey

Respondent I.D. No.:_____

Interviewer Class:_____

Interviewer I.D. No.:_____

Original Phone No._____ Page No._____ Col._____

New Phone No._____ (Received on:_____)

Respondent: 1. Primary 2. Alternate

Respondent: 1. Male 2. Female

Date of Interview_____

Time Interview Began:_____Ended:_____

Interviewer's Comments_____
_____

INTRODUCTION:

Hello, my name is _____ and I'm a University of Texas student. The College of Communication is conducting a public opinion poll of Austin-area residents. We randomly selected your home to ask your opinions about the media and several subjects in the news. Your opinions are important to the accuracy of our survey and we would appreciate your help. Your answers, of course, will be confidential.

(INTERVIEWING THE CORRECT HOUSEHOLD HEAD)

My instructions say that at your house, I'm to interview a

(SEX)____ adult head of the house. (If SEX matches person on the phone, say:) Are you that person? (Otherwise, say:) May I speak to that person? (If you are already speaking to the correct person, ask your first question. If a new person comes to the telephone, repeat your introduction, then begin.)

I'd like to begin by asking:

1. How often do you watch local evening TV news? Would you say:
   (Local evening TV news comes on at 6:00 P.M. and 10:00 P.M.)

   1. Never or seldom (Skip to Q4.)
   2. 1 or 2 days a week
   3. 3 or 4 days a week*
   4. Nearly every day
   5. Every day

2. Which local TV news do you usually watch?

    1. Channel 36, KXAN-TV, (Cable 4)
    2. Channel 24, KVUE-TV, (Cable 3)
    3. Channel 7, KTBC-TV, (Cable 2)**
    4. Channel 42, FOX-TV, (Cable 5)
    (5. Other_____)
    (6. Don't know)

3. Why do you usually watch that local TV news?

_____

_____

4. How often do you watch network TV evening news? Would you say:
(Network TV evening news comes on at 5:30 P.M.)

    1. Never or seldom
    2. 1 or 2 days a week
    3. 3 or 4 days a week
    4. Nearly every day
    5. Every day

5. How often do you read a daily newspaper? Would you say:

    1. Never or seldom
    2. 1 or 2 days a week
    3. 3 or 4 days a week
    4. Nearly every day
    5. Every day

6. How often do you discuss the news with your friends or family? Would you say:

    1. Never or seldom
    2. 1 or 2 days a week
    3. 3 or 4 days a week
    4. Nearly every day
    5. Every day

7. Do you have cable?

    1. Yes
    2. No (Skip to Q12.)

8. How often do you watch a home shopping channel on cable? Would you say:

    1. Never or seldom (Skip to Q12.)
    2. 1 or 2 days a week
    3. 3 or 4 days a week
    4. Nearly every day
    5. Every day

9. How many times have you ordered merchandise from a home shopping channel? Would you say:

    1. 0 times (Skip to Q12.)
    2. 1 time
    3. 2 to 5 times
    4. 6 to 9 times
    5. 10 times or more

10. What merchandise did you buy?

    _____

11. How satisfied were you with shopping from a home shopping channel? Would you say:

    1. Very satisfied
    2. Satisfied
    3. Somewhat satisfied
    4. Not satisfied

12. How often do you listen to radio?
    1. Never or seldom (Skip to Q18.)
    2. 1 or 2 days a week
    3. 3 or 4 days a week
    4. Nearly every day
    5. Every day

13. How familiar are you with the term "talk radio"? Would you say:

    1. Very familiar
    2. Somewhat familiar
    3. Not at all familiar (Skip to Q18.)

14. Some people say "talk radio" means radio programs that listeners can call in and voice their opinions on the air. How often do you listen to that kind of radio show?

    1. Never or seldom (Skip to Q18.)
    2. 1 or 2 days a week
    3. 3 or 4 days a week
    4. Nearly every day
    5. Every day

15. During the past three months, about how many times have you tried to call in on a "talk radio" show? Would you say:

    1. 0 or no times (Skip to Q17.)
    2. 1 time
    3. 2 to 5 times
    4. 6 to 9 times
    5. 10 times or more

16. About how many times have you talked on the air?

    1. 0 or no times
    2. 1 time
    3. 2 to 5 times
    4. 6 to 9 times
    5. 10 times or more

17. People have different reasons for listening to talk radio. In general, what is the main reason that you listen to talk radio?

_____

18. Now, I'm going to ask you about commercials on television. Some people pay close attention to television commercials, and others pay little attention. In general, what do you usually do when commercials come on during a TV program?

_____

_____

19. Now, I'm going to ask you about computers. How often do you use a personal computer at home or work?

    1. Never or seldom (Skip to Q27.)
    2. 1 or 2 days a week
    3. 3 or 4 days a week
    4. 5 or more days a week

20. Which of the following computer-related services do you use at least three times a week?

	Yes	No
A. Wordprocessing	1	2
B. Electronic mail	1	2
C. The Internet	1	2
D. Computer games	1	2
E. CD ROM	1	2
F. Online information services such as Prodigy, America Online, or Compuserve	1	2

21. How many times have you ordered merchandise through your computer?

    1. 0 or no times (Skip to Q24.)
    2. 1 time
    3. 2 to 5 times
    4. 6 to 9 times
    5. 10 times or more

22. What merchandise did you buy?

_____

23. How satisfied were you with shopping through your computer? Would you say:

    1. Very satisfied
    2. Satisfied
    3. Somewhat satisfied
    4. Not satisfied

24. Since you first began using computers, approximately, how much formal computer training have you received?

    1. None
    2. One-half day
    3. 1 full day
    4. 2 to 3 days
    5. 4 to 5 days
    6. More than 5 days

25. What is your primary source of information for learning about computers or computer-related products or services?

    _____

26. In general, how would you compare your computer comfort level with your circle of friends? Would you say you are:

    1. More comfortable than your friends
    2. Equally as comfortable as your friends
    3. Less comfortable than your friends
    (4. Don't know)

27. Now, I'm going to ask your opinions about some national and local issues. What do you think is the most important problem facing people in the United States today?

    _____

28. Austin has been growing during the past 10 years. Would you say Austin is:

    1. Too big
    2. About right
    3. Too small

29. How often do you go to downtown Austin? Would you say:

    1. Never or seldom (Skip to Q31.)
    2. One to three times a week
    3. 4 to 5 times a week
    4. Almost daily or more often

30. What are the main reasons you go downtown?

    _____

31. What changes, if any, would you like to see in the downtown area?

    _____

32. How likely would you be to go downtown if:

	More Likely	Less Likely	Wouldn't Matter
A. Parking were easier.	1	2	3
B. More stores were available for shopping.	1	2	3
C. More variety were offered in entertainment.	1	2	3
D. You felt safer.	1	2	3

33. After the city moves the airport, what do you think the city should do with the land at Mueller Airport when it's closed?

_____

34. Now, I'm going to ask you about violence on television. How do you feel about the amount of violence portrayed on television programs today, not including news programs? Do you think there is:

    1. Too much violence
    2. A reasonable amount
    3. Very little violence

35. As you may know, the major television and cable networks recently agreed to show a warning label before programs with violence are shown on TV. In your opinion, does this warning label go far enough to address the issue of TV violence, or not?

    1. Goes far enough
    2. Does not go far enough
    (3. Don't know)

36. Do you think the Federal government should do more to regulate violence on TV, should it do less, or is it doing about the right amount?

    1. Should do more
    2. Should do less
    3. It's doing about the right amount
    (4. Don't know)

37. Do you think there is a relationship between violence on television and the crime rate in the United States, or not? Would you say:

    1. Yes, there is a relationship.
    2. No, there isn't a relationship.
    (3. Don't know)

38. How many children, under 18, are there in your home?

    1. 0 (Skip to Q46.)
    2. 1 (Go to Q39.)

    3. 2
    4. 3   (Read:) For the next few questions, I want
    5. 4   you to think about the child who has the
    6. 5   next birthday coming up.
    7. 6 or more

39. How old will your child be on his or her next birthday?

_____

40. Is that child a boy or girl?

   1. Boy
   2. Girl

41. Do you have rules about your child watching TV?

   1. Yes
   2. No (Skip to Q43.)

42. What are those rules?

_____

_____

43. How often do you use the Motion Picture Association of America movie ratings, such as G, PG, and R, as guides to help you decide whether to let your child view a movie?

   1. Never (Skip to Q46.)
   2. Rarely
   3. Sometimes
   4. Often

44. Do you ever prohibit your child from watching a movie based on any of the movie ratings?

   1. Yes
   2. No (Skip to Q46.)

45. Which movies do you restrict?

		Yes	No
A.	PG	1	2
B.	PG-13	1	2
C.	R	1	2
D.	NC-17	1	2
E.	X	1	2

46. Now, I'm going to ask you some questions about the O. J. Simpson case.*** How familiar are you with the O. J. Simpson murder case? Would you say:

   1. Very familiar
   2. Familiar
   3. Somewhat familiar
   4. Not familiar at all (Skip to Q54.)

47. In general, how often did you pay attention to coverage of the case?

   1. Never or seldom
   2. One or two days a week
   3. Three or four days a week
   4. Five or six days a week
   5. Every day

48. From what sources did you get most of your news and information on the case?

    _____

49. Based on the information you received, what grade, A, B, C, D, or F, would you give:

	A	B	C	D	F	(Don't Know)
A. The fairness of Judge Ito's rulings.	1	2	3	4	5	6
B. The quality of media coverage.	1	2	3	4	5	6

50. Given all the information you've heard on the O. J. Simpson case, do you think O. J. Simpson is:

    1. Definitely guilty
    2. Probably guilty
    3. Probably not guilty
    4. Definitely not guilty
    (5. Don't know)

51. Why?

    _____

    _____

52. Did you think the jury in the criminal trial would:

    1. Definitely find O. J. Simpson guilty
    2. Probably find him guilty
    3. Probably find him not guilty
    4. Definitely find him not guilty
    (5. Don't know)

53. Why?

    _____

    _____

54. Now, I have just a few questions about your background. Generally speaking, do you identify yourself as a:

    1. Democrat
    2. Republican
    3. Independent
    (4. Other_____)

55. Do you consider yourself:

    1. Conservative
    2. Middle of the road
    3. Liberal
    (4. Other_____)

56. How old are you? (If respondent does not volunteer age, read categories.)

01. 18–22	07. 45–49
02. 23–24	08. 50–54
03. 25–29	09. 55–59
04. 30–34	10. 60–64
05. 35–39	11. 65–69
06. 40–44	12. 70 or older
	(13. Refused)

57. What is your zip code? (5 digits only.)

    _____

58. What is your marital status?

    1. Married
    2. Single
    3. Divorced or legally separated
    4. Widowed
    (5. Other_____)

59. What is the highest level of education that you've completed? (Read responses.)

    1. Some high school or less
    2. High school graduate
    3. Some college or technical school degree
    4. College graduate
    5. Some graduate or professional school
    6. Masters, M.D., or doctorate

60. What is your full-time title or position?

    _____

61. What type of company or organization do you work for?

    _____

62. What is your race or ethnic group?
    (If respondent does not volunteer race or ethnic group, read categories.)

    1. Caucasian or white
    2. African American or black
    3. Hispanic or Latino
    4. Asian American
    5. Other_____

63. Approximately, what is your household income? Please stop me when I read your correct income category. (If student is supported by parents, use parents' income.)

01. Under $10,000	07. $60-69,000
02. $10–19,000	08. $70–79,000
03. $20–29,000	09. $80–89,000
04. $30–39,000	10. $90–99,000
05. $40–49,000	11. $100,000 or more
06. $50–59,000	(12. Refused)

64. (DO NOT ASK SEX—JUST CIRCLE)
    Respondent's SEX is:

    1. Male
    2. Female

(DID YOU REMEMBER TO CIRCLE SEX?)

65. So that my professor can verify this interview, I'd like to double check
    your phone number. According to my records, your phone number is
    _____. Is that correct? (GET NUMBER FROM
    PAGE ONE.)

    1. Yes
    2. No (If respondent says no, ask for correct number and write in
       the blank.)_____

That's the end of our survey. Thank you very much for participating.

*On the questionnaire that was used for the survey, the first question did not include the re-
sponse choice "for 3 or 4 days." The question was originally designed to screen for non, low,
infrequent, and frequent viewers of local TV news for a separate focus group study. For the purposes of this example, "3 or 4 days" was inserted to ensure that the question was exhaustive.

**Channels 7 and 42 switched network affiliations after the survey was conducted. Channel 7 is
now affiliated with FOX, and Channel 42 is affiliated with CBS. Channel 42 also changed its call
letters.

***Questions on the O. J. Simpson case were updated for this example.

Appendix A.3

Intercept Questionnaire

Mall Walker Intercept Survey*
(Clip questionnaire to clipboard and identify senior citizens who are walking in the mall for exercise. Walk along side of mall walker as you say introduction and read questions.)

Introduction:
Hello, my name is Rachel Taylor and I'm a student at the University of Texas. I'm conducting an opinion poll for a course I'm taking in the College of Communication. Your opinions are very important to me and I would appreciate your help. Your answers, of course, will be confidential.

I'd like to begin by asking:
1. How many days a week do you usually exercise?
    1. 0 days
    2. 1–2 days
    3. 3–4 days
    4. 5–6 days
    5. 7 days

2. What is the main reason you exercise?
    _____
    _____

3. Do you usually exercise at the mall?
    1. Yes
    2. No (Skip to Question 5.)

4. Why do you exercise at the mall?
    _____

5. What is your main form of exercise?
    1. Walking
    2. Jogging
    3. Yard work
    4. Tennis
    5. Golf
    6. Swimming
    7. Other _____

6. How far are you willing to drive every day to exercise?
   1. 5 miles or less
   2. 6–10 miles
   3. 11–15 miles
   4. 16–20 miles
   5. 21–25 miles
   6. 26–30 miles
   7. 31 miles +

7. Where else do you exercise?
   1. Home
   2. Exercise facility/health club
   3. Neighborhood/neighborhood center
   4. Other
   5. Nowhere else

8. Who do you usually exercise with?
   1. Friends
   2. Children
   3. Spouse
   4. Alone
   5. Other

9. What do you usually do after exercising?
   1. Errands
   2. Meet with friends
   3. Work
   4. Eat
   5. Sleep
   6. Relax at home
   7. Relax where you're exercising
   8. Other _____

10. For how long do you usually exercise?

    _____

11. At what time of day do you usually exercise?

    _____

12. Do you have a current membership to an exercise facility/health club, YMCA, or country club?
    1. Yes (Skip to Question 14.)
    2. No

13. Would you be willing to pay to use an exercise facility or health club?
    1. Yes (Skip to Question 15.)
    2. No (Skip to Question 17.)

14. What type of facility is the membership for?

    _____

15. How much are you willing to pay for this type of membership?

    _____

16. What activities would you do at this type of facility?
    1. Walk
    2. Tennis
    3. Golf
    4. Swim
    5. Jog
    6. Aerobic activity (aerobics, Stair-master, stationary bicycle)
    7. Other _____

17. In general, what is your opinion of exercise facilities?

    _____

18. How many times in the past year have you used an exercise facility?
    1. 0 times
    2. 1–5 times
    3. 6–10 times
    4. 11–15 times
    5. 16 or more times

19. How would you rate your physical fitness?
    1. Excellent
    2. Good
    3. Fair
    4. Poor
    5. Other _____

Now, I have just a few questions about your background.

20. How old are you?
    1. 55 years or younger
    2. 56–60 years
    3. 61–65 years
    4. 66–70 years
    5. 71–75 years
    6. More than 75 years

21. What is your marital status?
    1. Single
    2. Married
    3. Widowed
    4. Other_____

22. If you do not mind, please tell me which category your income level falls in.
    1. Under $11,000
    2. $11–$19,000
    3. $20–$29,000
    4. $30–$39,000
    5. $40–$49,000
    6. $50–$59,000
    7. $60–$69,000
    8. $70,000 or more
    (9. Refused)

23. Respondent's Sex (Do not ask.)
    1. Male
    2. Female

Thank you very much for your cooperation. Have a nice day!

* This intercept questionnaire example was adapted from a questionnaire developed by Rachel Taylor for an independent study project when she was an advertising student at the University of Texas at Austin. The independent study was supervised by the first author. Permission to reprint granted by Rachel Taylor.

Appendix A.4

One-on-One Depth Interview Cover Letter and Questionnaire

Advance Letter: Minorities in Advertising

<Date>

Return Address

<Name and Address>

Dear <Name>:

I am a graduate student at The University of Texas at Austin in the Advertising Department. As a part of my thesis research, I am conducting an exploratory study of minorities in the advertising industry. I hope to learn about career influences, job satisfaction, minority roles in the industry, and any discrimination or barriers faced by minorities in the field. You were selected as a possible participant in this study because you are a minority in the advertising business and were referred by <NAME>, a former graduate student in advertising at U.T. Thirty individuals were chosen to participate in this study.

Your part in the study would consist of a 20-minute depth interview on the phone at a time that is convenient for you. If you elect to participate, I will ask you a set of open-ended questions about your career and experiences in the business. I will be taking notes as we are talking, and these will be summarized with the data collected from the other participants. In the final thesis report, experiences will be described without the inclusion of details that would allow identification of you as an individual or your agency. Your decision whether or not to participate will not affect your future relations with The University of Texas at Austin.

I hope that you will consider involvement in my research. I am very excited about the potential contribution my study will make to the industry. No study of this kind has been done, so this is truly a ground-breaking endeavor. I will be calling you within a week of your receipt of this letter to set up an interview time. Thank you for your consideration, and I look forward to talking with you soon.

Sincerely,

Kristin E. Kehl

Questionnaire
Minorities in Advertising: One-on-One Depth Interview *

Date: _____

Time:_____

Name: _____
Sex: M/F (Circle one.)

Race/Ethnic Group: _____

Statement of Consent:

My name is Kristin Kehl and I'm a graduate student at The University of Texas at Austin, Advertising Department. You are invited to participate in an exploratory study of minorities in the advertising industry as part of my thesis research. I hope to learn about career influences, job satisfaction, minority roles in the industry, and any discrimination or barriers faced by minorities in the field. You were selected as a possible participant in this study because you are a minority in the advertising business and were referred by _____. You will be one of 30 subjects chosen to participate in this study.

If you decide to participate, I will ask you a set of open-ended questions about your career and experiences in the business. I will be taking notes as we are talking, and these will be summarized with the data collected from the other participants. In the final thesis report, experiences will be described without the inclusion of details that would allow identification of you as an individual or your agency.

Your decision whether or not to participate
will not affect your future relations with The University of Texas at Austin. By giving verbal consent, you are indicating you have heard
the preceding statement of consent and have decided to participate.

1. How did you get into advertising in the first place?

2. Have you ever considered leaving the advertising field? What was the main reason for leaving or staying?

3. What do you like most about your current job?

4. What do you like least?

5. Do you participate in any minority professional associations? Which ones?

6. Do you feel the involvement has served your interests? How?

7. Approximately what percentage of the individuals at your agency are African American, Asian American, and Latino?

8. What is the highest level position in your agency held by a minority? (Discuss each minority group separately?)

9. What other positions in your agency are held by minorities?

10. Have you had a mentor-type relationship during your advertising career?

11. How would you describe it? (Probe.)

12. How did you meet this person?

13. Do you still keep up with him or her?

14. What do you see yourself doing in five years? Ten years?

15. What would you tell a young minority professional interested in advertising?

16. What role do you feel that your race or ethnic background has played in your work in advertising? (Probe.)

17. Demographics/Background Information:

Age: (19 and under) (20–29) (30–39) (40–49) (50–59) (60+)
(Circle one.)

Marital status: Single/Married (Circle one.)

Average hours worked per week: _____

Position: _____

Agency/Location: _____

Agency Description (accounts, mainstream/minority):

*Adapted from a one-on-one depth interview questionnaire that was developed by Kristin Kehl for her master's thesis, Minorities in Advertising: A Depth Interview Study, The University of Texas at Austin, May 1996. The thesis was supervised by the first author. Copyright 1996, Kristin E. Kehl. Permission to reprint granted by Kristin Kehl Lucido.

Appendix B

Telephone Survey Codebook

Media Use Survey Master Codebook

Variable		**Column**
V1	Respondent I.D. No.	(1–3)
V2	Interviewer I.D. No.	(4–8)
V3	Respondent: 1. Primary 2. Alternate	(9)

V4 1. How often do you watch local evening TV news?   (10)
    Would you say: (Local evening TV news comes on
    at 6:00 P.M. and 10:00 P.M.)
        1. Never or seldom (Skip to Q4.)
        2. 1 or 2 days a week
        3. 3 or 4 days a week*
        4. Nearly every day
        5. Every day

V5 2. Which local TV news do you usually watch?   (11)
        1. Channel 36, KXAN-TV, (Cable 4)
        2. Channel 24, KVUE-TV, (Cable 3)
        3. Channel 7, KTBC-TV, (Cable 2)**
        4. Channel 42, FOX-TV, (Cable 5)
        (5. Other_____)
        (6. Don't know)

V6 3. Why do you usually watch that local TV news?   (12–13)
        01 News anchors
        02 Already tuned to station
        03 Coverage of events/quality of coverage
        04 Habit
        05 Sports
        06 Weather

        97 No response/no opinion
        98 Don't know
        99 Other

V7 4. How often do you watch network TV evening news?   (14)
    Would you say: (Network TV evening news comes on
    at 5:30 P.M.)
        1. Never or seldom
        2. 1 or 2 days a week
        3. 3 or 4 days a week
        4. Nearly every day
        5. Every day

399

V8   5. How often do you read a daily newspaper?   **(15)**
Would you say:
1. Never or seldom
2. 1 or 2 days a week
3. 3 or 4 days a week
4. Nearly every day
5. Every day

V9   6. How often do you discuss the news with your friends **(16)**
or family?
Would you say:
1. Never or seldom
2. 1 or 2 days a week
3. 3 or 4 days a week
4. Nearly every day
5. Every day

V10   7. Do you have cable?   **(17)**
1. Yes
2. No (Skip to Q12.)

V11   8. How often do you watch a home shopping channel **(18)**
on cable?
Would you say:
1. Never or seldom (Skip to Q12.)
2. 1 or 2 days a week
3. 3 or 4 days a week
4. Nearly every day
5. Every day

V12   9. How many times have you ordered merchandise from **(19)**
a home shopping channel? Would you say:
1. 0 times (Skip to Q12.)
2. 1 time
3. 2 to 5 times
4. 6 to 9 times
5. 10 times or more

V13   10. What merchandise did you buy?   **(20–21)**
Do not code. Leave blank.

V14   11. How satisfied were you with shopping from a home **(22)**
shopping channel?
Would you say:
1. Very satisfied
2. Satisfied
3. Somewhat satisfied
4. Not satisfied

V15 12. How often do you listen to radio?   (23)
    1. Never or seldom (Skip to Q18.)
    2. 1 or 2 days a week
    3. 3 or 4 days a week
    4. Nearly every day
    5. Every day

V16 13. How familiar are you with the term "talk radio"?   (24)
    Would you say:
    1. Very familiar
    2. Somewhat familiar
    3. Not at all familiar (Skip to Q18.)

V17 14. Some people say "talk radio" means radio programs   (25)
    that listeners can call in and voice their opinions on
    the air. How often do you listen to that kind of radio
    show?
    1. Never or seldom (Skip to Q18.)
    2. 1 or 2 days a week
    3. 3 or 4 days a week
    4. Nearly every day
    5. Every day

V18 15. During the past three months, about how many times   (26)
    have you tried to call in on a "talk radio" show?
    Would you say:
    1. 0 or no times (Skip to Q17.)
    2. 1 time
    3. 2 to 5 times
    4. 6 to 9 times
    5. 10 times or more

V19 16. About how many times have you talked on the air?   (27)
    1. 0 or no times
    2. 1 time
    3. 2 to 5 times
    4. 6 to 9 times
    5. 10 times or more

V20   17. People have different reasons for listening to talk   (28–29)
radio. In general, what is the main reason that you
listen to talk radio?
01 Entertainment
02 Informative/educational/enriching/interesting
03 Sports
04 Specific personality
05 Specific topic
06 Just like to hear what other people like to say
07 To call in and talk
08 Dislike traditional radio formats

97 No response/no opinion
98 Don't know
99 Other

V21   18. Now, I'm going to ask you about commercials on   (30–31)
television. Some people pay close attention to television commercials, and others pay little attention.
In general, what do you usually do when commercials come on during a TV program?
01 Change channel
02 Don't watch them
03 Turn down sound/make mute
04 Do something else such as play games,
get something to eat
05 Watch them

97 No response/no opinion
98 Don't know
99 Other

V22   19. Now, I'm going to ask you about computers. How   (32)
often do you use a personal computer at home or
work?
1. Never or seldom (Skip to Q27.)
2. 1 or 2 days a week
3. 3 or 4 days a week
4. 5 or more days a week

20. Which of the following computer-related services do you use at least three times a week?

		Yes	No	
V23	A. Wordprocessing	1	2	(33)
V24	B. Electronic mail	1	2	(34)
V25	C. The Internet	1	2	(35)
V26	D. Computer games	1	2	(36)
V27	E. CD-ROM	1	2	(37)
V28	F. Online information services such as Prodigy, America Online, or Compuserve	1	2	(38)

V29   21. How many times have you ordered merchandise   (39)
through your computer?
   1. 0 or no times (Skip to Q24.)
   2. 1 time
   3. 2 to 5 times
   4. 6 to 9 times
   5. 10 times or more

V30   22. What merchandise did you buy?   (40–41)
Do not code. Leave blank.

V31   23. How satisfied were you with shopping through   (42)
your computer?
Would you say:
   1. Very satisfied
   2. Satisfied
   3. Somewhat satisfied
   4. Not satisfied

V32   24. Since you first began using computers, approx-   (43)
imately, how much formal computer training
have you received?
   1. None
   2. One-half day
   3. 1 full day
   4. 2 to 3 days
   5. 4 to 5 days
   6. More than 5 days

V33   25. What is your primary source of information for (44)
learning about computers or computer-related
products or services?
    1. People at work/co-workers
    2. Classes
    3. On the job
    4. Manuals/computer books/ online help/
       self-training
    5. Magazines
    6. Daily newspaper
    7. Family/friends
    8. No response/no opinion
    9. Other

V34   26. In general, how would you compare your computer (45)
comfort level with your circle of friends? Would you
say you are:
    1. More comfortable than your friends
    2. Equally as comfortable as your friends
    3. Less comfortable than your friends
    (4. Don't know)

V35   27. Now, I'm going to ask your opinions about some   (46–47)
            national and local issues. What do you think is the
            most important problem facing people in the United
            States today?
            01 Inflation/high cost of living/high prices
            02 Economy
            03 Unemployment
            04 Recession
            05 Energy problems/fuel shortages
            06 Crime
            07 Drugs
            08 Dissatisfaction with government, poor national leadership
            09 The President
            10 Congress
            11 Lack of trust in government
            12 Corruption in government
            13 Moral decline in society
            14 International problems/foreign affairs
            15 National defense
            16 Peace, war, nuclear war
            17 Race relations/civil rights
            18 Environment
            19 Poverty
            20 Education
            21 Family problems
            22 Big government
            23 The judicial system
            24 Apathy
            25 Government spending
            26 The deficit
            27 Health care
            28 Welfare
            29 Taxes

            97 No response/no opinion
            98 Don't know
            99 Other

V36   28. Austin has been growing during the past 10 years.   (48)
            Would you say Austin is:
            1. Too big
            2. About right
            3. Too small

V37   29. How often do you go to downtown Austin? Would   (49)
            you say:
            1. Never or seldom (Skip to Q31.)
            2. One to three times a week
            3. 4 to 5 times a week
            4. Almost daily or more often

30. What are the main reasons you go downtown?
    Use list below to code first and second reasons.

V38	1st Reason	(50–51)
V39	2nd Reason	(52–53)

    01 Work
    02 Business/banking/attorney/pay bills
    03 Sixth Street/clubs/entertainment
    04 Shopping
    05 Restaurants
    06 School

    97 No response/no opinion
    98 Don't know
    99 Other

31. What changes, if any, would you like to see in the
    downtown area?
    Use list below to code first and second changes.

V40	1st Change	(54–55)
V41	2nd Change	(56–57)

    01 Nothing
    02 More parking
    03 More stores for shopping
    04 Downtown shopping mall
    05 Sidewalk cafes/outdoor restaurants
    06 Improve appearance of buildings
    07 People living downtown
    08 Pedestrian walkways
    09 More greenways
    10 More historic emphasis
    11 Ease traffic congestion/enforce traffic laws

    97 No response/no opinion
    98 Don't know
    99 Other

V42	Code 1 for Record 1	(58=1)
	Leave 59 and 60 blank.	(59–60=Blank)
V43	Respondent ID (Repeat Respondent's ID.)	(1–3)

32. How likely would you be to go downtown if:

		More Likely	Less Likely	Wouldn't Matter	
V44	A. Parking were easier.	1	2	3	(4)
V45	B. More stores were available for shopping.	1	2	3	(5)
V46	C. More variety were offered in entertainment.	1	2	3	(6)
V47	D. You felt safer.	1	2	3	(7)

33. After the city moves the airport, what do you think the city should do with the land at Mueller Airport when it's closed? **Use list below to code first and second preferences.**

V48	1st preference	(8–9)
V49	2nd preference	(10–11)

01 Housing
02 Parks/recreational facilities
03 Continue use as airport
04 Industrial/factory/economic development
05 Shopping mall
06 Entertainment/restaurants/bars
07 Sell it
08 Shelter for homeless
09 Theme park/sports stadium

97 No response/no opinion
98 Don't know
99 Other

V50   34. Now, I'm going to ask you about violence on tele-   (12)
vision. How do you feel about the amount of vio-
lence portrayed on television programs today, not
including news programs? Do you think there is:
　　1. Too much violence
　　2. A reasonable amount
　　3. Very little violence

V51   35. As you may know, the major television and cable   (13)
networks recently agreed to show a warning label
before programs with violence are shown on TV.
In your opinion, does this warning label go far
enough to address the issue of TV violence, or not?
　　1. Goes far enough
　　2. Does not go far enough
　　(3. Don't know)

V52   36. Do you think the Federal government should do   **(14)**
more to regulate violence on TV, should it do less,
or is it doing about the right amount?
1. Should do more
2. Should do less
3. It's doing about the right amount
(4. Don't know)

V53   37. Do you think there is a relationship between   **(15)**
violence on television and the crime rate in the
United States, or not? Would you say:
1. Yes, there is a relationship.
2. No, there isn't a relationship.
(3. Don't know)

V54   38. How many children, under 18, are there in your home?   **(16)**
1. 0 (Skip to Q46.)
2. 1 (Go to Q39.)

3. 2
4. 3   } (Read:) For the next few questions, I
5. 4   want you to think about the child who
6. 5   has the next birthday coming up.
7. 6 or more

V55   39. How old will your child be on his or her next   **(17–18)**
birthday?

_____

V56   40. Is that child a boy or girl?   **(19)**
1. Boy
2. Girl

V57   41. Do you have rules about your child watching TV?   **(20)**
1. Yes
2. No (Skip to Q43.)

42. What are those rules?
Use list below to code first and second rules.

V58	1st Rule	(21–22)
V59	2nd Rule	(23–24)

    01 No inappropriate content such as violence
    02 No inappropriate content such as sex/nudity
    03 Limit number of hours allowed to watch
    04 Watch after homework is finished
    05 Watch after chores are finished
    06 Depends on grades in school
    07 No network TV, only PBS, Disney Channel, educational programs

    97 No response/no opinion
    98 Don't know
    99 Other

V60   43. How often do you use the Motion Picture   **(25)**
Association of America movie ratings, such
as G, PG, and R, as guides to help you decide
whether to let your child view a movie?
    1. Never (Skip to Q46.)
    2. Rarely
    3. Sometimes
    4. Often

V61   44. Do you ever prohibit your child from watching a   **(26)**
movie based on any of the movie ratings?
    1. Yes
    2. No (Skip to Q46.)

45. Which movies do you restrict?

		Yes	No	
V62	A. PG	1	2	(27)
V63	B. PG-13	1	2	(28)
V64	C. R	1	2	(29)
V65	D. NC-17	1	2	(30)
V66	E. X	1	2	(31)

V67   46. Now, I'm going to ask you some questions about   **(32)**
the O. J. Simpson case.*** How familiar are you
with the O. J. Simpson murder case? Would you
say:
    1. Very familiar
    2. Familiar
    3. Somewhat familiar
    4. Not familiar at all (Skip to Q54.)

V68 47. In general, how often did you pay attention to (33)
    coverage of the case?
     1. Never or seldom
     2. One or two days a week
     3. Three or four days a week
     4. Five or six days a week
     5. Every day

    48. From what sources did you get most of your news
    and information on the case?
    Use list below to code first and second sources.

V69 1st Source (34–35)
V70 2nd Source (36–37)

     01 Network News (ABC, CBS, NBC, including
      network news magazines)
     02 Newspaper
     03 Radio
     04 Friends/word-of-mouth
     05 News magazines such as *Newsweek, Time,* and
      U.S. News & World Report
     06 CNN
     07 Court TV
     08 Tabloid TV news shows such as *Current Affair*

     97 No response/no opinion
     98 Don't know
     99 Other

    49. Based on the information you received, what grade,
    A, B, C, D, or F, would you give:

		A	B	C	D	F	(Don't Know)	
V71	A. The fairness of Judge Ito's rulings.	1	2	3	4	5	6	(38)
V72	B. The quality of media coverage.	1	2	3	4	5	6	(39)

V73 50. Given all the information you've heard on the O. J. (40)
    Simpson case, do you think O. J. Simpson is:
     1. Definitely guilty
     2. Probably guilty
     3. Probably not guilty
     4. Definitely not guilty
     (5. Don't know)

V74   51. Why?   (41–42)

       01 Reasonable doubt
       02 Inconclusive evidence
       03 Troubled history of marriage
       04 History of spousal abuse
       05 Celebrity status
       06 Presence of high-powered defense attorneys
       07 Competence of prosecuting attorney
       08 Damaging evidence
       09 Too many technicalities
       10 Fear of racial trouble
       11 Blood evidence on Simpson's property
       12 DNA results
       13 Simpson's actions since murder
       14 Chase scene
       15 Location of trial in L.A.
       16 Racial issue
       17 Blind belief that he didn't do it
       18 Racial composition of jury
       19 Gender composition of jury

       97 No response/no opinion
       98 Don't know
       99 Other

V75   52. Did you think the jury in the criminal trial would: (43)
       1. Definitely find O. J. Simpson guilty
       2. Probably find him guilty
       3. Probably find him not guilty
       4. Definitely find him not guilty
       (5. Don't know)

V76   53. Why?   (44–55)
                01 Reasonable doubt
                02 Inconclusive evidence
                03 Troubled history of marriage
                04 History of spousal abuse
                05 Celebrity status
                06 Presence of high-powered defense attorneys
                07 Competence of prosecuting attorney
                08 Damaging evidence
                09 Too many technicalities
                10 Fear of racial trouble
                11 Blood evidence on Simpson's property
                12 DNA results
                13 Simpson's actions since murder
                14 Chase scene
                15 Location of trial in L.A.
                16 Racial issue
                17 Blind belief that he didn't do it
                18 Racial composition of jury
                19 Gender composition of jury

                97 No response/no opinion
                98 Don't know
                99 Other

V77   54. Now, I have just a few questions about your back-   (46)
                ground. Generally speaking, do you identify your-
                self as a:
                1. Democrat
                2. Republican
                3. Independent
                (4. Other_____)

V78   55. Do you consider yourself: (47)
                1. Conservative
                2. Middle of the road
                3. Liberal
                (4. Other_____)

V79   56. How old are you? (If respondent does not volunteer   (48–49)
                age, read categories.)
                01. 18–22   07. 45–49
                02. 23–24   08. 50–54
                03. 25–29   09. 55–59
                04. 30–34   10. 60–64
                05. 35–39   11. 65–69
                06. 40–44   12. 70 or older
                                          (13. Refused)

V80   57. What is your zip code?   (50–52)
                            Code last three digits.

V81   58. What is your marital status?   (53)
             1. Married
             2. Single
             3. Divorced or legally separated
             4. Widowed
             (5. Other_____)

V82   59. What is the highest level of education that you've   (54)
               completed?
             (Read responses.)
             1. Some high school or less
             2. High school graduate
             3. Some college or technical school degree
             4. College graduate
             5. Some graduate or professional school
             6. Masters, M.D., or doctorate

V83   60. What is your full-time title or position?   (55)

             1. Manager/executive/administrator/owner
             2. Professional (doctor, attorney, engineer, accountant)
             3. Technical/specialist/computer specialist
             4. Educator (university-college/high school or below)
             5. Student
             6. Secretary/clerical/sales/teller
             7. Homemaker

             9. Other

V84   61. What type of company or organization do you   (56)
               work for?
             1. Computer/high tech
             2. Government (federal/state/county/city
                 but not including universities)
             3. University/college/community college
             4. Public/private school
             5. Arts/music/entertainment
             6. Communication/media
             7. Retail
             8. Health
             9. Other

V85   62. What is your race or ethnic group?   (57)
(If respondent does not volunteer race or ethnic
group, read categories.)
1. Caucasian or white
2. African American or black
3. Hispanic or Latino
4. Asian American
5. Other_____

V86   63. Approximately, what is your household income?   (58)
Please stop me when I read your correct income
category. (If student is supported by parents, use
parents' income.)
1. Under $20,000
2. $20-$49,000
3. $50-$79,000
4. $80,000 or above
5. Refused

V87   64. Respondent's SEX is: (59)
1. Male
2. Female

V88   Record 2   (60=2)
Code 2 for Record 2.

*On the questionnaire that was used for the survey, the first question did not include the response choice for "3 or 4 days." The question was originally designed to screen for non, low, infrequent, and frequent viewers of local TV news for a separate focus group study. For the purposes of this example, "3 or 4 days" was inserted to ensure that the question was exhaustive.

**Channels 7 and 42 switched network affiliations after the survey was conducted. Channel 7 is now affiliated with FOX and Channel 42 is affiliated with CBS. Channel 42 also changed its call letters.

***Questions on the O. J. Simpson case were updated for this example.

Appendix C.1

Survey Printouts: Selected Frequency Tables

V7	*How Often Do You Watch Network TV Evening News?*				
		Frequency	**Percent**	**Valid Percent**	**Cumulative Percent**
Valid	1 NEVER OR SELDOM	178	38.6	39.1	39.1
	2 1 OR 2 DAYS A WEEK	84	18.2	18.5	57.6
	3 3 OR 4 DAYS A WEEK	54	11.7	11.9	69.5
	4 NEARLY EVERYDAY	66	14.3	14.5	84.0
	5 EVERYDAY	73	15.8	16.0	100.0
	Total	455	98.7	100.0	
Missing	0	6	1.3		
	Total	6	1.3		
Total		461	100.0		

V8	How Often Do You Read a Daily Newspaper?				
		Frequency	Percent	Valid Percent	Cumulative Percent
Valid	1 NEVER OR SELDOM	99	21.5	21.7	21.7
	2 1 OR 2 DAYS A WEEK	87	18.9	19.0	40.7
	3 3 OR 4 DAYS A WEEK	40	8.7	8.8	49.5
	4 NEARLY EVERYDAY	42	9.1	9.2	58.6
	5 EVERYDAY	189	41.0	41.4	100.0
	Total	457	99.1	100.0	
Missing	0	4	.9		
	Total	4	.9		
Total		461	100.0		

V9	How Often Do You Discuss News with Friends/Family?				
		Frequency	**Percent**	**Valid Percent**	**Cumulative Percent**
Valid	1 NEVER OR SELDOM	68	14.8	14.8	14.8
	2 1 OR 2 DAYS A WEEK	86	18.7	18.8	33.6
	3 3 OR 4 DAYS A WEEK	94	20.4	20.5	54.1
	4 NEARLY EVERYDAY	91	19.7	19.9	74.0
	5 EVERYDAY	119	25.8	26.0	100.0
	Total	458	99.3	100.0	
Missing	0	3	.7		
	Total	3	.7		
Total		461	100.0		

V10	Do You Have Cable?				
		Frequency	**Percent**	**Valid Percent**	**Cumulative Percent**
Valid	1 YES	346	75.1	76.2	76.2
	2 NO	108	23.4	23.8	100.0
	Total	454	98.5	100.0	
Missing	0	7	1.5		
	Total	7	1.5		
Total		461	100.0		

V21	What Do You Usually Do When TV Ads Come On?				
		Frequency	Percent	Valid Percent	Cumulative Percent
Valid	1 CHANGE CHANNEL	78	16.9	18.9	18.9
	2 DON'T WATCH THEM	66	14.3	16.0	34.9
	3 TURN DOWN SOUND, MAKE MUTE	35	7.6	8.5	43.3
	4 DO SOMETHING ELSE	78	16.9	18.9	62.2
	5 WATCH THEM	117	25.4	28.3	90.6
	99 OTHER	39	8.5	9.4	100.0
	Total	413	89.6	100.0	
Missing	0	47	10.2		
	98 DON'T KNOW	1	.2		
	Total	48	10.4		
Total		461	100.0		

V22	How Often Do You Use a PC at Home/Work?				
		Frequency	**Percent**	**Valid Percent**	**Cumulative Percent**
Valid	1 NEVER OR SELDOM	151	32.8	33.9	33.9
	2 1-2 DAYS A WEEK	32	6.9	7.2	41.1
	3 3–4 DAYS A WEEK	48	10.4	10.8	51.9
	4 5 OR MORE DAYS A WEEK	214	46.4	48.1	100.0
	Total	445	96.5	100.0	
Missing	0	16	3.5		
	Total	16	3.5		
Total		461	100.0		

V24	Use E-Mail at Least 3 Times per Week?				
		Frequency	**Percent**	**Valid Percent**	**Cumulative Percent**
Valid	1 YES	127	27.5	41.9	41.9
	2 NO	176	38.2	58.1	100.0
	Total	303	65.7	100.0	
Missing	0	158	34.3		
	Total	158	34.3		
Total		461	100.0		

V25	Use Internet at Least 3 Times per Week?				

		Frequency	Percent	Valid Percent	Cumulative Percent
Valid	1 YES	78	16.9	26.0	26.0
	2 NO	222	48.2	74.0	100.0
	Total	300	65.1	100.0	
Missing	0	161	34.9		
	Total	161	34.9		
Total		461	100.0		

V50	The Amount of Violence on TV?				

		Frequency	Percent	Valid Percent	Cumulative Percent
Valid	1 TOO MUCH VIOLENCE	342	74.2	76.2	76.2
	2 A REASONABLE AMOUNT	92	20.0	20.5	96.7
	3 VERY LITTLE VIOLENCE	15	3.3	3.3	100.0
	Total	449	97.4	100.0	
Missing	0	12	2.6		
	Total	12	2.6		
Total		461	100.0		

V51	Warning Labels Enough to Address TV Violence?				
		Frequency	**Percent**	**Valid Percent**	**Cumulative Percent**
Valid	1 GOES FAR ENOUGH	165	35.8	36.3	36.3
	2 DOES NOT GO FAR ENOUGH	257	55.7	56.6	93.0
	3 DON'T KNOW	32	6.9	7.0	100.0
	Total	454	98.5	100.0	
Missing	0	7	1.5		
	Total	7	1.5		
Total		461	100.0		

V61	Prohibit Child from Watching Based on Rating?				
		Frequency	**Percent**	**Valid Percent**	**Cumulative Percent**
Valid	1 YES	101	21.9	82.1	82.1
	2 NO	22	4.8	17.9	100.0
	Total	123	26.7	100.0	
Missing	0	338	73.3		
	Total	338	73.3		
Total		461	100.0		

V72	Grade Coverage of O. J. Simpson Trial				
		Frequency	**Percent**	**Valid Percent**	**Cumulative Percent**
Valid	1 A	68	14.8	17.5	17.5
	2 B	89	19.3	22.9	40.5
	3 C	89	19.3	22.9	63.4
	4 D	36	7.8	9.3	72.7
	5 F	78	16.9	20.1	92.8
	6 DON'T KNOW	28	6.1	7.2	100.0
	Total	388	84.2	100.0	
Missing	0	73	15.8		
	Total	73	15.8		
Total		461	100.0		

Appendix C.2

Survey Printouts: Selected Cross-Tabulation Tables

V24			Use E-mail at Least 3 Times per Week? *V87 Sex of Respondent Cross-Tabulation		

| | | | V87 Sex of Respondent | | |
			1 MALE	2 FEMALE	Total
V24 USE E MAIL AT LEAST 3 TIMES PER WEEK?	1 YES	Count	69	53	122
		% within V24 USE E-MAIL AT LEAST 3 TIMES PER WEEK?	56.6%	43.4%	100.0%
		% within V87 SEX OF RESPONDENT	47.6%	35.1%	41.2%
		% of Total	23.3%	17.9%	41.2%
	2 NO	Count	76	98	174
		% within V24 USE E-MAIL AT LEAST 3 TIMES PER WEEK?	43.7%	56.3%	100.0%
		% within V87 SEX OF RESPONDENT	52.4%	64.9%	58.8%
		% of Total	25.7%	33.1%	58.8%
Total		Count	145	151	296
		% within V24 USE E-MAIL AT LEAST 3 TIMES PER WEEK?	49.0%	51.0%	100.0%
		% within V87 SEX OF RESPONDENT	100.0%	100.0%	100.0%
		% of Total	49.0%	51.0%	100.0%

V50			The Amount of Violence On TV? *V87 Sex of Respondent Cross-Tabulation		

			V87 Sex of Respondent		
			1 MALE	2 FEMALE	Total
V50 THE AMOUNT OF VIOLENCE ON TV?	1 TOO MUCH VIOLENCE	Count	139	194	333
		% within V50 THE AMOUNT OF VIOLENCE ON TV?	41.7%	58.3%	100.0%
		% within V87 SEX OF RESPONDENT	66.5%	84.0%	75.7%
		% of Total	31.6%	44.1%	75.7%
	2 A REASONABLE AMOUNT	Count	62	30	92
		% within V50 THE AMOUNT OF VIOLENCE ON TV?	67.4%	32.6%	100.0%
		% within V87 SEX OF RESPONDENT	29.7%	13.0%	20.9%
		% of Total	14.1%	6.8%	20.9%
	3 VERY LITTLE VIOLENCE	Count	8	7	15
		% within V50 THE AMOUNT OF VIOLENCE ON TV?	53.3%	46.7%	100.0%
		% within V87 SEX OF RESPONDENT	3.8%	3.0%	3.4%
		% of Total	1.8%	1.6%	3.4%
Total		Count	209	231	440
		% within V50 THE AMOUNT OF VIOLENCE ON TV?	47.5%	52.5%	100.0%
		% within V87 SEX OF RESPONDENT	100.0%	100.0%	100.0%
		% of Total	47.5%	52.5%	100.0%

Appendix D.1

Telephone Survey Budget

Data Collection for 1,000, 10-Minute Interviews Using a Computer-Assisted Telephone Interviewing (CATI) System*

Wages

Administration	$ 5,600	
Field Manager	1,450	
Programmer	920	
Trainer	300	
Supervisors	2,250	
Interviewers	7,100	
Subtotal		$ 17,620

Fringe Benefits (27%)	$ 4,757

Services of Expendable Supplies

Telephone Cost and Equipment Rental	$ 2,700	
Sample	1,350	
Duplicating and Printing	350	
Computer Supplies	250	
Office Supplies	150	
Subtotal		$ 4,800
TOTAL DIRECT COST		$ 27,177
Grand Total		$ 27,177

*Administration includes questionnaire design with two or three open-ended questions, pretesting of questionnaire, computer processing and analysis, frequencies, and cross-tabs with basic demographics. Does not include consultation on results and written and oral reports with recommendations which may increase budget $5,000 to $10,000 plus expenses.

The sample consists of 4,000 telephone numbers generated through random digit dialing, which will be purchased from a company that specializes in sampling. The sample will have been screened for business, fax, and disconnected numbers. In general, 4,000 to 5,000 sample numbers will yield 1,000 completed interviews. Although interviewers may make a maximum number of five callbacks, on average, it takes three callbacks to complete an interview. (Inchauste, 1999)

Appendix D.2

Mail Survey Budget for Sample of 1,000*

Research Expert (Design and supervise survey, write and pretest questionnaire with cover letter, computer analyze data)	$5,000
Clerk (compile mailing list, prepare labels, assemble materials for four mailings, code questionnaires, input data, 120 hours)	960
Printing, Photocopying, Collating	
Letter and questionnaire photocopying and collating (6,250 pages @ $0.035)	219
Postcards	47
Postage	
Advance notification letter (@ $0.33)	330
Cover letter and two-page questionnaire (@ $0.33)	330
Stamped and self-addressed envelope to return questionnaire (@ $0.33)	330
Reminder postcard (@ $0.20)	200
Follow-up replacement cover letter, two-page questionnaire (@ $0.33)	248
Stamped and self-addressed envelope to return replacement questionnaire (@ $0.33)	248
Incentives	0
Supplies	
Labels (4,500)	33
Envelopes (4,500/$9.00 per 500)	81
Total	$8,026

*1. Budget does not include the written report and oral presentation, which may increase the budget by $5,000. Eliminating the cost of the research expert and clerk would reduce the cost of the mail survey to $2,020.

2. Printing, photocopying, and collating include costs for advance notification letter announcing forthcoming survey, original cover letter and questionnaire, reminder postcard, follow-up cover letter and replacement questionnaire for non-respondents, self-addressed envelope, labels.

3. Postage is for four mailings, including advance notification letter announcing forthcoming questionnaire, original cover letter and questionnaire, reminder postcard, and follow-up replacement questionnaire. Budget assumes follow-up replacement questionnaire will be sent to 75 percent of sample representing non-respondents. In other words, it is assumed that 75 percent of the sample will not respond and a new questionnaire will have to be mailed.

4. Even though this mail survey does not include an incentive to return the questionnaire, often mail surveys include a one dollar bill, promise of a donation to a charity, or other incentive to encourage a higher response rate.

5. Total cost of mail survey can be reduced by eliminating the advance notification letter, reminder postcard, or follow-up replacement cover letter and questionnaire. Eliminating these costs may reduce the response rate significantly.

Appendix D.3

Focus Group Budget

Budget for Two Focus Groups of Ten Participants Per Group

Moderator's Outline and Discussion Guide, Background Questionnaire	$ 1,500
Focus Group Facility Rental for 2 Groups per Night	800
Videotaping Discussion ($75 per group)	150
Recruitment of Participants (Recruit 14 for 10 to show at $900 per group)	1,800
Cash Incentives for Participants for 2 Groups ($50 per person)	1,400
Light Refreshments	100
Moderating Focus Groups	1,200
Analysis, Written Report, and Presentation	5,000
Assistant for Focus Groups to Set Up, Check Participants In, Distribute Cash Incentives, etc.	50
Total for two focus groups	**$12,000**

Depending on market, focus group facility, and expertise of research expert/moderator, these costs may vary.

Glossary

A priori   A method of knowing or explaining things that is based on theory and not experience.

Callback   When a respondent is not reached, the interviewer is required to call again at least two hours after the original call. Two to three callbacks or more may be attempted to reach the individual who was randomly selected to participate in the survey.

Case study   Case studies can be thought of as a study of a sample of one. Case studies can be used to study an individual, institution, organization, event, issue, or some type of phenomenon. The case study researcher examines his or her subject in depth, conducting hundreds of interviews and reviewing hundreds of contemporary and historical records, in order to understand everything about the research topic.

CATI   Computer-assisted telephone interviewing system in which the survey questionnaire is programmed into the computer and displayed on the computer screen. Interviewers enter responses directly into the computer

Census   When every individual in the population is surveyed.

Chi square   Most appropriate for nominal-level measurements, this statistic is used to evaluate the significance of a relationship between two variables. It answers the question: Are the results significantly different from what would have been expected?

Closed-ended   Survey question in which the response choices are provided for the respondent to select from.

Cluster sample   Type of random sample in which there is successive sampling of clusters and sub-samples of those clusters.

Code sheet   Based on the content analysis codebook and used to code individual commercials, TV programs, or news stories. Codes from the code sheets are compiled on a spreadsheet or entered directly into a computer file for processing.

Codebook   Used to code survey questionnaires or content for content analysis studies, this document specifies variables and their location in the data file, coding instructions, and codes. A survey codebook, which is based on the questionnaire, also includes categories and codes for open-ended questions.

Coding   In surveys, the process of assigning numerical codes to questionnaire responses; in content analysis studies, the process of assigning codes to media and communication content according to codebook instructions.

Coefficient of reliability   Expressed as a percentage and calculated from a formula that evaluates the amount of agreement between coders compared to the number of decisions made by coders.

Cohort   Type of longitudinal study in which respondents are defined by a common characteristic such as when they were born or grew up. The most well-known cohort today is the baby boomer generation, which was born between 1946 and 1964. A cohort study follows a generational group to understand their actions, attitudes, and beliefs over time.

Concept   Defined by researcher Fred Kerlinger as an expression of an abstraction that is formed by generalization from particulars. Examples of concepts might be achievement, intelligence, aggressiveness, media literate, or status.

Confidence interval   A statistical interval for a random sample that is expressed as a range of percentage points above and below the mean at a specified level of confidence. Although the mean of a random sample is not an exact match of the mean of the population from which it was drawn, 95 times out of 100, the sample mean will be one of the points in the confidence interval. Also called sampling error.

Confidence level   Probability level or level of certainty that is usually expressed as 95 or 99 percent confident that the random sample mean will fall within a specified confidence interval.

Content analysis   Research technique for the objective and quantitative analysis of the manifest content of media and communication.

Contingency   Type of survey question that is asked of those who were determined to be qualified to answer by the preceding filter question.

Control group   Group in experiment that was not exposed to the independent variable.

Copy testing   Type of research primarily conducted by advertisers to gauge reactions to advertising, its message, and any creative elements used to create the ad. Copy testing is conducted to answer the questions: Was the ad noticed? Was it understood? Was the ad effective? Was the ad remembered? Was it liked?

Correlation   Statistical analysis that shows two or more variables are related.

Cross-sectional   Research study that is conducted on a cross-section of the population at a specified period of time to gather information about a variety of characteristics.

Cross-tabulation   Analytical technique for comparing two or more variables and the relationship, if any, of the subgroups of the variables.

Deductive   Reasoning that moves from general to specific.

Dependent variable   Variable influenced by the independent variable.

Descriptive statistics   Mathematical tools for analyzing and summarizing large amounts of data.

Empirical   Systematically observing or collecting data or evidence for the purpose of describing phenomena or making inferences.

Evaluation research   Research to assess the effectiveness of a public relations campaign.

Executive summary   Section of a written business report that summarizes how the study was conducted and the most important findings.

Exhaustive   Requirement of closed-ended questions that response choices must be comprehensive with every possible answer included. Exhaustive response choices are often accomplished by including "other" as a possible choice on the list.

Exit poll   Type of survey conducted with voters immediately after they have voted. Results are used to predict the outcome of the election.

Experiment   Research method in which an independent variable is manipulated and its effects on the dependent variable are observed. Considered most powerful research method because causation can be determined.

Experimental group   Group in an experiment that is exposed to the experimental manipulation.

External validity   Addresses whether results of a research study can be generalized to the population of interest.

Extraneous variables   Variables unrelated to the study's hypothesis that may be responsible for the results.

Field experiment   Experiment conducted in a natural environment.

Filter   Survey question that is used to determine whether or not the respondent should be asked the follow-up contingency question.

Focus group   Small group discussion on a specific topic that lasts one and a half to two hours. Discussion is led by a moderator, and participants, who are selected because they possess characteristics required for the topic, are paid for their time.

Frequency   Method of statistical analysis that shows what percentage of the total each question response or content analysis category represents.

Hawthorne effect   Term that has come to symbolize experimental studies in which subjects change because of the attention they receive from participating in an experiment. Because these studies lack control groups, it is impossible to specify what effect, if any, the independent variable has on the dependent variable.

Independent variable   Variable that influences the dependent variable

Index of reliability   Expressed as a percentage and calculated from a formula that evaluates amount of agreement between coders compared to number of decisions made by coders. This formula differs from the inter-coder reliability formula because it takes into consideration the number of agreements that were due to chance.

Inductive   Type of reasoning that begins with empirical observations and moves to the general.

Inferential statistics   Mathematical tools for projecting from the sample results to the population from which the sample was drawn.

Intercept Face-to-face, non-random survey in which respondents are intercepted at the mall or other high traffic areas.

Inter-coder reliability Expressed as a percentage and calculated from a formula that evaluates amount of agreement between coders compared to number of decisions made by coders. Formula differs from index of reliability formula because it does not take into consideration the number of agreements that were due to chance.

Interviewer Trained individual who reads the questions and records the answers for a survey questionnaire.

Internal validity Research issue that addresses whether or not the measurement accurately represents the variable studied.

Interval One of four levels of measurements. Attributes or values are mutually exclusive and exhaustive, and can be placed in order. The distance between values is equal, and there is not a true zero.

Laboratory experiment Experiment that is conducted in a controlled environment; external validity is threatened.

Latent Underlying or hidden meaning. Content that is not coded in content analysis studies because the meaning is not apparent and it can be interpreted differently by different coders.

Level of measurement Refers to the precision of the measurement used in research studies. From least to most precise, they are nominal, ordinal, interval, and ratio.

Likert scale Type of attitude scale that measures intensity of agreement or disagreement with a series of words or statements that are used to describe an individual, organization, concept, or phenomenon.

Literature review A search for, review, and critical analysis of published and unpublished research studies that are relevant to the research question. The literature review should be a synthesis of what is already known about the topic and how it was learned.

Longitudinal Research study that is conducted over several distinct periods in time in order to compare changes over time. Trend, panel, and cohort studies are considered longitudinal.

Manifest Type of content coded in content analysis studies; content that can be objectively coded because its meaning is obvious.

Matching Process used in experimental studies to make the experimental and control groups equal. Usually used when random assignment of subjects to experimental and control groups is impossible. Subjects are matched on specific known characteristics and assigned to experimental and control groups.

Matrix Format used on a questionnaire that combines individual closed-ended questions on a related topic. The response choices must be the same.

Mean Statistic that represents one of three measures of central tendency that summarize data by reporting an average. Also known as arithmetic average, the mean is calculated by summing the number of cases and dividing the total by the number of cases.

Measurement Set of rules for assigning numbers, which represent values of varying degrees of precision, for reported or observed behaviors, attitudes, opinions, and other individual, group, organization, content, or issue characteristics.

Measures of association Statistics used to interpret the strength and direction of a relationship between two variables. Appropriate for ordinal, interval, and ratio-level measurements. In general, measures of association range from negative one to positive one, where zero can be interpreted as a lack of a linear relationship.

Median Statistic that represents one of three measures of central tendency that summarize data by reporting an average. The median is the midpoint or middle score, that is, the point where half of the numbers are above and half are below.

Mode Statistic that represents one of three measures of central tendency that summarize data by reporting an average. The mode is the most frequent score.

Moderator Individual who facilitates the focus group discussion by asking open-ended questions on the topic.

Moderator's Outline and Discussion Guide Focus group moderator's document that lists procedures and open-ended questions to be asked of participants.

Mutually exclusive Required for closed-ended survey questions and content analysis coding categories. Response choices and categories cannot overlap.

Nominal One of four levels of measurement, the attributes or values, which must be mutually exclusive and exhaustive, are sorted into groups and assigned labels.

Non-random sample Segment of the population that is selected without using scientific procedures. A non-random sample is biased and does not represent the population under study.

One-on-one depth interview One-on-one interview. Respondents are usually selected because they have certain information or hold certain positions in a company or organization.

Open-ended Survey question in which the respondent can supply an answer of his or her choosing.

Operational definition Used to assign meaning to the variable by specifying the operations or activities required to measure it.

Ordinal One of four levels of measurements. Attributes or values are mutually exclusive and exhaustive. In addition to being able to sort into groups and assign labels, they can be placed in order.

Panel Type of longitudinal study in which the same people are asked the same questions.

Perceptual mapping Analytical technique that uses survey data to visually represent consumer perceptions of a product, brand, or company in two or more dimensions.

Plus-one random sample Type of random sample in which the telephone book is used as a sampling frame and the last digit is altered by adding a one to it to reach unlisted phone numbers.

Posttest In an experimental design, posttest refers to measuring the dependent variable after the manipulation of the independent variable.

Precode Numerical values adjacent to the response choices for closed-ended questions, which will be used in the computer processing of the data.

Pretest Testing the survey questionnaire before it is finalized to ensure that question wording is understood and skip patterns are appropriate. In an experimental design, pretest refers to measuring the dependent variable before the manipulation of the independent variable. Also, pretest can refer to conducting a practice run of the experimental procedures.

Qualitative Type of research based on non-numerical and non-statistical procedures and analysis. Focus groups are a type of qualitative research used on the business side of media and communication. Ethnography, cultural studies, reception studies, and textual analysis are qualitative methods used on the academic side of communication. Academic qualitative research is grounded in the humanities rather than science, and it relies on interpretation, rather than measurement.

Quantitative Type of research based on measurement and on statistical procedures and analysis such as surveys and experiments.

Questionnaire Organized collection of questions designed to elicit valid information from survey respondents about the research topic.

Quota sample Type of non-random sample in which individuals are selected because they fit the characteristics of a population.

Random assignment Method of assigning subjects to experimental and control groups in order to make the two groups equal.

Random digit dialing One of several methods of selecting a random sample. A computer program is used to randomly pick the four-digit root numbers of a phone number and combine them with the telephone exchanges and area codes according to their representation in the population studied.

Random sample Segment of the population that has been selected according to statistical assumptions that make the sample representative of the population within a known amount of error.

Random selection Method of selecting respondents for a survey or elements for a content analysis in which there is an equal chance of being selected.

Range Statistic used to measure dispersion by calculating the difference between the highest and lowest score.

Ratio One of four levels of measurements. The attributes or values are mutually exclusive and exhaustive, and can be placed in order. The distance between values is equal and there is a true zero.

Reliability Required for scientifically based measurement. It addresses consistency of the question that measures the variable being studied.

Research Process of carrying out procedures for the systematic and objective observation, collection, processing, analysis, and reporting of information. Also the results of the process.

Research design Blueprint for the research study that specifies how the study will be conducted, and the results analyzed and reported.

Research question Describes what is being researched by setting forth a relationship between two or more variables in question form.

Respondents Individuals who participate in a survey by completing the questionnaire.

Response rate Percentage of respondents who completed the survey out of the total number of prospective respondents called less the non-working, business, fax, and modem numbers.

Response set When respondents give the same answer regardless of the question. This is potentially a problem in Likert-type scales when the intensity of agreement or disagreement is being measured.

Sample Segment of the population that has been selected for a research study through random or non-random methods.

Sampling Process of selecting segment of population to participate in study.

Sampling frame List of all the elements in the population, from which the sample will be drawn.

Secondary data analysis Analysis of data that have already been collected and used by a different researcher.

Simple random sample Segment of the population that is selected with the statistical assumption that every element of the population has an equal chance of being selected for the research study.

Skip interval Sampling frame divided by the sample size produces the skip or sampling interval, a standard interval that is used for drawing a systematic random sample with a random start point.

SPSS Statistical Package for the Social Sciences. One of several computer programs designed to process and analyze data collected from surveys, content analysis studies, and experiments.

Standard deviation One of several statistical measures of dispersion in which the variance is expressed in standard units.

Stratified random sample Random sample that sorts the population list by some key characteristic and draws sub-samples that are proportional to the representation in the overall population.

Subjects Individuals who participate in an experiment.

Survey Research technique that uses a standardized questionnaire to collect information about attitudes, opinions, behaviors, and background and lifestyle characteristics from a sample of respondents by telephone, mail, or in person.

Syndicated research Data that are made available for a subscription fee.

Systematic random sample with a random start point Random sample that uses a skip interval and random start point to select individuals for the sample. This sample will be representative of the population.

t-test Statistic often used in experiments to determine if there is a significant difference between the means of the experimental and control groups.

Table of random numbers Chart of numbers that lacks a horizontal, vertical, or diagonal pattern. Because numbers are displayed randomly, the table is used to pick a random start point for a systematic random sample with a random start point.

Theory Set of related concepts, variables, and hypotheses that explain phenomena.

Trend Type of longitudinal study in which different people are asked the same questions.

Unit of analysis In a content analysis study, the communication component, such as a commercial, magazine article, TV program, or TV news story that will actually be coded for analysis.

Unobtrusive observation Method of research that uses physical traces, archives, and observation without interacting with the individual that produced the subject that is being studied.

Validity Required for scientifically based measurement. It addresses whether or not the right question has been asked to get the answer that represents the phenomenon that is being researched.

Variable   Specific attitude, opinion, behavior, or demographic characteristic that can be measured such as level of education or frequency of reading a newspaper.

Variance   One of several statistics used to measure dispersion. It measures the average of the squared deviations from the mean and is reported in squared units.

Visual stimuli   Visual material such as advertisements, TV programs, prototypes that are shown to focus group participants, intercept respondents, or experimental subjects to gauge reactions.

Voluntary self-selection   Type of non-random sample in which individuals volunteer to participate because they noticed and filled out a questionnaire. Unrepresentative of the population studied.

Weighting   Statistical procedure for correcting the underrepresentation or overrepresentation of a demographic group in survey results.

References

American Association for Public Opinion Research. (1997, May). *Best practices for survey and public opinion research and survey practices AAPOR condemns*. Ann Arbor, MI: American Association for Public Opinion Research.

Anderson, C. (1996, July 24). Focus group believes Dole's age is a concern, Clinton lacks morals. *Austin American-Statesman,* Sec A.

Asher, H. (1988). *Polling and the public: What every citizen should know*. Washington DC: Congressional Quarterly Press.

Asimov, I. (1994). *Asimov's chronology of science & discovery*. New York: HarperCollins.

Austin American-Statesman (1995, August 28). Poll says computers in 41% of Texas homes, Sec. D.

Babbie, E. (1995). *The practice of social research*, 7th ed. Belmont, CA: Wadsworth.

Baltimore, D. (1997, January 27). [Letter]. *The New Yorker*.

Bandura, A., Ross, D., & Ross, S. A. (1963). Imitation of film-mediated aggressive models. *Journal of Abnormal and Social Psychology* 66(1).

Barboza, D. (1996, October 24). Nissan is changing the rules for car ads by rolling out entertaining spots using toy characters. The *New York Times*, National edition, Sec. C.

Becker, L. B. (1981). Secondary analysis. In G. H. Stempel III & B. H. Westley (Eds.), *Research methods in mass communication*. Englewood Cliffs, NJ: Prentice-Hall.

Berelson, B. (1952). *Content analysis in communication research*. New York: The Free Press.

Blalock, H. M. Jr. (1972). *Social statistics*. New York: McGraw-Hill.

Bower, R. T., & de Gasparis, P. (1978). *Ethics in social research: Protecting the interests of human subjects*. New York: Praeger.

Bruning, J. L., & Kintz, B. L. (1968). *Computational handbook of statistics*. Atlanta: Scott, Foresman.

Bureau of the Census. (1995, February 23). New Census Bureau African American report most comprehensive in 20 years. Press Release. Bureau of the Census Web site. <www.census.gov>

Bureau of the Census. (1996, February). *Current population reports, population projections of the United States by age, sex, race and hispanic origin: 1995–2050*, P25-1130. U.S. Department of Commerce.

Burrell Communications. (1997, July 28). Presentation to the Minorities and Communications Division Pre-Convention Program during the annual convention of the Association for Education in Journalism at the Burrell Communications Headquarters, Chicago.

Campbell, D. T., & Stanley, J. C. (1963). *Experimental and quasi-experimental designs for research*. Chicago: Rand McNally College Publishing Company.

Cantril, H. (1974). "The invasion from Mars." In W. Schramm & D. F. Roberts (Eds.), *The process and effects of mass communication* (2nd ed.). Urbana: University of Illinois Press.

Cohen, M. R., & Nagel, E. (1934). *An introduction to logic and scientific method*. New York: Harcourt, Brace.

Cohen, N., chairman, Mad Dogs & Englishmen. (1997, March 21). Presentation to The University of Texas at Austin advertising students and faculty during the students' annual New York agency tour.

Danielson, W. (1981). Data processing. In G. H. Stempel III & B. H. Westley (Eds.), *Research methods in mass communication*. Englewood Cliffs, NJ: Prentice-Hall.

DeFleur, M. (1997). *Computer-assisted investigative reporting: Development and methodology.* Mahwah, NJ: Lawrence Erlbaum.

DeFleur, M. L., Davenport, L., Gronin, M., & DeFleur, M. (1992). Audience recall of news stories presented by newspaper, computer, television and radio. *Journalism Quarterly 69*(4).

Dillman, D. A. (1978). *Mail and telephone surveys: The total design method.* New York: John Wiley.

Donohew, L., & Palmgreen, P. (1981). Conceptualization and theory building. In G. H. Stempel III & B. H. Westley (Eds.), *Research methods in mass communication.* Englewood Cliffs, NJ: Prentice-Hall.

Duhem, P. M. M. (1954). *The aim and structure of physical theory.* Princeton, NJ: Princeton University Press.

Editor & Publisher. (1988, May 14). Newspapers turn to research to sell NIE programs. *Editor and Publisher.*

Elliott, S. (1991, October 9). Debating the pros and cons of research vs. creativity. The *New York Times,* National edition, Sec. C.

Elliott, S. (1997, August 12). A new campaign for BMW of America by Fallon McElligott plays up the performance of its cars. The *New York Times,* National edition, Sec. C.

Elliott, S. (1997, September 5). *The Economist* wants readers to see it as bold, not bland. The *New York Times,* National edition, Sec. C.

Elliott, S. (1998, January 9). Advertising: A top woman executive who abruptly left Thompson re-emerges at D.M.B. & B. The *New York Times,* National edition, Sec. C.

Fidler, R. (1997). *Mediamorphosis: Understanding new media.* Thousand Oaks, CA: Pine Forge Press.

Fortini-Campbell, L. (1992). *Hitting the sweet spot.* Chicago: The Copy Workshop.

The Gallup Organization. (1995, October). Newsletter archive. *60* (22). Gallup Poll Web site. <www.gallup.com>

Goldberg, H. (1996, May 20). New census methods cut minority numbers. *Austin American-Statesman,* Sec. A.

Goodfellow, K. (1996, November 6). Quick calls: How America gets the news. The *New York Times,* National edition, Sec A.

Greenbaum, T. L. *The practical handbook and guide to focus group research.* Lexington, MA: Lexington Books, D.C. Heath.

Guilford, J. P. (1956). *Fundamental statistics in psychology and education.* New York: McGraw-Hill.

Halberstam, D. (1979). *The powers that be.* New York: Dell Publishing Company.

Harlan, C. (1996, April 17). Hispanic roles on TV still few, group finds. *Austin American-Statesman,* Sec A.

Hartley, R. F. (1995). *Marketing mistakes* (6th ed.). New York: John Wiley

Hastorf, A. H., & Cantril, H. (1974). They saw a game. In W. Schramm & D. F. Roberts (Eds.), *The process and effects of mass communication* (2nd ed.). Urbana: University of Illinois Press.

Hempel, C. (1965). *Aspects of scientific explanation.* New York: The Free Press.

Holmes, S. A. (1996, November 18). Quality of life is up for many blacks, data say. The *New York Times,* National edition, Sec. A.

Holsti, O. R. (1969). *Content analysis for the social sciences and humanities.* Reading, MA: Addison-Wesley.

Hoover, K. R. (1988). *The elements of social scientific thinking* (4th ed.). New York: St. Martin's.

Hovland, C. I., Lumsdaine, A. A., & Sheffield, F. D. (1949). *Experiments on mass communication.* Princeton, NJ: Princeton University Press.

Hovland, C. I., Lumsdaine, A. A., & Sheffield, F. D. (1974). The effect of presenting "one side" versus "both sides" in changing opinions on a controversial subject. In W. Schramm & D. F. Roberts (Eds.), *The process and effects of mass communication* (2nd ed.). Urbana: University of Illinois Press.

Inchauste, V., Director, Office of Survey Research, The University of Texas at Austin. Interviewed by first author, July 1, 1999.

Jones, J. H. (1981). *Bad blood: The Tuskegee syphilis experiment*. New York: The Free Press.

Kane, C. (1997, October 2). McDonald's starts a big campaign to revive its brand image. The *New York Times,* National edition, Sec. C.

Kaufman, L. (1997, August 18). Enough talk: Focus groups are old news. Today's marketers prefer crayolas, collages and surveillance. *Newsweek.*

Kehl, K. (1996). Minorities in advertising: A depth interview study. Master's thesis, The University of Texas at Austin.

Kerlinger, F. N. (1973). *Foundations of behavioral research* (2nd ed.). New York: Holt, Rinehart and Winston.

Kerlinger, F. N. (1986). *Foundations of behavioral research* (3rd ed.). New York: Holt, Rinehart and Winston.

Kolbert, E. (1992, August 30). Test-marketing a president: How focus groups pervade campaign politics. The *New York Times Magazine.*

Kurtz, H. (1997, August 13). Murder rate falls, but coverage of the crimes soars: Researchers say TV networks don't reflect reality by focusing news reports on homicides. *Austin American-Statesman,* Sec. A. Reprinted from *Washington Post.*

Lasswell, H. D. (1974). The structure and function of communication in society. In W. Schramm & D. F. Roberts (Eds.), *The process and effects of mass communication* (2nd ed.). Urbana, IL: University of Illinois Press.

Lewis, R. W. (1996). *Absolut book.* New York: Charles E. Tuttle.

Lindenmann, W. K. (1993, August). Public relations research: A look at what's happening on the commercial side of the fence. Paper presented at the Pre-Convention Workshop, Annual Association for Education in Journalism and Mass Communication Convention, Kansas City.

Link Resources Corp. (1986, March). *Viewdata/Videotex Report* 7(3). New York: Link Resources Corporation.

Lippmann, W. (1922). *Public opinion.* New York: Macmillan.

Lowery, S., & DeFleur, M. (1983). *Milestones in mass communication research.* New York: Longman.

Maso-Fleischman, R. (1996, November 18). Ethnographic research smooths Spanish-language ad strategy. *Marketing-News.*

Mauro, J. (1992). *Statistical deception at work.* Hillsdale, NJ: Lawrence Erlbaum.

McCombs, M. (1987). Effect of monopoly in Cleveland on diversity of newspaper content, *Journalism Quarterly* 64(4).

McCombs, M. E. (1992). Explorers and surveyors: Expanding strategies for agenda-setting research. *Journalism Quarterly* 69(4).

McCombs, M., & Poindexter, P. (1983). The duty to keep informed: News exposure and civic obligation. *Journal of Communication* 33(2).

Merrill, J. C. (1965). How *Time* stereotyped three U.S. presidents. *Journalism Quarterly* 42(4).

Meyer, P. (1991). *The new precision journalism.* Bloomington, IN: Indiana University Press.

Miller, D. C. (1977). *Handbook of research design and social measurement* (3rd ed.). New York: David McKay.

Mitchell, A. (1997, May 17). Survivors of Tuskegee study get apology from Clinton. The *New York Times,* National edition, Sec. A.

Naisbitt, J. (1982). *Megatrends: Ten new directions in transforming our lives.* New York: Warner Books.

The *New York Times*/CBS Poll. (1997, January 20). Public's assessment of presidents and problems. The *New York Times,* National edition, Sec. A.

The *New York Times*. (1997, January 20). How the poll was conducted. The *New York Times*, National edition, Sec. A.

The *New York Times*. (1999, February 13). The investigation: Starr's investigation finds grounds for impeachment, The *New York Times*, National edition, Sec. A.

Neuborne, E., & Kerwin, K. (1999, February 15). Generation Y. *Business Week*.

Newspaper Research Journal. (1983). Special Issue, *4*(4).

Noll, A. M. (1997). *Highway of dreams: A critical view along the information superhighway*. Mahwah, NJ: Lawrence Erlbaum.

Norusis, M. J. *SPSS: SPSS 6.1 guide to data analysis*. Englewood Cliffs, NJ: Prentice-Hall.

Oppel, R. (1996, November 1). Three steps toward improving public journalism. *Austin American-Statesman*, Sec. H.

The Pew Research Center for the People & the Press. (1998, March 27). Opinion poll experiment reveals conservative opinions not underestimated, but racial hostility missed. Washington DC: The Pew Research Center for the People & the Press.

Pickard, S., former account executive for Kenneth C. Smith Advertising, La Jolla, CA. (1996, September). Interview by first author, Austin, TX.

Poindexter, P. M. (1982, July). A content analysis of the Latino coverage in the *Los Angeles Times* and *La Opinion*. Marketing Research Department, *Los Angeles Times*. Photocopy.

Poindexter, P. M. (1986). The *Los Angeles Times* in Education pilot study. Special Projects Division, Los Angeles Times. Photocopy.

Poindexter, P. M. (1977). Newspaper non-readers: Why they don't read. Master's thesis, Syracuse University.

Poindexter, P. M., & Lasorsa, D. L. (1999). Generation X: Is the meaning understood? *Newspaper Research Journal 20*(4).

Popping, R. (1997). Computer programs for the analysis of texts and transcripts. In C. W. Roberts (Ed.), *Text analysis for the social sciences: Methods for drawing statistical inferences from texts and transcripts*. Mahwah, NJ: Lawrence Erlbaum.

Potter, W. J. (1996). *An analysis of thinking and research about qualitative methods*. Mahwah, NJ: Lawrence Erlbaum.

Prichard, P. (1987). *The making of McPaper: The inside story of USA Today*. Kansas City, MO: Andrews, McMeel & Parker.

Qualitative Research Council of the Advertising Research Foundation. (1985). *Focus groups: Issues and approaches*. New York: Advertising Research Foundation.

Quintanilla, M. (1990, May 25). 27 Southland students win trip to Orient. *Los Angeles Times*, Sec. E.

Reeves, R. (1984). George Gallup's nation of numbers. *Esquire's fifty who made the difference*. New York: Villard Books.

Rhoden, W. C. (1998, January 17). Golden goose just got much fatter. The *New York Times*, Sec. B.

Robertson, N. (1992). *The girls in the balcony: Women, men, and the New York Times*. New York: Random House.

Rogers, E. M., & Chaffee, S. H. (1994, December). Communication and journalism from "Daddy" Bleyer to Wilbur Schramm: A palimpsest. *Journalism Monographs* (148).

Rosenthal, A. (1992, April 25). Bush, asking for continuity, sounds like a revolutionary, The *New York Times*, National edition, Sec A.

Ross, C. (1998, February 9). Seinfeld shocker: $2 million price tag. *Advertising Age*, 1+.

Rubenstein, S. M. (1995). *The history of surveys. Surveying public opinion*. Belmont, CA: Wadsworth.

Rudestam, K. E., & Newton, R. R. (1992). *Surviving your dissertation: A comprehensive guide to content and process*. Newbury Park, CA: Sage.

Sabato, L. J., & Simpson, G. R. (1996). *Dirty little secrets: The persistence of corruption in American politics*. New York: Times Books.

Schramm, W. (1997). S. H. Chaffee & E. M. Rogers (Eds.), *The beginnings of communication study in America: A personal memoir.* Thousand Oaks, CA: Sage.

Schuman, H., & Converse, J. M. (1989). The effects of black and white interviewers on black responses. In E. Singer & S. Presser (Eds.), *Survey research methods: A reader.* Chicago: The University of Chicago Press.

Schweitzer, J. C. (1991). Personal computers and media use. *Journalism Quarterly 68*(4).

Sills, D. L. Stanton, Lazarsfeld, and Merton—Pioneers in communication research. In E. E. Dennis & E. Wartella (Eds.), *American communication research: The remembered history.* Mahwah, NJ: Lawrence Erlbaum.

Smith, A. (1980). *Goodbye Gutenberg: The newspaper revolution of the 1980s.* New York: Oxford University Press.

Smith, S. (1996, July 23). Hispanics debate classifications as 2000 census draws nearer. *Austin American-Statesman*, Sec. B.

Soruco, G. (1996). *Cubans and the mass media in south Florida.* Gainesville, FL: University Press of Florida.

Stacks, D. W. (1994, March). Motivating students to become receptive to research: How to overcome the fear of numbers in the introductory public relations course. *Teaching Public Relations.* Public Relations Division of the Association for Education in Journalism and Mass Communication, 36th edition.

Stamm, K. R. (1981). Measurement decisions. In G. H. Stempel III & B. H. Westley (Eds.), *Research methods in mass communication.* Englewood Cliffs, NJ: Prentice-Hall.

Stempel, G. H. III, & Hargrove, T. (1996). Mass media audiences in a changing media environment. *Journalism and Mass Communication Quarterly 73*(3).

Tankard, J. W., Jr., & Sumpter, R. (1993). Media awareness of media manipulation: The use of the term "spin doctor." Paper presented at the annual convention of the Mass Communication and Society Division, Association for Education in Journalism and Mass Communication, Kansas City, MO.

Taylor, R. (1995, Fall). Mall walker intercept survey. Department of Advertising Independent Study, The University of Texas at Austin. Photocopy.

Thomas, E., & Hosenball, M. (1999, February 8). The endgame. *Newsweek.*

Thompson, D. L. (1994). Daniel Starch. In E. Applegate (Ed.), *The ad men and women: A biographical dictionary of advertising.* Westport, CT: Greenwood Press.

Time Magazine, (1997, June 30). Pie chart. *Time.*

Townsend, B. (1988). Psychographic glitter and gold, in P. Wickham (Ed.), *The insider's guide to demographic know-how.* Ithaca, NY: American Demographics Press.

Unger, L. S., McConacho, D. M., & Faier, J. A. (1991). The use of nostalgia in television advertising: A content analysis. *Journalism Quarterly 68*(3).

Veronis, C. R. (1989, November). Some small newspapers have staff research help, too. *Presstime.*

Weaver, D. H. (1981). Basic statistical tools. In G. H. Stempel III & B. H. Westley (Eds.), *Research methods in mass communication.* Englewood Cliffs, NJ: Prentice-Hall.

Weaver, D., & Drew, D. (1995). Voter learning in the 1992 presidential election: Did the "nontraditional" media and debates matter? *Journalism and Mass Communication Quarterly 72*(1).

Webb, E. J., Campbell, D. T., Schwartz, R. D., & Sechrest, L. (1966). *Unobtrusive measures: Nonreactive research in the social sciences.* Chicago: Rand McNally College Publishing Company.

Westley, B. H. (1981). The controlled experiment. In G. H. Stempel III & B. H. Westley (Eds.), *Research methods in mass communication.* Englewood Cliffs, NJ: Prentice-Hall.

Wickham, P. (Ed.) (1988). *The insider's guide to demographic know-how.* Ithaca, NY: American Demographics Press.

Wilhoit, G. C., & Weaver, D. H. (1990). *Newsroom guide to polls & surveys*. Bloomington: Indiana University Press.

Williams, F. (1992). *Reasoning with statistics* (4th ed.). Fort Worth: Harcourt Brace.

Wilson, T. A. (1993, October). A study evaluating the relationship of The University of Texas at Austin and the African-American Community: Perceptions versus reality. Office of Public Affairs, The University of Texas at Austin. Photocopy.

Wilson, T. A., former PR consultant to Muse Cordero Chen. (1998, January). Interviewed by first author.

Woods, G. B. (1995). *Advertising and marketing to the new majority*. Belmont, CA: Wadsworth.

Zwarun, L. G. (1994). Advertising to Generation X: The rhetoric of rebellion. Master's thesis, The University of Texas at Austin.

Index